MANAGEMENT AND B

MANAGEMENT AND BUSINESS STUDIES

C. A. Leeds, B.Sc.(Econ.), M.A.
Economics Department, Stowe School

R. S. Stainton, B.A., M.Tech., Ph.D.,
F.B.C.S., F.I.M.A., F.O.R.
Henley Administrative Staff College

C. J. Jones, M.Sc., A.C.M.A.
Middlesex Polytechnic

MACDONALD AND EVANS

Macdonald and Evans Ltd
Estover, Plymouth PL6 7PZ

First published 1974
Second edition 1978
Reprinted 1979

©
MACDONALD & EVANS LIMITED
1978

ISBN: 0 7121 1298 7

This book is copyright and may not be reproduced in whole or in part (except for purposes of review) without the express permission of the publishers in writing.

Printed in Great Britain by
Fletcher & Son Ltd
Norwich

PREFACE

This book is designed as an introductory survey for students taking business studies for the first time, whether following courses in university, college or school sixth form, and for the general reader interested in management problems. It is intended to be of practical help also to students in industry in supervisory or junior management positions by drawing together material relevant to their studies. Research into problems of leadership and organisation during the past fifty years has resulted in the development of a framework of knowledge and techniques which can be applied to most management situations. This body of material cuts across the traditional classifications of arts (*e.g.* English and languages), social sciences and natural sciences as it is in fact drawn from all three sources. Interdisciplinary studies are now considered to provide the best introduction to business and management training, so that both "literate" and "numerate" qualities can be developed together, along with the ability to be equally at ease when dealing on the one hand with facts or objects in the sequestered environment of a research laboratory or library, and on the other with the more unpredictable material of living human beings, as well as with the ability to discover the respective merits and purposes of "quantitative" and "qualitative" modes of operations.

The "art" of management is the product of intelligence, aptitude, knowledge and experience. Essential qualities for gaining people's co-operation are the abilities to lead, communicate and make correct decisions. Although experience is a great educator, learning merely by this method may result in costly mistakes. The aim of this book is to help to bridge the gap between theory and reality by guiding the student towards an understanding of how theoretical knowledge and techniques can be related to practical situations and problems.

Acknowledgments

Various people have read parts of the text and made helpful comments. We would like to thank Ian F. S. Robinson, M.Sc., A.R.C.S., D.I.C., M.I.Chem.E., F.R.I.C., formerly Director of Studies, The Management Centre, Bournemouth College of Technology; Desmond Graves, M.A., M.Phil., A.M.B.I.A., Fellow of the Oxford Centre of Management; Basil Banks, Management Consultant,

Peter Naylor, Industrial Relations Officer and Stephen Dunn, B.A., M.Sc.(Econ.), Research Assistant, London School of Economics.

October 1978 C.A.L.
R.S.S.
C.J.J.

CONTENTS

Preface v

Introduction 1

CHAPTER	PAGE
I Background to Industry and Trade	4
Basic economic activity	5
Basic entities of industry and commerce	6
Forms of Business Organisation	9
The sole trader and partnerships	9
Joint stock companies	11
Co-operative movement	13
Public corporations	14
The Legal Background to Business	15
English law	15
Important legal concepts in business	16
Law of torts	17
Law of contract	18
The sale of goods and consumer protection	20
Contracts of service and employment	22
Race and sex	23
European Community law	24
II Economic Principles and Industrial Formations	25
Supply, Demand and Price Determination	25
Micro and macro studies	25
Basic economic problems	25
Supply conditions	26
Factors of production	28
Opportunity cost	29
Allocation of resources in an industry	30
Demand conditions	32
Principle of diminishing marginal utility	33
Relationship between price, supply and demand	35

	Demand and supply elasticities	37
	Exceptional demand and supply conditions	41
	Revenue and costs	42
	Forms of competition and monopoly	44
	Theories of the firm—an evaluation	49
	Economies of scale and the size of firms	51

Industrial Structure and Monopolies

Forms of industrial expansion	54
Multi-national corporations and European companies	56
Monopolies and their control	59
Competition in the European Community	64

III Macroeconomics and International Trade — 66

Concepts Governing the Working of the Economy: Employment Theory and Industrial Location — 66

Trade cycle and business fluctuations	66
The national income	68
Economic indicators	70
Mathematical forecasting	72
Aggregate demand and supply	74
Consumption, savings and investment	75
The multiplier and the accelerator	77
Introduction to employment	80
The classical approach	80
The depression years 1920–39	81
Keynes and the general theory of employment	82
Present-day employment problems	83
Location of industry	84
Regional planning	85
European Community regional policy	87

Government and Management of the Economy — 88

Types of economy and economic aims of Government	88
Summary of developments in the economy, 1945–72	92
Public finance	94
The Budget and fiscal policy	96
Types of taxes	96
Value Added Tax	98

International Economic Relations — 99

Advantages of international trade	99

CONTENTS ix

    Terms of trade 101
    Balance of payments 102
    The gold standard 104
    Floating exchange rates 105
    Factors determining exchange rates 106
    The fixed exchange system ("managed flexibility") 107
    Gold and the financing of world trade 108
    Problems of dollar and sterling currencies 108
    Special Drawing Rights and Stand-by Credits 109
    The Eurodollar market 110
    International monetary reform 111
    Trade restrictions and efforts to secure their removal 113

IV Money, Banking and Investment 117

    Money and Banking 117

    The nature and function of money 117
    Types of money and methods of payment 118
    Functions of deposit banks 121
    The creation of deposits 122
    The Bank of England and the history of banking 124
    Techniques of monetary policy—open market operations, bank rate and other methods 125
    Recent banking developments 128

    The Finance of Foreign Trade 131

    The money market and the bill of exchange 131
    Documentary credits 133
    The E.C.G.D. and the Amstel Club 133
    International banking 134

    Monetary policy and inflation 136

    The value and quantity of money 136
    The rate of interest 139
    Inflation and deflation 142
    Index numbers 143

    Investment Management 145

    Sources of short-term finance 146
    Long-term capital 147
    Capital market 150
    The Stock Exchange 151
    Investment and unit trusts 151

General Principles in Portfolio Management	152
Choosing shares	156
The timing of investment	159

V Company Accounting — 161

Introduction	161
Presentation and Measurement of Financial Performance	162
The balance sheet	162
Balance sheet examples	163
Transaction recording and profit measurement	165
The profit and loss account	168
Cash flow	170
Depreciation	173
Intangible assets	175
Accounting Systems and Techniques	176
Accounting conventions	176
Ratio analysis	179
Calculation of ratios	182
Using ratios	188
Inflation accounting	189
Management Accounting	190
Budgeting	191
Budgetary control and standard costing	193

VI Management Information and Data Processing — 195

Data and Information	195
Exception reporting	196
The Computer	197
Trials and tribulations	197
Human similarities	199
Binary base	199
Computer decisions	200
Data input	201
Memory	204
Program instructions	204
Computer output	206
Permanent copy	206

CONTENTS

Audio and visual records	207
Man/machine conversation	208
High-level languages	209
Organisation of data	210
The data needs of management	211
Computer justification and data bank	213
Commercial documentation and credit control	213
Distribution by value	216
Levels of reporting	217
Factors of control	218
Management Information System	220
VII Production and Marketing	**224**
Functions Associated with Production	224
Purchasing	224
Production planning and control	226
Value analysis and work study	228
Patents and registered designs	231
Tenders	232
Functions Associated with Marketing	232
Market analysis and research	232
Product planning	234
The sales function	236
Channels of distribution	238
Commodity markets	240
Advertising and promotions	242
Public relations	245
Forecasting	245
Stock control	250
Automated warehousing, vehicle scheduling and depot siting	251
VIII Industrial Relations and Personnel Management	**253**
Trade Unions, Collective Bargaining and the Law	253
History and legal background	253
Structure and function of trade unions	256
Powers of unions	259
National collective bargaining (the formal system)	261
Strikes, causes and effects	263
The informal system and the shop steward	264

Wage productivity agreements	266
Reform measures	267
European trade unions	271
Personnel Management	274
Recruitment and selection	274
Induction records and labour	276
Training, welfare and health	277
Industrial Sociology	279
Needs and motivation	279
The Classical School	282
The Hawthorne Studies and the Human Relations School	282
Informal groups	284
The Systems School	286
Worker participation and involvement	288
Conflict and bargaining	292

IX Leadership and Decision Making 295

Leadership	295
Leadership types	295
Delegation	300
Span of control	301
Business objectives and responsibilities	302
Innovation—research and development	305
Decision making	308
Deciding between alternatives	309
Levels of decision	321
Decision types	322
Corporate planning	323

X Organisation and Communications 325

Organisation	325
Company ownership	325
Chairman and Managing Director	326
The Board of Directors	327
Organisational structure	329
Functional relationship	331
Staff responsibilities	332
The specialist barrier	333
Employee roles	334

CONTENTS xiii

Structured conflict	334
Management responsibilities	335
Measurement of management performance	337
Time span	339
Centralisation or decentralisation	343
Communications	348
Horizontal and vertical communications	348
Communication nets	351
Committees	352
Perception, semantics and communication	354
Report writing	357
Persuasion	358

XI	Business Mathematics and Operational Research	360
	The beginnings	360
	Operational research techniques	361
	Statistics	361
	The average	362
	The sample	362
	Variation	364
	Normal distribution	365
	Area under the curve	367
	Identifying the source	368
	Statistics used properly	369
	A distribution problem	369
	The Theory of Queues	371
	Queue characteristics	373
	Queue control	374
	Mathematical analysis	374
	Some queue equations	376
	Simulation	377
	Modelling	377
	Mathematical models	378
	Data collection	379
	Simulation objectives	380
	An example of simulation	381
	Linear Programming	382
	Identifying the problem	382
	Objectives	384

	Mathematical expression	384
	Linearity	386
	Reality	386
	Relaxing the constraints	388
	An application of linear programming	388
	The "mix" problem	389
	Transportation	394
	Summary	395
	The Theory of Games	395
	Definition of a game	395
	Zero sum games	396
	Non-zero sum games	397
	Dominant strategies	398
	Saddle points	398
	Mixed strategies	399
	Critical path planning	400
	New product launch	403
	Resource allocation	405
	P.E.R.T.	406
XII	A Case Study	408
	Questions	414

Appendix I Questions from Examination Papers 417
Appendix II Bibliography 422
Index 425

Introduction

Brief history of management and business studies

Before 1939 there was relatively little formal education in management in Britain. There was an attitude of general contempt towards any idea of professionalism in management, and opposition to any form of systematic training in the subject. Instead the gifted "amateur" was held in high esteem, someone with innate ability in leadership or someone who had mastered the necessary skills and qualities as part of his general schooling and university training, and hence was ready to cope effectively with any task involving the making of decisions, whether in government, business or the armed services. Non-technical subjects which trained the mind, such as history and classics, were considered superior to any specialised training relating to the actual job in which one was eventually to be involved. Business, in fact, as a field of human activity, was not thought worthy of the intellectual effort directed to pure science, the arts or other fields of traditional higher learning, and the belief prevailed that management as a subject could not be taught at all.

Since 1945 progress in management education and training has been spectacular in comparison with former times, particularly during the 1960s. In the late 1940s the Administrative Staff College at Henley was established. In 1949 a scheme was launched for part-time courses leading to a Diploma in Management Studies and to graduate membership of the British Institute of Management. Staff-training centres for individual companies were developed and staff colleges for particular industries opened in increasing numbers. Technical colleges widened the scope of their short courses for managers.

Courses available

Postgraduate studies in management can now be taken at a number of specialised institutions such as at Henley, the Cranfield College of Management and the London and Manchester Business Schools. Universities and colleges now undertake a number of undergraduate courses in business studies. One specific type is a sandwich course which combines academic study with a period of practical training in industry. Supervision and foremanship have become more intricate and are now seen as part of management. Impetus to this type of training was given by the *Industrial Training Act*, 1964, and resulted in the creation of the National Examinations Board in Supervisory Studies (N.E.B.S.S.), which awards certificates after appropriate courses have been taken.

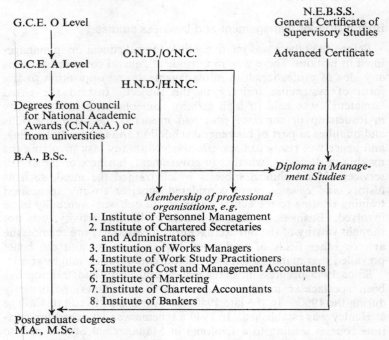

Possible routes in the study of Management and Business Studies

For school-leavers there are now opportunities to take a course of studies to prepare for work in industry or the professions through the Ordinary National Diploma (full-time) or the Ordinary National Certificate (part-time), approximately equivalent to G.C.E. A Level standard, and through the Higher National Diploma (full-time) or the Higher National Certificate (part-time), taken after three or four years and equivalent to a pass degree. To take the Diploma in Management Studies, candidates without several years experience in industry or commerce are frequently required first to have obtained H.N.D. or H.N.C., a degree from the Council for National Academic Awards (C.N.A.A.) or from a university, or the qualifying certificate of an approved professional body, and preferably to have had some experience in industry or commerce as a preliminary qualification. An alternative route is via the passing of the Advanced Certificate

INTRODUCTION

of the N.E.B.S.S., provided one has reached foreman rank, is over twenty-seven years of age and has been specially recommended.

As business studies became well established at the 18-plus level, with a reasonable amount of agreed knowledge available, attention was then turned to promote the subject at school level. As a result a two-year G.C.E. A Level course for 16- to 18-year-olds has become established with the main object of giving sixth-formers a knowledge of commerce and industry in Britain.

I. BACKGROUND TO INDUSTRY AND TRADE

Management is the effective organising of men, and the creation of the right conditions to achieve a certain objective. It thus applies to any work involving groups which is beyond the capacity of one individual. Examples are the running of governments, businesses, professional activities, non-profit organisations and private affairs.

This book is concerned with the application of management to "business," defined as any enterprise engaged in applying its resources profitably to satisfy an economic need. Its essential task is the use and co-ordination of productive resources (plant, materials, etc.) and financial and human assets to the best possible advantage, or, in other words, to their optimum capacity. This applies at any level of the hierarchy of a business unit, from the managing director to the foreman, and also to any of the functional or specialised areas such as production or personnel. A useful adage for remembering the ingredients of a successful business are the four Ms—Men, Money, Merchandise and Method. The objectives and responsibilities of the firm are discussed in detail in Chapter IX.

The business enterprise does not work as a closed system. Various factors, given below, act as constraints and must be taken into account.

1. *Political and legal.* These comprise the regulations and activities of the Government and local authorities which establish one particular type of framework in which business operates.

2. *Economic and commercial.* These consist of business competitors, the markets in which the business buys and sells, and allied commercial organisations.

3. *Social and cultural.* These include the local community and its organisations; the grouping of people, their attitudes, beliefs and behaviour which in the aggregate are reflected in the social institutions confronting business; private pressure groups; and the general climate of opinion.

4. *Technological and scientific.* This refers to the existing state of knowledge in technology and science.

In various chapters of this book consideration is given to these four groups of constraining factors.

Basic economic activity

The present pattern of the way in which needs are satisfied is the result of a long process of historical development. In the primitive societies, man was economically self-sufficient as he was able to provide for his simple wants independently of others. These were primarily the acquisition of food supplies and the obtaining of raw materials for making clothes and for building shelter to protect him from the cold and to keep him in good health.

By early Neolithic times, food-gathering was supplemented by trapping and hunting activities. Later, nomadic (wandering) families developed into organised tribes in settled locations. As food became more plentiful, there was time to make, repair and improve tools, pots, weapons, etc. Craftsmanship developed, and though at first each man made all his own goods, basic specialisation soon took place, each concentrating on the craft in which he excelled. Early trading originated when a family's surplus goods were exchanged for whatever other acceptable goods or services their neighbours could offer.

When man had acquired ample supply of the basic survival needs, he then began to covet a better standard of accommodation, food, clothing and so on. As his wealth increased, so his requirements developed. Though one man can more or less accurately assess the extent of basic human needs, the measurement of other wants is highly subjective, varying considerably from one society to another according to values, ideas and tradition. In a marked degree the luxuries of one age become the necessities of another. For example, due to the pace and pressures of modern living in many occupations, adequate rest and recreational activities become absolutely necessary at regular intervals, whereas they are not essential for people with less demanding occupations in more rural-pedestrian environments of the present, and were not essential in the past.

Instances of the transmuting of luxuries into "psychological" necessities that have been mentioned are easy to find. Examples are cars, tobacco, alcohol, television, washing machines and refrigerators, which, though not part of the absolute survival needs of man, have in time become so plentiful and cheap as to be very much part of the total culture and life in developed societies.

Some things which satisfy our needs and desires come to us without effort as "free" goods, such as sunshine and fresh air or uncultivated fruit (see Fig. 1). However, the majority of our wants are supplied by the work of specialists, whether craftsmen, factory owners, farmers or hairdressers, etc., who produce material goods

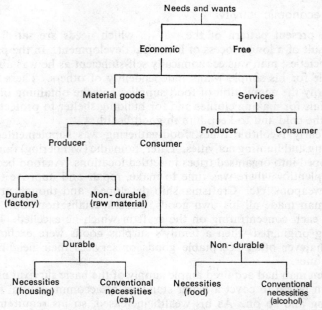

FIG. 1. *Types of goods and services which satisfy our needs and wants*

or perform services such as cutting our hair. There are two broad groups of goods which can be made: consumer goods, which directly satisfy our requirements, and producer (capital) goods such as factories, machines and tools, which facilitate the production of consumer goods. A useful distinction is also made between durable goods, which can be used over and over again, and non-durable goods, such as coal or bread, which can be used only once.

Basic entities of industry and commerce

Business serves as a form of middleman between the undeveloped resources and the consumer. It encompasses all the supplies, organisations and institutions which are directly or indirectly related to the production and distribution of goods and services for the satisfaction of consumer wants. In broad terms, the business world comprises three basic units:

1. an establishment which occupies a particular site, *e.g.* a factory, mine, hotel, shop or farm;
2. a firm, which owns one or more establishments;
3. an industry.

In fact it is not easy to say exactly what constitutes an industry or a firm because the use of different criteria provides different answers. For example, one attitude is that there is no conclusive way of defining an industry, since in practice some employers find they have interests in common with certain other employers and come to consider themselves part of the same industry. An industry is usually thought of as a grouping together of firms which produce similar products for the same markets. Yet dissimilar firms can have other links through the materials employed or the processes used. The position is complicated by the firm which diversifies into a number of industries.

A distinction can be made between industry (the output of producer and consumer goods, sometimes called primary and secondary production), commerce and other agencies which provide services to industry. Although some of this third category are definitely regarded as business activities and some, such as the hotel or tourist trade, are loosely considered as industries, others, such as the fire service and police force, basically are not.

Direct production covers the process of utilising raw materials for the manufacture of finished goods. This includes not only the primary activities, such as agriculture and mining, concerned with extracting resources from the earth, but also the mechanical processes involved in changing their shape or form so that they become marketable commodities suitable for human use or consumption.

Commerce comprises all aspects of trade which enable goods to pass along the productive chains, from the purchase of raw materials to the sale of finished consumer goods (*see* Fig. 2). The trader, a specialist in buying and selling, provides a personal link between producer and consumer, and overcomes the difficulties which exist when producers have to find buyers and buyers have to find the appropriate producers. Trade can be divided according to the scope of the business (whether wholesale or retail) and the geographical limit (whether home or overseas). It is concerned also with the organisation of distribution, including all the activities and auxiliary services necessary to ensure safe delivery of goods from the factory to the consumer. Commerce covers the processes involved in the removal of obstacles to the exchange of commodities. These are mainly those of person (through trade), space or distance (transport), time (warehousing), finance (banking) and information (advertising and publicity).

Certain occupations cannot be classified as "directly productive" in the same sense as farming or manufacture; or as aids to production

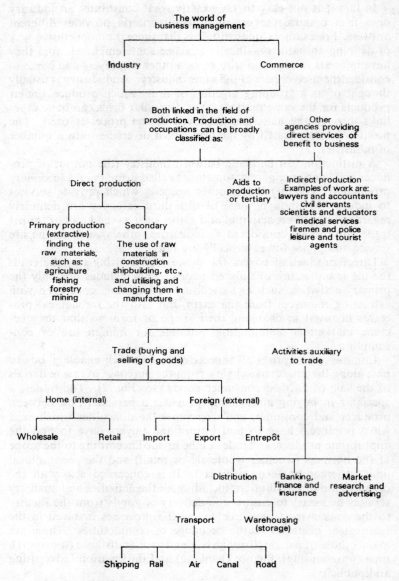

FIG. 2. *Classification of industrial and commercial activities*

in the commercial sense of providing some service which helps to enable goods to pass along the chain from their raw material state till they reach the consumer. In spite of this, such occupations contribute indirectly to the purpose of industry by giving the necessary health, training or direction to men and women who are in the industrial category. For example, by seeking to build up the mental, spiritual or physical well-being of these men and women, workers in the church and the legal profession, or in the fields of recreation, tourism, sport and entertainment, perform services necessary towards the satisfaction of the needs and desires of their fellow creatures.

FORMS OF BUSINESS ORGANISATION
The sole trader and partnerships

There is a variety of legal and organisational forms through which business enterprises may operate in different industrial societies (*see* Fig. 3). The diversity of type is to some extent a consequence of the diversity of modern times and historical circumstances. As the scale of production increased new forms of enterprise evolved, each type best fitted to the time and trade.

The oldest, simplest and most popular form is the one-man business, owned by an individual known in law as a sole trader. This proprietor provides the capital, runs the business and accepts full responsibility, bearing any loss and reaping any profit. The desire for independence and the limited funds necessary to start are generally the reasons which tempt people to adopt this form of business. It flourishes in circumstances where personal attention to customer needs are important and call for specialised skill and individual discretion. Examples are found in farming, retail shopkeeping, hotel management, hairdressing and the professions (such as medicine, architecture and the law). Any person carrying on a business under a name other than his own was soon to be made to register with the Registrar of Business Names (*Registration of Business Names Act*, 1918), and the true name of the trader, and his nationality if not British, had (and still has) to appear on all material bearing the name of the business. A Certificate of Registration must be shown at the main place of business.

Some of the drawbacks are that limited capital may prevent expansion, illness may prevent proper management and little scope may exist for specialisation and the division of labour. These restrictions may be overcome by the second form of organisation, known as the partnership and governed by the *Partnership Act, 1890*. Any number between two and twenty may form a partnership (a maximum of ten for banking purposes), and they are often members of the same family. Typical examples of partnerships are solicitors, accountants, dentists, small manufacturers and retailers.

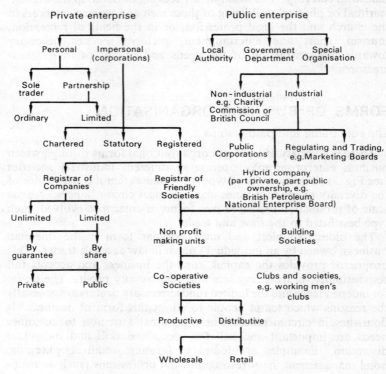

FIG. 3. *Forms of business organisation*

In 1907 the *Limited Partnership Act* was passed enabling the liability of partners to be limited if they took no active part in the business, provided there was one general partner with unlimited liability. They must be registered. They are few in number as the private limited company can provide better advantages.

Partnerships suffer from two of the drawbacks with which the sole trader also has to contend. The liability for debts incurred in the business is unlimited, which means that all one's private personal assets may be taken to pay off one's creditors. Further, since the

BACKGROUND TO INDUSTRY AND TRADE

firm has no legal existence apart from its members, the death of one may result in the dissolution of the partnership.

Joint stock companies

The alternative to being a sole trader or forming a partnership is to establish a company, the typical business unit today. It is formed for two chief reasons: to limit a trader's personal liability, and to persuade other people to invest in the business.

In Britain, companies first became important during Tudor times in the area of foreign trade. The method of formation was by Royal Charter. This was not easy to obtain, and usually conferred a monopoly of trade within a certain area, as with the Hudson's Bay Company or the British South Africa Company. Incorporation was a crucial step in the establishing of a company. Once formed, it had a separate existence and a distinct identity from its members, the shareholders. Though the shareholders who contributed capital had only restricted powers and no voice in the day-to-day management of the business, they had two distinct advantages over members of a partnership. Since shares could be transferred, the holders could always sell what they had bought and recover the investment, though not necessarily the same amount as originally paid. Secondly, the provision was included in the charter of most early companies that shareholders had only limited liability for the debts of the company, to the extent of each individual's share in it, and not, as with a partnership, to the limit of his personal wealth.

Another method of forming a company which developed in the 18th century was incorporation by special Act of Parliament. This was used by companies formed to undertake large public utility works such as canals, docks, waterworks and railways. Few of these companies exist today because the industries have been nationalised.

During the Industrial Revolution in the early part of the 19th century it was extremely difficult and expensive for business firms to obtain permission to form a company. There was also opposition from the general public to the granting of joint-stock-company status as they tended to associate companies with the idea of monopoly and there was at the time a popular dislike of exclusive privilege. Yet industry was developing beyond the bounds of the sole trader or partnership. After 1815, many illegal companies were formed, trying to adopt, for example, the device of transferable shares, or attempting to limit the liability of members by forming a trust. Eventually a series of *Companies Acts* in 1844, 1855 and 1862 permitted manufacturing firms to form companies with limited liability by a simpler and cheaper method than had been used before. This was the system of incorporation by registering documents with a Registrar of Companies under conditions laid down by statute.

Unlimited companies are comparatively few in number, confined mainly to persons preferring this form of organisation for family estates and other forms of property. Some organisations are limited by guarantee, for example, non-trading and professional bodies such as the Chambers of Commerce, Trade Associations and charitable bodies. This means that the liability of members is limited to the amount they have agreed to contribute in the event of the company winding up.

The majority of companies are limited by share. Despite the company legislation of the 19th century, many average manufacturing businesses remained as partnerships or family businesses for some time, or, if they formed companies, did not appeal to the general public for capital. Eventually the *Companies Act* of 1907 recognised legally a distinction which had been developing between private and public companies. It stipulated that a private company must have at least two members and a maximum of fifty, that it was to be precluded from inviting the public to subscribe capital, and that the right of members to transfer shares was restricted.

Private companies are more numerous than public companies, and are cheaper and simpler to form. The latter have much larger capital, and are the more usual legal form adopted by big business enterprises. Private companies tend to be the family type of manufacturing or retailing business run by members of the family or close business associates.

The numerous company statutes which insist on full publicity of a company's affairs, and other legislation relating to business organisation, are designed to make successful fraud and dishonesty difficult. They are also intended to generate confidence in members of the public so that they will be encouraged to participate in business and thus to aid its development.

The *Companies Act* of 1948 contained detailed provisions for many matters, such as the formation of companies, the keeping of accounts, the publication of prospectuses and the allotment of shares to the public. It exempted private companies from having to file annual accounts in the Board of Trade Companies House. Two-thirds of registered companies are in this category.

The *Companies Act* of 1967 requires companies to give fuller information about their affairs (particularly in relation to subsidiary

BACKGROUND TO INDUSTRY AND TRADE

and associated companies), their investments, the salaries of their directors and contributions from their accounts to political persons or parties. The exempt private company was abolished, which meant that all private companies now had to file annual accounts with the Registrar of Companies. These disclosures are aimed at protecting both the shareholders and the public interest.

The *Companies Act*, 1976 provides that an investment of over 5 per cent of the shares of any company must be placed on public record. The rule does not apply to the monarch, any other head of state or their family or to any government.

The persons forming a company (the promoters), having settled preliminary details among themselves, are required to file a number of documents with the Registrar of Companies. The first is the Memorandum of Association, which defines the company's powers and regulates its relations with the outside world. It states the name and objects of the proposed company, its address and the amount of its authorised share capital. The second important document is the Articles of Association. This contains the internal regulations of the company, defining such matters as the rights of various classes of shareholders, the way meetings are to be conducted and the method of appointment of directors.

If everything is in order and the proper fees have been paid, the Registrar will issue a Certificate of Incorporation. Private companies may then begin business immediately, as they do not have to seek capital from the general public. Public companies, however, must wait until the public has subscribed for sufficient shares to provide adequate capital for trading purposes. When this has occurred, the company can start trading as soon as the Registrar has issued a Trading Certificate. Each year the company must send an annual return to the Registrar and usually a balance sheet has to be enclosed. If shareholders feel affairs of the company are being mishandled, they may ask the Department of Trade to investigate.

Co-operative movement

The co-operative movement developed because of the poor conditions of the working classes. The success of some workers in forming a co-operative in Rochdale in 1844 (called the Rochdale Pioneers) led to the creation of similar societies throughout the country. Today co-operative societies exist in manufacturing, wholesaling and retailing. In retailing, the customers are shareholders and receive a share of profits in the form of dividends based on the value of the goods they purchase. Shareholders in the Co-operative Wholesale Society, founded in 1863, are retail societies.

The Co-operative movement, strongest in the North and Midlands, is a social force as well as a business enterprise, reflected in its interest in education and welfare, democratic organisation and links with the Labour Party.

Public corporations

Limitations of private enterprise, already discussed, led to Government creating public corporations, a form of organisation which is not part of a government department, but is subject to varying degrees of state control. The most important are those which in the public interest operate major nationalised industries established since 1945, such as coal, electricity, gas, steel, railways, commercial road transport, postal services and the aircraft and shipbuilding industries. Capital is raised by the issue of stocks or the raising of other types of fixed interest loans.

Each corporation is under the supervision of a Minister responsible to Parliament for its operation, but he can only lay down lines of general policy. Corporations are usually organised on normal business techniques and are self-governing as far as their day-to-day activities are concerned. At the head is a board appointed by the Minister from persons of experience and ability in industry and commerce.

Each board submits to the appropriate Minister an annual report with accounts, which is in turn presented to Parliament, so permitting matters on the conduct of the corporation to be discussed. Some parliamentary supervision is exercised through scrutiny of the reports of its special Select Committee on nationalised industries, and publicity can be given through debates on their activities and questions in the House. Control by Parliament is, in practice, limited. Consumers' Councils in some undertakings, such as gas and electricity, protect consumers' interests and bring their views to the attention of the Board.

In the 1970s the Labour Party developed the idea that publicly owned companies should actively compete with private ones. The 1975 *Industry Act* created the National Enterprise Board, a state holding company, partly to extend "public ownership into profitable areas of manufacturing industry." Through the British National Oil Corporation, the government exercises participation rights in the exploitation of Britain's offshore oil resources.

THE LEGAL BACKGROUND TO BUSINESS

Without an efficient legal system to protect us we would have to rely on our own strength. The existence of the law compels participating parties to honour their bargains, facilitates trading exchanges, assures the worker of his wage for work done and the property owner of interest and rent from those who use his property.

The law today is complicated and involved and few businessmen would try to solve important legal questions affecting their businesses without the advice of the legal profession. There are certain rudimentary and important elements of law which relate specifically to commerce and industry, and this is a brief introduction to them. Knowledge of the law helps one to avert difficulties with other people, and possible loss of time, money and effort. Company law has been covered in the preceding section, and law relating to trade unions and industrial relations is discussed in Chapter VIII. Section 177 of the *Companies Act*, 1948, stipulates that every company, public or private, must have a secretary. He is the chief administrative officer and is responsible for seeing that the affairs of the company are run in accordance with the law.

English law

There are two sources of law, English law and law of the European Community. English law can be subdivided into civil law and criminal law. Civil law governs relationships between individuals and the choice of whether or not to proceed against the wrongdoer rests with the victim. In contrast, an offence is a criminal one if it is considered to affect the public as well as the victim. The police may take action even if the victim does not desire it. In this section some of the implications of civil law are discussed.

The remedy of a civil action is primarily the award of monetary damages as compensation. The basis of English law is the "common law." This developed gradually after 1066 as the commissioners or judges of the King replaced local customs by a standardised type of law throughout the country. In time, however, judges became rigid in their interpretation and people felt they were not able to obtain satisfaction in cases where they considered that altered circumstances required new laws. The practice developed of petitioning the King and then the Chancellor for the settlement of disputes to which the common law did not apply. The Chancellor dealt with these cases on the basis of common fairness and from this developed what came to be known as "Equity" (that is, a system of law based on principles of justice and coexisting with and correcting common law). Since 1875 both types have been administered in the same courts: the practice of Equity being covered by "case law" or "judge-made law," as it originates from case decisions. The most important form of law is statute law, based on Acts of Parliament.

Important legal concepts in business

Legal rights are enjoyed by legal persons only and the latter alone are subject to legal duties. In English law everyone, irrespective of age, sex, nationality or occupation is a legal person. Some persons, for example, the under-eighteens, do not enjoy full legal capacity. A group or association of persons may also be treated collectively in law as a legal person, the body being known as a corporation, which is free to own property in its own name and enter into contracts, etc. Forms of corporation have already been discussed.

A distinction is made in law between ownership and possession. Possession is a matter of fact, and relates to the circumstance of someone having actual custody of something and being able to exercise control over it and to exclude others from control. Ownership, on the other hand, relates to the person recognised in law as entitled to the control and use of something. Ownership is more difficult to prove than possession, and the possessor will be protected by the law as long as someone else is not able to prove that he has a better title to something.

A person's possessions may be either tangible (things in possession) or intangible (things in action). The former may be divided into, first, permanent immovable objects such as land, trees and buildings, and, secondly, chattels which are movable such as furniture and clothing. The ownership of most chattels may be changed by simple delivery. However, some, such as ships and shares, need certain other formalities, and land can only be transferred through the handing over of a document in the form of a deed known as a Conveyance. Things in action relate to ownership of something which the possessor cannot physically control, but which is useful and represents a right enforceable at law, for example, debts, *i.e.* money due from customers. Other forms are negotiable instruments such as patents, copyrights, stocks and shares, bills of exchange, cheques and goodwill. When a business is sold the buyer will pay not only for the tangible assets but some agreed amount for the goodwill, that is, the reputation and trade connections which the former owner has built up.

Law of torts

Tort is the breach of some duty imposed by law. Certain duties are obligatory for all of us, such as exercising care in the interests of others and not interfering with their property or attacking their reputation. Generally, in tort, the broken obligations are towards people in general, while in contract, they are towards specific persons. A tort is a civil wrong and the normal remedy for it is to bring an action for damages by way of compensation. A person may also, through what is called "vicarious liability" be responsible for the torts of another. The most frequent instance of this in modern law is the liability of a master for the acts of his servants committed during the course of their normal employment, whether or not they were specifically instructed to do the particular deed which represented the wrongful act.

The newest and most important tort today is "negligence." A person is guilty of negligence if he does something which a reasonable man in his circumstances would not have done, or if he omits to do something which a reasonable man in his circumstances would have done. This tort is not concerned with any one particular right of others, but with the general duty to observe care. For example, a car driver owes a duty of care to the general public by driving with reasonable caution and skill, and the owner of business premises has the duty to the people using them of ensuring that they are safe. But if a person freely and voluntarily accepts a risk, knowing the danger, and gets hurt in the process, he may not succeed in getting damages. People also owe a duty of care to themselves, and where two parties are negligent and one is injured, then the amount of damages the injured party could recover would be reduced in proportion to his amount of contributory negligence.

Under the *Occupiers Liability Act*, 1957, an occupier of premises owes a "common duty of care" to all his visitors. This involves taking such precautions as will ensure that the visitor will be reasonably safe in using the premises for the purpose for which he has been permitted to use them. If a visitor enters premises without permission, or stays on when his permission has expired, he will be treated in law as a trespasser, and the owner is exempted from almost all liability for his safety. Since the case of *Herrington* v. *British Railways Board* in 1971, it has been held that there is some duty of care owed to a trespasser, usually depending on whether or not sufficient care had been taken to prevent that person from trespassing in the first place.

A person is trespassing if, without lawful justification, he enters and remains on land in possession of another. Trespass is actionable but the plaintiff is entitled only to nominal damages if no damage has been done. However, trespassers cannot be prosecuted, since trespass is not a criminal offence unless made so by Act of Parliament, *e.g.* in the case of restricted areas. Private nuisance occurs when a person in some way interferes with some other person's enjoyment of land. This may take the form of allowing some obnoxious "thing" such as smoke, dust, noise or smell to escape on to the adjoining land, or of blocking a free flow of light by erecting some kind of structure on his own land. Redress is by action for damages or an application to a court for the issue of an injunction. A public nuisance, caused by some obstruction to people in general on the public highway, is a criminal offence and would be handled by the police.

Wrongful interference with the goods of another person also comes under the law of trespass. A party may not sell or keep for himself goods which do not wholly belong to him, *e.g.* he may not sell or withhold goods partly paid for on hire purchase (conversion), nor may he refuse to return something held for repair, or after a period of lease has elapsed (detinue).

Action can be taken in cases of malicious falsehood, when statements are published which are untrue and cause loss to the person about whom, or about whose property, they have been made. Where these statements directly affect someone's reputation, they may be actionable under "defamation of character," which comes under two headings: "libel," which consists of a defamatory statement made in some definite material form such as on television or in a book, when no actual damage need be proved, and "slander," whereby a defamatory meaning is conveyed by spoken words or gestures, in which case damage must usually be proved.

Law of contract

Business transactions are customarily based upon agreements known as contracts, which are enforceable at law. They are made between two or more parties, and they give legal backing to the acquisition of rights by one party through agreed acts or forbearances on the part of the other party.

A contract is not legally binding unless certain requirements are met. Probably the most important is the offer by one party of something to another party (*e.g.* the selling of a car for a certain price) and the precise and absolute Acceptance by the party to whom the offer was made. The Offer and Acceptance together become an Agreement. Another most important feature is Consideration.

BACKGROUND TO INDUSTRY AND TRADE

This is defined as "some right, interest, profit or benefit accruing to one party, or some forbearance, detriment, loss or responsibility, given, suffered or undertaken by the other." Consideration gives a contract the element of "bargain." Both parties must be ready to give something for the benefits they expect to receive in return. In other words, it binds an Agreement. To enforce a contract, the person taking the action must show that he has provided something himself.

Certain contracts must be made in a specified form. For example, contracts concerning conveyance of land and leases for more than three years are unenforceable unless made by Deed under seal. Other contracts, too, must be in writing to be enforceable at law. These include bills of exchange and promissory notes, hire-purchase agreements, contracts of guarantee, assignments of copyright, insurance and assurance contracts and transfers of shares in a company incorporated under the *Companies Act*, 1948. However, verbal contracts are usually just as valid as those in writing, though there may be difficulty in proving the exact terms of the contract. The tendering of money for goods or service constitutes a contract, as, for example, with shop purchases or bus fares.

Agreements between persons are thus valid in law only if the parties intend, by means of contract, to enter into legal relations with each other and if both have the capacity to do so. Particular categories of persons are debarred from binding themselves by contracts in certain circumstances, including minors (persons under eighteen) and those suffering permanent or temporary impairment of faculties, such as mentally disordered persons and drunkards. A minor can enter into perfectly valid contracts concerning the purchase of essential goods and goods appropriate to his station in life, and also beneficial contracts regarding education, employment, service and so on. Whether something is essential depends on the circumstances of the case, such as the standard of living and the nature of one's occupation.

No contract is valid unless it is both legal and possible. Certain contracts are illegal, as, for example, those of an immoral nature, or contracts to commit a crime or civil wrong. In certain cases, a contract may be invalidated if it results from a genuine mistake, misrepresentation or fraud.

The respective rights and duties of parties to an Agreement are not satisfied until the contract is discharged. This may occur when the contract has been satisfactorily fulfilled, or has lapsed in an agreed time span, or if the parties agree under certain conditions to cancel it, or by subsequent impossibility. This last contingency may arise from a change of law, the death of one of the parties contracted to acts of personal service, the bankruptcy of one of the parties, or the non-occurrence of an event which is the essence of a contract. A contract may also be discharged by the substitution of a new Agreement for the old one.

The terms of a contract will contain conditions (essential parts of the contract) and warranties (collateral stipulations, non-vital parts of the contract). If a condition is broken, the innocent party may repudiate the contract, consider it discharged, claim monetary damages or seek enforcement of the contract. The contract may have specified an amount of money to be paid in the event of a breach. Where the parties have not agreed on the damages in advance, or the Court considers that the damages agreed do not represent a fair estimate of the loss suffered, the Court has to assess damages. Sometimes, where the loss could not be covered by the award of damages, the Court may grant an order for "specific performance" or may issue an "injunction" either restraining the other party from doing something or compelling him to perform some specified action. However, if the breach is only a slight breach of warranty, the injured party may only be entitled to damages as compensation.

The sale of goods and consumer protection

The law regarding the sale of goods is now contained largely in the *Sale of Goods Act*, 1893, as amended by the *Law Reform (Enforcement of Contract) Act*, 1954, the *Supply of Goods (Implied Terms) Act*, 1973, and the *Fair Trading Act*, 1973 (*see* p. 63). The meaning of "goods" is all personal possessions and all movable material things, including animals, minerals and crops but not money, shares or debts. A contract of sale is one where the transfer of title in goods from a seller to a buyer is in return for a money consideration called a price. A barter transaction is not considered a contract for the sale of goods. These contracts provide two main protections for the buyer. It is a pre-requisite that the seller has the right to sell the goods in the first place; if he is not the owner he cannot pass title to the buyer. The rightful owner of goods wrongfully sold in this way can reclaim them. An example of an exception to this is goods sold in "market overt," *i.e.* in an open and public market in daylight. This includes all shops in the City of London and properly constituted markets elsewhere. Secondly, the buyer of goods has protection against purchases which are subsequently found not to be the ones ordered. For example, when goods are sold by sample the quality of the goods supplied must correspond with that of the sample, or, if goods are sold by description, they must conform to the descriptive statement.

There is no condition as to the suitability of goods for any particular purpose because it is one principle of the law that the buyer should beware (*caveat emptor*). However, if the buyer has indicated the purpose for which the goods are required and relies on a dealer in that kind of commodity to choose accordingly, there exists an implied warranty that the goods will be reasonably fit for the purpose indicated. Also, since the *Trade Descriptions Act*, 1968, every trade seller must substantiate every claim made on behalf of his goods. This restricts the tendency of traders to make exaggerated claims for their goods and services. *The Supply of Goods (Implied Terms) Act*, 1973, guarantees the consumers' basic rights in every transaction for the purchase of goods.

The *Misrepresentation Act*, 1967, is designed to protect people who enter a contract on the basis of a false statement when the statement was honestly but negligently made. People whose profession or business it is to give advice or opinions—such as valuers, bankers, doctors, accountants, architects and estate agents—are particularly likely to find themselves in a position where they can be sued for making a negligent misstatement unless they made it clear that the statement was without legal liability or unless the circumstances in which it was made were purely social, for example, at a cocktail party. There is also liability in tort for such statements.

The seller also has certain rights, requiring the buyer to accept the goods and to pay for them. If the seller has not been paid but still has the goods in his possession, he may exercise "seller's lien," which means that he may act as if he still retained ownership, but he may not dispose of the goods as he wishes except in special circumstances and can only bring an action against the buyer. (The buyer, however, may be able to sue for non-delivery if the seller has insufficient reason for retaining the goods.) But once possession has passed to the buyer, the seller's right of lien is lost and his only remedy is to bring an action for the amount he should have been paid. If possession, however, has merely been given to a third party (such as a carrier) and the buyer is found to be insolvent, the unpaid seller has the right to stop the goods in transit. As soon as they are again in his possession his lien will be restored.

It is the buyer's right that the seller must observe any conditions or warranties, observed by the seller, and must effect delivery of the contracted quantity of goods, or must make them available at the agreed time and place. It can be noted that the *Hire Purchase Act*, 1965, entitles *every purchaser* who makes a "door-step" agreement to three days' grace in which to have second thoughts on a hire-purchase contract (*see* p. 63 for details of the *Fair Trading Act*, 1973).

Contracts of service and employment

When an employee works under a contract of service for an employer, the latter is responsible for (*a*) the provision of a safe system of work, (*b*) the wrongful acts of the former committed while working and (*c*) the insuring of the employee under the National Insurance (Industrial Injuries) scheme. The employer is entitled to tell his employee not only what to do but also how to do it. If a contractor has agreed to perform a certain task for a client the latter is not responsible for items (*a*) to (*b*) above, and is only entitled to tell the contractor what to do, not how to do it.

Though this form of contract may be terminated in the same way as any other, there are certain methods of cancelling a contract of service which are special. For example, every contract of service, with the exception of those made for a definite period of time, may be terminated by either side giving notice. Secondly, the employer may end the engagement of the employee by paying him the wages he would have received for the period of notice. However, the employee has no right to terminate the contract by paying the employer his own wages, and strictly speaking he should work out his full term of notice. Thirdly, the employer may dismiss the employee without notice if it can be shown that he has been guilty of a breach of contract through some misconduct (drunkenness, violence, theft, wilful disobedience or gross negligence). Fourthly, the contract automatically becomes null and void if there is a change in the persons of a partnership or if a company goes into liquidation.

The *Contracts of Employment Act* of 1963 provides that each employee is entitled to written particulars of his employment, with details concerning his rates of pay, holidays, etc., within thirteen weeks of starting the job. Employees who have been employed continuously for at least two years and then become redundant are entitled to a redundancy payment from their employer under the *Redundancy Payments Act*, 1965. An employee is not entitled to demand a reference or a testimonial from his employer or ex-employer (although he is allowed to ask for one). However, if the employer deliberately gives a reference which is unfair to the employee, the latter may sue him for damages for defamation of character. The *Employment Protection Act*, 1975, and the *Redundancy Payments Act*, 1965, protect workers in the case of redundancies. Employers must consult a trade union before implementing redundancies and workers affected may be entitled to receive a sum of money.

An employer has certain duties to employees which exist in the absence of any agreement of the parties to the contrary. He has to pay the agreed remuneration to his employee, who, however, is not entitled to demand to be given work to do, except when piece-rates are used, or when his employment is of the kind where future employment depends on the publicity secured by former work, such as that of an actor. The employer must pay all reasonable expenses incurred by his employees on his behalf, and has a duty to care for the safety of persons working for him, providing them with reasonable and safe premises, tools, materials and equipment. In addition employers, particularly in factories, are compelled by statute to provide specific safety appliances, devices and other arrangements for the protection of employees. Many Factory Acts grant special protection to women and children.

An employee must perform all duties personally and not use a substitute, must obey all legitimate orders, must render careful service and must be prepared to compensate the employer for any form of loss for which he was responsible. The employee has a duty to be loyal to his employer, and also not to divulge information likely to be of value to others.

Race and sex

The *Race Relations Acts* do not fit neatly into the categories of tort and contract which have been discussed in this section, as they cover various aspects of both fields. Though these Acts come under civil law, they tend to operate in a quasi-criminal manner, since proceedings are enforced by the Government-appointed Commission for Racial equality rather than the normal courts.

The *Race Relations Act* of 1965 aimed to promote equal opportunities in employment, housing and services, etc. In 1968 another *Race Relations Act* made racial discrimination unlawful in housing, employment and the provision of goods, facilities or services such as insurance and credit in regard to colour, race and national origins. The Act also banned unlawful discrimination in relation to the publishing or displaying of advertisements regarding vacant jobs and in terms of membership of trade unions and employers' and trade organisations.

As these Acts were slow in having the desired effect, stronger provisions were provided for in the *Race Relations Act* of 1976. Indirect discrimination was now also illegal. This meant applying a test which would, even accidentally, discriminate against people on a racial basis, *e.g.* if an employer only gave jobs to people "with good English accents." There are exceptions to the Act as, for example, where a particular job is held to require a particular race, such as Chinese waiters in a Chinese restaurant—then race becomes a "genuine occupational qualification."

Under the *Equal Pay Act* of 1970, equal pay for men and women in jobs became law from 29 December 1975. Under the *Sex Discrimination Act*, 1976, it is unlawful for employers to discriminate in opportunities for recruitment, training and promotion either on grounds of sex or on grounds of marriage.

European Community law

The European Community or Common Market originated in 1957 when six countries, Belgium, France, West Germany, Luxemburg, Italy and the Netherlands, signed the Treaty of Rome. It is a customs union, and also possibly the first step towards full political integration of Western Europe. In 1973 it was enlarged by the addition of Britain, Denmark and Eire.

On 17 October 1972 Parliament passed the *European Communities Act*, which provided that on Britain's entry into the European Community all existing and future European law automatically became part of British law. Perhaps the most significant part for businesses is Section 9, which modifies considerably existing company law in Britain. For example, a company or person acting as agent for it is now liable for any contracts made before the company was formed. Also every company must now show various particulars on all business letters and order forms of the company. It must mention the place of registration of the company, the address of its registered office and, in the case of a limited company exempt from the obligation to use the word "limited" as part of its name, the fact that it is a limited company. Obligations for enforcing this body of law falls mainly on governments, firms and other corporate groups. Under Article 177 of the Treaty of Rome, all courts in Common Market countries may, and final courts of appeal must, refer points of Community law to the Court of the European Community for a ruling. This means that in future British traders, businessmen and farmers may be involved in disputes at Luxemburg, the Court's headquarters.

A considerable volume of Community law, dealing with economic, commercial, industrial and social matters, has been developed. It covers custom duties, agriculture, transport, the regulation of the coal, steel and nuclear industries, and the movement of labour, services and capital between member countries. Certain aspects of this law are covered in various chapters of this book. Problems of competition and monopoly are discussed in Chapter II, regional policy and labour mobility in Chapter III. Much of the law is in the embryonic stage, regarding such aspects as proposals for a European Company.

II. ECONOMIC PRINCIPLES AND INDUSTRIAL FORMATIONS

SUPPLY, DEMAND AND PRICE DETERMINATION

Micro and macro studies

Chapters II and III cover the areas of economics known respectively as Microeconomics and Macroeconomics. Microeconomics is the study of the behaviour of individual economic units such as households, firms and industries, and of such problems as the output of a specific product, the number of workers in a particular firm and the revenue or income of a certain family. It concerns the parts rather than the whole, the trees rather than the forest.

Macroeconomics refers to the structure of the economy as a whole, or to relationships between the major subdivisions which form part of the economy, such as the sum total or aggregate of businesses, households, etc. (an aggregate being a collection of specific economic entities which are regarded as one unit). It involves target planning, *i.e.* the fixing of quantitative aims for the growth of the whole economy or specific industries, and it is concerned with efforts to control the economy by the use of figures relating to national income, savings, investment, output and employment levels, etc.

Sometimes economists tend to specialise in macro- or microeconomics. But too exclusive a concern with either of these approaches leads one to forget that principles of economic behaviour at one of these levels of analysis may not be valid at the other. If at the micro level a farmer had a large harvest in one particular year, his income would be greater than usual. But if at the macro level all farmers had a bumper harvest, they would in general be worse off financially than usual, as prices vary inversely with total output and the surplus supplies would result in reduced prices.

Basic economic problems

Given existing limits of technology at particular times in history, man's wants have tended to outpace his ability to satisfy them by the adequate supply of goods and services. Commodities that cater for our desires are relatively scarce, being quickly consumed or used up, and can be replaced only by constant effort, or in some cases, like a rare painting, cannot be replaced at all.

Economics is the study of the problem of scarcity and the necessity for choosing between alternatives. If all wants could be easily satisfied there would be no economic problem and no compulsion for economising. As they cannot, a decision has to be made as to which wants should be satisfied first. Societies tend to recognise only those individual wants which are supported by the offer of something in return; this solves the allocative problem of apportioning resources or producer and consumer goods among various competing claimants. These types of wants are known by economists as "effective demands," taking the form of the offer in exchange for goods and services of other goods and services (as in a barter or primitive economy) or of some form of money as we know it today in the market economy.

Important economic concepts relating to money, demand and supply are Value and Utility. Value is an estimate of what a price ought to be, and this valuation varies from person to person. The economist, however, is interested in "value in exchange," aspects of value which can be measurable. This is done through the use of money. Hence if 10 units of commodity A exchange for 1 unit of B the price of 1 unit of B would be 10 times greater than that of 1 unit of A. The exchange value of something is determined by the interaction of demand and supply. It is the estimate placed upon something because of its ability to satisfy some want. Utility is the attribute of anything that can satisfy a want. Something may possess utility without possessing value. For example, the utility of water is enormous, but its value is usually low. Value is not synonymous with Price. Price is merely value expressed in terms of money. Except in conditions of barter, the price of a commodity is definite and clear, and usually the same for all purchasers.

Business is undertaken not only to satisfy people's demands but to make a reasonable profit so that it is worth while to continue to supply goods or services. An understanding of the factors influencing demand and supply, the two chief determinants of price, enable one to appreciate the reasons for the different sizes of firms in industry and the problems of trying to produce goods at the cheapest and most efficient level of production.

Supply conditions

Supply in economic terms does not mean the available potential resources of a region, *e.g.* coal underground, but the amount of goods

ECONOMIC PRINCIPLES

or services on offer for sale in the market at a given price. Though scarcity is important in relation to supply, it is a relative and not an absolute term. One cannot say whether something is economically scarce except in relation to the demand for it. The first folios of Shakespeare's works or genuine Rembrandt paintings are numerically scarce, but are economically scarce only if many people want them (which constitutes Demand), and this is reflected in the high price some people are prepared to pay to obtain them. The chief

TABLE I
RELATIONSHIP BETWEEN PRICE AND QUANTITY

Price (pence)	Quantity supplied
50	500
40	450
30	400
20	300
10	100

determinants of supply are price, costs of the factors or means of production, techniques and methods of production, the price of other goods and, particularly for agricultural products, weather conditions.

Generally firms are willing to offer more of a commodity or service for sale at a high price than at a low price. There are two basic reasons for this. First, higher prices are likely to mean greater profits. Secondly, higher prices may be necessary to produce a greater amount of certain items, particularly in the short term, due to the need to attract factors of production away from other industries, and these factors may be less efficient or more expensive.

Table I gives a supply schedule showing the relationship between prices of an item and the different quantities which a firm might be willing to produce and sell at these prices. Later, when considerations of demand have been discussed, the supply schedule is illustrated in graphical form.

The next condition of supply is the technique of production. For example, new inventions, more efficient machines and improved organisation can all have a decisive effect on supply conditions. Technique is often a question of the size or scale of the operation. Up to a certain output, firms will benefit by gaining economies or "cost-savings." In other words, the larger the firm, the cheaper the goods that can be produced. Beyond a certain point, however, diseconomies will start. Other aspects of technique involve the degree to which specialisation and division of labour are employed.

Some commodities can only be produced jointly, though the second one may be a by-product of the first. Examples are wheat and straw, pork and bacon, petrol and fuel oil, beef and hides. An increased demand for one of the items in joint supply will result in an increased supply of both items. As there is now a larger supply of the second, its price will tend to fall. Similarly a decreased demand for one will lead to an increased price for the other. Changes in weather conditions can seriously affect the output of agricultural products. Good or bad harvests may depend on an adequate supply of rain and sunshine.

Factors of production

No production can occur unless the economic resources (inputs, commonly called the factors of production) are available. They are usually grouped into four categories: land, the cost of which is called rent; labour, which commands a wage or salary; capital, for which interest has to be paid; and lastly the entrepreneur, whose reward is profit. In economics a "normal" profit is often regarded as "cost" as it forms part of the price a consumer has to pay for a product or service. The businessman or accountant estimates profit as a residual to cost, defining it as the difference between cost and selling price.

Each factor has distinct characteristics. Land is distinctive in being strictly limited in supply, not geographically mobile, and subject to the Law of Diminishing Returns. It includes all natural resources, such as forests, farmland and mineral deposits, as distinct from man-made resources. The law, which is shortly explained, may also apply to labour and entrepreneurial ability, and, in a sense, to capital, but not necessarily so soon as with land. Labour is not only a factor of production but the reason why economic activity takes place, since people are also consumers. In the use of labour, ethical and moral problems need consideration, quite apart from the economic. Its supply depends on the size and age composition of the population, and such aspects as the age for retirement from work or for leaving school. Capital can be broadly defined as money or those goods that can be bought with it, which help in the production of other goods such as equipment, machines, factories and transport facilities. The fourth factor, the entrepreneur, is the person who initiates production, takes the decisions, bears the risks involved and organises and co-ordinates the other factors. In large companies it is difficult to see the entrepreneur as a distinct factor since much of

ECONOMIC PRINCIPLES

the responsibility rests with salaried managers while the ultimate risk in terms of money lies with the shareholders.

Sometimes the factors are divided into two: capital (including land and labour) and management. Alternatively, factors can also be classified as specific or non-specific. A specific factor is one, such as highly specialised labour or capital equipment, which can only be applied to a limited range of uses. Non-specific factors are those which are adaptable to alternative uses. Specific factors are relatively immobile, while non-specific factors are more mobile, which means they are more easily transferred from place to place (regional mobility), or from one use to another (occupational mobility).

Opportunity cost

Economists are concerned not only with money costs but also with opportunity or real costs, which are the alternatives that have been forgone as a result of following a particular course of action. The

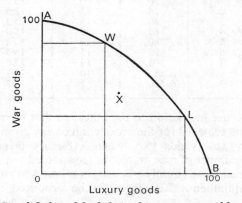

FIG. 4. *Simplified model of choice between war and luxury goods*

true cost of a new television set is the alternative of a holiday or a new car which could have been enjoyed instead. The opportunity cost of a resource is equal to the earning power of that resource elsewhere or the maximum value of its contribution in the best alternative use. If a factor is paid less than its opportunity cost, the tendency is for it to be transferred elsewhere. At the national level, Fig. 4 illustrates a possible choice facing a country between utilising its resources for producing weapons of war or producing luxury goods. At maximum efficiency it could choose any combination on the production possibility curve A–B, point W indicating a preponderant production of war goods and point L indicating a preponderance of luxury goods. It is possible that if its resources are not used to their maximum it could be producing at point X.

Allocation of resources in an industry

In every industry, the units of production—land, labour and capital—can usually be arranged in different proportions. It is assumed that a relationship exists between the amount of factor inputs and the rate of production, and this is called a "production function." The entrepreneur, in planning production, has to decide how much of

TABLE II
INCREASING AND DECREASING RETURNS IN PRODUCTION

Men employed	Total output	Marginal product	Average product
1	10		10
2	25	15	12·5
3	40	15	13·3
4	60	20	15·0
5	80	20	16·0
6	95	15	15·8
7	105	10	15·0
8	115	10	14·3
9	120	5	13·3

each factor to use in relation to the others so that the most efficient combination is achieved for the production of any given commodity. Let us study how yields vary when a factory owner gradually increases the number of men employed (considered a variable factor, and all assumed to be equally efficient) in relation to a fixed amount of capital equipment. Results might be produced as shown in Table II.

Column 3 gives the addition to total output resulting from employing one more man. The table illustrates the way in which total output could change as production increases; up to the point where 5 men are employed, average output rises, which results in increasing returns to scale. Beyond that point, returns to scale are diminishing. If the return to the total output was constant with each successive man employed, production would be taking place under conditions of constant returns. As the number of men is increased from 1 to 9, the *total* product continues to increase, but both *average* and *marginal* products reach a maximum and then start to fall. These movements are illustrated in graphical form in Fig. 5.

ECONOMIC PRINCIPLES

The average product rises so long as the marginal product is greater, and falls when the marginal product is less than the average product. It follows that where average product is at a maximum, marginal product equals the average product. From Fig. 5 it can be seen that the marginal product curve cuts the average product curve

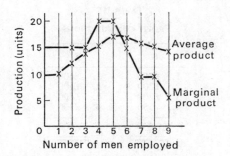

FIG. 5. *Increasing and decreasing returns in production*

between 5 and 6. When 5 more men after the first man are employed the optimum has been exceeded, as indicated by the drop in the average product. It is demonstrated from this experiment that the maximum amount of labour which the owner should employ is 5 men. This is an illustration of the law of diminishing returns, which states that as the amount of the variable factors of production are increased in relation to one fixed factor, successively smaller returns to total output will at some point by yielded.

As production requires at least two factors, one factor cannot be entirely replaced by another, but it may be substituted at the margin. For example, wheat can be produced by employing much labour and little land (intensive farming) or by using little labour and much land. How much of each factor an entrepreneur uses depends on its cost relative to its productivity. Factors should be extended to that level where their marginal returns are equal. In other words the value of the extra product resulting from the last pound spent on labour, machinery or land must be the same. If marginal contributions prove to be unequal then he will find it necessary to reallocate resources from the less profitable to the more profitable and thus raise profits till the marginal returns are equal.

An example of the above is a firm which invests eight separate sums of £100 between two alternatives A and B. Table III shows the profit contributions which the firm earns, totalling £2,850.

As marginal contributions are unequal at £150 and £300, £100 could be taken from A and allocated to B, yielding the results shown in Table IV.

Profit has increased by £50 as a result of re-allocating capital resources between A and B in the ratio of 5:3 instead of 4:4. Marginal returns of A and B are now equal at £200.

TABLE III
PROFIT CONTRIBUTIONS

A	B
1. £400	1. £600
2. £300	2. £500
3. £200	3. £400
4. £150	4. £300
£1,050	£1,800

Demand conditions

As with supply, the chief determinant of demand is price. However, whereas a direct relationship exists between supply and price, there is normally an inverse relationship between price and demand. Demand may be expressed by means of a table or demand schedule, Table V being an example. This shows how much consumers are

TABLE IV
PROFIT CONTRIBUTIONS
(ALTERNATIVE)

A	B
1. £400	1. £600
2. £300	2. £500
3. £200	3. £400
	4. £300
	5. £200
£900	£2,000

prepared to buy at several different prices. It is usually found that a rise in price decreases demand while a reduction in price increases demand.

Other important considerations influencing demand, particularly preferences and incomes, also affect the shape and position of the demand curve which is shown graphically in Fig. 6 (p. 36). It slopes down from left to right, not only because some people will buy more

ECONOMIC PRINCIPLES 33

of an article at the lower price than at the higher one, but because, at the lower price, poorer people will buy for the first time.

Price changes can influence demand in one of two ways. A price fall represents an increase in real income, because the consumer can now consume as much as before for less expenditure. As a result he may spend more money on articles whose prices have not fallen.

TABLE V

RELATIONSHIP BETWEEN
PRICE AND DEMAND

Price (pence)	Quantity demanded
50	100
40	150
30	200
20	300
10	500

This is called the "income effect." Secondly, as the price of an article falls the satisfaction per unit of money increases and the consumer is therefore prompted to re-allocate expenditure so that more satisfaction is bought at the lower price and less through higher priced goods. This is called the "substitution effect."

Perhaps the most important factor influencing demand is the tastes and preferences of the consumer. The tastes of one person may differ over time, and tastes will certainly differ between persons at any one point in time. Subsidiary influences on tastes include changing fashions and the impact of advertising. Not only is industry concerned with the production of goods to satisfy existing wants or new ones which may spontaneously arise, but also it is increasingly preoccupied with "demand creation." Various techniques are used to persuade the consumer to buy goods which the producer wants to sell. Examples are new styles in cars, dresses and popular music.

Principle of diminishing marginal utility

In relation to tastes, choices or preferences, the concept of Utility needs more detailed study. From observations of human behaviour, economists have evolved certain principles regarding people's spending habits. It is assumed that each individual acts rationally in his best interests to arrange his income in such a way that maximum satisfaction is obtained from the way it is spent. While the basic utility is the main advantage to be derived from the consumption of some goods or services, there is the additional attraction of a marginal utility derived from each successive unit purchased. This cannot be measured exactly because it is a subjective valuation varying according to individual tastes. However, a person will tend, unconsciously perhaps, to make purchases in such quantities that the marginal utility he derives from each commodity per price is equal. Total utility for the consumer is greatest when for each commodity or service purchased, the ratio of its marginal utility to its price is the same.

One difficulty with this approach is that not all people know exactly, or bother to calculate, the personal satisfaction derived from each unit of all goods purchased. As a result they do not act like calculating machines to equalise their marginal utilities relative to price.

An important aspect of utility is the principle known as "diminishing marginal utility." This means that the greater the amount of a commodity consumed in a given period, the less is the utility derived from the consumption of each successive unit. In terms of price, it means that the purchaser is usually unwilling to pay as much for additional amounts of the same item. For example, on a hot day a thirsty person might be prepared to pay 60p for his first pint of beer, whereas he might consider successive pints to be worth very much less (although, whatever his own personal valuation of the beer, he would have to pay the standard price charged). This principle explains the shape of the normal demand curve. For example, customers at a pub might buy more beer as prices were lowered. Eventually saturation point would be reached when further lowering of prices would not make the drinkers buy more. Hence the demand curve tends to flatten out at lower prices.

Naturally this law, as with all economic laws, operates only in normal situations where "other things remain the same." For example, continuing the illustration of beer, the principle of diminishing marginal utility would assume that the purchaser drank the same kind of beer in the same place, that he kept the same company of friends, was not celebrating some special event, was not an alcoholic, and that his consumption of other things remained the same throughout the evening. Given special circumstances it would be quite possible for successive pints of beer to have increased utility for the drinker, in contrast to the normal situation where there is usually decreased utility after the second or third pint.

Another factor affecting the demand for, say, product A, given the price as fixed, is a change in the prices of related goods. Here there are three possible situations, competitive, joint and composite demand. Where two commodities can be substituted for each other or interchanged, they are said to be in competitive demand. Examples are butter and margarine. An increase in the price of butter will cause an increase in the demand for margarine and hence in its price.

Where two goods are complementary or inter-related, they are said to be in joint demand. The use of the one implies the use of the other. An increase (or decrease) in the demand for one will result in an increase (or decrease) in the demand for the other. Examples are tennis racquets and balls, tea and sugar, cars and petrol.

Commodities are in composite demand when they have several different uses. Nylon fibre is required by the clothing industry, carpet makers, hosiery producers and many others. An increased demand for any one use will increase the price of nylon and affect the price of everything made from it.

Money Income is another important determinant of demand. For example, the rise in average income per head and the alteration in the distribution of income closely affect the size and direction of demand. Another factor affecting the total demand is the number of consumers and the general population trends. When the population is rising because of a higher birth rate there is an emphasis on commodities demanded by the young; but if an increase in population is due to increased longevity resulting in a large part of the community being composed of older people, then demand trends are different.

Relationship between price, supply and demand

Figure 6, showing relations between price, supply and demand illustrates normal tendencies under competitive conditions. However, there are limitations, which are explained later.

Price tends towards that level where supply and demand are equated. If the price was 40p, there would be an excess supply and accumulated stocks, leading to a price fall. On the other hand, if the price was 10p, there would be an excess of demand over supply, leading to a price rise. Any one particular demand or supply curve shows the amounts demanded or supplied at particular price levels. However, at a given price, there may be a change in either demand or supply conditions.

An increase in demand (given the conditions of supply) or a decrease in supply (demand being unchanged) will lead to a rise in price. Conversely, a decrease in demand (supply being the same) or an increase in supply (with demand unchanged) will lead to a fall

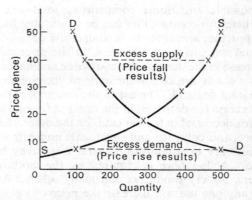

Fig. 6. *Demand and supply relationships and the equilibrium price*

in price. If we take one example in Fig. 7, it can be seen that increase in demand from DD to D'D' leads to rise in price from OP to OP'. The result is an extension of supply from OQ to OQ'.

Figure 8 illustrates an increase in supply from OQ to OQ' which has the effect of reducing the price from OP to OP', leading to an increased demand.

The relationship between supply and demand can be classified into four general laws, which indicate tendencies and are not without exception.

1. Price tends towards the level at which demand is equal to supply (after a period of oscillation).
2. A rise in price tends to decrease demand and increase

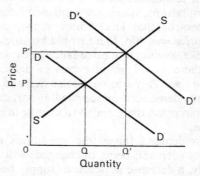

Fig. 7. *Effect of increase in demand on price*

ECONOMIC PRINCIPLES

supply, a fall in price tends to increase demand and decrease supply.

3. If demand exceeds supply, price tends to rise; if supply exceeds demand, price tends to fall.

4. A larger quantity of a commodity will usually be demanded at a lower price and a larger quantity will be offered for sale at a higher rather than a lower price.

In the very short term, the dominant factor in price is demand (derived from utility). In the longer term, the dominant factor is supply (costs of production). The long term is the period when all costs become variable.

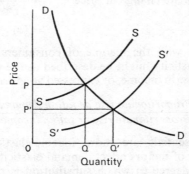

FIG. 8. *Effect of increase in supply on demand*

Demand and supply elasticities

The extent to which demand is affected by a change in price of a commodity is termed "price elasticity of demand." Elasticity of demand arises in two ways. First, existing customers buy more as price falls, and secondly, new customers are tempted to make purchases. The opposite occurs with a price rise. Some stop buying an article altogether, others buy fewer than before.

If a small price change causes a relatively large change in the quantity demanded, demand is said to be elastic. If, however, the change in the quantity demanded is relatively small, or in other words, if a given change in price leads to a less than proportionate change in demand, demand is inelastic. Price elasticity of demand can be expressed as a ratio.

$$\frac{\text{Proportionate change in quantity demanded}}{\text{Proportionate change in price}}$$

When as a result of a price change, this ratio is greater than 1, demand is said to be elastic. If this ratio is less than 1, demand is inelastic. If the ratio is equal to 1, demand is said to have unity elasticity. In Fig. 6 the demand curve is inelastic (and fairly steep) at the higher price of 50p, and gradually becomes more elastic until virtually a horizontal line. The elasticity of demand over the price range from 40p to 50p can be calculated as follows:

(a) Proportionate change in quantity demanded $= \dfrac{150 - 100}{100} = \dfrac{1}{2}$

(b) Proportionate change in price $= \dfrac{50 - 40}{40} = \dfrac{1}{4}$

Elasticity $= (a) \div (b) = 2$

Demand varies with the income of consumers as well as with prices. Income elasticity might be described as the responsiveness of demand to a change in income, or expressed as a formula.

$$\dfrac{Proportionate\ rise\ or\ fall\ in\ demand}{Proportionate\ rise\ or\ fall\ in\ income}$$

Generally inessentials are more income-elastic than essential items. A number of factors affect demand elasticity. The first consideration is the degree to which substitution is possible. If good substitutes are available, demand tends to be elastic. If there are no good substitutes, demand tends to be inelastic, as with certain staple food items such as bread, salt and potatoes. Another influence is the degree of necessity. Valuation of this naturally depends on customs, income and tastes. Tea and coffee, beer and wine, and bread, rice and potatoes are consumed in different proportions, depending on people's habits and preferences. Television sets and cars may be regarded as necessities, luxuries or just plain handicaps, depending on people's incomes and their priorities in life. Rich people tend to have a less elastic demand than poor people for most items, being less affected by comparatively small changes in price.

The element of time is another factor. Demand for an item may be inelastic in the short run as a result of an increase in price. However, if in the long run substitutes have been made available, demand will become elastic. Lastly, it is important to consider the proportion of income involved in expenditure. For items which are very cheap, even a 100 per cent increase in price may have little effect on demand.

ECONOMIC PRINCIPLES

The elasticity of supply measures the responsiveness of supply to a rise or fall in price. Expressed as a formula it is:

$$\frac{\textit{Proportionate change in quantity supplied}}{\textit{Proportionate change in price}}$$

Supply is said to be inelastic if this ratio is less than 1; and it is elastic if the ratio is greater than 1.

The time element is important. Perishable goods, bulky goods and

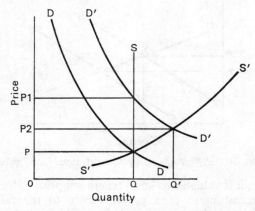

FIG. 9. *Inelastic supply and increased demand*

those whose production takes a long time or involves the use of highly specialised factors are in relatively inelastic supply. Optical glasses are an example, for their supply cannot be readily increased in the short run. Easily stored goods, those which can be produced in a short time, and those whose output can be increased without adding to the existing plant tend to show an elastic supply. Also, if a producer can close down with little loss, if the employees can readily find other work, and if the materials, equipment and machines are convertible to other uses, the easier will be the contraction in output following a fall in demand. In summary, the degree of the elasticity of supply depends on the flexibility or mobility of the productive resources—raw materials, men and money.

The short term is the period during which supply is restricted to the quantities available in the market. An example is perishable goods, where supply is limited to the quantities delivered for the day. Supply is completely inelastic (shown by vertical straight line SQ in Fig. 9) and hence an increase in demand from DD to D'D' results in a price increase from OP to OP1. Eventually as more factors of production are brought in or better use is made of the existing resources, supply becomes more elastic, as the curve S'S' shows and the price drops to OP2.

The most important contribution of elasticities of demand and supply to the study of business problems is the value of the concepts in estimating the effects of price changes. A businessman may have to decide, in a certain situation, whether to raise or lower his prices.

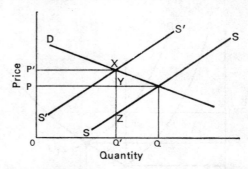

FIG. 10. *Effect of tax on demand, supply and price*

For example, it is valuable to know whether a price reduction would increase demand more than proportionate to the fall in price, resulting in increased revenue, or whether the price reduction would result in such a small increase in demand that less revenue would be made than before. If it is known that demand is inelastic at the ruling price, it would benefit the firm to raise its price till demand became elastic, as that revenue would increase and costs would fall.

The Chancellor of the Exchequer is interested in knowing the effect upon revenue of imposing certain taxes. The incidence or distribution of the effects of a tax between consumers and producers is determined by the relationship between the elasticity of demand and supply. If demand is more inelastic than supply, the greater share is borne by the consumer.

In Fig. 10 a tax XZ has been imposed which has the effect of moving the supply curve upward by the amount of the tax, from SS to S'S'. Producers will now require a higher market price to bring forward any given quantity of the commodity. In this particular case, the demand is elastic and the producer will suffer a price fall (YZ) greater than the price increase borne by the consumer (XY). The price will rise from OP to OP' and the quantity supplied will fall from OQ to OQ'. The price does not rise by the full amount of

ECONOMIC PRINCIPLES

the tax. Though the tax is equal to the amount XZ, the price rises by the amount XY. The burden of the tax is shared, the consumer bearing the amount XY, the producer the amount YZ. The Government once increased a tax on whisky, only to find that whisky had an elastic demand, so that they received less in revenue after the imposition of the tax than they had done before it.

The reader might draw diagrams illustrating the situations where, first, demand was entirely elastic, and hence all the tax was borne by the producers, who experienced a fall in price equal to the amount of the tax, and, secondly, where demand was altogether inelastic and the producer was able to pass on to the consumer the full effects of the tax.

Elasticity in demand or supply contributes to stability of prices. Where both are elastic, no great change in price is necessary to keep them in step with each other. Price fluctuations are more frequent in agriculture than in industry.

Exceptional demand and supply conditions

An exceptional demand curve will be one which slopes up from left to right. This means that the demand for the product will be greater at a higher than at a lower price. There are a number of cases where this might occur.

1. Certain cheap necessities (*e.g.* bread, potatoes, milk) may be in increased demand by poorer income groups if there is a price rise. Demand for such items increases with a fall in real income resulting from a price rise, and decreases with a rise in income resulting from a fall in price. These are known as Giffen goods.

2. Under extreme inflationary conditions or in a rising stock exchange "bull market," people may buy more goods or shares as prices increase, anticipating bigger rises in the future.

3. Sometimes more of a product is bought when its price is high, on the assumption that price automatically reflects quality. Such articles of ostentation or snob appeal include expensive cars, jewellery and rare pedigree dogs.

Note that some economists deny the existence of exceptional demand conditions. When more goods are demanded at higher prices the situations are interpreted as a change in tastes resulting in a shift of the demand curve to the right.

There are also circumstances when the supply of labour to a particular occupation decreases, as a result of higher wage rates, resulting in a backward-sloping supply curve as in Fig. 11. Higher rates of pay generally encourage a person to work overtime, the increased reward obtainable inducing substitution of work for leisure. However, this is not always the case, and the worker may prefer to maintain his existing standard of living by earning the higher wage rate but working fewer hours, thus being able to enjoy increased leisure rather than more goods. This may particularly apply to the female labour force, where the urgency of earning is less, or to disagreeable manual jobs where workers are satisfied with a certain wage packet once obtained and have no desire to work further.

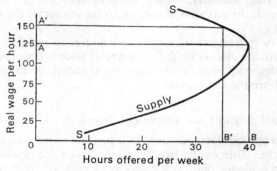

FIG. 11. *Effect of higher wage rates on supply*

For example, a worker at a wage rate of 75 pence an hour may only work 35 hours a week, obtaining a wage of £26·25. At the higher wage of 125 pence he works 40 hours obtaining £50. However, if the wage is increased to 150 pence an hour he may decide to work only 35 hours since now he can obtain roughly the same wage as before—£52·50 for working fewer hours.

Revenue and costs

Average revenue is the total revenue obtained from the sale of a commodity divided by the quantity sold. It is, in fact, the price per unit, and also the firm's demand or sales curve. Marginal revenue is the additional revenue obtained by selling one more unit of the commodity.

Costs of production can be divided into two groups.

1. Variable (*prime costs*), which vary directly with output (number of men employed, cost of raw materials, interest on short-term loans, research, administrative costs, advertising and sales costs).

2. Fixed (*supplementary costs*), which can be varied only in the

long term (rent for plant site, depreciation, land, building, insurance charges).

In the short-term period, some factors can be altered in quantity, but large-scale alterations in the structure of a business can take place only over the long term. In the latter case the entire scale of operations is being changed and all costs become variable.

When a business is producing nothing, it will nevertheless be incurring fixed costs, which are the same as its total costs. See Table VI. When the firm starts to produce, variable costs will be incurred, increasing according to the level of production and thus causing total costs to rise.

TABLE VI

COSTS AND REVENUE OF A FIRM PRODUCING UNDER CONDITIONS OF PERFECT COMPETITION

(see Fig. 12, p. 45, for graphical representation of these figures)

Output	Fixed cost	Variable cost	Total cost	Average cost	Marginal cost	Average revenue (£s)	Total revenue	Marginal revenue	Profit or loss
0	60	0	60	—	—	—	—	—	—
10	60	20	80	8	2	5	50	5	−30
20	60	50	110	5·5	3	5	100	5	−10
30	60	90	150	5	4	5	150	5	0
40	60	160	220	5·5	7	5	200	5	−20
50	60	260	320	6·4	10	5	250	5	−70

Three basic concepts in understanding cost are Total, Average and Marginal. Total costs include fixed and variable costs. Average cost is the cost per unit and is determined by dividing the total cost by the number of units produced. The economist includes what is known as normal profits in the average costs of a firm. This is a minimum level of profit which just makes it viable to stay in the same business and which is regarded as a cost of production. Where a firm has a small output, its average cost will be high because its fixed costs will be "distributed" over a low number of units. This is because certain inputs are indivisible, e.g. the cost of basic equipment remains the same whether 1 or 10,000 units are produced. As output expands, fixed costs comprise a smaller proportion of overall costs and the average cost per unit falls initially. When a firm is producing at the lowest possible average cost, it is said to be at its optimum or most efficient size.

After a certain point the law of diminishing returns comes into force—in other words, the firm is now operating under conditions of increasing costs. Some of the reasons are discussed later in this chapter, in the section on Economies of Scale.

Marginal cost is the addition to total cost of production resulting from the expansion of output by one unit. Now any producer who wishes to maximise profits will continue to produce more as long as his revenue from the sale of extra units exceeds the cost of producing them. Maximum profits occur when production is expanded to the point where marginal cost is equal to marginal revenue. *See* Chapter IX for further discussion of marginal, fixed and variable costs.

Forms of competition and monopoly

The classical economists such as Alfred Marshall and A. C. Pigou favoured a market system known as "perfect competition." It assumed the conditions of a perfect market. First, all units of a commodity sold in a particular market were considered homogeneous, *i.e.* identical to each other. Thus all buyers were indifferent as to whom they bought from, and all sellers were indifferent as to the buyers to whom they sold. Many buyers and sellers existed who had access to all relevant information and easy communication was possible between all persons in the market. It was also assumed that there was perfect mobility of the factors of production and consumers, and freedom for firms to enter or leave the market.

As there were many buyers and sellers representing only a minute part of the total market, each individual's activities were unable to influence price, which was uniform throughout the market. The firm's demand or sales curve would consequently be perfectly elastic. Economists tended to consider this the ideal situation in industry as competitive conditions would force industry to produce goods at the lowest cost and hence lowest possible price, thus resulting in maximum consumer satisfaction. The most obvious examples, where such conditions virtually existed, were the market for such agricultural commodities as wheat, and trading on the stock exchange.

In much of industry in the 19th and early 20th centuries, price was also the key factor in equating supply and demand conditions, most products being unbranded. Let us assume an actual condition where perfect competition exists in an industry. The firm's demand curve is perfectly elastic and hence a horizontal straight line, and it will be the same as the price line of its product. Since the firm produces such a small part of the whole supply that it cannot influence price by changes in output, its marginal revenue will be the same as the price or average revenue and will be constant whatever the output. The firm will maximise profits where marginal cost cuts the marginal revenue curve and this occurs when MC = MR = AR (Price.) At the market price of £5 the firm will produce 3,300 units.

The imaginary cost and revenue structure of a firm in Fig. 12 will make these points clear. Note that at output of 3,300 units the firm is earning normal profits which are included as part of its costs. This is the long-term equilibrium position, where the cost curves of all firms are the same as those of the marginal or least efficient firm in

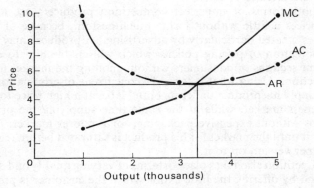

FIG. 12. *Perfect competition*

the industry. In the short run the most efficient firms may earn abnormal profits by charging a higher price than £5. However, in the long run, conditions of free entry for other firms would, as output increased, decrease the price to £5. Firms which cannot cover their costs at this price would go out of business.

In the late 19th and early 20th centuries, the theory of perfect competition became less appropriate as an explanation of how firms behaved. As a result of changing market conditions, virtually all industry today falls between the two extremes of perfect competition and full monopoly. Complete monopoly exists in an industry where there is only one seller of a product. This is discussed in detail later. In a typical industry between one-quarter and one-third of all output is produced by the three largest companies, the rest being shared out among a large number of smaller producers. Proportions vary widely from industry to industry. Examples of highly concentrated industries in Britain are man-made fibres, oil and tobacco. In contrast, industries where less than 10 per cent of output is produced by the three largest firms are printing, furniture and building.

Competition does not exist merely in terms of price. One form of imperfect competition is where products which are physically very similar are differentiated by means of brand names so that producers are able to create mini-monopolies for their products within the same market. Another form is oligopoly, where few competitors exist in an industry and little or quite considerable product differences may exist, as, for example, with soap powders and motor cars. The Ford Motor Company is the only manufacturer of the Capri but not the only manufacturer of cars.

In both forms of imperfect competition producers are able to vary prices a little without losing much custom, because of brand loyalties created particularly by advertising. A producer may adopt a combination of pricing policies which will enable him to attract different sections of consumers without spoiling the market for any one section. Using what is termed "concurrent discrimination," he may supply his product under its brand label at a high price to reach the richest market, while at the same time supplying the product, perhaps without expensive packaging, for a poorer market. Or he can wait until the market for his product is saturated before releasing a cheaper version on to it.

Competition also takes place in terms of varying quality and design, etc., and by offering the little extras which the customer is prepared to pay for, such as prompt service and delivery facilities. Firms compete in trying to bring out something that stands out from the products of its rivals. This form of competition is called technological or the competition of innovation, and it covers new products, new methods and even new forms of organisation. An example was the discovery by Pilkingtons of a "float" process which made glass more cheaply and hence, for a time, seriously affected business projects of other producers throughout the world.

The economists' model of conditions of imperfect competition can be contrasted with the model of perfect competition. Note that both models assume competition only in terms of price, and that other conditions such as technology, taste and income remain the same. In fact, such static conditions rarely exist as the business world is essentially dynamic, with changing conditions being the normal rule.

Under conditions of imperfect competition or complete monopoly, it is possible for a firm to make maximum profit by restricting output and charging a high price, since a point would by reached where $MC = MR$ below the output at which average costs were lowest (optimum firm size). It would not benefit the entrepreneur to expand output to this point since price would be lower and reduced profits would be made. In Fig. 13 it has not been possible to illustrate this particular point owing to the scale of the diagram and the output where MC = MR is virtually the same point as lowest average costs. However Fig. 13 illustrates certain points concerning pricing and output strategies under such market conditions. As under perfect competition, average revenue is the same as the demand curve, but the fact that it is downward-sloping from left to right illustrates

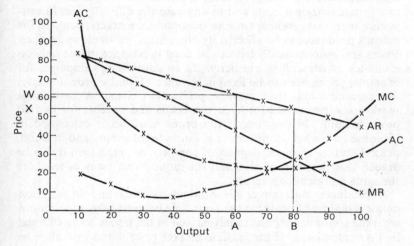

FIG. 13. *Imperfect competition*

that price has to be reduced to sell increased output. Maximum profit is made just below output OB. (*See* Table VII.)

Output could be expanded to just over 90 units (where MC = AR) resulting in reduced profit. Such increased output may be necessary for essential products or services, and since private firms might be reluctant to do this, this is an argument put forward in favour of nationalised industries. When an industry operates under increased costs, *e.g.* output past OB, pricing would generally be based on marginal cost pricing. This applies, for example, to the electricity industry which charges more for peak-rate usage since extra output involves much higher costs in connection with the provision of new plant.

Output could be expanded to over 100 units where AR = AC (the "break-even" point where neither a profit nor loss is made). Given a different cost structure, where a firm operates under decreasing costs, benefits from economies of scale and has heavy unchangeable fixed costs (sunk costs), work might be undertaken, *e.g.* tenders, export orders, based on marginal cost pricing. In this case, however, MC would be below AC, and although a specially reduced price is made (example of price discrimination) this will benefit the firm as long as the additional revenue covers or exceeds the variable costs. (*See* pages 315–17 for more details.)

Generally, industrialists use full-cost or cost plus pricing rather than the economist's marginal analysis techniques. Few firms attempt to estimate marginal costs and in any case the difficulty lies in estimating marginal revenue, since in oligopolistic markets, demand for a firm's products can be affected by other firms' products and prices. Prices and output usually have to be fixed in advance, based only on estimates of demand or elasticity. In an advertising campaign, for example, prices need to be fixed in advance. Usually probable sales are estimated and then average production costs. A percentage mark-up is then added for fixed overheads and another for desired profit margin. In practice, if the profit mark-up is calculated in response to market conditions (*e.g.* estimates of supply and demand, possible future changes, degrees of competition, etc.) then it can be argued that this method is merely the industrialist's way of reaching the same marginal cost result.

A producer must cover his production costs and in addition obtain a margin of profit; at the same time he must take into account what the consumer expects to pay as well as the prices being charged by his competitors. If the feasible market price is too low, then he must find ways of decreasing production costs. There is a "normal" rate of profit in every trade, and if a supplier charges less than the price which will produce it, he is likely not only to spoil the market for all other suppliers, but to make an insufficient profit for himself.

TABLE VII

COSTS AND REVENUE OF A FIRM PRODUCING UNDER CONDITIONS OF IMPERFECT COMPETITION

Output	Total costs	Average cost	Marginal cost	Average revenue (£s)	Total revenue	Marginal revenue	Profit or loss
0	800	—	—	—	—	—	−800
10	1,000	100	20	84	840	84	−160
20	1,140	57	14	80	1,600	76	460
30	1,230	41	9	76	2,280	68	1,050
40	1,310	32·7	8	72	2,880	60	1,570
50	1,430	28·7	12	68	3,400	52	1,970
60	1,590	26·4	16	64	3,840	44	2,250
70	1,810	25·8	22	60	4,200	36	2,390
80	2,100	26·0	29	56	4,480	28	2,380
90	2,490	27·5	39	52	4,680	20	2,190
100	3,010	30·1	52	48	4,800	12	1,790

ECONOMIC PRINCIPLES

If he charges more than the normal rate he is in danger of losing custom. Ideally, resources would be allocated in an optimal manner and public interest maximised if prices show us the value of alternative production at the margin, in other words if prices equalled marginal cost.

The price behaviour of large manufacturers may be very different from that portrayed by the theoretical operation of supply and demand. In practice world prices are published and therefore only infrequently altered. If an increase in demand occurs, with no immediate matching in supply, the result is usually a "waiting list," rather than an increase in price. Also in some cases where falling demand occurs, manufacturers may increase, rather than reduce, their price, to protect profit margins. This happened with motor cars in the early months of 1967. Other aspects of pricing such as "break-even analysis" are covered in Chapter IX.

Theories of the firm—an evaluation

Microeconomic theory, as outlined in this chapter, provides a useful basis for analysing the behaviour of economic units such as firms and markets, as long as the limitations are recognised. The classical economists formulated their theories during the heyday of private enterprise in the early 19th century. They used mainly the deductive method of reasoning, which implied taking for granted certain overriding general assumptions, such as the merits of a perfect competitive economy and non-intervention of the Government in industrial affairs. Other problems were solved by reasoning based on these general propositions. It was assumed that perfect competition was the norm or ideal state of affairs, and other conditions could be judged according to the degree to which they departed from this position. Economists in Britain have tended to follow the assumptions of the classical economists in building models of how firms determined their prices.

In practice such models are only of limited value in understanding actual business behaviour, though they provide a useful starting point and basis from which to make the attempt. Due to developments in technology and science, greater Government intervention in industry and changing patterns of world trade, firms have grown in size and complexity. Since they operate in a dynamic setting where change is the rule rather than the exception, it is necessary for them to adopt a variety of business aims and objectives in addition to the profit maximisation motive, and to adapt constantly their organisation and price structure as the environment changes, affected as all firms are by the activities of Government, competitors and consumers, etc. Some of these constraints on a firm were mentioned at the start of Chapter I. It must be noted that large businesses also try to modify the environment in which they work through their marketing and public relations policies, etc., and large multi-national companies, discussed later in this Chapter, can have a considerable impact on the international scene.

Various writers have argued that classical economic theories were unsound or had only limited applicability to conditions of Britain and the United States, having no relevance to continental Europe. From the onset the Government have in fact increasingly limited freedom of enterprise and interfered with the operation of the price mechanism by various regulatory enactments. One American academic, Veblen (1857–1929), argued that realistic analysis in economics should not be based on the notion of equilibrium, popular with the classical economists, but on the process of change. Later economists such as J. A. Schumpeter and J. K. Galbraith also argued that growth in terms of studying change, new technology and new products was a more fruitful approach than studying price, costs and profits in a vacuum.

A third approach to economics that was developed in the United States was "institutionalism." One exponent, J. R. Commons, argued that since all costs are eventually incomes, in the process of production and exchange each pressure group will try to obtain the incomes it wants. This produces conflict, and eventually a settlement is reached, often with scant regard for the economy. Institutionalism stresses that the standard of living and the organisation of an economy depend on the interaction, conflict and resolution of the views of private pressure groups (trade unions, employers, consumers, etc.) with those of public pressure groups and Government bodies (public authorities, local authorities, etc.) or between entities within these two broad groups. This view is helpful towards an understanding of both problems in macroeconomics and the relationships between the three large entities of Government, management and unions, which are discussed in Chapters III and VIII.

Today numerous theories of firms have been put forward, in part reflecting the fact that they differ in their structures, philosophies and priorities, etc. It is now advocated in micro economic studies that more emphasis should be placed on practical problems in the running of an organisation, such as marketing, production, industrial relations, pricing and costing, and on theories applicable to business and management techniques stemming from such subjects as industrial sociology, psychology and the quantitative aspects of economics like accounting, statistics and operations research. These topics are in fact covered in Chapters V to XI. It should be noted that most modern economists use both inductive and deductive methods in formulating their theories.

Economies of scale and the size of firms

A characteristic of industry is the large number of small firms with fewer than 100 employees. The market for a particular commodity or service may be small or limited to a certain region. On the other hand, it may cater for personal tastes and requirements, so that no large-scale economies are possible, as, for example, with certain dress models. Some activities require little capital, *e.g.* painting and decorating and the running of cafés, and can be undertaken even though shortage of funds will restrict expansion.

Personal reasons are also important in explaining the existence of numerous small firms. Some businessmen like to be independent, to be their own boss and to maintain full control over the activities of an enterprise. The expansion of a firm means the sharing of responsibility. Another reason is lack of ambition—the preference for leisure and freedom from anxiety to the higher income with heavier responsibility which a larger business would entail. Shortage of managerial ability can also restrict growth. As a firm expands, its organisation and co-ordination become more difficult. As departments multiply and grow in size, the task of welding them into an integrated smoothly working team becomes more difficult.

Despite the continuance of a large number of small firms, there has also been a growth in the number and importance of industries with over 10,000 employees, accompanied by a movement towards fewer but larger plants in most of them. There are numerous reasons for the growth of firms. The key is to be found in the conditions of supply and demand which have been analysed.

Economies of scale or savings in costs, *i.e.* reductions in cost per unit of product produced, are made when the size of a production unit (machine, factory, blast furnace, etc.) is increased. They are customarily classified as Internal or External. Internal economies apply to an individual firm and are sometimes known as Technical, Managerial, Marketing, Financial and Risk-bearing.

Technical economies refer to the plants or product lines and are related to the process of manufacturing. Some industrial processes require expensive equipment which it is not economic to produce for small outputs, or for technological reasons will not function for them. For instance, if three main processes of production are used, it is possible to calculate the average output per process. The first process may produce 60 units per hour per man, the second process

400 units and the third 1,000 units. The most efficient use of the whole combined process will require that the machines operating the last two parts of the process are fully worked. Only if an output equivalent to the lowest common multiple of all the processes (6,000 units per hour) is achieved, can this be done. This would mean the use of 100 men in the first operation, fifteen machines in the second and six in the third.

Some types of capital equipment can only be employed efficiently in units of a certain minimum size, and this may be too large for the small firm. Examples are a rolling mill, blast furnace, car assembly line and power press. Such indivisibility of plant means that small enterprises cannot make use of large specialised equipment unless they combine for this purpose. In agriculture, a number of small farmers might jointly use one machine, say a combine harvester.

Costs do not always increase proportionately with size. If the dimensions of a ship are doubled, its theoretical capacity is increased by eight times. The larger ship will not require many more staff to operate her and will not need eight times the fuel and power to propel her through the water. Another source of economy is the fact that if the cost of building a ship or furnace is related to its surface area, the output of the ship or furnace is related to its volume, and the cost of an increase in size does not increase at the same rate as output. This accounts for the tendency of certain industries such as steel, oil refining, chemicals and car manufacture to operate in large units.

Managerial economies mean that a large firm can engage specialist managers to look after each aspect of the work. Many tasks can be delegated, leaving time for the top management to concentrate on overall policy. Big firms can also afford the salaries that will attract the best man in their fields.

There are also marketing economies. Because a large firm buys in large quantities, it will obtain the best discounts from suppliers. It will also have other advantages. For example, it can employ expert buyers and a specialised sales force. Financial economies can also be important. A large firm can borrow from banks upon better security and can raise capital more easily through the issue of shares and debentures than a small firm, since it will have a wider reputation and more influence with those who have money to lend or invest.

There are also risk-bearing economies. The amount of reserve manufacturing capacity or of stocks that need to be kept will often be proportionately less if the capacity and output of the firm are large. The greater the number of instances, the lower the risk of errors in judgment. Thus in a large firm, where the same operation is repeated more often than in a small one, uncertainty can be reduced.

Large firms are able to reduce the risks of a decline in demand by means of diversification. They may manufacture a variety of products and have a number of different markets. Demand fluctuations between regions or between home and overseas trade may offset one another. A small firm, on the other hand, is more vulnerable to changes in market conditions.

In practice there is no one optimum size because the capacity for control differs with each entrepreneur or manager. Usually, in the last resort, a balance is made between the technical and managerial optima. The concept of the optimum, however, gives a clue to the peculiarities of business structure, the forms and scale of organisation, etc. For example, the rise of the big store and the multiple shop is closely connected with the optimum aspect of marketing.

External economies benefit all firms in an industry. There may be certain advantages of an industry concentrating in a certain area: for example, the provision of efficient transport facilities, the supply of trained labour, or the availability of specialist services, which would not be possible if the firms were scattered. Market information also is easier to obtain in a large industry, as it becomes feasible to issue various trade and technical publications. Firms are saved much independent research which they might have been forced to undertake in a smaller industry.

Economies of scale apply particularly to the international field in matters of marketing, research, development and administrative services. In Britain about thirty-five of the largest firms account for a quarter of all exports. Few small firms can afford the marketing organisations and distribution networks to penetrate foreign markets. The big firms do not, in fact, just sell abroad but expand by setting up branches overseas. Some of the advantages are:

1. to jump tariff barriers;
2. to overcome a home shortage of some factor, say management, capital or labour;
3. to expand where factor costs are lower;
4. to benefit from tax advantages.

Another important reason is the personal desire for greater profit and the satisfaction of being in a successful, expanding firm. Improved communications have led to wider markets and hence larger firms. This tendency has also been encouraged by advances in technology where firms require large capital reserves for research expenditure and for the adoption of mass production and automated methods.

The desire for power is another factor, the urge to dominate a market, or to match the power of a rival in dealing with suppliers or customers. Imperial Chemical Industries Ltd. (I.C.I.) was created in 1926 partly to enable the British chemical industry to cope with rivals overseas on an equal basis and partly to provide access to economies of scale.

INDUSTRIAL STRUCTURE AND MONOPOLIES

Forms of industrial expansion

The legal forms of business organisation have been described in Chapter I while this section discusses the varied forms of structure adopted within organisations. Both aspects can be seen summarised in Fig. 14.

Firms can expand in two ways.

1. *Natural growth*.
2. *Merger*—integration with another firm.

Examples of the first are the Ford Motor Company and International Business Machines Ltd. (I.B.M.); examples of the second are Trust Houses and Forte's (Trust Houses Forte Ltd.—T.H.F.), and Cadburys and Schweppes (Cadbury Schweppes Ltd.). In the second category come various types of permanent combination created by some process of acquisition, amalgamation or take-over, etc. Though the different parts of the whole organisation may exist separately in name, they are really under the financial control of a central organisation. The year 1972 in Britain was a record one for mergers and take-overs, in terms of both number and value. Recently many firms have preferred growth by acquisition to growth from within.

An amalgamation occurs when companies merge into one company. One method is a compulsory take-over when one firm forces another to amalgamate by superior monetary power. This is in contrast to the mutual agreement of two companies to merge voluntarily. A third method is the formation of a holding company. A holding company is one which has shares in other enterprises, which are termed "associated companies" if the holding firm does not have a controlling interest, or "subsidiary companies" if it has more than 50 per cent of the shares. The distinction is that in the latter case one company takes over complete possession of another, which loses its identity (though it may retain its own name), while in the former it does not. An enterprise is most likely to be taken over by another business when its assets are undervalued and the buying firm believes it can make better use of the resources. (The term "undervalued assets" refers to poor financial record or return for the capital employed, usually reflected in low price on the stock exchange if the company shares are quoted.) In fact, an important

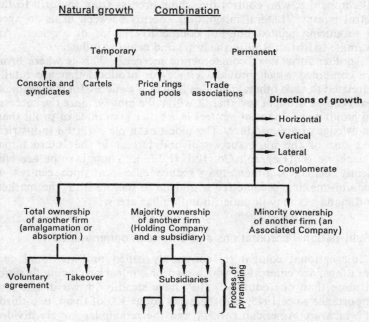

FIG. 14. *Types of business expansion*

reason for mergers is the belief that the whole to be created will be more successful financially than the firms would be separately.

Of the numerous types of combination, the commonest form is "horizontal integration." This is the coming together of two or more firms which make similar products and are at the same stage of production. An example is Unilever, where manufacturers of soap, detergents, toothpaste, frozen foods and margarine were brought under unified control. Another type of combination is "chains." These are formed by firms at the same stage of production, turning out the same product or operating a similar service, but working in separate local markets. Examples are found in retailing (chains of grocers, shoe shops, chemists, supermarkets) and in the hotel industry. Many of these combinations have been formed by growth rather than merger.

Amalgamations between firms which operate at different stages of production are known as "vertical integration." This may be backward towards sources of supply, or forward towards the market. In some cases production is completely integrated, as notably in the oil companies, who control the whole process from the drill to the petrol pump. "Lateral integration" occurs between firms engaged in producing related but not competitive goods or services. An example is British Rail in the hotel and catering industry.

Another form is a "conglomerate merger." This is where firms are combined which provide services or products that are totally unrelated to each other. The idea is that, if a successful management team can be brought together, it will make money, since the successful handling of financial matters is a better guarantee of profit than knowledge of any product. The oldest example is Litton Industries, and one of the most successful and largest is the International Telephone & Telegraph Co. Ltd. (I.T.T.). Though some are efficiently managed, others may reduce efficiency since centres of decision-making become fewer and more remote from the market, and managers may flounder in unfamiliar areas.

Multi-national corporations and European communities

International companies, commonly called multi-national corporations, are enterprises which own or control producing facilities in more than one country. They have steadily grown in size and importance since 1945, and there are about 300 of them, two-thirds of which are American owned, and the remainder largely divided among the British, Dutch, Swiss and Japanese. Examples in Europe are Royal Dutch Shell, Philips, I.C.I., Unilever and Volkswagen and, in Japan, Mitsubishi. The power and influence wielded by these companies are enormous, since about 75 per cent of all industrial assets in the non-Communist world is controlled by them. General Motors, the largest, has total annual sales which exceed the annual net income of most countries in the world.

Often they manufacture their products where labour is cheapest and channel profits to that country where taxation is lowest. The ability of the big corporations to switch large sums of internal funds from country to country can have a serious effect on a nation's balance of payments. Tax havens include Luxemburg, Liechtenstein, the Bahamas and Singapore.

Many multi-national companies are largely technologically based. As a result, enormous capital investment is needed in research and development and vast markets are required for standard equipment sold around the world. Corporations operating in different countries try to standardise their design, parts and products, so that in the event of any local domestic disaster a flow of products can be maintained from some other country or source.

The management of these vast organisations is a great problem. The main link with foreign subsidiaries is the chief executive and his central services in head office. The local manager must be able to merge the skill and knowledge of his own imported labour staff, usually in key positions, with the cheaper and less skilful home labour force. It is an exercise in successful co-operation between races and nationalities in that a local manager must be able to plan and operate according to local knowledge, never forgetting his allegiance to the company as a whole, and the capital and materials made available to him. He must know when to refer to the parent company for advice and how best to serve the host country, although, naturally, his own country's interest must come first.

Generally these companies do become committed to their host countries overseas, economically, politically and socially, and play a large part in their future growth. Often their tremendous influence and power are resented and feared by governments, but as they bring prosperity, they gradually become accepted. American expansion has been noticeable in the last twenty years. One of the principal reasons is that American domestic anti-monopoly laws make oversea expansion easier than at home. In fact more than twenty American companies earn over half their revenue from overseas rather than home markets. In the beginning there was just simple oversea marketing, which evolved to oversea manufacturing subsidiaries, then to the combination of the subsidiaries by international division, and finally to co-ordination at board level.

Such a company not only operates in many countries, but has complete industrial organisations in them, employing local staff and having both multi-national and central management and share ownership. More and more the companies are coming to view Europe as one entity, as several different countries make parts for the same machines (*e.g.* tractors), which are eventually assembled as a completed product in America. Close to 70 per cent of manufacturing exports of the Western world are inter-company shipments from U.S.-based parent companies to their subsidiaries abroad.

Other arguments advanced for expansion abroad have been to avoid tariff duties, and to reduce labour and marketing costs, etc., by producing goods near to the actual customer.

Two opposing views are popularly held about the future of these companies.

1. They will go bankrupt unless the trend is changed to smaller, completely transnational companies with the biggest concerns being split into component parts by a sort of reverse take-over bid. This belief is based on the premise that there cannot be infinite growth in a finite world.

2. Twenty years from now 300 companies will completely dominate world business and something approaching a true world economy will emerge.

The last decade has witnessed the gradual growth of Euro-companies. The size and cost of modern technological projects have become too formidable, not only for companies, but for many nation states. This has led to increased collaboration in capturing a market, and in obtaining the cash for development, sharing its costs and cutting down on the risks involved. In 1962 Britain and France agreed to work together to launch the Concorde project. Since then the VFW 614, the F 28 and the European airbus have become major joint projects. In the computer industry, Siemens of Germany, France's CII and Philips of Holland have agreed to become partners.

One problem is the lack of a uniform European company law, and particularly tax law. Sometimes the formation of a European company becomes virtually impossible. For example, under French company law, a foreign company cannot take over a French company without the consent of every single shareholder. E.E.C. rules for merger preclude some of the more vigorous British take-over activities. The formula has been one by which two independent parent companies set up a series of jointly owned subsidiaries. European companies developed through merger up to the present are Unilever, Royal Dutch Shell, Agfa-Gevaert, Fokker-VFW and Dunlop-Pirelli. Most mergers, however, have been within individual countries of the Community.

One way of overcoming the problem of achieving cross-frontier mergers is the possible creation of a European company, Societas Europea, based on a law that would be uniform throughout the E.E.C. and interpreted uniformly by one body; this is at present being investigated by the European Parliament and the Economic and Social Committee. The idea is that its headquarters would be anywhere in the Community; details would be entered on a European register kept by the Court of Justice, and it would be taxed by the country in which its management was centred. The proposed law would operate parallel to national company legislation and would not replace it. One feature would be the co-management principle, which would guarantee workers' participation and introduce people who would seek to support the Community's policies in relation to competition and social matters.

Monopolies and their control

Industries may be either broadly competitive or monopolistic in character. Complete monopoly presupposes one firm in an industry, the sole supplier of a given product or service to any given market, which is able to earn long-run surplus profits without attracting competition. Under monopoly conditions, in contrast to perfect competition, since the aim is higher profits, this can be achieved by restricting output and charging higher prices. An example of this is the marketing of diamonds. Some monopolies confer little actual power due to the existence of other forms of competition. British Rail monopoly is restricted by road haulage, national bus corporations, airline companies and the car. In another sense competition always exists in business since producers compete for the allocation of a buyer's income.

Monopoly power may arise from one or more of the following causes.

1. Control of a factor of production, *e.g.* diamonds.

2. Legal privilege. This can be conferred by patent on inventors, by copyright on writers and by statute on public corporations, *e.g.* the Gas Board and certain Marketing Boards.

3. Large-scale production, which prevents small producers from competing successfully. A few companies now dominate the world motor-vehicle industry.

4. Exclusion of competitors by price-cutting, price-fixing agreements or combinations.

Combinations may be of a permanent character (*e.g.* mergers and take-overs) or terminable. In the case of the latter, loose associations may be formed where members retain their independence and freedom to leave the group whenever they think it opportune. Firms may come to an understanding to regulate output or fix prices or divide market areas in order to avoid cut-throat competition. This may be in the nature of an informal "gentleman's agreement" or a trading association, formally constituted, with a body of rules. A further stage is the Pool, where the businesses concerned agree to arrange output or sales collectively in accepted proportions, according to the volume of business undertaken. This was done by British railway companies before 1939. A joint selling agency might also be formed, called a cartel, popular in Germany before 1939. Sometimes following a general rise in costs, firms in an industry may raise prices in unison or follow the action of a "price leader." Though price competition became less important during the inter-war period 1919–39 as a result of numerous trade agreements, such restrictive practices have been greatly reduced by modern legislation.

Before 1914 combinations were widespread among firms responsible for such products as soap, tobacco, whisky and cement. However, in general the staple industries (coal-mining, iron and steel, cotton, wool, textiles, shipbuilding and engineering) remained in the hands of numerous, independent firms. They were responsible for a large share of total industrial output and British industry was generally more competitive than American or German. One explanation was the preoccupation of major British industries with the export markets and the absence of duties on imports.

After the First World War slump conditions in Britain and the loss of foreign markets left the staple industries with much excess capacity. They started experimenting with a variety of restrictive schemes for regulating prices and output. These failed to equate supply and demand at profitable levels of prices. By the late 1920s more drastic remedies were sought by means of rationalisation, *i.e.* consolidation of interests within an industry, or co-operation among groups of manufacturers, in order to remove surplus capacity.

In Britain almost the only remedy against restraint of competition before 1948 was to resort to an action at common law, which was difficult. The courts were inclined to view restrictive arrangements as legitimate business tactics. These practices were affirmed by a decision of the House of Lords in 1937 upholding the use of a trade-association tribunal for blacklisting or fining price-cutters.

In theory limitations on the power of monopolies already existed. A monopolist might be satisfied with less than maximum profits to avoid attracting possible new competitors into the market. He might wish to retain the goodwill of the public rather than to maximise profits and to be regarded as an exploiter of the consumer—a role in which the monopolist is frequently viewed. Indeed, in extreme cases of public criticism, the Government could step in to nationalise or control the firm. However, without taking this measure, the Government can, by means of taxes, subsidies, rationing or setting up of statutory bodies, regulate the advantages of monopolistic enterprise in the public interest. Though many restrictive practices had been adopted by industry as a defence against depression, they had a harmful effect on economic growth when they were used as a means of avoiding financial difficulties instead of the management making the effort to introduce cost-reducing innovations.

Most countries had some form of legislative control against the concentration of power in any one company. A form of monopoly called the Trust originated in the United States with the Standard Oil Company (1882). In the U.S.A. the Sherman and Clayton Acts of 1890 and 1914 provided for criminal prosecution for a variety of restrictive practices. Various ways have been found, however, of getting round these laws. European countries had laws against cartels. After 1945 it was argued that the British Government's full employment policy might be frustrated by private restriction aimed to limit output and keep up prices, and similar legislation was advocated in Britain as applied abroad.

In 1948 a Monopolies Commission was established to report on cases referred to it by the Board of Trade, and to decide whether or not monopoly power was being used in the public interest. Monopoly power was defined as that possessed by a company controlling one-third of the market. The public interest included "production by the most efficient means, in such volume and at such prices as will best meet the requirements of home and overseas markets."

Eventually a wide variety of restrictive practices were discovered. An interesting one was the agreement by the Electric Lamp Manufacturers' Association that bulbs should not be produced that lasted more than 1,200 hours. It also fixed prices and retail margins, and enforced them with fines and a collective boycott of offending traders who resorted to price-cutting. Approximately a third of the goods sold in retail in Britain were subject to Resale Price Maintenance (R.P.M.), the manufacturers stipulating the prices at which the retailers or wholesale outlets were required to sell, even though they were not owned by the manufacturers.

The *Restrictive Trade Practices Act*, 1956, forbade manufacturers' associations to enforce price maintenance on retailers. It established a branch of the law to keep a record of restrictions on competition, such as collective agreements concerning prices, conditions of supply and process of manufacture. The court could decide to prohibit any of them considered not in the public interest. If a restrictive agreement was considered to fall under one of seven conditions or "gateways" it was permissible: for example, if it lessened unemployment, protected the public from injury, protected small businesses or gave the public substantial benefits.

This Act had certain weaknesses. There was a rapid growth of open price agreements—agreements among companies to keep each other informed about their prices and the quality of goods supplied. Such exchanges of information could have the same effect as formal arrangements not to compete, if companies used one another's prices as a basis for setting their own. There was also no provision for protecting the public interest in regard to mergers or take-overs that created a monopoly position. An increase in mergers followed the Act; for example, when price restrictions were discontinued in cable-making following a report of the Monopolies Commission in 1952, the majority of the companies were acquired by either one of the big electrical companies—Associated Electrical Industries or British Insulated Callender's Cables Ltd. (although it is interesting to note that the A.E.I. was itself taken over later by the G.E.C.—General Electric Company).

The Monopolies Commission was restricted in its powers to monopoly goods only. Yet monopolies did exist in services, and might include cinemas, stockbrokers, estate agents, lawyers and banks. It was also difficult in many cases for a panel of judges to judge whether, in a certain monopoly position, the advantages to the public outweighed the disadvantages.

The *Resale Prices Act*, 1964, prohibited individual manufacturers (and not merely associations) from enforcing R.P.M. unless they could make out an exceptionally strong case for exemption. R.P.M. might be allowed to continue, for example, if it could be shown that its abolition would lead to a large reduction in the number of retail outlets, or an increase in retail prices.

The *Monopolies and Mergers Act*, 1965, gave certain powers to the Board of Trade. It could refer to the Monopolies Commission any merger, within six months of completion, which was claimed to strengthen a monopoly or where the assets taken exceeded £5 million.

As a result of criticism of the 1956 Act, and to make its operation more flexible and its enforcement more effective, the *Restrictive Trade Practices Act*, 1968, was passed. Among its provisions were the following.

1. The Board of Trade was permitted to exempt from registration agreements:
    (*a*) concerning projects of substantial importance;
    (*b*) made at the Government's request in connection with prices and incomes policy.
2. The Board of Trade could order the registration of any class of information agreements.

The Government, since the war, has tended to encourage a certain concentration of industrial power in Britain. Owing to a relatively small home market, firms rely on exports if they become big, and they need to be big to compete overseas. The primary aim of the state-financed Industrial Reorganisation Corporation (I.R.C.), created in January 1966, was to encourage and improve the structure of British industry by giving financial assistance in reorganising firms into stronger units to make them more competitive internationally. An example was a £15 million loan to two large firms, English Electric and Elliott-Automation Systems, who pooled their resources in 1967 to form one of the best-equipped European groups in the field of automation and control systems. There was also the case of Leyland Motor Corporation and British Motor Holdings, which in 1968 together formed British Leyland. The I.R.C. was abolished by the Conservative Government in 1970.

A major change in legislation occurred with the *Fair Trading Act*, 1973. An Office of the Director-General of Fair Trading was created covering consumer protection, monopolies and mergers and restrictive practices. As this organisation now has a larger staff and greater financial resources at its disposal than any organisation created for this purpose in the past, it is in a stronger position to survey the whole field of competition and industrial structure and to take appropriate measures. It now includes the Monopolies Commission (which has been renamed the Monopolies and Mergers Commission), the Registry of Restrictive Practices and a new Consumer Protection Advisory Committee. Complaints received from the courts, the Weights and Measures Inspectorate or consumers about unfair trade practices may be referred to the Consumer Committee. Criteria which have been the basis for judgment by the Monopolies Commission in the past as to whether a trading practice adversely affected consumer interests have been:

1. giving inadequate information to consumers about their rights and obligations in a contract;
2. confusing consumers about the nature, quality or quantity of goods involved in a transaction;
3. pressurising consumers unduly or making inequitable transaction terms or conditions.

If this Consumer Committee also finds the practice unfair, the Director-General can make a recommendation for action to the Secretary of State for Prices and Consumer Protection. Reference might also be made to the Registry of Restrictive Practices, which now has broader powers covering service industries such as banking and the nationalised industries, with provisions for studying restrictive practices of both management and trade unions. The existence of a monopoly has been redefined to cover a market share of one-quarter of the goods of that description in Britain. Local as well as national monopolies are now liable for investigation.

Competition in the European Community

One objective of the European Community under Article 85, paragraph 1, of the Treaty of Rome is the promotion of fair competitive conditions. Open frontiers are acceptable within the Community provided that all undertakings face equal conditions. Agreements between undertakings on price-fixing, restrictions on production, marketing, investment, sources of supply and bargaining rights are prohibited. This means the exclusion of state monopolies involving legal or practical discrimination, and the prevention of state aids which distort competition.

However, it is possible for exemptions to be made under Article 85, paragraph 3, if specific agreements help to improve production or distribution, or to promote technical or economic progress. Certain types of co-operation which are not restrictive have been allowed by the Commission, such as a sole dealership agreement and agreements covering joint research, joint advertising and selling. But the Commission has ruled against agreements when it has found evidence of price-fixing, as in the case in 1969 when fines were imposed on several companies for alleged price-fixing of aniline dye-stuffs.

There are various ways in which member governments interfere with the operations of intra-Community competition. One is by the state tobacco monopolies which operate in France and Italy. Another is by ensuring that public sector contracts through a variety of mechanisms go mostly to companies in their own countries. The Community is trying to get legislation to make compulsory the general publication of public works contracts, whenever they are worth more than £1 million.

Article 86 declares illegal the abuse of a dominant position in the European Community in so far as it is liable to affect trade between member states. In the Continental Can case, January 1972, the Commission held that Continental Can's acquisition of a Dutch competitor constituted an abuse of a dominant position. It stated that enterprises were in such a position when they were able to take decisions without paying much attention to competitors, buyers or suppliers. The Commission is generally opposed to these types of mergers which result in the elimination of actual or potential competition.

There has been gradual progress in harmonising laws regarding unfair competition. In Britain there is no law relating to this concept in the continental sense, and no legal restrictions on, for instance, the giving away of articles to promote goods or services. However, in Belgium, Luxemburg, Netherlands and Germany, restrictions on various forms of non-price competition, such as premiums, samples gifts, competitions, forms of deferred rebates, special offers, clearance and seasonal sales, diminish the effectiveness of many marketing techniques. Much of the legislation was aimed against the large retailers, and was intended to protect the consumer. A recent French law imposes discriminatory taxation on large-scale retailers. However, it may result in protecting traders against competition from enterprising newcomers to the market. There is in fact an Italian law of 1971 which restricts entry into retailing.

There is some ambiguity in the emphasis on creating competitive conditions in the European Community. During the 1960s the chief European concern was to create industrial and commercial units of a size capable of operating in an international context, particularly in view of the challenge from large American companies.

III. MACROECONOMICS AND INTERNATIONAL TRADE

CONCEPTS GOVERNING THE WORKING OF THE ECONOMY: EMPLOYMENT THEORY AND INDUSTRIAL LOCATION

A general knowledge of the working of the economy and of the factors determining the level of employment can be useful to business. Greater awareness is shown of the variables on which the economy functions and how the variables interact. Firms are able to see more clearly their role in the economy and the problems that occur when it is freely fluctuating, particularly the detrimental effect on trade and industry, and the need for some form of Government action to prevent the waste or overuse of resources, to stabilise the economy and to give a more even pattern to growth.

Trade cycle and business fluctuations

The "trade cycle" is the term for the phenomenon of regular changes in the pattern of business activity. The four phases are known as: depression or slump (a period of high unemployment and excess plant capacity); gradual recovery or reflation (when the economy is expanding and many resources are gradually becoming utilised); boom period (when all resources are fully employed but continuous demand results in inflation), and recession (a period of increased unemployment of resources, reduced demand, and lower wages and prices). These periodic fluctuations have been a prominent feature of the economy since the early part of the 19th century.

Statistics of output, employment, prices and incomes show that the long-term expansion of economies has not been achieved by a consistently upward movement but through a series of oscillations on a generally rising level. Given the quantity of resources one year after another in an economy, output tends to rise due to the increased efficiency with which resources are used. In addition the discovery of new techniques, etc., steadily increases the capacity or potential output of the economy.

The length of each cycle (from peak to peak) has usually covered a time span of about five to ten years. Since 1945 the fluctuations have been less extreme in Britain and the United States partly due to improved economic knowledge and techniques of control. Also incomes and prices are cushioned against slumps by the organised resistance of trade unions and employers. This resistance to cuts in wages and prices accentuates the effect of a recession phase on output and employment.

The recovery period (the second phase) may well be slow because businessmen have little incentive to invest money when demand is low, resources are already under-employed and profits meagre. However, the Government may implement various monetary and fiscal policies to help a quicker recovery. For example, monetary restrictions may be lifted, bank rate reduced and official restraints on bank lending removed. This will lead to relaxation on restrictions in hire-purchase finance, extending to the fiscal sphere by means of lower taxes. At the same time Government spending will be increased.

Consumer goods industries are often the first to recover from stagnation, particularly those durable sectors where a large proportion of sales are credit financed. Idle resources are mopped up rapidly and gradually the gap between actual and capacity output diminishes. Unemployment declines rapidly. Excess stocks accumulated during the "stop" period run down. Firms expand production. Eventually plans are made to increase productive capacity, *i.e.* by a higher level of investment in fixed assets. Thus increased activity takes place in capital goods industries.

In the third phase (the boom period) we have reached almost the peak of resource utilisation. Bottlenecks appear in various areas and industries and cause inflation in terms of rising wages and prices. This phase can only continue as long as the reserves of gold, convertible currencies or borrowings exist or if the country is exporting sufficiently to maintain a favourable balance of payments.

The warning indicators of an approaching balance of payments deficit relate to those factors leading to an adverse balance of trade, which is an excess (in terms of value) of imports over exports. This may be caused by inflation. Usually domestic inflation creeps into foreign trade and relatively imports look cheaper and exports dearer. The excess of purchasing power has to be satisfied from imports, while rising prices make the country an attractive market for foreign manufacturers and divert home-produced goods away from the export market. Thus imports increase and exports decrease and eventually an adverse balance of trade develops.

To maintain solvency the Government has to let out the excess pressure by deflating. This is the fourth phase—the stagnation period. Output remains roughly static while capacity increases. The amount of unemployed resources increases, measured by the gap between capacity and actual output. Wages and prices tend to drift up roughly parallel with the increase in capacity, ending up with wages relatively higher than prices. This accounts for the increase in real wages or standard of living which is continually happening.

New product launching should generally be timed to coincide with a period of expansion in the economy or in the industrial sectors likely to provide a market outlet. The same applies to promotional expenditures to aid sales expansion on existing products. The depth of the slump is the time for planning so that arrangements can quickly be put into action when the "Go" signal comes. Deflationary periods are usually the best time to embark on programmes of major building expansions. Prompt delivery and keen prices are then offered by plant manufacturers. Expansion by "take-overs" can be effected more cheaply then, as share prices are usually at a low level. It is also true that money loans may be less available and interest rates high at such times.

Market share enlargement is easier when business is expanding. If it is contracting, existing suppliers hang on grimly to the share of the market they already have. In planning a major sales growth it is wise to ensure that the increased market expenditures and productions coincide with an expansion phase in the economy, or at least in that sector of it which forms the market.

Shortage of finance will frequently cause trouble for firms. When Government restrictionist schemes are introduced this means higher interest rates and reduced availability of credit. New equity finance (ordinary shares) can be raised more cheaply, in terms of cost of annual dividend, while share prices are high and yields low, before the introduction of Government restrictive measures which adversely affect company profitability and cause a decline in the share market.

A firm's industrial relations and training policy should also take note of the trends of the economy. Pre-expansionary phases can be used to recruit and train new staff before the labour market becomes tight. When unemployment is low and hence labour scarce, management–worker relations will be very much dominated by the strong bargaining power of the unions, with prospects of strike threats and pressure for higher wage rates.

The national income

Economic statistics are needed to indicate the current trend of the economy as a basis for policy and to provide means by which the effects of past policies can be judged. National income statistics are used in conjunction with numerous other economic data relating to the level of employment, prices, industrial production, the trade balance, etc.

National income figures give an indication of the economic welfare and the capabilities of a country, provide a standard of comparison of the economic performance compared with past years, and enable comparisons to be made between the relative prosperity of different nations, either as a whole or per head of the population. They give the most complete picture of the whole economy, the respective contributions of its different sections and the changes in income which have taken place among them. They thus provide important information for the Government control of the economy.

Details of the national income are obtained from many sources, such as private tax returns, companies' income and expenditure accounts and reports, and Government returns and reports. By dividing the national income by the number of the population (or of the actively employed population), the average income per head of the country can be obtained. Three methods can be used for calculating the total of a country's income in a year.

In the Income Method is included the total of all money incomes earned in exchange for goods and services, *e.g.* wages, profit, rent, interest. "Transfer payments" must be excluded, which result in no increase in actual production, such as retirement pensions, students' grants, interest on Government securities, money from sales of second-hand goods and unemployment benefits. The Output Method measures the money value of all goods and services produced. Property income from abroad must be added, and dividends paid to foreign owners of U.K. shares as well as rents paid to overseas property-owners must be deducted. Any stock appreciation in value during the year must also be deducted, since, like transfer payments, it represents no actual production. Both these methods show the Gross National Product at factor cost, that is the full cost of producing the items in the national income, ignoring the effect of indirect taxes and subsidies. The Expenditure Method shows the total amount of money spent on consumer goods and on gross capital investment. The value of imports must be deducted, since they were not produced in the country, and the value of exports (items produced but not purchased) must be added. The result is the Gross National Product at market prices. To convert it to factor cost, taxes on expenditure (which are proceeds paid to the Government) need to be deducted, and subsidies (which are paid by the Government to producers and enable them to sell goods at a lower price than they would normally) have to be added.

All three methods result in the Gross National Product (G.N.P.), which is the same as the gross national income. To calculate the national income or Net National Product (N.N.P.), one must deduct depreciations, *i.e.* the amount of the country's capital worn out during production.

When gross investment exceeds depreciation, the economy is growing or expanding. A stationary or static economy is one in which gross investment and depreciation are equal, as the country is producing just enough capital to replace what is consumed in producing that year's output and no more. A declining economy exists when gross investment is less than depreciation.

Factors which determine the level of the national income and hence contribute to economic growth include the supply of natural resources, capital and labour, the age and sex distribution of the population, its intelligence and general inventiveness, the state of technical knowledge, the distribution of wealth and the country's capacity for saving and spending. While high consumption means a high national income at the present time, a high degree of saving will usually mean a sacrifice in the standard of living and a low national income now, with the prospect of better welfare and higher national income in the future.

Since national accounts are prepared only once a year and have to be retrospective, they are historic accounts in that they give last year's figures. To find out what is happening in the current year and what is likely to happen in the immediate future, information can be obtained from two sources, economic indicators and mathematical forecasting.

Economic indicators

These, as shown in Table VIII, are key variables in the economy which provide some idea of the way it is behaving at the present time.

Useful sources of information, especially as to indicators, are *The Economist, The Financial Times, Economic Trends* (H.M.S.O.) and *Economic Progress Report*, issued monthly by the Central Office of Information.

Important indicators are:

1. Unemployment and unfilled vacancies, which show the supply of available labour and the demand for labour.
2. Balance of payments. This consists of:
    (*a*) the visible trade balance, *i.e.* the difference between imports and exports, measured on a monthly basis;
    (*b*) invisibles.

TABLE VIII

TYPICAL ECONOMIC INDICATORS

	Published monthly (months or monthly average)	Unit	1971	1972	1972 1st qtr	1972 2nd qtr	1972 3rd qtr	1972 4th qtr	Nov	Dec	1973 Jan	
1	Exports f.o.b.[1]	£m	733	761	728[6]	769	686[7]	861[2,7]	850[2,7]	838[2]	881[2]	1
2	Imports f.o.b.[1]	£m	707	819	768[6]	786	780[7]	939[2,7]	947[2,7]	921[2]	958[2]	2
3	Visible balance[1]	£m	+26	−58	−40[6]	−17	−94[7]	−78[2,7]	−97[2,7]	−83[2]	−77[2]	3
4	Official reserves (end of period)[3]	£m	2,526	2,167	2,715	2,673	2,337	2,167	2,262	2,167	2,171	4
5	Unemployed (excl. school-leavers and adult students)[4]	'000s	737	816	870	834	807	752	756	727	705[2]	5
6	" "	% of all employees	3·2	3·6	3·8	3·7	3·6	3·3	3·3	3·2	3·1	6
7	Retail sales (vol)[4]	1966 = 100	103·8	110·0	106·3	108·5	111·8	113·7	113·0	115·2		7
8	Retail prices (not seasonally adjusted)[5]	Jan 1970 = 100	113·2	121·2	117·8	120·1	122·0	125·0	124·9	125·6		8
9	Average earnings[4]	Jan 1970 = 100	119·4	128·6	125·4	130·5	135·2	135·2	142·5[2]			9
10	Industrial production	1963 = 100	124·9	128·6	122·3	128·9	130·0	133·3	133·6	133·9[2]		10
11	Manufacturing production	1963 = 100	126·7	130·5	125·4	129·5	132·1	135·0	135·5	135·9[2]		11

1. On balance of payments basis 2. Provisional
3. Calculated at old rate (£1 = $2.40) up to end-November 1971 and at new middle rate (£1 = $2.6507) from end-December 1971
4. Excluding Northern Ireland   5. The 16 January 1962 = 100 index rebased on 20 January 1970
6. Affected by miners' strike   7. Affected by dock strike

3. Industrial output.
4. Retail prices or the Department of Employment's "cost of living."
5. Wage Rates. (Both 4 and 5 are useful for measuring the degree of inflation.)

Advance warning of possible restrictive policies are three simple statistics given by 1, 2 and 4 above. These are the unemployment

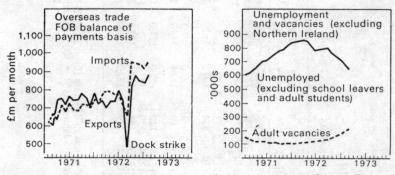

FIG. 15. *Two specimen economic indicators in chart form. Figures published up to 12 March 1973 are included in the charts.* (*Source:* Economic Progress Report No. 38, *April 1973.*)

percentage, the rate of increase in the cost-of-living index and the monthly trade figures (as in Table VIII and Fig. 15 which shows two specimen charts).

Mathematical forecasting

This involves taking the national income figures for the last year (and previous years) and projecting forward mathematically from them. However, numerous problems are involved. Forecasting tends to be based on certain conditions, but as soon as these conditions cease to exist the forecast is no longer reliable. Examples are changed political and economic alignments between countries, and changed monetary or economic conditions in the one country.

Another major difficulty is that the national accounts are by no means accurate and the Central Statistical Office lists them as "estimates" because of the difficulties involved in measurement. For example, "double counting" must be avoided, such as adding together both the value of the steel used in making a car and the value of the completed car, since it is only the value of the finished product which is required in calculating the national income. Problems arise over activities which do not directly exchange for money. For example, there are various unpaid "do-it-yourself" jobs like gardening and housework, while other forms of work may be paid in kind, such as free housing or food rather than money. Capital depreciation is difficult to estimate. Lastly information, such as that contained in some tax returns, can be inaccurate.

The standard of living of a country and its rate of economic progress and growth are chiefly determined by the size of the national income. However, this is not a reliable indication unless account is taken of changes in money values and population. It is important to distinguish between real national income (the volume of goods and services) and money national income (the value of the goods and services). An increase in national income may be due simply to price inflation, not to increased output of goods, leaving the people materially no better off. If the population increases, the real income may increase proportionately, leaving the average income per head the same as before. After price rises and increases in population among which the national income is shared have been taken into account, economic growth entails the production of more goods and service per head each year. This makes available opportunities for higher standards of living and consumption.

The real national income per head in Britain was over 50 per cent higher in 1965 than in 1945, having risen by about $2\frac{1}{2}$ per cent per year. Account must also be taken of how the wealth is distributed. If it is concentrated in the hands of a small governing or land-owning élite, a country may have a high national income but a low standard of living. The composition of the national income is also important, for a country may spend considerable amounts on matters like defence and military production which make no direct contribution to welfare.

To a greater extent firms today are trying to anticipate Government policy by using national independent forecasts (e.g. National Institute of Economic and Social Research, N.I.E.S.R.) and supplementing them with their own forecasting departments. This is not an easy task as few firms have the means to create expensive economic intelligence units, forecasting methods are far from completely reliable and it is difficult to quantify how much value they are to the firm. Also action taken by Government may come when it is not practicable for the firm to alter its short-term objectives and it is possible that Government policy will clash with that of business.

Apart from using present sales and production and cost figures, the businessmen, when making forecasts, must take general economic trends into account. In this respect a knowledge of economic theory,

Government policy and the effects of foreign trade will help them to a better understanding of those indicators which give a general picture of economic trends.

Aggregate demand and supply

In Chapter II the factors determining the individual consumer's demand for a given commodity were discussed; they were price, income and taste. At the micro-level when the prices of some goods increase relative to others, consumers will reduce their demand and may switch to cheaper commodities. However, at the macro-level, when all prices rise, factor incomes increase in the same proportion, since someone must receive as income the additional money spent when prices increase. Similarly whereas at the micro-level taste referred to consumers' preferences between one commodity and another, now at the macro-level it refers to their preferences between consumption and saving. In the short run these are fairly slow to change. Thus given prices and the consumers' preferences, their total demand for goods and services will depend on their total incomes.

After allowance has been made for the discrepancies in the different methods of calculating the national income, the totals of the country's income, output and expenditure will be the same. The value of the total volume of output of goods and services is the same as the total income, because all expenditure on goods and services goes to some factor of production or another as income or payment.

It is now necessary to provide a theoretical explanation of how fluctuations occur in an economy and of the role of certain variable factors which interact upon each other.

One can illustrate the workings of a simple economy by making the assumptions that there is no foreign trade and no government intervention or expenditure. The flow of money can be considered a circulation between firms which produce goods (national output, production or aggregate supply) and households which earn incomes (total income), which are then used up in being spent (national expenditure or aggregate demand) on the goods and services produced.

The problem in an economy is to match total (aggregate) demand to the total output of goods and services. If there is a lack of demand for goods and services, that is if the public are unwilling or unable to buy them, firms will reduce output, may lower their prices to get rid of surplus stocks and will possibly increase their exports if the oversea demand justifies it. If, however, aggregate demand is greater than current output, firms will try to expand output, may increase prices and may start importing if possible.

It is only when aggregate demand is exactly equal to the current level of national output (or aggregate supply) that firms will not be compelled either to reduce or to increase the quantities and/or prices of the goods they produce. This situation can be called the macroeconomic equilibrium, the counterpart to the supply and demand equilibrium for the market of a single commodity which was discussed in Chapter II.

In the short run (three to five years), aggregate supply changes little whereas aggregate demand can change considerably, and it is this factor which determines the level of employment. If an economy is to avoid large-scale unemployment on the one hand and inflation on the other, aggregate demand must be sufficient to absorb the full-employment level of output and no more.

Consumption, savings and investment

Now it is necessary to discuss in detail the determinants of the aggregate demand of the community for goods and services. One factor is the community's demand for home-produced consumer goods, termed consumption (c). In a closed society where no foreign trade took place, stable equilibrium would exist if all earned incomes were spent on consumption expenditure (*see* Fig. 16 for a simplified diagram of the flow of wealth). However, if some people wanted to save rather than spend money, this would represent a withdrawal of income from the flow of wealth, and income would exceed consumption. The result would be decreased consumption, lower incomes and a fall in economic activity.

Consumption refers to income payments by households to firms, in exchange for which households receive consumer goods and services; saving represents that part of income which is not spent on consumption. If the average income level is high, then greater consumption is possible. When a consumer has a very low income, it is spent on basic necessities, but as his income rises, he is able to save some of his earnings. The degree to which a person saves rather than consumes depends partly on his mode of living and beliefs, on prevailing attitudes, on advertising and the availability of outlets for funds (*e.g.* in property), on the provision of financial facilities (*e.g.* hire-purchase companies) and on the existence of such services as pension schemes and free education which may discourage saving.

The other factor determining aggregate demand is investment spending. This includes money spent on producing capital items such as factories, machinery, schools and roads, net additions to stocks (consumer goods, raw materials, etc.) and replacements for worn-out capital goods. This can be regarded as an "injection" which is the counterpart of the "savings withdrawal" from the national income. If these two are equal, then the economy can be said to be in equilibrium again. However, if savings are greater than investment, firms will receive a smaller volume of income to pump into the next circuit of the circular flow. National income will fall

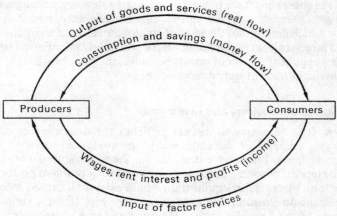

FIG. 16. *The flow of the national wealth*

and unemployment increase till savings and investment are equal again. This process is called deflation. In the reverse position, when investment is greater than saving, and at a particular point of time when, say, the national income is £30 million and firms receive income, say, of £35 million, then national income will rise to £35 million. The additional funds may come from past savings or from abroad. Planned savings and investment are most unlikely to be equal at the same moment in time because savers are not identical with investors, and the factors which govern savings and investing are not closely related.

Another clear gap between income and consumption expenditure is taxation, the countervailing injection being Government expenditure. Government output and expenditure form an important part of the community's aggregate supply and demand for goods and services. By appropriate policies in regard to its own production or spending and to the level of spending in the economy, the Government can influence the total volume of output and help to bring about overall equilibrium between the overall supply and demand (*see* the section on Public Finance, pp. 94–6).

MACROECONOMICS

Another pair of withdrawals and injections are imports (for which expenditure has to be paid to other countries) and exports (where the expenditure from abroad helps to generate income in the country). Savings, taxation and imports are leakages from the income flow which would cause a contraction of total income and hence of aggregate demand. However, the corresponding injections are investment, Government expenditure and exports. These three, together with consumption, are the main determinants of aggregate demand. This condition can be summarised by the equation:

$$y = c+i+g+e$$

where

y = national product or national income (aggregate demand);
c = consumption;
i = investment, including demand for additions to stocks as well as for durable equipment;
g = Government's demand for goods and services;
e = demand by customers overseas for our exports.

It is the interaction of these variables that determines the nature of the fluctuations of economic activity in the community. In the macro-economic equilibrium position total leaks or withdrawals from the system (savings plus imports plus taxation) equal the total injections (investment plus exports plus Government expenditure). *See* Fig. 17.

The multiplier and the accelerator

In contrast to consumption and savings plans of households, investment programmes are likely to fluctuate greatly. In fact, levels of output, employment and prosperity fluctuate more in capital goods industries, *e.g.* shipbuilding and heavy engineering, than in consumption industries.

There are various reasons for this. First, it is difficult to estimate the life or durability of capital goods, though their cost is written off over a period of years by means of depreciation. The necessity of replacing capital goods as they wear out has to be considered. There is also the risk of new innovative techniques which may render existing capital equipment obsolete. Then, too, the expectation of future profitability is influenced by the size of current profits, any variability of current profits causing investment fluctuations, because profits are a major source of funds for investment. Also the level of demand and of availability of money for the purpose of investment is determined partly by the willingness of savers to part with money in the form of loans to businesses.

Another factor is the expected yield relative to cost that is likely to result from use of the capital equipment over its expected life span (marginal efficiency of capital). Another factor is the rate of interest, that is the cost of borrowing the money for the investment. The higher the rate of interest on loans, the less attractive is the prospect of borrowing for the purpose of investment. However, changes in

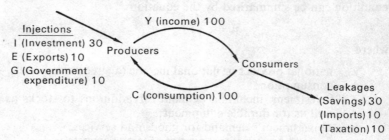

FIG. 17. *Circular flow of income*

the estimation by businessmen of the expected yield are generally more important in accounting for fluctuations in investment decisions than movements in interest rates. Estimations of the future earning power of an investment may be arrived at after the consideration of such factors as the current income, the likely future price level, the course of stock exchange prices and Government policy.

The multiplier and the accelerator, described below, help to explain the widely differing fluctuating rates between industries producing capital goods and those producing consumer goods, and and provide some idea of the way in which the trade cycle works, accounting for the good and bad years of business operations. In addition they explain why fluctuations in the level of aggregate monetary demand lead to a series of changes in the level of national income instead of just one.

The level of investment is the most important element in determining real income, because an increase in investment creates not only a demand for goods but also the productive capacity for higher levels of output in the future. It is possible to calculate a factor called the "multiplier," which measures the effect on income and consumption of a given increase in investment. If, say, £10 million is invested in a building project, it will be passed on, in terms of income of £10 million, to the staff, who will in turn spend it, setting up an expanding cycle throughout the economy. If the increase in income is not spent but is all saved, there will be a multiplier of 0 (zero), a most unlikely event. If all the income, in the form of wages, salaries, etc., is spent (*i.e.* implying a marginal propensity to consume of 1 and a marginal propensity to save of 0), then the multiplier would be infinity. The size of the multiplier in practice lies between these hypothetical extremes. If out of £100 million extra income $\frac{4}{5}$ of the extra income was spent and the remainder saved, the marginal propensity to consume would be $\frac{4}{5}$ and the marginal propensity to save would be $\frac{1}{5}$. As £20 million of the extra income is now saved, £80 million expenditure generates a further £80 million of income. If the same marginal propensities exist, £16 million will be saved and £64 million spent in the next period. Those who received the extra £64 million as income would spend £51·20 million and save £12·80 million. Eventually, as national income expands in a series of decreasing increments, the final extra income would be £500 million. This is found by adding up the totals at each successive level:

£100 million + £80m + £64m + £51·20m and so on.

We shall find that income has not increased by just £100 million (the original injection of investment) but by a multiple of it. In this case the total is £500 million, five times the size of the original injection of investment, and the multiplier will be 5. Equilibrium is restored with £100 million of the extra savings exactly balancing the original increase in investment. The multiplier is always the reciprocal to the marginal propensity to save (M.P.S.). As the M.P.S. is $\frac{1}{5}$, the multiplier is 5. We could also follow the same process in the reverse direction if a fall in investment took place, and study the effects on income.

The theory of the accelerator shows the effect of a change in demand for consumer goods on investment, and how a certain small change in demand for a consumer good will cause a proportionately greater change in the capital investment required to produce that commodity.

If a factory produces television tubes and has 100 machines with an effective life of ten years, ten machines will have to be replaced each year and the producers of the machinery must have the capacity to meet this replacement demand. If the demand for television tubes increases by 10 per cent one year, there will be an immediate need for ten new tube-making machines in addition to the ten replacement machines. Thus a 10 per cent increase in consumer demand leads to a 100 per cent increase in the demand for capital goods, from ten to twenty tube-making machines. If demand stays constant at the new level during the following year, production of the machines will contract sharply. Until the extra machines wear out after ten years, only the annual replacement of ten machines will be needed.

Introduction to employment

A person is unemployed if he is willing to work but no work that he is capable of doing is available. People unable to find work for long periods tend to become apathetic and depressed, and the resultant low morale can cause repercussions throughout the community. Also unemployed labour and capital represent wasted potential production, and poverty conditions can seriously effect the efficiency of the labour force when it does eventually find work.

"Full employment" usually means that only about 2 per cent of the labour force is registered as unemployed and seeking work. This 2 per cent includes those affected by seasonal variations in demand, such as in the tourist trade, fishing and harvesting, and those who are temporarily out of work while changing jobs (transitional unemployment). These seasonal and transitional forms of unemployment are regarded as unavoidable (although conference centres can help problems in the tourist trade). A form of temporary unemployment which is avoidable is called "cyclical," *i.e.* it relates to the upward and downward trends in business activity during the trade cycle. Until the great depression of 1929 these "cycles" used to occur every seven to ten years, wartime excluded.

The classical approach

Till the mid 1930s the views of the "classical" economists such as John Stuart Mill and Marshall were generally accepted as pointing to the best way of coping with problems in the economy. These economists believed that in normal conditions the price system under capitalism was capable of providing the maximum use of resources. This was in accordance with a principle known as Say's Law (after J. B. Say, a French economist), which stated:

    1. that the act of producing goods generated an amount of income equal to the value of the goods produced, *i.e.* supply creates its own demand;

    2. that income would be spent either on consumption or investment (the equality of funds saved and funds invested being assumed).

Unemployment was considered to be only a temporary phenom-

MACROECONOMICS 81

enon which, when it did occur, would be solved by the following economic forces.

1. The rate of interest. The classical economists believed that if there was unemployment in the economy due to a fall in investment then the rate of interest would fall. This would be due to the fact that the demand for loanable funds, which is derived from the investment requirements of businessmen, is greater than their supply, *i.e.* the community's savings. There would thus be less incentive to save and it would be cheaper to invest. More investment leads to more employment opportunities, and therefore to more funds being available through saving for investment at a mutually acceptable interest rate. Eventually savings would equal investment, at the full employment level of income.

2. Wage conditions. They believed also that unemployment could be relieved by a lowering of wage rates. This was supposed to encourage total demand and to make it more profitable for businessmen to employ labour.

3. Deflation. Unemployment caused by a decline in the demand for exports abroad would be corrected by automatic deflation of the economy, resulting from the deficit in the balance of payments under the gold standard. It would result in an outflow of gold, a fall in the money supply and in spending (in accordance with the quantity theory discussed in Chapter IV) and a fall in prices, including export prices. Eventually demand for exports would increase. For a fuller discussion see the section on International Trade on pp. 104–5.

The depression years 1920–39

Until the 1920s there was usually no permanent unemployment in the U.K. and so the classical theory seemed to work in practice, although slowly. There seemed no necessity for Government intervention in the economy to secure full employment. These assumptions were proved wrong by the persistence of widespread unemployment during the inter-war period at a level of 14 per cent, rising during the depression years 1929–32 to over 20 per cent of the total labour force.

The classical theory became discredited for the following reasons.

1. The remedies it provided for the problems of persistent general unemployment (*i.e.* lowering of the wage rates, lowering of prices and lowering of interest rates) did not work. During the depression years, the areas particularly affected by unemployment were the locations of the heavy capital or staple industries, such

as coal, textiles, steel and shipbuilding, which had been the basis of our export trade before 1914. The situation was aggravated by the fact that whenever a slump in the main industry occurred other dependent specialised industries in that area also suffered; and general regional unemployment was the result.

2. Countries refused to abide by the rules of the gold standard.

3. Changes in wage conditions were not sufficient to secure movement of labour, particularly when there was no adequate information on job opportunities elsewhere, and when close family and social ties had been established in an area. Often it was the younger or more skilled labour which was prepared to move out of depressed areas, leaving behind the unskilled or those skilled in only limited activities.

During the 1920s and 1930s the Government worked on the principle of the balanced budget, adjusting expenditures according to changes in revenue. As income taxes are linked to the level of income, and this declines when there is a slump, Government revenue automatically declines at times when there is insufficient demand. This meant that Government expenditure had to be cut, one result being the reduced salaries of Government employees. Total demand consequently decreased even further, aggravating the unemployment problem.

Keynes and the general theory of employment

In 1936 John Maynard Keynes wrote *The General Theory of Employment, Interest and Money*, attacking the theories of the classical economists, and declaring that capitalism contained no forces or mechanisms capable of guaranteeing full employment. Some of his important arguments were as follows.

1. *Income*. Savings and investment were made equal by changes in the national income rather than by changes in the rate of interest. If savings were greater than investment, national income would fall, which would eventually reduce savings to the level of investment.

2. *Full employment of resources*. The equality of savings and investment was just as likely to occur at a low as at a high level of business activity. There was therefore no natural tendency towards full employment of resources in the economy.

3. *Investment*. Where resources were under-utilised, deficiency of demand was the chief cause. Business expectations reflected in investment were the main determinant of employment: hence the level of income, consumption and savings.

4. *Government intervention.* Government management of the economy by the use of fiscal or budgetary policies was essential, so that Government expenditure or taxes could be reduced or increased to ensure that investment in the economy was at the desired level to create full employment.

Reference point 2 above, the fact that equilibrium can occur at any level of employment has certain implications for business. Equilibrium when resources are under-utilised will mean a waste of scarce resources. If they are over-fully employed there will be an excess bidding-up of prices and the value of money will decline. Under- or over-utilisation of resources poses problems for those trying to organise production and distribution.

It was as a result of the severe economic depression of the interwar period, and of the general acceptance of the economic theories of Keynes, the ideas contained in the Barlow Report (1940) and the proposals of Lord Beveridge for full employment that the British Government gradually assumed responsibility for managing the economy as declared in a White Paper published in 1944.

Present-day employment problems

After 1945, Britain had a situation of near-full employment for many years. Unemployment increased during the late 1950s but did not become a serious problem until the early 1970s, when unemployment figures rose steeply to reach $1\frac{1}{2}$ million by 1977. However, its nature is very different from the type experienced in the 1930s, which suggests that new policies are needed to cope with the problem. Individual payments of benefit by the Government enable a reasonable standard of living to be maintained, and unemployment is therefore not the destroyer of human dignity and self-respect that it was in the 1930s.

As long as present attitudes and policies relating to employment are held by the Government and by employers and employees, there will always be a sizeable pool of men unable to get work. Not only are technical advances today relieving the burden of labour, they are also reducing the number of labourers required. Even with capital investment and expansion, increased productivity and efficiency will in many cases be achieved by machines, not men. Such a position exists in the docks, where modernisation and mechanisation, plus excessive wage demands, have led to a declining work force while the volume of goods handled has increased.

Yet there is the possibility of full employment for all if arrangements can be made for sharing work, reducing working hours and giving opportunities for more leisure. The idea of such a system is unpopular, however, with employed workers because, although it would provide work for others, it would mean a drop in their own pay. Overtime has been a contributory cause of unemployment and it is difficult to change since it is part of a deep-rooted industrial tradition in Britain. In one week in December 1969, when unemployment was increasing, 19·54 million hours of overtime were worked, which, in terms of jobs, would have provided work for 486,000 people.

Location of industry

Numerous factors may influence a businessman's choice of site for a new factory or firm, varying from economic considerations (the optimisation of the supply and demand conditions) to a personal liking for an area, as shown, for example, in the choice of Oxford for the site of the Nuffield car factory. However, in the case of an extractive industry there is generally little choice of location. Chalk quarries are tied to their raw materials and agricultural siting depends on climatic and geological factors.

A principal factor is the cost of building and the price of land. Much depends on the type of production, whether heavy industry, processing, assembly, finishing, etc. Where raw material input is a large element in total production, it is important to be near the source of supplies of the raw materials. Sufficient and suitable labour must be readily available.

Access to adequate power and energy is essential, exemplified by the heavy concentration during the 19th century of the staple industries (coal, steel and textiles), engineering and shipbuilding in areas providing good access to water and coal. The costs of various services are likely to be cheaper in an area if there are a large number of firms there using them. This has been described as the external economics of a firm, and is discussed in Chapter VII. For example, if a hydro-electric plant is built to provide power for a number of firms, the services of that plant will also be available to other firms that move into the same area.

Changes in technology may result in new processes requiring different combinations of factor inputs. During the 20th century the increasing availability of electricity, particularly after the establishment of the national grid in the 1930s, and the increasing use of other fuels such as gas and oil have meant that coal is no longer of such overriding importance in industrial location.

Supply factors such as nearness to raw materials have become less important compared with the need to be near large centres of population as market outlets and near transport facilities, *e.g.* road, railway, river or canal. This has been particularly relevant for service industries.

Nearness to seaports or airports is an advantage for firms likely to export a large proportion of their products. Firms connected with "footloose" industries (orientated towards neither markets nor raw materials) are generally the easiest for which to find a new location. They include light industries such as clothing, light engineering and some food trades. They use so little fuel power that their total costs are not much affected by differences from place to place in the price of these items. They have tended to be concentrated in the Midlands and the south-east.

Regional planning

A businessman may also be guided in reaching his decision by the offer of financial inducements by the Government to locate his firm in a particular area. Since the 1930s the Government has given particular attention to industrial location and to the importance of balancing the distribution of the population and preventing widespread unemployment, all problems of regional planning, which aims at securing an even development of a country's resources.

A shortage of work in some localities can be offset by an abundance in other places. However, unemployment will persist if workers are not prepared to move to new jobs or are incapable of learning new skills. This was particularly evident in the 1930s when considerable disparity existed in the levels of unemployment between different regions of Britain. The areas with a higher than average level of unemployment were those which had declining staple industries such as shipbuilding in Northern Ireland, coal-mining in south Wales, heavy engineering in central Scotland, or had been reorganised so as to require a smaller labour force (like the steel and tinplate manufacture in south Wales).

One undesirable fact was the concentration of two-fifths of the population in several large conurbations of which London was the greatest. Prosperous areas in terms of secure, well-paid employment with good conditions were Greater London, the west Midlands and south-east England.

Regional imbalance creates two problems. First, wages and production costs are pushed up in the more prosperous regions by firms competing for scarce resources such as labour, when ample supplies may be available elsewhere. Second, industrial imbalance between regions can introduce social imbalance. Expanding areas attract younger workers, resulting in increased birth rates, while other regions may have a predominantly aged population. Housing shortages, overcrowding in schools and hospitals, and traffic congestion can occur in the more prosperous areas, the resulting social costs being borne by the taxpayer. In contrast housing may be poor in a depressed region and social capital, *i.e.* amenities and community facilities, may be out of date.

Methods used by successive Governments in regional planning have included the following.

1. Incentives to induce firms to migrate to areas in need of development (a policy of "taking work to the worker"). Such measures were first introduced by the Government in the 1930s but were extended by the *Distribution of Industry Acts* after 1945, the *Local Employment Acts* of 1960 and 1963, and the *Industrial Development Acts* of 1966. They designated areas of high unemployment which today include most of Scotland and Wales, northern England, Merseyside and large parts of Cornwall, Devon, Nottinghamshire and Derbyshire. Inducements include the provision of regional development capital grants for plant and machinery, etc., depreciation allowances, a Regional Employment Premium or Government subsidy of £1·50 per week for male employees, loans at favourable interest rates, help for transferring key workers and removal grants. Local planning permission is required for new building while for larger industrial buildings an industrial development certificate is required from the Department of Industry, which is unlikely to be granted in areas of high employment. The *Industry Act*, 1972, provided for selective financial assistance for projects likely to provide employment in assisted areas.

2. The encouragement of the movement of labour. The Government has tried to encourage workers to move location to find work or to train in new jobs. Occupational mobility is assisted by the *Industrial Training Act*, 1964, and Government Training Centres which offer retraining programmes. However, human and social problems are involved. Migration implies an initial waste of social capital, such as housing and roads, in areas of emigration and a corresponding burden in areas of immigration.

3. The creation of New Towns such as Corby, Crawley, Stevenage and Harlow to relieve overcrowding elsewhere.

4. The allocation of funds under the European Regional Development Fund, set up by the E.E.C. (1975) to assist special projects

in areas experiencing particular economic problems.

5. The establishment between 1964 and 1966 of advisory bodies in ten regions into which the country was divided. In each was an Economic Planning Board, composed of staff of Government departments whose function it was to identify and select remedies for individual regional problems, and an Economic Planning Council, composed of part-time members of the community with specialised local knowledge.

European Community regional policy

The nine countries of the expanded Common Market agreed in October 1972 to co-ordinate their regional policies and to create a special Regional Fund financed from the Community budget. Countries of the Community are pledged by the terms of the Rome Agreement to the equalisation of working and other social conditions between its various regions. It committed them to improving the living and working conditions of the people. The foundations for basic agreement have been made on certain aspects of industrial relations, such as rules for dismissal and social security benefits, especially in regard to pensions and unemployment benefits.

Workers can change residence from one member state to another and take up offers of employment actually made. Co-ordinated arrangements are made by which these migrant workers and their dependants can qualify for social security benefits as a result of their contributions, irrespective of the member states in which they were made. Italians have made the most of the opportunities for working abroad, particularly in Germany. Freedom of movement of labour within the Community is virtually complete. However, member countries may still, with Community authorisation, give preference to nationals in some areas and in occupations where labour surpluses remain. One barrier to foreign nationals seeking work is the lack of mutual recognition of professional qualifications, thus allowing countries to maintain priority for their own nationals.

In the past the European Community has concentrated the use of resources on agricultural areas rather than on older industrial areas. Britain and Italy have paid out more in regional aid to industry than all the other Community members combined. Britain hopes to gain from the Regional Fund for her own declining industries, which will in part offset contributions from Britain to the common agricultural policy.

The Community aims to reduce disparities between various regions by mitigating the backwardness of the less favoured ones. The European Investment Bank has helped by making loans to aid in developing backward areas. Areas in the Community are designated as "central" and "peripheral." At present there is no limit to regional aid from national governments to the latter, which include the Mezzogiorno in southern Italy, West Germany's frontier area with East Germany, south-west France and West Berlin. The rest of the Community is the "central" areas where regional aid, above that which is available in the country as a whole, must be limited to 20 per cent of the after-tax cost of investment from January 1972. All aid must be "transparent," which means that it is measurable as a percentage of the cost of the investment. Thus present British regional aid such as regional investment allowances and the regional employment premium might be classed as "opaque" and not permissible under Community rules.

GOVERNMENT AND MANAGEMENT OF THE ECONOMY

Types of economy and economic aims of Government

Three basic economic problems are:

1. What variety of goods should be produced and in what quantities.
2. How this should be done, and how the goods should be distributed.
3. How our capacity can be expanded to produce more resources in the long run.

Different methods have been tried to solve these problems, but in any society there are three groups on which decisions hinge, the consumer, the firm and the state. Each has a vital role.

Under a primitive or undeveloped system production and distribution are based on barter trade (the swapping of goods for other goods) and subsistence farming (*i.e.* concerned with producing basic survival needs only). Such an arrangement still exists today in parts of Asia, South America, the extreme north of Canada and Alaska, and Africa, where there are tribal or communal systems.

The second system, the "command" economy, is broadly one of state-directed economic activity. An extreme form exists in Communist countries today—Russia, China and those in Eastern Europe. The basic means of production are owned and managed by the state, which for the most part determines what shall be produced, whose wants shall be satisfied first, and what shall be the price of the goods.

The price mechanism is unimportant as a means of allocating goods.

The third economic system, predominant in Britain and North America during the 19th century, has had various labels, such as capitalism, market or price economy, and private enterprise or individualism. Such writers as Adam Smith advocated the system of *laissez-faire* (abstention from interference), which implied that the Government should confine its role in society primarily to one of preserving order, and raising money for this purpose through taxation to pay for necessary administration by officials, the judicial system and the armed forces. They believed that in the absence of Government economic restrictions, enlightened self-interest under conditions of free competition would realise both individual and public welfare. The problem of what goods should be produced and in what quantities was decided by the way consumers spent their money, and through bargaining between individuals. The free forces of supply and demand determined the price of goods and services. The price theory of perfect competition underpinning this system has been discussed in detail in Chapter II.

The drawbacks of this system in Britain during the past 120 years led to the Government gradually becoming the prime force in economic affairs. This resulted in the fourth type of economic system, the "mixed economy." This does not imply here an economy part industrial and part agricultural, though this is a possible meaning of the term and would be applicable to Britain. In this context it means a system where economic resources are owned partly by private enterprise and partly by the state, with planning by the Government playing an important role in managing a country's economy. A brief account is given below of some of the reasons for the increased Government involvement in economic affairs.

During the 19th century it was realised in Britain that the interests of the individual and of society did not necessarily coincide since unrestricted competition often resulted in the waste of resources and the duplication of facilities, as during the boom years of railway construction.

The price mechanism tended to allocate goods and services on the basis of demand, which meant desire backed by ability to pay, rather than on the basis of need. A penniless man dying of starvation has a desperate "need" but no "demand" for food.

The system of individual bargaining was not always a satisfactory criterion, since the bargaining power of individuals was not always equal. For example, competition between unorganised workers for jobs forced their wages down to the bare minimum and private monopolies existed, able to restrict competition and control supply and then charge high prices for goods.

The price mechanism made no allowance for social costs and benefits. The productive process entails many costs which may not be incorporated into the cost and price structure of firms. A firm might avoid the expense of properly disposing of waste materials by polluting nearby lakes or rivers with such wastes, thus destroying the beauty and recreational value of these places. In this case it is shifting a portion of those costs which it might be expected to bear on to society as a whole. As a result of these "spillover" effects social costs (or benefit) may diverge from private costs (or benefit).

When the benefit to be gained from a service is diffuse, indiscriminate and indivisible, the service has to be provided collectively. The state has to make provision for maintaining law and order, and for defence of the country from external threats. A citizen cannot buy his own share of these services. As the benefit cannot be directly allocated to individuals it is best to pay for them by taxation. The same applies to the legal system, the standardisation of weights and measures, and a unified currency system.

Other important factors for the rise of "mixed economy" were discussed earlier in this chapter. Note should be given to the important role played in this development by the growth of Socialist ideas and the power of the Labour Party, which was committed to a wider distribution in ownership of wealth, and Government ownership of some of the key industrial sectors of the country. Briefly it can be said that this system is an attempt at avoiding both the extreme fluctuations likely under a free economy and the rigidities of a controlled economy. The Government attempts to take responsibility for certain areas which are considered important (*e.g.* defence and the supply of many essential services) and allows freedom of choice in other areas.

From time to time the Government issues statements of its economic and social objectives, as in the British White Paper on Employment Policy (1944) and the planning document "The Task Ahead" (1969). Priorities are constantly changing. The following are the possible aims of a Government today:

1. Satisfactory level of employment.
2. Achievement of a surplus in the balance of payments.
3. An equitable distribution of income and economic social security for all.
4. Stable prices.
5. Adequate rate of economic growth.

6. Healthy state of industrial relations.
7. Balanced geographical distribution of industry and population.

The problem is that it is usually difficult for a country to achieve all economic aims at the same time. For example, the preservation of full employment and the promotion of economic growth make it difficult to achieve stable prices, and consequently inflationary pressure can have detrimental effects on the balance of payments.

Since the various economic aims conflict, the Government must decide the extent to which any particular one should be sacrificed to another, and its choice will depend on the current economic position and its own list of priorities. The pursuit of material growth to the exclusion of other considerations might indicate that modern industrial societies have their priorities wrong. Once a reasonable level of material welfare has been achieved, more attention could be focused on improving the "quality of life."

The British Government has generally relied on one or a combination of the following practices to regulate the economy and to balance aggregate demand and supply.

1. *Fiscal or budgetary policy.* (*See* p. 96.)
2. *Monetary policy.* This involves the Government's ability to influence the quantity and price of credit through such measures as control of the money supply, hire-purchase restrictions, changes in the Minimum Lending Rate which influences other interest rates, open market operations and Government funding operations. The Central Bank also regulates foreign exchange transactions and influences the exchange rate (see Ch. IV).
3. *Public enterprise.* As the State owns or has a substantial financial interest in many industries, the Government can directly influence pricing, investment and employment.
4. *Legal controls.* Two broad types are as follows. (*a*) Creation of a legal framework within which private enterprise can operate, *e.g.* legislation on monopolies. (*b*) Direct regulation of specific activities, e.g. measures to limit income and price increases and limitation of new Stock Exchange issues. Statutory controls can be on a permanent basis, usually associated with wartime policies, or implemented temporarily, as those introduced by governments in 1967 and 1972. The Government may not resort to legal measures if it can persuade people voluntarily to act in a particular way or to implement its recommendations, as was tried in 1965 and early 1972 when the Government attempted to persuade firms and unions to co-operate against inflation.

5. *Planning.* A distinction is made between (*a*) authoritative or normative planning, when the state determines how the price system will work, and (*b*) indicative planning. Here the Government and industry try to co-ordinate their policies, exchanging information about their respective intentions. A knowledge of forecasting probable public spending helps industry to estimate future demands, while information provided by industry helps Government to see likely sources of strength and weakness in the future economy. Policies can then be initiated as a strategy for the country's future.

Summary of developments in the economy, 1961-77

Since 1961 Britain has introduced a form of indicative planning which owed much to knowledge of its working in France. However, due to the possibility of a balance of payments crisis, and debts to its neighbours for support of its currency, no British Government can follow through a national policy completely of its own choosing.

Another limitation is the desire of various sectors of the economy, firms, workers, political parties, etc., to co-operate with or frustrate Government policies. A major problem since 1945 has been to find a successful formula for a smooth working relationship beween businessmen, the Government and the trade unions. At times they have each seen their respective aims as opposed to the others, which has hampered the creation of mutual confidence and an understanding of each other's problems. In addition Britain's growth record since 1945, compared with those of Japan, France and Germany, some of our main competitors, has been poor. This was the main reason why the Government invited representatives of employers and labour to join in working out a medium-term economic plan.

In 1962 the National Economic Development Council (N.E.D.C. or "Neddy") was created, composed of members of the Government, the nationalised industries, the T.U.C. and the C.B.I. For three years it concerned itself with the problems of identifying the obstacles to growth. In 1964 it recommended that the Government should set a target of 4 per cent growth for the whole economy over the next few years. The Council's report *Conditions Favourable to Faster Growth* (April 1963) was very influential. Its recommendations on education and training, labour mobility and redundancy, regional policy, balance of payments, taxation, and prices and incomes led to the *Industrial Training Act*, 1964, the *Redundancy Payments Act* and earnings-related unemployment pay, selective employment tax and the National Board for Prices and Incomes. In 1964 Economic

Development Councils ("Little Neddies") were created for various industries. Their composition is tripartite as in the N.E.D.C., and amongst their objectives is the consideration of ways of improving the economic performance and efficiency of their own industry.

In 1962 the National Income Commission, created by the Conservative Government, aimed to plan wages by consent and to control cost-push inflation as well as demand-pull inflation (on which attention was focused in the 1950s). The trade unions refused to co-operate so its effect was limited, and in April 1965 it was replaced by the National Board for Prices and Incomes, composed of trade unionists, businessmen and independents, to whom the Labour Government referred proposed wage and price increases.

In 1964 the new Department of Economic Affairs was given responsibility for general planning and the Government's National Plan, published in September 1965, aimed at a target of 25 per cent growth in national production by 1970. However, it contained no strategy to take into account external problems or unexpected events which would nullify any estimates. Balance of payments difficulties and inflationary pressures as a result of incomes rising faster than output in early 1966 meant that devaluation or deflation was necessary.

In July 1966 the Government was forced to abandon the National Plan and return to traditional fiscal and monetary techniques, combined with a statutory freeze on wages, prices and dividends to curb demand, check inflation and protect the balance of payments. Government measures had some success but further economic problems in 1967, including the effects of the Middle East War and the dockers' strike, led to devaluation of the pound in November.

In 1968 the Government again tried to curb price and wage increases through statutory controls, but this policy of compulsion was vigorously opposed, both by the Labour Left and the Conservative Opposition, and the Prices and Incomes Act of 1968 was abandoned in 1969. Reliance was now placed on "voluntary restraint" within recommended guidelines, and price control. The Department of Economic Affairs was abolished and responsibility for overall planning returned to the Treasury. In 1971 the National Board for Prices and Incomes was dissolved by the Conservatives, and its functions merged with those of the Monopolies Commission in the Commission for Industry and Manpower.

A wage explosion had followed the abandoning of statutory controls and orthodox Keynesians assumed that an inverse relationship existed between unemployment and the extent of inflation, as Professor Phillips had described in his model of the "Phillips Curve". Following this approach, the Conservative Government in 1970 hoped that mounting unemployment would eventually be curbed by lower wage increases, which in turn would come about through "voluntary restraint" of the trade unions and Government opposition to wage increases in the public sector. To revive the economy, the Government lowered interest rates and increased public expenditure. Most of the resultant "boom" that followed came from increased demand for consumer goods, rather than a revival in manufacturing industry, met partly by increased imports.

The Government faced the unpleasant realisation by 1972 that unemployment continued to increased while inflation went on to reach a record rate of about 25 per cent. The theory of the Phillips curve was partially discredited. The balance of payments, in a healthy surplus in 1970, was by 1973 registering a huge deficit. Reasons for this included Britain's higher inflation rate than most other countries, a sharp rise in the price of essential imports, particularly oil, and a fall of some 15 per cent in the value of sterling between June 1972, when the pound was floated, and mid-1973.

At the end of 1972 the Government belatedly introduced a statutory incomes policy, embodied in the Counter-Inflation Act of 1973, which also created the Price Commission to supervise price controls. The Government's downfall was eventually caused by its resistance to the miner's wage claim, which resulted in a damaging strike and a shortened working-week for Britain as a result of a declaration of a state of emergency.

In 1974 the new Labour Government permitted large wage settlements, including that of the miners, and from October a voluntary incomes policy was operated for a time, the "Social Contract". In return for TUC co-operation in getting trade unions to accept annual wage claims in step with cost-of-living increases, the Government agreed to control prices and to help the lower-paid and pensioners.

Serious balance of payments difficulties were met in 1976 by a large I.M.F. loan, while severe public expenditure economies were enforced, to reinforce the government's policy of controlling inflation. By 1977 Britain's economic prospects had improved, reflected in a healthy balance of payments position and success in reducing the inflation rate.

Public finance

Public finance covers the income and expenditure accounts of public authorities—the Government, public corporations, the nationalised industries and local authorities.

Until the 19th century, Government expenditure was limited to a narrow range of services. During the last hundred years, as responsibilities and functions of public authorities have increased, there has been considerable increases in Government (public) expenditure, which now accounts for about 40 per cent of the Gross National Product (G.N.P.). The pattern of Government spending has also changed. For example, the state intervenes extensively to achieve specific social and economic ends. There has been an enormous growth in "social expenditure," which now takes up about one-third of total public spending, the main forms being education, health, unemployment and sickness benefits, pensions and national assistance.

The Government is the biggest customer of industry. About one-sixth of goods/services produced are bought by the public sector (central or local authorities). Demand springs from Government interest in many vital fields, such as defence and national welfare.

DISTRIBUTION OF GOVERNMENT SPENDING %

	1860	1960
Defence	40	30
Interest (N.D.)	39	15
Civil government	20	21
Social services	1	34

Some part of Government expenditure is covered by borrowing, particularly during war-time. The British National Debt originated in 1694 when William III received a loan of £1,200,000 from the new Bank of England to finance his wars. It has steadily increased in size, largely as a result of successive wars and increasing commitments in the economy, and in 1965 was £29,000 million. A large part is made up of long- and medium-term securities with fixed maturities or dates on which the Government promises to repay. Another part is in the form of undated stocks where the Government has no obligation to repay. About 20 per cent is in the form of short-term loans or Treasury Bills. These securities are marketable and ownership can be freely transferred on the stock exchange, and on the discount market in the case of treasury bills. A further 20 per cent takes the form of non-marketable securities, such as national savings certificates (and stamps), development bonds and defence and premium bonds.

These non-marketable securities are widely held, and a large proportion of them are in the hands of institutions such as banks, insurance and building societies, trade unions, pension funds and local authorities. Since this type of debt is simply one owed by the people collectively, *i.e.* the state, to the people individually, the community as a whole is neither richer nor poorer. However, about 10 per cent of the debt is owned by individuals, Governments and institutions abroad and this part does constitute a burden. The payment of interest and capital must be made in foreign currencies, and exports are required to pay for these foreign currencies which might otherwise have been used to buy imports.

The Budget and fiscal policy

In Britain the term "the Budget" refers to the tax proposals announced by the Chancellor of the Exchequer in March or April each year. Taxes may be adjusted at other times in an "Interim Budget" or by the use of the Chancellor's "regulator" powers to vary expenditure tax rates by up to 10 per cent between budgets. At one time the Budget was regarded purely as a balance sheet. When revenue equalled expenditure each year, this was regarded as evidence of sound finance. The aim of the Budget was to raise revenue through taxes so that the Government could meet its estimated expenditure for the following year, usually decided by about January.

Today the Government makes use of fiscal policy to regulate the economy. If total demand of the community, reflected in consumption and investment spending at the full employment level, is greater than the income or output, the Government can by use of the Budget help to curb demand by increasing taxes and reducing Government expenditure. Alternatively, if total spending is less than income or output, the Government can encourage demand by reducing taxes, and increasing Government expenditure. The Government's ability to influence the economic climate through investment decisions of the public sector is due to its considerable purchasing power. The technique of "deficit-financing" refers to Government spending in excess of revenue in order to stimulate a depressed economy. "Surplus-financing" is the collecting of more revenue by taxes than is necessary to meet expenses, and is applied to reduce consumer demand for goods and services during periods of inflation.

Types of taxes

Taxes can be broadly classified into two categories, direct and indirect. Direct taxes, collected mainly by the Inland Revenue, are of varied forms. Income tax raises about three-quarters of the total revenue from direct taxation. Surtax was a tax levied in addition to the standard rate of tax on earned income; it was abolished on 1 April 1973. There is also capital transfer tax, stamp duties on various legal and commercial documents, capital gains tax (which is levied upon the increase in the value of an asset between the times when it was bought and sold) and corporation tax (a tax on company profits). Allowances are made for capital expenditure and there is provision for relief for trade losses. Capital Transfer Tax is a tax on transfers of personal wealth (or "gifts") whether they take place during a person's lifetime or on his death.

Most indirect taxes are collected by the Customs and Excise Departments. Revenue comes from taxes on oil and petrol, duties on tobacco and alcoholic drinks and V.A.T. (Value Added Tax, *see* below). V.A.T. is useful not only as a source of revenue but also for restricting demand for goods wanted for the export trade. There are also taxes on betting and gaming. Selective employment tax (operative 1966–73) was a tax on all industries except agriculture, mining, transport and utilities (*e.g.* gas and electricity). Manufacturing industries received a refund of the tax after one to four months.

Taxes can be classified according to their effect. With progressive taxes the higher income groups pay not only more than the lower income groups but proportionately more. Thus the first £100 may be subject to tax at a rate of, say, 15p in the £, and the next £100 at 20p in the £. Income taxes and capital transfer tax are examples. Proportional taxes are those which are at a uniform rate, say of 10 per cent of income. A regressive tax is one which falls more heavily on the poor than the rich; such taxes existed in Europe in feudal times. Indirect taxes which are not regressive in form tend to be regressive in effect; an example is a tax on cigarettes, which takes a greater proportion of a poor man's income than of a rich man's. The fourth type is the flat rate or poll tax, when everyone pays the same amount.

There are certain elements of sound taxation, depending on the criteria used for evaluating their effects. Good taxes should not be a disincentive to work or inflationary in nature. Among the principles of taxation can be mentioned the following:

1. *Equity.* This is interpreted today as ability to pay and equality of sacrifice. Progressive taxes accord best with this view, sometimes defended on the grounds of the law of diminishing marginal utility. An illustration of this would be if the taking of £20 from a man earning £80 per week caused him the same loss of satisfaction as would the removal of £4 per week from a man earning £30 per week.

2. *Certainty.* The taxpayer should know how much tax he has to pay and when he has to pay it.

3. *Convenience.*

4. *Economy*. Costs of collection should be small in relation to revenue obtained.

5. *Flexibility*. A tax should be capable of being altered easily to meet changing financial conditions.

At one time taxes were paid in arrears. The Pay As You Earn (P.A.Y.E.) system which replaced it was regarded as more convenient.

Value Added Tax

Value Added Tax (V.A.T.), a uniform tax on goods and services, was adopted by the E.E.C. in 1967. It is a way of collecting money by instalments from everybody involved in producing each item, as it moves from the raw material through to the final consumer. Each firm is liable to tax on the value of its sales, but its liability is reduced by a tax credit equal to the amount of tax paid on the supplies purchased.

TABLE IX

How V.A.T. is calculated

	Total value	Gross tax liability 10%	Total price	Tax credit	Net tax actually paid to Government
1. Sale of raw materials to manufacturers	100	10	110	0	10
2. Sale of final products to retailers	300	30	330	10	20
3. Sale of goods to consumers	500	50	550	30	20
If the whole of the final output was exported then lines 2 and 3 would be:					
4. Sale of goods for export	500	0	500	10	−10

On 1 April 1973 the British system of indirect taxation was extensively changed with the replacement of both purchase tax and selective employment tax by V.A.T. The aim of the standard rate of 10 per cent in conjunction with a lower rate on certain essentials was to raise the same revenue as the two taxes abolished. In 1974 the standard rate was reduced to 8 per cent.

V.A.T. is essentially a tax on the consumer, since a taxable trader is able to take credit for the tax charged to him and to collect from his customers the tax charged by him. If during an accounting period, normally every quarter, the "input tax" (tax charged to the firm by its suppliers) is greater than the "output tax" (tax charged to customers on sales), perhaps because the firm is stocking up or has purchased expensive equipment, it will be entitled to claim a refund of the difference from the Customs and Excise.

Some goods are zero-rated, which means that there is no tax on their purchase. This includes children's clothing, foods (with a few exceptions), sweets, newspapers, periodicals and books, newspaper advertising, new construction, fuel, fares, medicines on prescription and exports. Firms dealing with these are registered and can claim refund of tax already paid on their own purchases.

Some other items are also exempt. This means that although they are not able to claim refund of the tax already paid on goods (for raw materials, etc., used in production), the final product will be exempt from further tax. This includes all firms with a turnover of under £5,000 a year involving some half-million traders, and a number of items outside the scope of the small retailer such as domestic rents, education, health and postal services, insurance, betting and gaming, banking and transactions in land and old buildings.

The main argument in favour of V.A.T. is that it is more neutral than purchase tax and S.E.T., and will help towards the E.E.C. ideal of the free movement of final products, capital and labour in a competitive free-enterprise economy. When V.A.T. came into force, certain items became cheaper, *e.g.* furniture, as a result of the changeover from Purchase Tax but, in the case of other items, increased prices soon negated any benefits from a lower rate of tax payable. One major drawback is that considerable clerical work is involved which places a burden particularly on the very small businesses which cannot afford specialist staff.

INTERNATIONAL ECONOMIC RELATIONS

Advantages of international trade

International trade originated when nations exchanged products for others which they could not produce themselves or which could only be produced at exorbitant cost at home. It differs from internal trade in a number of ways. For instance, greater risks are involved when a firm has to estimate the size of a market where the people have customs, habits and tastes differing markedly from those of its usual customers. Different languages, currencies and methods of conducting business are some of the other complications. In addition, legal restrictions and the reluctance to move are two of the reasons why capital and labour movements are less frequent when political frontiers are involved.

As a result of specialisation and exchange in domestic (internal) trade people can enjoy higher standards of living. In the same way if countries specialise, concentrating on producing goods and providing services for which their resources and human skills are best fitted,

TABLE X

A AND B PRODUCTS OF RICE AND STEEL

Country	Rice	Steel
A	400	100
B	100	400
Total Production	500	500

the total output of both goods and services is increased, economic growth is promoted, and the resultant trade enables everyone to enjoy a wider variety than would be possible under a policy of self-sufficiency.

The practical advantages of this can be illustrated if we consider two imaginary countries, A and B, which produce just two products, rice and steel, and devote an equal amount of time and expenditure of resources to producing each of them, as shown in Table X.

TABLE XI

A AND B PRODUCTS WITH OPPORTUNITY COST RATIOS

Country	Rice	Steel	Opportunity cost ratios
A	100	250	$1:2\frac{1}{2}$ (4:10)
B	50	100	$1:2$ (5:10)

If A then specialises in producing rice only and B specialises in steel only, total production could be 800 units each of rice and steel, a net gain of 300 units of each item to be shared between them. In this the benefits are obvious, as A is better at producing rice and B is better at steel production. However, the situation could be that A has an absolute advantage in producing both goods. Even so, both countries can still gain by specialisation and trade if there is some difference in the relative or opportunity costs of producing these goods. This is known as the "law of comparative costs."

The opportunity cost ratio is the cost of using factors to produce so much of one of the goods rather than the other and in this case the rate at which each country can change steel into rice internally. Now it can be seen from Table XI that A has a relatively greater advantage in producing steel and, without trade taking place, A values 1 unit of rice at $2\frac{1}{2}$ units of steel, the cost ratio being 4:10. In country B, however, 1 unit of rice must be given in return for 2 units of steel, the ratio being 5:10.

To benefit from the principle of comparative costs A now specialises in steel and B in rice, the commodity in which it has the less comparative disadvantage. Trade will only take place between A and B in terms advantageous to both, and as A can produce 1 unit of rice by giving up $2\frac{1}{2}$ units of steel, it will only be interested in trading with B on any terms by which it gets more than 1 unit of rice for less than $2\frac{1}{2}$ units of steel. Since B can produce 2 units of steel by sacrificing 1 unit of rice, it will only benefit from terms where it obtains more than 2 units of steel for 1 unit of rice. By exchanging 1 unit of rice for between 2 and $2\frac{1}{2}$ units of steel (limits determined by the opportunity cost ratios 5:10 and 4:10) both countries are better off than if they had decided to continue producing these goods themselves.

Terms of trade

Within the limits set by the opportunity cost ratios, the manner of sharing the gains from specialisation and trade between the two countries depends on conditions of supply and demand. On a world level, the actual rate at which a constant quantity of a nation's goods are exchanged for those of other countries is called the "terms of trade." They can be calculated by the formula:

$$\frac{\text{Index of export prices}}{\text{Index of import prices}} \times 100$$

If, subsequently, export prices rise relative to import prices so that a given volume of exports pays for an increased volume of imports, the terms of trade are said to be favourable. If a rise in import prices takes place this signifies a deterioration in the terms of trade.

For example, if Britain's export prices rise by 5 per cent she will earn more foreign money only if the demand for her exports is fairly inelastic, in that the export sales do not change, or fall by less than 5 per cent. If import prices fall by 5 per cent she will spend less foreign currency on imports only if demand is inelastic and the amount bought does not increase more than 5 per cent. If the demand for both exports and imports is elastic, favourable trade movements might make Britain worse off, as her expenditure abroad would rise and her income from abroad would fall.

Balance of payments

Each nation's record of its transactions with other countries is known as the Balance of Payments. Since 1970 two broad classifications used in presenting the British balance of payments have been (*a*) Current Account, and (*b*) Investment and other capital flows.

The current account is split into visible and invisible items. Visible trade refers to the export and import of goods, and the difference between the values of these two amounts is known as the balance of trade. Normally Britain has a deficit here, imports exceeding exports, but in 1970 there was a small surplus of £3 million. "Invisible" items refer to the import and export of services. Britain provides financial services for other counties such as banking and insurance, and shipping facilities for carrying their goods, and also offers tourist amenities. Also included is the return or earnings on investments such as royalties, interest, dividends and profits. Since Britain's foreign investments abroad exceed sums invested by foreigners here, there is a net gain to the balance of payments on this item. There is a net debit under Government items, due to Government grants to developing countries under aid programmes, military expenditure abroad, etc. Overall, though, Britain does well on "invisibles" with a net gain being made.

Under the heading "Investment and other capital flows" are included various flows of capital, many of which were once included as monetary movements in the balance of payments. Examples are public sector or Government lending or borrowing overseas on a long-term basis, and overseas investment in the U.K. private sector and British private investment abroad. This could take the form of the purchase of foreign stocks and shares, or the starting of businesses abroad. Some of these funds may be liquid assets, such as bank deposits of overseas holders, which can be withdrawn at short notice.

At the end of the account is shown how the Government finances a deficit in the balance of payments or allocates any surplus which has been made. A deficit can be met by reducing the country's assets, selling foreign investments and running down the reserves of foreign currency and gold. Alternatively, or in addition, the country can incur additional short-term liabilities, receiving loans or gifts from abroad, or borrowing from international institutions such as the International Monetary Fund and the Bank for International Settlements. Certain countries, including Britain and the United States, have created a pool of $6 billion available on a stand-by basis to offset speculative movements (U.S. billion=a thousand millions). Other measures including special drawing rights and "swop arrangements" are discussed later.

All the above measures are only temporary expedients since in the long run a country must correct the underlying causes of deficit by expanding exports or reducing imports. The alternative is to face national bankruptcy. One reason for the deficit could be inflation, which results in a reduction of export sales abroad because of high prices or their diversion to satisfy domestic demand, and an increase in imports which may be cheaper than the home-produced goods.

Various solutions can be tried. Deflationary measures through fiscal, monetary or incomes policies may help to reduce domestic prices or at least stabilise them. Invisible imports can be curbed when the Government limits the amount that can be spent on foreign goods and services. This used to be £50 a year in Britain but was increased in 1970 to £300. A measure which was successful in curbing imports was the requirement in 1967 that importers had to deposit sums of money in advance with the Government. A more drastic remedy was the imposition by Britain in 1964–6 of a 10 per cent surcharge on imported goods, while in 1971 the United States imposed a surcharge of 15 per cent. Import controls have the advantage of being approved in the articles of the I.M.F. and of GATT as stopgaps for short-term balance of payment problems, whereas the use of tariffs and quotas (*see* pp. 114–15) are generally unpopular and contrary to the rules of GATT.

In the last resort a country may try devaluation. This involves altering the rate of exchange so that the domestic currency does not buy so much foreign currency, making exports cheaper and imports dearer. In 1949 the £ was devalued in terms of the dollar from $4·03 to $2·80, and in 1967 from $2·80 to $2·40. Devaluation succeeds only under certain conditions. It would fail, for example, if competitive devaluation was applied by other countries, if there was an inelastic demand by other countries for the bulk of our exports, if our export goods were in inelastic supply, or if the amount of goods imported did not decrease perceptibly (due to an inelastic demand for them). It would succeed if the demand for imports and exports was elastic, resulting in increased exports and reduced imports.

In the very long term the only answer is increased output achieved through improved efficiency in industry and improved management–labour relations, etc., thus making possible higher export levels and the reduction of unnecessary imports, since firms would then be able to satisfy home demand.

The gold standard

The cost of international trade transactions whether in goods or services has to be met by a form of payment acceptable to the countries involved. As countries use different currencies, each country likes to be paid in its own currency. However, unless effective substitutes are found, delays seriously affecting trade may occur if shortages of the appropriate currency arise. In addition, a system has to be created to determine the value of one currency in terms of another.

In the 19th century these problems were solved when countries adopted the gold standard. This meant that each national currency was exchangeable for gold at a fixed price, and that the note issue and coinage were fully or substantially backed by gold reserves in the central bank. Until 1914 Britain supplied sovereigns as well as gold bullion in exchange for notes, and the pound was equal in value to the defined weight of gold in the sovereign. This established the exchange rate of sterling with currencies of other gold-standard countries. If the gold content of the sovereign was five times that of the gold dollar, the exchange rate would be about 5 dollars to the pound. The exchange rate would deviate from parity by an amount approximately equal to the cost of transporting gold between the two countries. If the currency exchange rate varied further, countries would find it cheaper to send gold than currency. For example, if £1 in London could be exchanged for the same weight of gold as $5 in New York, it would be unprofitable for Americans to pay much more than $5 for each pound bought in the foreign exchange market with which to buy necessary imports from Britain.

In the 1920s many countries adopted a form of gold standard known as the gold exchange standard. This enabled some countries to declare gold parities with other gold-standard currencies, while holding their reserves not in gold but in other major currencies. In those days Britain played an important role in international trade dating back to the Industrial Revolution, and the City of London provided excellent financial facilities. Prior to 1939 sterling was the major reserve currency and provided the medium in which international transactions were carried out. The system had the advantage of economising in the use of gold.

The gold standard had two advantages, stable exchange rates and an automatic corrective mechanism for balance of payments deficits. If one country's imports exceeded its exports, the effect would be a decline in the amount of money in circulation in relation to a given stock of goods as a result of an outflow of gold in payment, since the note issue was automatically linked with the gold reserves. This would result in deflation, *i.e.* falling prices. Eventually the prices of exports would become cheaper and more competitive and would exceed imports. This would start a chain reaction in the other direction. Increased exports result in a gold inflow, and hence an increase in the amount of money relative to the quantity of goods and a price rise. Exports gradually tail off again and imports start increasing when prices are at their peak, resulting in a repetition of the cycle.

The system collapsed in 1931 because of the unstable trade conditions after 1918, highlighted by the Great Depression, following the Wall Street crash (1929). The gold standard did not permit countries to employ independent internal monetary policies to cope with such problems as unemployment. This was one of the factors which led to gold-standard countries failing to observe its conditions. They restricted the movement of gold artificially; they did not expand their economy in inflationary policies when they had excesses of gold, but accumulated gold reserves in economic stagnation. Countries also applied tariffs and quotas, etc., restricting trade and disturbing the price mechanism.

Floating exchange rates

During the 1930s countries adopted generally the system of free (flexible or floating) exchange rates, which meant allowing the external value of their currencies to find their own level in the foreign exchange markets. The merits of this were that it gave policy-makers greater freedom because a balance of payments disequilibrium became impossible, and made monetary and fiscal policies to control such a disequilibrium unnecessary. If, for example, imports exceeded exports the price of foreign exchange to buy the excess imports would rise, thus curbing the demand.

Apart from currency depreciation as a means of remedying a balance of payments deficit (under floating exchange rates), another solution would be domestic policies to curb demand (if rates are fixed), thus creating unemployment and a decline in business activity. The balance of payments' problem arises when governments maintain fixed exchange rates so as to avoid domestic economic problems such as unemployment. To even out fluctuations in the exchange rate brought about by capital movements and to help to stabilise the value of the pound, the Treasury created the Exchange Equalisation Account in 1932. It bought sterling when other countries wished to sell it to keep up the exchange rate, and sold it in the market when other countries wished to buy it to keep down the rate.

The main argument against floating exchange rates was their supposed uncertainty, which might result in stricter capital controls being imposed to restrict capital flow and subsequently comprehensive trade restrictions. This system was not generally popular with export and import traders since constantly fluctuating exchange rates meant it was difficult to know in advance how much they would actually receive for their goods or how much they would have to pay. It was also disliked by bankers as it encouraged speculation. But spot (or present) rates and forward (or probable future) rates tend to be similar as a result of a consensus of all the various market transactors. If there were a great difference between spot and forward rates, large speculative profits could be made. But in a free market these speculative transfers would force spot and forward rates to be closely aligned. Only if expectations fluctuated widely would the rates fluctuate in relation to each other.

Factors determining exchange rates

The main factors determining why currency is bought and sold in the foreign-exchange market, and hence the rate of exchange and value of a currency, are the forces of demand for and supply of the currency. Funds are required by British people to pay for imports, invisibles, investment and speculative dealings.

An important consideration is the price of home-produced goods compared with the price of similar goods abroad. If foreign goods were cheaper British people would buy them in preference to home goods, while exports would decline if expensive relative to the prices of these items produced abroad. In a free exchange market the reduced demand would lower the value of the pound sterling so that eventually British goods would be the same price as those of other countries. An extreme version of this is known as the Purchasing Power Parity Theory, which, in brief, can be shown as:

$$\text{Foreign exchange of } £ = \frac{\text{Foreign prices}}{\text{British prices}}$$

Though there is much truth in this theory it is an over-simplification of the problem. Not all goods enter foreign trade, and such factors as indirect taxes may change internal prices but not affect exchange rates, while the theory ignores capital movements for investment or speculative purposes.

In addition to relative prices, other forces affecting the rates of exchange include:

1. Likely returns in terms of interest or dividends through investment in Government stocks, shares or business ventures abroad.

2. Political factors and Government budgetary and monetary policies which affect exports, imports and capital flow.

Free exchange rates tended to discourage international trade and by 1945 most countries were agreed that a new system was necessary, and were determined to maintain full employment and stable price levels, which had been impossible under the gold standard. Since 1944 the dollar had supplanted sterling as the primary world reserve currency due to the wealth of the United States and the poverty of the rest of the world at that time. Sterling continued as a second reserve currency financing about 25 per cent of world trade. As the gold standard had been abandoned, and gold, dollars and pounds represented different units of exchange, the problem arose of how they could be reduced to a comparable basis of valuation in terms of each other without returning to the other alternative of fluctuating exchange rates.

The fixed exchange system ("managed flexibility")

As a result of the Bretton Woods Conference in the United States in 1944 plans were made for the post-war trading structure. The International Monetary Fund was created in 1947 with the aim of combining the advantages of both the gold exchange standard and freely floating exchange rates in the Fixed Exchange or Reserve Currency System. Exchange rate parities between countries were fixed rigidly in the short run while scope for adjustment was permitted in the long run, after prior consultation with the I.M.F. through devaluation. Governments were able to carry out their own internal policies to promote full employment.

Member countries each had a quota, expressed in dollars, which they contributed to the fund in their own currencies and gold. The I.M.F. acted as banker, allowing members to buy other currencies with their own currency, and made loans to members in temporary balance of payments difficulties. Each country was required to ensure by appropriate policies that its currency did not deviate by more than 1 per cent on each side of the established par value. While each currency was expressed in terms of the dollar, the dollar itself was fixed to gold at the official rate of \$34 per ounce of gold, the price fixed in 1934. The United States undertook to sell gold in exchange for dollars at this rate.

A weakness in the reserve currency system was the difficulty which countries experienced in changing their exchange rate parities, particularly those which run the reserve currencies, the United States and Britain. Because changes in parities are usually made in jumps, by means of devaluation or revaluation of currencies, there is a tendency for speculation to take place against the currency of that country when it is undergoing financial difficulties.

Gold and the financing of world trade

The demand for gold has been so intensified since 1945 that for the first time in history it has outstripped the amount newly mined. South Africa produces 75 per cent of the non-Communist world's gold and it is sold through the gold market in London. In addition to stocking official monetary reserves and its use in the "London gold pool" (a free market that meets shortages to stabilise prices), an increasing amount has gone into non-monetary uses, particularly as it seemed undervalued at the 1934 price of $34 an ounce; this price survived till 1971, when a modest increase took place, which is explained later. About half the world's annual output has been used for industrial purposes. A large amount goes into private hoards or to speculators. Although in Britain, the sterling area and the United States the ordinary citizen is not allowed to hold gold, many nations in Europe, Asia and the Middle East permit private collections of gold. The basic motive for holding it is not so much to make money as to have some precaution against losing it through devaluation, inflation or various other forms of political insecurity. The French, for example, have suffered fourteen devaluations since 1914, reducing the franc to one two-hundred-and-fiftieth (0·004 per cent) of its value in that year. Gold remains the eternal steady standard of measure and is still the only international currency in many parts of the world. The first reaction of many people in a crisis is to go out and buy gold.

Problems of dollar and sterling currencies

Despite the shortage of gold after the war, there was little difficulty, until the late 1960s, in finding funds to finance world trade because of the willingness of the United States to supply finance in the form of dollars by running an almost permanent balance of payments deficit. The prosperity of the world has in fact been due partly to this policy. However, from 1966 there have been world monetary crises, partly the result of increased deficits in the United States balance of payments because of the cost of the Vietnam war, and the refusal of other countries to devalue or revalue their currencies when necessary.

In March 1968 there was a rush to convert dollar holdings into gold and by this time some 3,000 tonnes of gold, nearly 2 years' production, had gone into private hands. As a result a two-tier gold market was introduced, where the rate continued to be $35 an ounce for official transactions, while a second market was introduced where private demand and supply were brought into line at a free price. This rate naturally fluctuated considerably and soon became much higher than the official rate.

The objections to raising the price of gold include the fear of the resulting inflationary impact, the fact that the benefits of a gold revaluation would be unequally distributed, mainly helping gold-producing countries such as South Africa and the U.S.S.R., and the dislike of a continued reliance on a metal, the supply of which ultimately depends on the speed at which it is mined.

Sterling is in just as vulnerable a position. As a result of the Second World War, Britain had sterling liabilities of £3,700 million, while reserves of gold and convertible foreign currencies were about £600 million. She was thus an international banker with short-term liabilities very much in excess of her reserves. In financial crises such as an adverse balance of payments which worsens the ratio of assets to liabilities, foreign confidence becomes undermined and the situation aggravated by the liquidation of sterling balances held by non-sterling area countries. These balances are liquid funds held by overseas depositors from countries who are members of the sterling area formed in 1931.

Special Drawing Rights and Stand-by Credits

By 1968 it was clear that the current supply of international finance, gold, dollar, sterling and international credit facilities was barely adequate for financing trade. The phenomenon since 1945 of the volume of international trade having risen more rapidly than the means of paying for it has been called the "international liquidity problem." There was a certain self-contradiction in a system which depended upon deficits being incurred by key currency countries if an adequate flow of reserve currencies into other countries' reserves was to be maintained. Hence other reserves had to be created through multi-national action.

Eventually the rules of the I.M.F. were amended and in 1970 it permitted an initial issue to members of $3,500 million of Special Drawing Rights (S.D.R.s). These are units of international currency devised by the I.M.F. They are book entries with the I.M.F. distributed on the basis of the quotas on which members may call when losing reserves or in other balance of payments difficulties. S.D.R.s carry interest and a gold guarantee. They cannot be used in trade for buying goods and services, but they may be transferred to other members in exchange for foreign currencies. One day this new form of international money "paper gold" may gradually phase out the reserve roles of national currencies such as the dollar and sterling. Whether it will eventually oust gold itself as a monetary factor is more problematic. Gold has already lost its monetary role in national currencies.

Credit is also increased by mutual assistance between central banks. "Stand-by credit" would entail a country in surplus issuing credits to one in deficit. A country required to support its own currency in the markets within 1 per cent of par can ask another for a "swop." The Bank of England can pay sterling for dollars, which are then used in the London market to buy pounds, often with the effect of raising the price of sterling enough for the Bank to buy back dollars and repay the "swop."

As from 1st July 1974 S.D.R.s have become the world's principal reserve unit, gold and the former reserve currencies having reduced roles. The value of S.D.R.s is fixed as a composite of a "basket" of 16 chief currencies. The S.D.R.s are daily valued by the I.M.F., according to changes in the exchange rates, weighted by their relative importance in international transactions. It is hoped that the S.D.R., replacing gold as the world's basic money, will develop into a generally acceptable form of international liquidity and standard of value.

The Eurodollar market

This is a large market in dollars held outside the U.S.A. and dates from the sharp rise in U.K. interest rates in 1957 and the imposition of restrictions on the use of sterling credits to finance trade between non-sterling countries. Supplies were available because of the U.S.A. balance of payments deficit and the relaxation of exchange controls in Europe, which allowed a surplus pool of funds to accumulate for trading purposes. Demand came as a result of the need of international and large national corporations for funds. Instead of raising funds on the London or New York markets a company or individual can now raise them in Eurodollars. This international market has no exact location, but its principal European centre is London and comprises most of the world's leading banks and finance houses.

Some business corporations are today so large that a single national money market is no longer adequate for their financial needs. Although many corporations are now international, their financial headquarters are normally collated in one building and one centre.

This predilection for one financial centre is greatly aided by the existence of a market which transcends nations, and loans can be raised in any currency and placed in any nation.

We now have the Euromark, the Eurofranc and even the Euroyen. This perhaps points the answer to the dilemma. Even if the United States were to achieve a surplus, other countries would thus be in deficit, and this deficit, although no longer in dollars, would continue to finance the market. As long as the international monetary situation remains imperfect, as long as countries therefore have to run deficits, there will be funds for the Eurodollar market.

In 1968 dealers involved formed the Association of International Bond Dealers (A.I.B.D.), which has since, meeting monthly, formed a set of rules and regulations by which the market is now governed. There still remain technical problems. Companies floating new issues are often not closely vetted and many near bankrupt firms have managed to raise funds. There is also the problem that when the market is buoyant so many new issues are often floated that there is little hope of them all receiving the funds required. Dealing has now begun in long-term securities (Eurobonds) and in shares (Euroshares).

International monetary reform

The system of more or less fixed exchange rates decided at Bretton Woods to prevent the competitive devaluations which disrupted trade in the 1930s has broken down. This has been due to the strain of inflation, divergent national social policies, actions of multi-national companies and the failure of countries to abide by the rules of the I.M.F.

The expansion and extension of international business have outgrown the rules of the game that have served since 1947. The 1960s have witnessed the production and marketing by subsidiaries of parent multi-national companies replacing straight trade as the main method of commercial trade between Western industrial countries. Banks have developed a corresponding flexibility of operation across national boundaries to match these developments.

The general principle had been for exchange rates to be changed if a country had a deficit in its external payments of some £500 million a year. The volatility of the present system has led to an instability with which the Bretton Woods arrangements are unable to cope. Movements of single currency across the exchanges have taken place, not of £500 million a year, but of £500 millions a week. The greater ability of business and banking in moving funds today has meant that it is difficult for conventional foreign exchange controls to insulate any one country from monetary crises abroad.

Countries have been reluctant to alter their parities by devaluation or revaluation of their currencies according to I.M.F. rules to cover situations when the need arises. This has been primarily for prestige rather than for economic reasons, as was the case with France and Germany in 1968 and Japan in 1972.

The drawbacks of a system of unlimited flexibility as experienced during the 1930s have already been described. In fact, despite this, most exchange rates are now floating, the trend away from fixed rates having developed in the early 1970s. In 1972 Britain floated the pound sterling, intended as a temporary measure.

A foreign currency crisis is caused when a currency is overvalued and large international companies, banks and private investors who hold spare funds sell that currency to guard against the risk of devaluation. It has been argued that one cause of the present instability of the international monetary system has been the nature and expansion of the Eurodollar market. This is because a large pool of money can be moved at short notice out of weak currencies and into those offering better interest rates and security of value. This can create problems for a country applying a restrictive monetary policy and high interest rates to curtail demand, since a sudden influx of funds can have an expansionary and an inflationary effect on the economy.

One response has been the introduction of a two-tier exchange rate system, separating current from capital transactions. France and more recently Italy have adopted this system. It means, particularly if the rate for money flows is allowed to float, that speculators are unlikely to benefit from moving into that currency due to a rise in the rate of exchange when a large demand for it occurs. The expression "dirty floating" refers to intervention, when no official parities are maintained, by monetary authorities such as the Bank of England to keep exchange rates higher or lower than would occur under normal market forces. "Smoothing" means intervention to prevent sudden large changes from day to day.

The problems of international liquidity and disruptions of trade would be partially solved if agreement could be reached concerning greater international supervision of exchange rate movements. An alternative to either devaluation or floating exchange rates would be to have a system of more flexible exchange rates, frequently adjusted.

Another factor which has accentuated the problem of financing world trade has been the trade surpluses accumulated by the oil-rich countries of OPEC since the early 1970s, especially as a result of marked oil price rises in 1973. By 1977 most of the rest of the world was in deficit. Remedies need to be found to prevent the collapse of the world international monetary system. On a system of fixed exchange rates, rules could be enforced by which a country was required to revalue or devalue its currency once its official reserves had reached a predetermined high or low level. This system since 1945 had more or less broken down in any case. On the present system of floating exchange rates countries in surplus have been reluctant to take appropriate remedies to help the deficit countries. The United States, West Germany and Japan were less effected by oil price rises because of their stronger economies, ability to attract OPEC investment and to match increased import costs by comparable export expansion. These countries are reluctant to expand and reflate their economies to a marked degree for fear of inflation, although such measures would help to expand the exports and reduce the unemployment problems of the deficit countries. While Japanese exports have been a factor causing deficits in certain western countries, Japan has discouraged imports by various rules and regulations. Surpluses of the OPEC countries are by no means all spent or re-lent. The failure of the O.E.C.D. countries to sufficiently co-ordinate their policies, and the seriousness of the world situation, led to the economic summit in London (1977).

One remedy is for the richer western countries and the oil-rich countries to extend credit to deficit countries either through bilateral aid or investment or through institutions such as the I.M.F. and the World Bank. The willingness of OPEC to do this may depend in part on what aid and trade arrangements the West is prepared to offer the less developed countries (*see* page 116). In addition, the I.M.F. could be given powers to lend greater sums and to impose more stringent conditions on borrowers.

Trade restrictions and efforts to secure their removal

Countries try not to be too reliant on international trade. Supplies may be cut off from other countries in time of war, and fluctuations in demand, supply and price abroad can have a harmful effect on domestic economies.

From 1846, when the Corn Laws were repealed, until 1914, Britain was a free-trade country. Duties were imposed only for revenue purposes, balanced by equivalent excise duties on similar home-produced goods. Protectionism started with the McKenna duties on luxury goods, 1915, and the *Safeguarding of Industries Act*, 1921, which was imposed for strategic reasons to protect industries essential in time of war or suffering from the depression which followed. Examples of protected items were iron and steel, agriculture, aircraft, chemicals and scientific instruments.

Due to the interdependence of countries in trade, the depression which started in the United States in 1929 affected all countries outside the Soviet bloc. A 70 per cent reduction in the volume of American trade brought about a 64 per cent decline in the value of all international trade, even though American trade accounted for less than one-eighth of it. Efforts were made by countries to maintain domestic employment by protecting their producers against foreign competition. Various methods were used. First the flow of goods was restricted by means of tariffs (or high customs duties) and quantitative restrictions. The latter can take the form of quotas (in which the volume of imports is restricted) or exchange control regulations, where limits are placed on the amount of foreign exchange available for trading. Britain in 1932 imposed tariffs ranging from 10 per cent to about 30 per cent on most imports. Excepted goods were most foodstuffs and certain raw materials such as rubber and cotton. This did not apply to the Commonwealth. Under the Ottawa Agreements manufactured goods from Britain received preferential entry into other Commonwealth countries, while raw materials and food from the Commonwealth received preferential treatment in Britain. Under the conditions of multilateral trade which had prevailed, each country had not had to balance its exports and imports with each individual country with which it traded. Deficits with one country could be offset by surpluses with another. Now, however, bilateral trade agreements took the place of multilateral trade, reducing trade virtually to barter.

Other protectionist arguments have been to improve the balance of payments, or the agricultural interests against the dumping of cheap excess produce of another country. One reason advanced in favour of the prevention of an influx of cheap products from low-wage countries, such as India or Hong Kong, is based on the idea that this is unfair competition with British industries, which have better working conditions and a better-paid labour force. This can be specious reasoning since the whole point of trade is to take advantage of variations of production costs in different areas. The same argument has, in fact, been used by some in the United States to protect their own labour against cheaper goods from Europe.

Another obstacle to free trade is the artificial encouragement of exports by such aids as bounties or taxation exemption. There are also invisible tariffs, stringent regulations stipulating high standards of quality for imported goods.

Since 1945 efforts have been made to remove barriers to the free flow of goods and hence to promote the growth of international trade and co-operation. Important institutions have been established:

the International Monetary Fund (concerned with the provision of funds), which has already been discussed, and the General Agreement of Tariffs and Trade, a treaty arrangement made in 1947. Members agreed to negotiate trade concessions within a regulated framework, an important rule being that the most favoured nation clauses should prevail. Thus concessions negotiated between some members had to be extended to all.

GATT-type negotiations have helped the growth in trade between the advanced countries, but have done little to help the less developed nations, who have called GATT a "rich man's club." For example, the Kennedy Round negotiations, completed in 1967, planned substantial cuts in the trade barriers between industrialised nations between 1968 and 1972, but the benefits for the developing countries are negligible.

A serious issue is the widening chasm in wealth between the "developed" countries (the "haves"), located mainly in Europe and North America, and the "developing" countries (the "have-nots"). More than one hundred countries, located mainly in Africa, Asia and South America, are poor in wealth, having low *per capita* incomes, whether involved in subsistence activities or industry. In the last decade these countries have received a falling share of the total world trade (from a third in 1950 to a sixth in 1969), yet trade is crucial to their economic development and growth. The GATT arrangements are biased against these countries in that they assume complete equality among the contracting parties; in reality great inequality exists since the real power lies with the rich industrialised states. Due to the United States, a waiver clause was included in GATT to allow protection of domestic agriculture, which militates against the interests of the poorer countries.

The developing countries have difficulty in selling their commodities, since the tariffs increase their prices and hence reduce the demand. The commodities most affected are cereals, meat, vegetables, oils, textile fibres and sugar. The developed countries permit duty-free entry for primary products such as tropical fruits and tea if they do not compete with their own agricultural products. World demand for basic commodities has grown less than the demand for industrialised goods. Many poor countries are too dependent upon exports of one or two basic items, *e.g.* 99 per cent of the exports of Mauritius and 66 per cent of Ceylon consist of sugar and tea respectively.

Exports of developing countries come from the sale of commodities. Earnings tend to be unpredictable; for example, agricultural crops may at any time be subject to disease, drought, etc. On the other hand, if the crop is abundant, a glut can also prove to be a catastrophe since world prices of the crop fall dramatically. When poorer countries have attempted to diversify by moving into the processing and manufacturing stages of production, the problem has again been how to sell. Heavier tariffs are imposed if primary products are processed and import restrictions are severest of all on manufactured goods.

Another problem is that the prices of manufactured goods have increased much more than the prices of primary goods. While poorer nations pay rising prices for the essential manufactured goods they need to import, earnings from their exports have not brought in a corresponding revenue.

Between 1961 and 1967 20 per cent of the world's people from the developed nations added to their annual income $161,000 million, an amount far greater than the total income of the remaining 80 per cent. It is estimated that the average income in the rich countries is now twelve times higher than in the poor countries.

In 1964 the United Nations Conference on Trade and Development was created, which acts as a form of pressure group uniting poorer countries together in their demands for a removal of obstacles to trade with the rich countries, and hence for a paving of the way for faster economic development for themselves. It has called for 1 per cent of the G.N.P. of rich countries as the minimum amount which should be transferred annually to poorer countries.

In the 1960s, termed the Development Decade, a conscious effort was for the first time made by the richer developed countries to formulate programmes of aid for the economic development of the poorer nations, thereby supplementing the work of the U.N. agencies. Early hopes were not realised, partly as a result of the failure of the West to agree on appropriate strategies. Agreement is still needed between the North and the South on problems of trade, aid, outstanding debts of the poorer countries and the demands of the latter for a "new international economic order" whereby the developing countries have a greater say in the distribution of the world's wealth. Developing countries tend to argue that much of their economic difficulty is a legacy of European colonialism or is the result of neo-colonialism.

Increased scarcity of certain mineral resources has led to a two-fold division of developing countries into the resource-rich countries including OPEC and the very poor countries of the Fourth World.

IV. MONEY, BANKING AND INVESTMENT

MONEY AND BANKING

The nature and function of money

It has been said:

> *Money's a matter of functions four,*
> *A medium, a measure, a standard, a store.*

Money serves as a medium of exchange for goods or services received and acts as a common measure of value or unit of account for all economic items. This saves the necessity of calculating the value of one commodity in terms of another commodity. Money also represents a store of value since it can be turned into goods or documents of title to goods. Lastly it acts as a standard for deferred payments, making it possible for a debt to be measured and agreed for payment at a later date.

The commodity chosen as money must possess certain qualities if it is to carry out these functions. In early societies the commodity used had also to be desired for its own sake; that is, it had to have intrinsic value in addition to monetary value. This explains the use of certain commodities as money such as cattle, rice, salt, cowry shells, furs, etc. The particular object chosen varied with time and country.

Characteristics of good money first noted by Adam Smith were: divisibility, indestructibility, stability of value, homogeneity, cognisability, acceptability and portability. The mnemonic "Dishcap" provides a useful memory aid. In whatever form money may be, its acceptability as a means of payment is the most important characteristic. Hence money is defined as anything which is generally acceptable in immediate settlement of a debt. Stability of value is also important if money is to act effectively as a store of value and as a standard for deferred payments.

This list of desirable features explains why, as civilisation developed, men turned to precious metals to serve as money, particularly gold and silver. They are portable, as they have a high value relative to weight, they are divisible without loss of value, they can be stored without deterioration and they are in limited supply.

Types of money and methods of payment

Developed societies today make use of the following: metal coins, paper money and bank money (bank balances or deposits). At one time standard coins circulated. These contained their full face value in pure metal, gold or silver. One disadvantage was the gradual reduction of the coinage when rulers were tempted to enrich themselves by putting less of the precious metal into the coins, or when people profited through clipping the edge of the coins. From about 1343 until the reform of the coinage in 1544, the silver content of the penny in Britain fell from 22 grains troy to 10 grains. This affected the acceptability of money and led to the formulation of Gresham's Law (generally attributed to Sir Thomas Gresham, Elizabeth I's Royal Agent in Flanders), which stated: "Bad money tends to drive out good." Thus when a variety of coins are in circulation, some of which have a higher metal content than others, people will tend to hoard the coins with the greater metallic content and to use the debased coinage as currency. From 1663 coins were milled at the edge to prevent clipped and underweight coins being circulated. However, standard coins are no longer used, having been replaced by token coins whose metallic content is less than their face value. In Britain these coins consist of silver or cupro-nickel, copper and nickel-brass.

The next step was the introduction of paper money. As metallic money could be stolen easily, the habit developed of leaving gold and silver in a place of safety. This led to the issuing of deposit receipts, a written evidence of a "promise to pay." In time these I.O.U.s came to be regarded as the equivalent of money and to be passed from hand to hand, in the knowledge that the holder could at any time exchange the receipt for gold at the goldsmiths who had issued it. The goldsmiths began to make out their deposit receipts as payable "to bearer" instead of to a named person. Because of the confidence of the people in the convertibility of the receipts, only a small number were cashed, most of them remaining in circulation. During the 17th century they came to be called banknotes. Thus the greater part of a goldsmith's holdings of gold and silver lay idle, since only a small proportion was needed to meet daily demand. But it was necessary to retain some gold on hand, because paper was not sufficient for some transactions. When goods were brought from abroad, paper had to be converted into gold and shipped overseas. The goldsmiths discovered that it was not essential to keep an ounce of gold in the vaults for every claim to an ounce which circulated in the form of paper money. Acting as bankers they started the practice

MONEY, BANKING AND INVESTMENT

of issuing banknotes for more than the gold originally deposited with them. The era of convertible paper currency—the right to convert banknotes into gold on request—ended in 1931 when Britain left the gold standard.

It may seem remarkable that the total value of bank deposit money was considerably greater than the supply of coins and banknotes by the Bank of England. The reason for this was that since the time of the goldsmiths the banks had been creating money in the form of bank deposits representing loans to customers, and thus issuing promises to pay sums which, in aggregate, were greater than the cash they actually had.

Most of the money used today has no intrinsic value, in contrast to the early days when money was first used. The precious metals gold and silver are not available in sufficient quantities to meet modern needs and have only a limited use as an international means of exchange.

Token money consists of coins and notes. Token coins issued by the Royal Mint have a metallic value less than the circulating value and are only limited legal tender, *i.e.* they can only be legally offered in payment for a debt up to a certain amount. English banknotes on the other hand are unlimited legal tender, but are token in the sense of no longer being convertible into gold.

There is no clear division between what is money and what is not. Money is basically what money does, and if it is accepted in payment for goods and services it is acting as money. Hence in addition to coins and banknotes, there are numerous other forms of payment which act as money in a limited sense, and largely obviate the need to transfer the commodity known as money at all.

Today the greater part of the money supply consists of bank money (or bank credit): credit balances of the accounts of customers of deposit banks (which can also be referred to as clearing banks, commercial banks or joint-stock banks). Payment is made largely by cheque. This is a written instruction to a bank to transfer money to a named payee or to bearer, and is signed by the payer or drawer. Open cheques can be cashed across the counter of the bank on which they are drawn, but crossed cheques have to be paid into a banking account. Another form of money apart from token and bank money is "near" or "quasi" money, assets that can easily be turned into money at short notice, such as savings certificates, building society share deposits and postal orders.

The method by which debts are settled when cheques are drawn on current accounts is briefly as follows: If both drawer and payee (debtor and creditor) are members of the same bank in the same town, the matter could easily be settled by debit and credit entries in their respective accounts. If claims have to be offset between local branches of different banks in the same town, these branches may arrange to work out net claims on each other and to offset them by drafts drawn on their head offices. The head office of each bank arranges to offset claims between branches of its own in different areas. Cheques drawn on other banks in different towns are sent to head office in London and then to the Central Clearing House. Eventually the net amounts owed or receivable by the various banks are settled by transfers from or to their accounts at the Bank of England by means of ledger entries. Thus the physical transfer of money is avoided.

Some methods utilise bank deposits. Examples are bills of exchange, standing orders (regular payments of the same amount made by a bank on behalf of a customer to the same payee, *e.g.* a club to cover a regular subscription) and telegraphic transfers (a swift method of transferring credit from one account to another account abroad). Banks and other agencies also issue Travellers' Cheques, which provide some security and avoid exchange complications when money is drawn abroad. In 1961 the commercial banks introduced the Credit Transfer system (now called the Bank Giro), which enabled a person to pay a number of bills with one cheque. If creditors are willing to accept payment in this way, and the bank has all the required information, it will pay the various bills for a client by means of book-keeping entries, co-operating in this task with other banks.

Credit cards represent yet another tendency to replace paper and coin by transfers through the banking system as they enable one to purchase at many places without payment. Examples are Access issued by the Joint Credit Card Co. Ltd. (formed by Lloyds, Midland and National Westminster Banks), Barclays, Diners Club and American Express. Eventually details of the transaction are sent to the Credit Company, which pays the amount to the firm concerned. After a discount has been deducted, the customer receives a monthly statement of all items bought with the card. He then issues a single cheque to the Credit Company for services bought from a variety of different shops and restaurants. If preferred, extended credit facilities can be obtained, a customer having to pay off only part of the amount owing each month. Credit cards must be distinguished from cheque or bank cards, which enable holders to draw money up to a certain amount from major British banks and from banks abroad displaying the Eurocheque sign. Twenty-eight countries are in the Eurocheque system, including the European Community, five states in Eastern Europe, Turkey, Morocco and Iceland.

Some people who do not have bank accounts use the Post Office services to transfer money. At one time postal and money orders were used quite frequently, but now the Post Office Giro system offers its facility to small customers who do not use a commercial bank's services by making standing order payments, and it also enables an account holder to transfer money to another person. It is a restricted banking service open to everyone over eighteen years. No cheque book is available and it does not offer overdraft facilities.

Functions of deposit banks

Banks are dealers in money and credit, though their activities can be said to cover anything that is natural and profitable for a bank to do. The chief form are the Deposit Banks. However, they do not carry out a full range of financial services, and so there are a large number of specialist credit and finance institutions.

Recent amalgamations have reduced the number of commercial banking groups. Of the "Big Four" the largest is Barclays, which absorbed Martins in December 1969. The second is the National Westminster, formed by the amalgamation in January 1970 of National Provincial, Westminster, District and Coutts & Co. The third largest is Midland followed by Lloyds. Other banking groups are Williams & Glyn's Bank, formed from the two banks of Glyn, Mills & Co. and Williams Deacon's, which merged in September 1970 with another group, the National and Commercial Banking Group, formed in 1968 and consisting of the Royal Bank of Scotland and the National Commercial Bank of Scotland. All these banks, apart from the Scottish banks, which operate their own system and rules, are subject to controls operated by the Bank of England and are members of the Clearing House system. Certain private banks are still operating in London today.

One old banking function was the provision of a safe deposit for valuables. Another, which is now restricted to the Bank of England and Scottish and Irish banks, was the issuing of banknotes. The chief function of banks is the acceptance of money on current and deposit accounts, and the organisation of the cheque system, an efficient method of settling debts. As money in a current account can be withdrawn on demand, frequently by cheque, the customer earns no interest on it. However, deposit accounts, which are subject to seven days' notice of withdrawal that banks may insist upon, particularly with large sums of money, earn a small interest. Banks may also provide special savings accounts, which earn a higher interest on the first £250 and then deposit rate thereafter.

Banks provide a variety of other services concerned, for example, with executor and trustee work, income tax services, advice on investments and the buying and selling of securities, the issue of foreign trade letters of credit, acting as references, carrying out standing orders and conducting foreign business for clients through branches or correspondence banks abroad.

The most profitable function is the lending of money to customers by way of (*a*) a loan account repayable over a definite period, (*b*) an overdraft of a current account, when interest is paid on the amount overdrawn for the time the overdrawn amount lasts and (*c*) a discounting of a bill of exchange.

Commercial banks are companies which exist to make profits for their shareholders by borrowing money at lower rates of interest than they charge to borrowers. Basically the banks only lend on a short-term basis, usually providing trade and industry with working capital, *i.e.* money to replenish stock, pay current expenses or take advantage of favourable financial opportunities. Creating deposits in order to lend at a profit involves certain risks. First the loan may not be repaid, and secondly there may be a run on the banks for cash. In practice a joint stock bank prefers not to lend if there is any risk of inability to repay and seeks to cover itself by demanding some form of collateral to be deposited at the bank in return for a loan, *e.g.* an insurance policy, marketable stocks and shares, or deeds of a property. The bank also considers the personal reputation and standing of the borrower, the purpose for which the loan is needed and the length of time required. In addition the bank has to consider the general credit situation in the country as a whole and to try to reconcile the conflicting aims of (*a*) adequate liquidity and (*b*) maximum profitability when considering its lending policy.

These objectives pull in opposite directions, the shorter the loan period the greater the bank's liquidity but the less it will earn by way of interest. Experience has in part determined what is a suitable distribution of assets, as shown by bank failures in the past. Loans are divided among different types of borrowers for different periods, and different types of loans are kept fairly close to carefully worked out ratios or percentages. Sometimes these ratios are applied by an arrangement between the bankers themselves (as in Britain) or by enforcement of minimum legal reserve ratios (as in the United States).

The creation of deposits

The ability of banks to create deposit money depends first on the willingness of customers to deposit cash with them, secondly on the fact, based on experience, that these deposits need be only fractionally backed by notes and coins, and thirdly—and most important—on the banks' lending operations. We will now discuss these forms through a survey of some of the items in a bank's balance sheet (*see* Fig. 18).

Current liabilities
Current, deposit and other accounts
Balances with subsidiary companies
Taxation

Proposed final dividend

Capital and reserves
Capital
  Authorised:
  Issued:
Reserves

Current assets
Cash and short-term funds
Cheques in course of collection
Special deposit with the Bank of England
Investments
Advances and other accounts after provision for bad and doubtful debts

Fixed assets
Investments in subsidiary companies
Trade investments
Premises and equipment

FIG. 18. *A specimen bank statement of accounts*

The bank's current liabilities take the form partly of money on current, deposit and other accounts. Regarding the current assets to meet these liabilities, about 8 per cent used to be held as assets in notes and coins to meet demand, or in deposits at the Bank of England. This was the cash–credit ratio, the relationship between the actual indebtedness of the banks and the quantity of cash available to meet calls on demand. It meant that the banks were able to create credit, called Bank Deposit money, up to $12\frac{1}{2}$ times the amount of the original deposits.

Very short-term loans (money at call or short notice up to fourteen days) were made to local authorities and to the money market, chiefly to the discount houses, which borrow from the banks to purchase treasury and commercial bills. A small percentage of the bank's assets were composed of treasury bills and commercial bills of exchange, which the banks purchased from the discount houses. These liquid asset reserves (cash, short loans and bills) formed about 28 per cent of total assets and made up the liquidity ratio. The banks also invested money in long-term Government securities. The most profitable, but least liquid of the bank assets, were the advances or loans made to the customers. The cash ratio and the liquidity ratio were replaced by a single reserve ratio in September 1971, discussed later in the chapter.

The Bank of England and the history of banking

Banking in England was begun after the Norman Conquest by the Jews, and then by Italian merchants, the Lombards who traded in Lombard Street on open benches. (The Italian for "bench" was *banco*, from which came the English word "bank.") Modern English banking dates from the time of the London goldsmiths, who used to provide a safe deposit for values and later for money. Public confidence in them was frequently shaken by their attempt to make quick profits through lending out large sums, and then being unable to meet demands for cash. By the 1670s the goldsmiths were lending not only to merchants but also to the Crown. In 1672 Charles II suspended repayments, which weakened the goldsmiths and hardened them against lending again to the king. William III later needed money to finance a war against France but the goldsmiths would only advance it to him at an exorbitant interest. In 1694 a Scotsman, William Paterson, and some other financiers were given a charter to found the Bank of England in exchange for the loan of £1,200,000 at 8 per cent interest per annum. This was the beginning of the National Debt.

At first the business of the new bank was chiefly the receiving of money on deposit. Eventually it became the Government's bank, holding Government funds, raising new issues of treasury bills and other Government securities, keeping records, paying interest on its loans. In 1751 it undertook the administration of the National Debt. By the end of the 18th century it was becoming the bankers' bank, for the London banks found it convenient to keep accounts at the Bank of England.

The first development that led to it becoming a central bank was controversy over the correct method of note issue. In the 18th century the issue of notes had been regarded as the most important of banking functions. Some banks issued an excessive number of notes, and there were frequent bank failures. In 1797 the Bank of England refused payment of its notes in gold, which thereby became inconvertible currency. After 1815 two schools of thought developed: the Banking School, which believed that the size of the note issue should be left to the discretion of bankers, and the Currency School, which held that the amount of notes issued should be tied to the amount of gold held by the bank. A compromise was adopted in the *Charter Act*, 1844, which provided that no new bank could issue notes and that an existing bank on amalgamation or bankruptcy lost the right of note issue. Its provisions gradually resulted in the Bank of England obtaining a monopoly of the note issue. The Act of 1844 also stated that the latter could issue notes to the value of £14 million against securities—the fiduciary issue (notes permitted to be issued without gold backing)—and that any issue above this sum had to have gold or silver backing. In 1890 the Bank undertook to discount fifteen-day bills for the discount houses at not less than bank rate, and one of its important functions today is as a lender of last resort, when borrowers are unable to obtain funds from the deposit banks. During the 20th century its work and responsibilities have greatly increased because of the expansion in Government expenditure, the management of the currency following the suspension of the gold standard (1931) and the introduction of exchange control (1939). Today the Bank acts as agent for the Government in administering exchange control, and manages the Treasury's Exchange Equalisation Account, which holds Britain's official reserves of gold, sterling and foreign currency that are used to support the sterling rate of exchange. It also acts as financial adviser to the Government on international financial problems.

As well as implementing the Government's monetary policy and acting as banker for the Government and for commercial banks, it does so also for overseas central banks and international organisations such as the International Monetary Fund (I.M.F.). In addition there remains a small amount of private and commercial business, a legacy from the days when the Bank of England was active in general banking.

Techniques of monetary policy—open market operations, bank rate and other methods

One way of attempting to regulate the economy is by techniques affecting the supply of money. The ability of an individual commercial bank to lend money and hence create deposits is limited first by the amount of cash available and secondly by the supply of acceptable collateral securities. Two traditional instruments used by the Bank of England, acting on behalf of the Government, have been open market operations and bank rate changes.

Open market operations occur when the central bank's broker buys and sells treasury bills and other Government securities in the open market. Securities are sold if the Bank wants to restrict credit. The buyers pay for these securities through cheques drawn on their accounts at the commercial banks. These cheques are then sent to the

Bank of England and the debts are settled by a reduction in the commercial banks' deposits. This represents a loss of cash, an important source of liquid assets, and the commercial banks will then be forced to restrict their lending. If an expansion of credit is wanted, the broker will buy securities and the reverse process will take place. The scope today is more limited than before since many of Britain's biggest industries are nationalised, and have to resort to fixed interest financing, being unable to issue equities.

Bank rate served three functions. First, it was the chief rate on which overdraft and other interest rates were based. Secondly, it was an important means of Government control of the economy. Changes in bank rate were followed by changes in other short-term rates of interest and helped to reinforce open market operations. Bank rate increases tended to reduce the amount of borrowing, while bank rate decreases tended to increase the amount of borrowing. Thirdly, it was the rate charged to discount houses when the Bank of England acted in its capacity as "lender of last resort." This would occur when the banks called in their loans from the discount houses (due to Government open market operations) and the latter were forced to turn to the Bank of England to obtain the necessary funds to repay their loans to the commercial banks. Bank rate was higher than the current short-term rates of interest and was hence a "penal" rate. The discount houses would then have to raise their own interest rates to cut their losses, and the commercial banks would follow suit.

For the last twenty years bank rate has been losing importance in regard to its first two functions. If the Bank wanted to stop a flow of "hot" money from the country, bank rate would be increased, while if the Government wanted to stimulate the economy, the rate would be lowered. But a conflict in aims could occur when the Government wanted to stop hot money and stimulate the economy at the same time. In any case, to the extent that a high bank rate increased the liquidity of the banking system by attracting foreign funds, it achieved the exact reverse of monetary restraint. And in a period of expansion accompanied by inflation, the added cost of credit as a result of high bank rate was only a limited disincentive. Borrowers were also able to obtain loans at high rates from other financial institutions when the banks were under severe credit control.

Since 1945 the Bank of England has resorted to other methods in addition to varying bank rate and open market operations. To control the movement of money in and out of the country, it has operated directly on interest rates in the money market. To control credit, it has increased its powers by such means as directives and the "special deposits" system, which are explained below.

The Government, through the Bank of England, makes suggestions and requests to the banks from time to time concerning lending policies. They may be of a qualitative nature, when banks are asked to restrict their loans to activities in the national interest, by, say, looking favourably upon applicants for loans for financing exports and discouragingly upon applicants for loans for the purchase of consumer goods. The requests would be of a quantitative nature if the banks were asked to limit their total advances to a specified level or ceiling. If necessary the Treasury can issue a special directive (under Section 4 [3] of the *Bank of England Act*, 1946) to reinforce its requests and recommendations.

These methods were effective as long as the banks created credit on the basis of their cash reserves, but banks also based their credit policies on their holding of liquid assets, of which treasury bills were the most important. Thus another form of control to reduce the commercial banks' holdings of treasury bills is for the central bank to divert the supply of bills by selling them to other financial institutions or to resort to the use of "funding" (which is the conversion of short-term into medium- and long-term debt by issuing fewer treasury bills and more bonds). This funding of short-term debt held by banks, by replacing short-term securities (treasury bills) with long-term securities, which are not classed among the liquid assets, will reduce the liquid asset ratio of banks, and cause them to contract deposits. It was first used for this purpose in 1951. However, an older objective of funding was to obviate the need for the Government to redeem maturing bills at frequent or inconvenient intervals.

Funding adds to the cost of Government borrowing, since short-term borrowing is cheaper and tends to disrupt the structure of interest rates. Hence a new device of "special deposits" was first used in 1960 to restrict bank liquidity and to make it easier to implement open market operations. When in operation, it obliges the banks to deposit a certain percentage of their total deposits with the central bank. This policy was not entirely successful as banks tended to raise cash by selling securities, thus maintaining their liquid asset and total deposit levels. Government-imposed limits on consumer loan terms or hire-purchase regulations can also be considered as part of monetary policy. Since 1945 the Government has made frequent changes in minimum down-payments and maximum repayment periods as a means of cutting down consumers' demand for durable goods.

Recent banking developments

In September 1971 extensive new monetary and banking regulations were introduced. One major change was the Bank of England's policy in the gilt-edged market. The authorities' main concern used to be with the management of the national debt with the aim of increasing the demand for gilt-edged securities, to provide funds for current requirements and for refunding of a continuous flow of maturing debt. As a result the Government was concerned to keep all interest rates stable and at a level which reduced the burden of public debt. Thus the Bank of England, to stabilise the price or interest rates of funds in the money market, undertook continuous smoothing operations. This involved either the purchase or sale of treasury bills depending on the position.

By their commitment to maintaining a given level of interest rates the authorities had relinquished control of the money supply (discussed in detail later in the chapter) and were prepared to accept limitation on competition among banks. However, the Bank of England stated in September 1971 that it was no longer prepared to buy stocks outright except those of one year or less to maturity. The aim was to limit fluctuations in available funds arising from official operations in gilts, and to allow greater freedom for prices to be affected by market conditions.

An end was made to Government-stipulated ceilings on each bank's lending policies. In place of direct quantitative controls such as the treasury directive, the Government was to rely on varying interest rates and on the powers of the Bank of England to cut down excess liquidity by calling each Thursday a uniform percentage of all banks' assets into idle "special deposits" with it. Focus would be on controlling the money supply rather than bank lending as formerly.

Before discussing other changes, a brief coverage is given of certain banking developments over the last twenty years. In the 1950s the commercial banks accounted for a high proportion of sterling and foreign currency deposits of the U.K. banking sector and provided most of the loan facilities to industry and individuals. By the end of the 1960s many of the non-clearing banks, comprising the merchant banks, finance houses, British overseas and Commonwealth banks, and American and other foreign banks, now accounted for a greater amount of funds deposited and loans made. Much of the new business resulted from an increase in foreign funds associated with the London Euromarkets. Overseas banks and multi-national companies, etc., had invested funds on deposit for short-term lending with acceptance houses and the exchange banks in a variety of currencies. As a result an international market in loanable funds has developed (details were given of the Eurodollar market in Chapter III).

The growing activities of various financial institutions were a contributory factor to the decline of the effectiveness of traditional monetary policies of the Government. Credit restrictions imposed on the deposit banks encouraged the growth of financial institutions which carried on activities similar to deposit banks but which were not subject to credit controls. Businessmen unable to borrow from banks could resort to other methods of raising finance, which could involve, say, a building society, insurance company or other financial institutions. Since foreign banks could switch funds in and out of sterling comparatively easily, this raised problems relating to interest rate policy and balance of payments.

Gradually the authorities reacted to the changing financial environment by developing new monetary controls and extending them to a wider range of financial institutions. From 1965 onwards the Government gradually extended credit controls on lending to members of the Finance House Association and to overseas banks. In 1968 a Cash Deposits Scheme was started to give the deposit banks power in certain circumstances to demand deposits from some of the non-clearing banks.

From September 1971 the commercial banks were required to keep not less than $12\frac{1}{2}$ per cent of their sterling deposit liabilities (called eligible liabilities) in specified reserve assets, such as cash at the Bank of England other than special deposits, treasury bills and money at call. They could not include in this cash in their tills (about $6\frac{1}{2}$ per cent of deposits) and certain other funds. The interpretation of the observance of this ratio was stricter than that applied to the previous 28 per cent ratio, as it now had to be maintained as a minimum ratio on a day-to-day basis. However, the banks now had considerably more liquid funds to lend to customers or to invest in the longer-term gilt-edged market.

This minimum reserve ratio of $12\frac{1}{2}$ per cent was also applied to all types of banks, defined as deposit-taking institutions. This covered merchant banks and small banks in so far as they attracted sterling deposit liabilities. Only savings banks, the Post Office Giro and building societies were not subject to the new regulations. Finance houses were required to maintain a ratio of 10 per cent of eligible liabilities while the discount houses were now required to keep 50 per cent of their funds in officially defined public debt. Thus the divisions, as regards lending or deposit regulations, between banks and near-banks, and within the banking system between the clearing banks and the rest, were removed.

The Government also aimed to introduce a more competitive banking environment. The clearing banks abandoned their collective agreements whereby they promised not to compete with one another in deposit or basic overdraft interest rates, which had previously been linked to bank rate. Now they were able to determine what were called their base rates, to which borrowing and lending rates were to be linked.

Since the deposit banks, as a result of the new system of monetary controls, are able to increase their share of business relative to other financial institutions by increasing their efficiency, this should eventually increase the size of the banking industry. Already they have started to play a greater role in the capital market, providing medium-term funds to both industrial and personal customers.

As a result of the Government's new policy of competition and credit control in September 1971, the bank rate ceased to have any direct influence on rates of interest offered by banks to borrowers and lenders. The only function left to it was that of governing the money market. To make this particular role more effective, and to discard the other former functions, bank rate was replaced in October 1972 by a new rate, "the minimum lending rate" at which the Bank will lend as a last resort, which will be based on the average rate of discount for treasury bills at the weekly tender plus $\frac{1}{2}$ per cent and rounded to the nearest $\frac{1}{4}$ per cent above. This does not exclude the possibility of a special change in the rate if the Government considers it necessary to give a lead to interest rates during a period of economic crisis.

This means that changes in bank rate will no longer need to be interpreted as signalling major shifts in Government monetary policy and will enable the Bank of England to have more freedom to influence short-term rates through such devices as the weekly treasury bill tender. It manipulates the treasury bill rate in two ways. First, it operates directly on the bill rate daily by open market operation. If the market is short of money, and the Bank lowers its buying price for bills, bill rates increase. Secondly, it exerts a further influence on bill rates and on longer-term interest rates by adjusting the "mix" of Government debt financing.

A new development is the growth since 1971 of money shops and in-store banking points (*i.e.* retail and consumer banking). Major participants include American banks, U.D.T. and Bowmaker. They maintain normal shop opening hours, provide cash and credit facilities and possibly give financial advice and savings facilities.

THE FINANCE OF FOREIGN TRADE

The money market and the bill of exchange

The money market can be considered the mainspring of the City's life, for it is only by its function of lending and borrowing and giving short-term credit that international trade can be transacted so swiftly and efficiently. Trade would have been severely hampered if every stage of production, transportation, marketing and resale had to be paid for as a separate transaction of business, accompanied by the passing of hard cash. Through the money market these payments can be made without the actual handling of money, and delays and stoppages in the flow of business can be averted. Also without the knowledge which members of this market have of foreign firms, bad debts could occur, with a loss of confidence and a general falling off of business.

The institutions which comprise this market are the British and overseas banks, merchant bankers and acceptance houses, the discount houses, the bullion brokers, the head offices of the big insurance companies, and the Bank of England.

Bills of exchange are used particularly to finance international trade. Such a bill is an order addressed by one person to another and requiring the addressee to pay a certain sum of money on demand or at a fixed future date. Bills of exchange enable the exporter to obtain cash as soon as possible after dispatching the goods, while enabling the importer to defer payment until the goods reach him, or later.

An illustration will make their use clear. If a French tyre manufacturer wanted to buy rubber from Malaya, he might not have the cash available for some time to pay for it, nor a supply of Malayan currency in which to pay. The rubber planter, on the other hand, would want money immediately and not in French francs. Through the London market a bill of exchange can be arranged so that the rubber planter is paid immediately and in sterling. The French manufacturer's bank, through its London branch, will approach a merchant bank or an acceptance house. If the manufacturer has a good record, the bill will be accepted. This is done by endorsing it with the name of the bank or acceptance house, thus guaranteeing payment should the buyer of the goods default. The bill now becomes a valuable saleable commodity, and the planter can either hold the bill to maturity and collect the total debt, say £500, or receive immediate cash, but a reduced amount, by discounting the bill with a discount house. The discount is deducted from the face value of the bill, and is calculated at an agreed rate per cent for the period the bill has to run. Its current worth becomes closer to its face value as the bill approaches maturity.

Rules regarding bills of exchange are governed by the *Bills of Exchange Act*, 1882. Clean bills are used where there is complete trust between importer and exporter. No documents are attached to them as they are sent direct to the importer. Documentary bills are accompanied by documents of title to the goods. The documents to accompany the bill are agreed upon by the importer and exporter when drawing up their contract.

The commercial banks play only an indirect role in financing trading by (*a*) lending to the discount houses who form the intermediaries, and (*b*) discounting bills of exchange. The discount houses borrow short-term funds from the commercial banks to finance these trade bills on a long-term basis and make profit by charging a higher rate of discount than they have to pay the banks for borrowing. Some funds also come from the acceptance houses and overseas banks.

When a bank negotiates a bill of exchange, it pays the face value of the bill less discount to its customer. This is the same process as discounting, but with foreign bills it is called "negotiation." Usually the bank requires a signed undertaking from its customer that he will reimburse the bank in the event of the bill being dishonoured. Sometimes the bank also requires additional security and will only advance a proportion of the face value of the bill, the remainder being handed to the customer when the bill is finally paid.

When funds are not required immediately or when the bill is not sufficiently attractive for negotiation, the exporter may hand it to his bank for collection. The bank then acts as the customer's agent, taking instructions from him to collect the proceeds of the bill. There are uniform rules for collection of bills which have to be observed by bank and customer.

Treasury bills are Government bills of exchange. The Government is the largest borrower on the money market and issues bills generally for ninety-one days in denominations of £5,000, £10,000, £50,000 and £100,000. Most of these are bought by the discount houses but some are issued to the commercial banks and to Government departments.

Money market operators have a margin between short loans or call money interest rates and the market discount rate as their area for profit. The market rate is the rate at which first-class bills are rediscounted between members of the market. In the last resort, if money is short in the market, operators are forced "in the bank," which means they are forced to pay the rate of interest charged by the Bank of England in order to obtain credit.

Documentary credits

Foreign business transactions can be settled through the normal banking system as each British bank has accounts with banks throughout the world. Foreign banks also hold sterling balances in British banks, therefore transactions are settled by offsetting one debt against another.

The two most important methods of settlement offered by the banks are bills of exchange and documentary credits. But transactions may also be settled on open account; or by telegraphic transfer whereby the importer's bank directs the exporter's bank to transfer some of the balance on its account to the person named in the transfer; or by mail transfer, which is similar except that the instructions are sent by mail and not telegraph; or by banker's draft.

Documentary credits are letters of credit which may be either a personal or a commercial credit. Personal credits enable the businessman travelling abroad to obtain money without having to take large amounts of cash with him, and commercial credits enable a firm or person to obtain money provided the conditions laid down in the letter of credit are fulfilled.

Uniform customs and practice for documentary credits were codified by the International Chamber of Commerce and adopted by the British banks in 1963. A contract is drawn up between the importer and the exporter whereby the importer arranges for his bank to send a letter to the exporter undertaking to pay when the bank receives the documents specified in the letter. These documents, the invoice, bill of lading (when goods are sent by ship) and insurance certificate provide proof that the exporter has sent off the goods. The bank establishing the credit can make it either a revocable or an irrevocable credit. The terms of an irrevocable credit cannot be changed without the consent of all parties, whereas those of a revocable credit can.

A sight credit is where the beneficiary can obtain payment immediately, and an acceptance credit is payable upon the maturity of the bill of exchange. Red clause credits authorise advances to the beneficiary to enable payment to be made for produce before shipment.

The E.C.G.D. and the Amstel Club

The Export Credits Guarantee Department (E.C.G.D.) plays an important role in guaranteeing firms against loss in connection with their export contracts. Businesses which benefit particularly are those wishing to expand into new markets abroad and to develop business with new buyers, or those where export credit tends to be substantial in relation to capital. Insurance policies are issued covering the whole of an exporter's business for twelve months or three years ahead. The department was established by the Government in 1919 at a time when political and financial upheavals in Europe had greatly increased the risks of foreign trading.

In 1959 a group of leading financial institutions known as the Amstel Club entered into reciprocal agreements for the finance of imports and exports between their respective countries. The eleven member countries comprise Britain, the United States, Switzerland, France, West Germany, Holland, Belgium, Austria, Italy, Norway and Portugal. The British member is United Dominions Trust Limited, which formed a new company, International Finance & Services Limited. The new company, after certain procedures have been completed, offers credit to the buyers of British goods abroad and, on shipment of the goods, immediately pays the exporter the amount due.

International banking

Merchant banks finance trade rather than trade on their own account. Some of the well-known ones are Barings, Rothschilds, Schroders and Warburgs. One important function is the accepting of bills of exchange. They also act as issuing houses for companies making share issues and as expert managers of investment trusts, manage the investment of pension funds, carry on foreign exchange business, provide loans to industry, and assist with take-over bids in industry, amalgamations and mergers of firms.

The British overseas banks are still the City's most important earners of foreign exchange. Their branches, stretching across five continents and over seventy countries, were first developed in the 19th century when banks were needed to service the capital Britain was investing abroad. At this time, when British goods dominated world trade, sterling was the only international currency and London's banking skill was the only one capable of starting banking systems in newly developing countries. They cover four main areas. Asia and the Middle East is served by Hongkong and Shanghai, Chartered, National and Grindlays, the Ottoman Bank and their subsidiaries. Africa is divided between Standard and Barclays Bank International (formerly Barclays D.C.O.) though National and Grindlays also operate in East Africa. In 1971 the Bank of London & South America, which operated mainly in South America, amalgamated with Lloyds Bank (Europe) to form Lloyds Bank International.

The break-up of the British Empire, the forces of nationalism and socialism, nationalisation schemes, political unrest and war, etc., have affected overseas banking. Today they face increased competition from local banks, who get favoured treatment from their governments and from the American banking mammoths, Bank of America, Chase Manhattan and First National City. Sometimes there is a demand by a local government for greater control, perhaps even for a separate bank in the country with local shareholders holding a controlling interest. However, the banks believe the essence of the operation is that they remain branch systems transcending national frontiers. They are gradually diversifying into wider markets, forming large international banking chains and taking an increased share of the international deposit market, thus reducing their reliance on sterling as a currency.

Multi-nationals have been increasing their share of the European market and have made heavy demands for capital to increase their expansion. Parallel to this the bigger American banks have been acquiring a greater share of business in Europe. Another development in times of credit restrictions has been the tendency for oil companies and other multi-nationals to become "near-banks" themselves. For some years multi-nationals have lent out working cash through the market, using the banks less and less as intermediaries. They have become even "nearer-banks" by starting direct lender–borrower relationships, cutting out the market altogether.

In response to this invasion during the 1960s European banks reorganised themselves, numerous mergers taking place and several cross-frontier groupings being formed. The European Banks International Company (E.B.I.C.) comprises the Amsterdam–Rotterdam Bank, Deutsche Bank, Midland Bank and the Société Générale de Banque (Belgium). The Orion Group includes Chase Manhattan and the National Westminster. Barclays is a member of Société Financière Européenne (S.F.E.). They are thus able to mobilise larger funds at less cost. Only Lloyds of Britain's Big Four banks is not yet a member of the general Euro-groupings. The S.F.E. can best be described as an international merchant bank. It provides medium- and long-term finance by loans or equity participations; it negotiates mergers and regroupings, etc.; and it undertakes research into problems of a technical, fiscal, legal or administrative nature which confront companies wanting to expand abroad.

The British Bankers' Association used to have only clearing banks and the main deposit banks as members. In 1972 it widened its membership to include merchant banks, discount houses, accepting houses, some of the issuing houses and finance houses. The Association will represent British banking in the Fédération Bancaire, the European Federation of banking trade associations.

MONETARY POLICY AND INFLATION

The value and quantity of money

Traditional explanations of the value of money have been the quantity theories, of which three main versions can be identified. First there is the "equation of exchange," where $MV = PT$, a simplified version of the formula of Fisher, an American economist. It is useful in identifying the different factors which may influence the value of money, or in other words the price level. It is in a sense a truism or tautology, true by definition, since expenditure by purchasers equals the value of the goods sold to them by sellers. From the consumers' viewpoint, total spending is equal to the money they hold (M) multiplied by the number of times each unit of it changes hands during a given period, called the Velocity of Circulation (V). From the producers' viewpoint, expenditure of the community is the volume of trade or or number of goods and services exchanged (T) multiplied by the price (P). The equation can also be expressed as $P = MV/T$, which confirms the generalisation that prices tend to rise, causing a decline in the value of money, if money expenditure (MV) increases in relation to the volume of trade (T).

The two other theories were put forward by classical economists, who assumed conditions of full employment. These were the "rigid" and "flexible" variations of the quantity theory. The "rigid" or crudest form was that the value of money varied inversely with the supply of money (M). This was based on the observation that prices rose as the supply of money increased. It assumed that money circulated with a constant velocity (V) against a constant volume of goods (T), or that any change in one would be cancelled out by a change in the other.

This was naturally not true in all circumstances. For example, if an economy suffered from unemployment, the result of an increase in the quantity of money and consequently in expenditure would not necessarily lead to higher prices but to the use of idle resources and an increased output. An increase in the supply of money could also be cancelled out by a fall in the average velocity of circulation, if money was hoarded or retained as idle balances, and hence would not lead to increased expenditure or prices. Thus prices would not rise so long as the increase in M was accompanied by a sufficient fall in V, or a sufficient rise in T, or a partial movement in both.

Once full employment is reached the "rigid" theory applies. T cannot now alter because all resources are employed, and all changes in M must exert their full effect on P. Thus if M goes up by 10 per cent, so will the supply of money. However, this assumes that V will remain constant. This may apply but not if inflation becomes serious, when people start to spend their money rapidly to avoid being left with depreciating currency. In this case the strict version of the quantity theory does not apply. Since T must be constant, prices will rise more than in proportion to the increased supply of money. This situation is explained by the third or "flexible" version of the quantity theory. As M rises, it is argued, prices will rise too, but no attempt is made to estimate by how much.

If total demand and price level depended only on the quantity of money, their control would be comparatively easy, but it has been found that economic fluctuations occur in conditions of stable money supply. The change in emphasis from a static economic world to a dynamic one showed the importance of money as a store of value especially in times of uncertainty. Thus there was a change in emphasis from V to its opposite, the demand for money to hold. During the 1930s Keynes and a number of Cambridge economists modified the quantity theory by introducing a number of variables relating to the demand for money. The Cambridge equation is $M = KRP$, where M is the quantity of money, R is the national output, $P =$ is the price level and $K =$ is the proportion of R which the community desires to hold in money.

Keynes split the demand for money into three: the transactions demand, the precaution demand and the speculative demand. The first covered money held to facilitate purchases, the second, that held for expediency, and since these generally would not consume all income the third category was possible, comprising money which could be held for speculative purposes, for investment at the right moment. Classical economists had thought that inflation (*i.e.* lowering of the value of money) was a pure monetary phenomenon. Keynes in contrast demonstrated that V and T were not constant, and that prices were not solely determined by the supply of money. Since the velocity could in theory change, it was argued that the price level would not necessarily be reduced just by reducing the money supply. The Cambridge equation helps to illustrate the effect of a change in the demand for money. Though people cannot through their own actions increase (or decrease) the total quantity of money, they can adjust their level of spending to increase or reduce their individual balances. Keynes popularised the idea of fiscal techniques for stimulating demand and for curing deflation.

The continued limitations of fiscal policy in controlling inflation described in Chapter III led in the 1960s to the attempt by Milton Friedman and the Chicago school to reintroduce monetary policy via a modernised version of the quantity theory. They argued that if velocity is not stable it is at least predictable, and arrived back at the former conclusion that if the money supply (M) can be controlled then so will the price level (P).

The supply of money used to be regarded as the total of coins and banknotes in public circulation plus bank sterling current accounts, which were payable on demand. The renewed interest in the money supply by the authorities in 1970, the Bank of England and the Treasury, led to a redefinition of the supply of money. The above was called M1, the narrowest definition, which has been discarded as the most widely used indication of the money stock. M2 includes such growing components of total banking liabilities as (*a*) deposit accounts (repayable in cash after seven days' notice of withdrawal) and (*b*) foreign currency accounts with the deposit banks and discount houses, which can be regarded as liquid for practical purposes. M3 adds all resident deposits with the U.K. banking sector in sterling or foreign currency. It has risen rapidly since September 1971 as banks have tried in the more competitive environment to attract new depositors by offering special facilities and competitive rates of interest.

During balance of payments deficits the money supply will decline or grow less quickly, as currency will be required to pay for imports, etc., from abroad. In the case of a surplus the opposite will occur. Hence the external position must be taken into account when changes in the supply of money are studied. In 1969 the British Government adopted a new monetary concept, Domestic Credit Expansion, which has owed much to the Chicago school in stressing the effects of changes in the supply of money in an economy. D.C.E. is a broader concept of money and is an attempt to measure not only the change in the level of M3 but also changes in bank lending in sterling and non-sterling currencies to residents and non-residents and Government borrowing from abroad, in order to estimate a figure which is close to the supply of money in the hands of individuals.

One result of new thinking on this subject was an effort by the Labour Government in 1968 to control the growth in the money supply, *i.e.* cash in the hands of the public plus current deposits in the banks. As a result of deliberate sales of gilt-edged stocks by the Bank of England, Britain had by September 1969 experienced nine months in which the money supply had risen by under 2 per cent. This compared with approximately 10 per cent in the previous two years.

If this quantity theory more closely fits reality than the Keynesian theory, then monetary policy will be more important than fiscal policy in managing the economy, and conversely if the Keynesian model more closely describes the real position. Monetarists tend to argue that stricter control of the money supply would help in curbing inflation. The money supply should grow at the same rate as the estimated underlying growth of the economy, any excess rises in the supply resulting in inflation. If the money supply grows at a lower rate than the rate of growth of the economy, then increased unemployment is likely. But Government's ability to control the domestic money supply is limited in part since some people can always adjust their money holdings by exporting or importing balances from one country to another.

The rate of interest

The rate of interest is the price of loanable funds. There is a spectrum of rates ranging from the very short-term "overnight" rate to the long-term rate on Government stock where the capital sum is irredeemable, *i.e.* never repaid. Short-term rates are paid for funds borrowed to tide over shortages of cash for a period of time up to a year. It includes treasury and commercial bills of exchange. Long-term rates are paid for funds to finance capital investment and includes Government stock (bonds) and industrial stock (debentures).

The rate of interest will depend on the supply of and the demand for loanable funds. Government monetary policies play an important part in influencing the supply of funds which are forthcoming, for example, when variations are made in the volume of issued notes and coins, or by open market operations. The money can also be varied by expansion or contraction in bank credit or in trade credit allowed by such financial institutions as hire-purchase companies. The part of people's earned incomes which are not spent but are saved are known as "active balances." Investors are more willing to supply funds when interest rates are high and might fall in the future, than if interest rates are low. Such funds will help to finance industry directly through investment in Government stocks or industrial shares or debentures, or indirectly by being placed in various financial institutions such as banks, building societies or insurance companies, which will relend or invest the money in Government or industrial securities as explained above. The volume of loanable funds can also be supplemented through "disentanglement," if stocks are liquidated or capital assets sold by firms. A certain amount of funds are neither spent immediately nor saved; these are known as "idle balances." They are retained for everyday transactions, unexpected expenses or speculation.

The sources of demand for loanable funds come from a similar area as the supply. The Government is a major borrower of funds, to finance public debt. Industry requires funds to finance the purchase of stocks of raw materials or machinery, or the construction of buildings, etc. (called "re-entanglement"). There is also a demand from the people who wish to make purchases in excess of the amount of the cash resources they are prepared to put down in immediate payment. Consumer credit for purchase of such items as cars, television sets, etc., is made possible by the use of such facilities as bank loans and hire-purchase arrangements. Naturally borrowers of funds are more anxious to do so at low interest rates than high. One problem a Government has in operating an economic policy to control inflation is that if it tries to control the supply of money in general circulation to curb demand, this may result in higher interest rates, which will increase the cost of borrowing funds for Government and industry, and may jeopardise any target the Government has of achieving a higher annual growth rate. How the various forces influencing the supply of and demand for loanable funds interact will determine the rate of interest.

There are a number of reasons for varying rates of interest. Some types of investment are secure (*e.g.* Government stock), others are fairly safe (*e.g.* well-established reputable industrial companies), but others may be highly speculative. A high rate will have to be paid to the lender as compensation if there is some risk that the money will not be repaid. The time factor is also important. Long-term rates are higher than short-term rates to compensate the investor for the loss of the use of his money for alternative purposes, or for the depreciation in the value of money over a period.

Interest rates will vary depending on (*a*) the general political and economic conditions which affect the current price of stocks, and (*b*) Government policies. There is an inverse relationship between current rates of interest and the prices of different stocks. When stock prices are high, interest rates are low, and vice versa. This will be made clear by the following illustration. Government stock may be issued initially at the nominal value of £100 at a fixed and guaranteed rate of interest of, say, 4 per cent per annum for ten years. At the end of this period the £100 is repayable. If subsequently market value falls by, say, 20 per cent (reflecting perhaps a slackening of the economy and a lack of funds in industry) £100 worth of bonds will now cost £80 to buy. This means that the real rate of return or yield for subsequent purchasers of this stock will be 5 per cent. This can be calculated by dividing the nominal value of the stock (£100) by the market value (£80) and multiplying by the rate of interest:

$$\frac{100}{80} \times 4 = 5\%$$

The difference between the level of short- and long-term rates gives opportunities for profit-making to various kinds of financial institutions. For example, commercial banks and building societies borrow from creditors on a short-term basis at low interest rates and lend to other people on a long-term basis at higher rates. This means that their debts are withdrawable on demand or at very short notice while their assets are mostly not so easily realisable.

Imagine you are taking investment decisions in a financial institution. You have the choice of purchasing either Government long-term (10 years) stock at $6\frac{1}{4}$ per cent or short-term (7 days) stock at $6\frac{1}{4}$ per cent. Your decision would be based on expectations concerning the future rate of interest. You would purchase long-term stock if you expected interest rates to fall and short-term stock if you expected interest rates to rise. From the point of view of the Government, if it expected interest rates to fall, short-term borrowing would be preferred, so that it had no long-term commitments which would prevent it from taking advantage of favourable rates of interest in the future. If it expected interest rates to rise, it would prefer to borrow on long term.

But all these rates tend towards equilibrium during any given period, with the yield on all bonds being approximately the same, regardless of the time to maturity. If, for instance, M.L.R. increases from 7 per cent to 8 per cent, short-term rates will rise and the supply of funds to the short market will increase, the supply of funds to the long market decreasing accordingly. The cost of borrowing has now risen in the short market, and although the supply of funds has increased, the demand for them will diminish. Demand will now switch to the long market where the rate is lower. The increased demand and the decreased supply of funds in the long market will push the rate up to that obtained in the short market.

Although there is a tendency towards an equilibrium of rates, individual rates obviously differ for the reasons already given. Another factor for the continuing differentiation is the imperfection of the market. Building societies specialise in the property market, and their activities will not usually affect the discount houses dealing in treasury bills or the investment houses trading in long-term equity capital. Moreover, moving from market to market and from one type of bond to another is costly, involving such expenses as brokerage fees.

Inflation and deflation

The purchasing power of many of the world's major currencies varied little from year to year before 1914. However, apart from the period 1925–31 when prices fell in Britain, there has been a steady increase annually in the price level. Both inflation and deflation express situations where the amount of money available to the community is out of balance with the amount of goods produced by it. Inflation means a rising price level and a falling of the value of money, as denoted by the popular expression "too much money chasing too few goods." Deflation is the opposite of inflation, a period of recession and falling prices, too little money and too many goods.

Since 1945, with full employment of resources being the general situation, inflation has been a major problem, not only in Britain but in most of the developed economies of the world. In Britain from 1952 to 1964 the average annual rate of price increase was less than 3 per cent; during the last few years, however, it has been 7 per cent. This situation has been described as demand-pull inflation, where demand exceeds the supply; when money coming forward to buy goods and services is greater than the amount available from current production and imports. Thus prices are forced to rise. Some reasons for this are an increase of Government expenditure over Government income, and the expansion of bank credit to meet expanding private investment, the latter caused perhaps by a wave of optimism, new inventions or a rising demand for exports.

Cost-push inflation is caused by wage or salary increases, often the result of strong trade unionism, which can threaten strikes, or of increased prices of imported raw materials. Thus it can be seen that adverse terms of trade can cause inflation, as they necessitate an increase in exports to pay for a given amount of imports.

Inflation can give a boost to an economy since high profits encourage investment, which helps to maintain growth and fuller employment. This is preferable to deflation. However, inflation can have harmful effects, leading to a reduction in the level of real income and to a redistribution of wealth from people whose income and assets do not rise as rapidly as prices to those whose income and assets do change correspondingly. Rising prices tend to benefit the ordinary shareholder, organised labour, property speculators and all who have to pay out incomes, including the entrepreneur and debtors.

MONEY, BANKING AND INVESTMENT 143

They adversely affect a sizeable section of the community such as creditors, old-age pensioners and others with fixed incomes, wage-earners, civil servants, salaried and professional groups and Government lenders of money. Savings also are discouraged by inflation since their value falls as prices rise. This may perpetuate inflation by encouraging expenditure on consumption and aggravate a deteriorating balance of payments situation caused by increased imports and the driving of savings abroad. The introduction of various wage or pension schemes since 1974 related to the cost of living index have helped to improve matters.

Anticipated inflation where future prices have been correctly estimated is not so harmful as unanticipated inflation, which causes hardship and can have a damaging effect on the economy. However, there is always the danger that creeping or gradual inflation may give place to runaway, galloping or hyper-inflation, where all confidence in the monetary system is lost. This occurred in Germany in 1923 and in Brazil in the 1960s. For possible remedies *see* Chapter III.

Index numbers

An index number is a measure over time intended to show the average change in price, value or quantity of a group of items; an example is the *Financial Times* Industrial Ordinary Share Index. Real income, income measured in terms of the actual volume of goods and services produced, is measured by use of index numbers which enable the effects of changes in the value of money to be measured.

Retail price index numbers are based on sample items likely to be

	Percentage	
	1962	*1968*
1. Food	31·9	28·9
2. Alcoholic drink	6·4	6·5
3. Tobacco	7·9	6·8
4. Housing	10·2	12·3
5. Fuel and light	6·2	6·4
6. Durable household goods	6·4	6·0
7. Clothing and footwear	9·8	9·1
8. Transport and vehicles	9·2	12·2
9. Miscellaneous	6·4	6·1
10. Services	5·6	5·7
	100·0	100·0

purchased by the average family. A base year or starting-point is chosen, and the average level of prices at the base year is represented by 100. The main Department of Employment index is based on prices in January 1962. Previous base years have included 1947 and 1914. Some goods are relatively more important than others, and so compilers assign them "weights" that correspond to their relative significance in an average family budget, and goods and services are divided into ten classes (*see* p. 143).

From this list a comparison can be made of the appropriate weighting assigned to each category in 1962 and 1968. In subsequent years the same quantities of the same goods are priced and used in a calculation similar to that used here, which is simplified to cover only three commodities, and describes a hypothetical period of two years when prices went down. In this example, it is assumed that bread is five times and butter twice as important as meat in the budgets of most consumers.

	Year 1		Year 2	
Bread	6p = 100	Bread	4p	$4 \times \frac{100}{6} = 67$
Butter	12p = 100	Butter	12p	$= 100$
Meat	14p = 100	Meat	18p	$18 \times \frac{100}{14} = 129$
	3)300			3)269
Average index number = 100		Average index number = 98·6		

After a system of weighting has been applied the results are:

	Year 1	Year 2	Change in index	Weights	Product of % & weight
Bread	6p	4p	67%	5	335
Butter	12p	12p	100%	2	200
Meat	14p	18p	129%	1	129
					8)664

Weighted index number = 83

A major drawback to the weighting method is that it is difficult to ascertain exactly what the average family does consider important. One family attaches importance to a television set, another to a car. Sometimes such items may be considered more important than an adequate amount of basic necessities, such as food, clothing and housing.

INVESTMENT MANAGEMENT

Money should be productively utilised rather than left idle when, due to inflation, it would quickly dwindle in value. Spare money can be donated to various worthwhile charities, or invested in a variety of savings schemes. From an industrial standpoint, money can be either employed in one's own business or invested in someone else's. A knowledge of the merits of different forms of investment and the general principles involved is valuable. It helps one to make the best possible use of personal finances, to know the various options available in raising finance for one's own firm, and to understand the basic factors involved in the investment policy of a large organisation in which one is employed. Numerous large organisations such as insurance companies have funds which need to be profitably employed, while large businesses usually run pension funds, which, if not managed by an outside specialist firm, will be managed by a pensions fund manager.

Basically money invested in one's own business should obtain a higher rate of profit than if it was invested in stocks and shares or other forms of savings. Two forms of finance or investment management are discussed in this chapter.

1. *Raising of capital.* This involves the financing decision, *i.e.* determination of the best financing mix or capital structure of the firm. Firms basically calculate the cost of capital by taking the weighted average cost of the various main sources of capital, debentures, preference and ordinary shares and retained earnings. The cost of capital so derived is the rate at which forecast returns from the investment, after due allowance for risk, are discounted to bring them to their present value.

2. *Security analysis.* This is basically concerned with the evaluation of the worth of various companies and sound portfolio management, depending on the respective merits of various forms of investment, stocks and shares, etc. Another form of investment management discussed in Chapter IX relates to investment decisions by the organization. In that section, the concept of Discounted Cash Flow is introduced. Discounted Cash Flow (commonly known as D.C.F.) is a useful analytical tool for the appraisal of capital investment projects.

Sources of short-term finance

Capital is classified as long-term if required for sinking in permanent (fixed) assets such as land, building, plant and machinery; medium-term if wanted for more than a year; and short-term if required for everyday business transactions, called "net current assets." Examples of such working or circulating capital are cash, marketable securities, debtors and stocks.

A man in business can use his own money and/or some external source of funds to found or expand his firm. A sole trader or partnership may obtain funds by borrowing from a private individual, a building society or a bank. Usually the larger the enterprise the easier it is to obtain external finance, particularly for a public company. An important source of funds for large or small firms is the ploughing back of profits into the business, which are consequently not distributed to the owners or shareholders. It includes allowance for depreciation and for replacement of existing machinery as it wears out. Such funds are termed "cash flow." Unpaid taxes can be regarded as a form of financing in the short term. While the salary earner has to pay tax as the income is earned, business taxes are collected in the following year. The tax left in the business constitutes part of its working capital.

The payment of cash immediately for materials or finished products is rare in business. Firms if creditworthy usually obtain the credit terms customary in the type of trade they are in. For example, monthly payment is normal in engineering. This form of credit is termed "trade credit." Bills of exchange in the export and import trade can be regarded as another source of finance, usually self-liquidating over three months. Bank loans are an important source, usually linked to the purchase of fixed assets. They can extend for as long as ten years, but as there is always the chance of their being called in at short notice, perhaps because of a credit squeeze, they are regarded as current liabilities. Short-term finance at a lower interest rate is provided by means of a bank overdraft.

Hire purchase has become a popular method of raising money during the last ten years. It is used frequently to purchase items such as cars, delivery vehicles, metal and wood-cutting machines, computers and earth-moving machinery. It is usually considered a medium-term financing method. Usually the seller who wants payment sells the machine to a finance company (industrial banker), which makes out the hire-purchase contract for the buyer. This may be a small business and a new concern which has not yet acquired funds to purchase outright. The interest charges are an allowable business expense for tax purposes. The repayment of capital borrowed is not, since it is an accumulation of capital. Some finance houses have links with banks. For example, since 1958 Barclays have had a large stake in United Dominions Trust. Some have expanded into the leasing of equipment business, for example, Bowmaker. Leasing involves only hiring the equipment and may be chosen where the life of a machine is short, or when it becomes quickly outdated. Leasing enables a company to benefit by the use of both equipment and capital. It prevents the tying-up of valuable working funds which can be profitably utilised elsewhere. Rental payments are tax-deductible; leasing helps to combat the effects of inflation and ensures fixed costs for a known period.

A mortgage from a bank or insurance company, etc., up to about 70 per cent valuation can normally be raised on industrial property buildings at reasonable rates of interest above bank rate. Such mortgages are usually repayable over a specific period, which in the case of a bank is normally up to five years.

In the future certain firms called factors are likely to play a greater role in financing British industry, especially in export markets. On receipt of an invoice a factor forwards the cash sum to the client, who uses it to pay wages or regular bills. It is a great help to a company in a seasonal trade or to a heavy exporter, who usually has to wait months for payment. Factors also offer other services, the simplest being the sales aspect of accounting. The factor looks after the sales ledger, handling all the invoices and chasing up the payment. Thus the client has just one debtor, the factor, who is a reliable payer. Most factors also offer a guarantee against bad debts.

They are closely associated with banks. For example, International Factors, the first and largest group in Britain, is owned by Lloyds. They can be particularly helpful abroad. For example, the largest factoring groups, International, Portland and H & H are part of international networks, or have links with overseas factors. Through them advice can be given to exporters on the credit reliability of foreign customers, and currency complications can be removed. Thus they can help to make the selling of goods abroad as simple as selling goods to a buyer on the other side of town.

Long-term capital

The most important source of funds for companies is by the issue of ordinary (equity) shares (which give the purchaser rights of ownership), preference shares and debentures, for amounts over £300,000. Ordinary shares may be issued with or without voting rights, while preference shareholders have no voting rights but have a priority rating for repayment in the event of liquidation of the company. Shares have a nominal or par value, usually a multiple of 5p and commonly 5p, 10p, 20p, 25p, 50p or 100p. This value represents the price at which the shares were originally offered for sale, but depending upon the present fortunes of the company, they will be selling on the stock exchange at their current market values, which will almost certainly be different from par. However, since it is with the money received from the original sale of the shares that the company assets have been purchased, the market value of the shares is of no direct benefit to the company. Even so, a company will prefer to have its shares valued highly by the investor, or owner, because if it were to require additional capital for expansion it would be able to offer more shares for sale, nominally at par value but in fact at market value, so reaping in more cash with reduced liability. If we suppose that a new issue of 20p shares can be offered and sold at 50p, any future dividend paid on these shares will appear more attractive than it really is. A declared dividend of 25 per cent, *i.e.* 5p per share, will in reality be 10 per cent of the actual price paid for the share. If the company continues to do well and the share value increases to, say, 80p, the return of 5p reduces to $6\frac{1}{4}$ per cent of the share value, but the shareholder would be well compensated by his increase in share value of 30p. A company with such a growth performance would probably be considered a safe company in which to invest, and so an increasingly high share value would make it relatively easy to secure loans, which is another way of raising necessary capital.

Preference shares, as the name implies, are those shares to which preference is given whenever there is insufficient profit for dividends to be distributed or if the company becomes bankrupt. In the latter case the assets of the company will be sold, the creditors will be paid first, and then any cash left over will be divided first among the preference shareholders and finally among the ordinary shareholders as a fixed amount per share. This means that less risk is incurred in holding preference shares and as a result the holder expects to receive a lower rate of return on his shares, say, 6 per cent. This is normally a fixed return no matter what the fortunes of the company may be. If there are insufficient profits to pay the 6 per cent, then whatever is available is paid to the preference shares.

The ordinary shareholders receive the remainder of the distributed profit in the form of dividends after the preferences have been satisfied. This could mean that they receive nothing, but it is much more likely that they will receive proportionately far more than the preference shareholders. In fact, although equity bears greater risk in times of difficulty, nevertheless it is a recognised hedge against inflation in that, as prices rise, so it can be expected that profits, dividends and the market value of shares will experience corresponding gains. In this respect preference shares are not so attractive a form of investment.

Debentures or loan capital is another form of finance. A debenture holder is a creditor, not a shareholder, since he lends money to a company in return for a fixed annual interest. This must be paid before any distribution of dividends is made to the shareholders. In deciding what proportion of its funds should be raised by preference shares or loan capital, a company has to balance the greater flexibility of the former against the lower cost of servicing the latter.

When interest rates are falling, debenture fixed-interest charges become an increasing burden. The problem is to decide on the amount of fixed interest, or debt, which a firm can stand in bad times, when the alternative of raising capital through ordinary equity shares (where the dividend varies with profits) does not constitute such a financial burden on a company. A firm's choice of the amounts of capital to be raised by these two methods is sometimes known as the "debt-equity" decision.

There are a number of institutions which under certain conditions are able to provide long-term finance. The Industrial and Commercial Finance Corporation Limited (I.C.F.C.) is the largest single source of long-term finance in small and medium-sized amounts in Britain. It is owned by the Bank of England, the English clearing banks and the Scottish banks. It exists to help small and medium-sized businesses with less than £200,000 capital. Finance is provided in any, or a combination of any, of the following forms: ordinary shares, redeemable or irredeemable preference shares, unsecured or secured loans and debentures, leasing and plant purchase facilities. The Finance Corporation for Industry Limited makes funds available to firms with capital exceeding £200,000 in cases where normal sources are inapplicable. An example is the financing of the early stages of a new product, which is not likely to interest traditional lenders of funds. The Government played an important part in encouraging the establishment of these institutions.

This method of finance is appropriate where the amount of capital required is too small for a public issue, or where the financial needs are temporary. In the latter case, if there had been a public issue of shares, the company would be over-capitalised when the particular needs had been satisfied.

Capital market

This is the market for medium- or long-term loans. The most important institutions are the London Stock Market, the New Issue Market and various specialist finance corporations.

The new issue market is concerned with the issuing of new securities. There are a number of ways of issuing shares to the public and the choice will be made according to the size of the issue and the market conditions. For small issues it is often convenient to make arrangements for private placing, *i.e.* for their purchase, privately by one investor or a few, or by a number of institutional investors via a stock exchange placing. Usually the company's broker will act as an intermediary in such transactions.

For large issues the usual method is a public issue by prospectus. Since there are a number of problems in trying to sell a large number of shares to the public, use is made of an issuing house which specialises in share issues. Frequently the issuing house will be the main underwriter. This means that it guarantees to buy any shares not sold to the public. It will pass on some of the responsibility to sub-underwriters. The issue is advertised to the public. Information on the company and the issue will be in a prospectus. According to stock exchange regulations, this must be published in at least two London daily papers. An alternate method is an "offer for sale." Here the shares are offered to the public not by the company, but by some intermediary to whom the issue has been sold, usually an issuing house.

A public company whose shares are already quoted on the stock exchange can raise fresh capital by means of a "rights" issue. Shareholders are offered the right to purchase new shares in some stated proportion of their existing holdings. For example, they may be offered one new share for every two existing shares. If the new shares are not wanted, the rights can be sold to an investor who does want them.

Other institutions linked to the new issue market are institutional investors, who control money entrusted to them by the public. These include investment and unit trusts, insurance companies, pension funds and trade unions. Insurance companies have large funds built up from life assurance premiums and pension contributions. They may grant loans and mortgages to firms, and are substantial holders of Government and industrial securities. Many large firms have pension schemes and may be directly responsible for the safe investment of these funds or use the services of a specialist firm, *e.g.* a merchant bank. The trade unions also often have surplus funds for investment from pension and welfare schemes.

The Stock Exchange

A stock exchange is basically a market, where investors buy and sell stocks, shares and debentures. In March 1973 the various provincial stock exchanges merged with the London Stock Exchange to create a U.K. Stock Exchange, liaison with the trading floors in the provinces being maintained through the six former regional exchanges. There are two groups of members, the brokers, who act as agents for the public, and the jobbers, who have no contact with the public in these transactions but specialise in certain groups of securities which they hold and act as intermediaries between brokers whose clients wish to buy and sell respectively. The broker is always quoted two prices by a jobber, who does not know initially whether the broker wishes to buy or sell securities. For example, the jobber may say 102p to 105p, which means he is prepared to buy at the first price and sell at the second. The jobber is naturally influenced by supply and demand conditions. If buyers are numerous he will raise his price, hoping to attract sellers. If on the other hand there are many sellers, he will lower his price, hoping to attract buyers. It is intended that the difference between the two prices (the jobber's turn) will protect him against market fluctuations and enable him to make a living. The Stock Exchange might be compared to a barometer, which registers daily what investors think of the position and the prospects of various securities.

Part of the Stock Exchange's role is to vet all securities before they can be quoted. A company which wishes its shares to be dealt with on the market has to apply for permission from the council which governs the Stock Exchange. This is only given if certain strict conditions are fulfilled and so provide the investor with some protection against investment in an insecure enterprise, though it can give no guarantee that a business will succeed.

The Stock Exchange is a vital part of the City since it provides the means by which a large part of industry and commerce is financed. It enables men to find capital to start new enterprises or to expand existing businesses and to buy securities in the knowledge that they can be sold again if necessary, and it provides them with a source of unearned income.

Investment and unit trusts

An investment trust is not strictly a "trust" in the legal sense but a company whose shares, like those of other companies, are traded on the Stock Exchange. However, it does not run a business itself but invests in a selection of the shares of other companies. On average, the return from investment trusts has been higher than from individual shares. This is partly because some of their capital is generally raised by issuing fixed-interest investments. This results in ordinary shareholders doing disproportionately well when profits are rising, because the fixed-interest lenders receive the same return. However, when profits fall, ordinary shareholders do disproportionately badly. Ordinary shares are only suitable for people who wish to invest several hundred pounds in one company, to keep buying and selling costs down and on a fairly long-term basis; they are sometimes rather difficult to obtain. Because investment trusts were unsuitable for small investors, unit trusts developed in size and number in the 1950s. Here the smallest initial amount required is usually between £25 and £100, or only a few pounds if added to an existing investment or invested regularly each month. In contrast to investment trusts, unit trusts are trusts in that their operations are not controlled by the *Companies Act* but by the *Prevention of Fraud (Investments) Act*. Although its managers are responsible for investing money subscribed by the public in a wide range of shares, the shares are actually held by a trustee, which is often a bank or similar institution.

GENERAL PRINCIPLES IN PORTFOLIO MANAGEMENT

The ideal investment would be one which was absolutely safe, extremely profitable and easily and quickly cashed. However, the most profitable types of investment provide no security of capital invested. Thus one is forced to make some kind of compromise when choosing an investment.

The basic types of investment fall into three categories. There are first, fixed capital investments, where money invested is guaranteed but the amount of income can vary. Because they can be cashed at short or immediate notice they are often called "liquid" investments. Examples are British savings bonds and local authority loans. They are useful as an emergency fund and as short-term savings. Bank deposit accounts provide the speediest means of getting one's money back, but the rate of interest is low. Building society accounts, National Savings Certificates and Post Office and trustee savings bank accounts give a higher rate of interest, but the money is not so accessible.

The second type is fixed income investments, in which the amount of interest is guaranteed but the value of one's capital can vary. They are normally bought and sold on a stock exchange at prices which fluctuate. They are mostly called "stocks," and are issued by the

Government, local authorities, Commonwealth and foreign governments, public utilities and companies. There are two chief forms. Irredeemable ("undated") stock provides a fixed annual interest for ever, examples being most company preference shares and undated Government stock. With preference shares, compared to investment in Government stock, there is an element of risk, in the event of bankruptcy of a company. The redeemable type (for example, company debenture stock or dated Government stock) guarantees a fixed interest annually and the repayment of the capital at the end of a definite period. These stocks are usually based on a nominal value of £100, on which the fixed income is paid. But the actual value varies, depending on supply and demand conditions, which in turn depend mainly on the interest rate, the prevailing cost of long-term borrowing, how soon stock, if it is redeemable, is due for repayment, and how reliable the borrower is considered to be.

The third type are investments guaranteeing neither capital nor income, which on average appreciate steadily in value. The commonest investments are ordinary shares and houses. However, there are many more, such as jewellery, antiques, silver, paintings, racehorses, vintage cars, postage stamps. These items cannot be considered a homogeneous category in other ways. For example, a variable income, on a regular basis, may be obtained on shares and rent from property, while no money can be obtained from the others unless sold.

Though shares are a riskier form of investment than Government stocks, they have proved in practice during the last fifty years to be a more remunerative form of investment both in terms of income and capital. For example, since 1932 the share market in Britain and the United States has advanced at an average minimum annual rate of 8 per cent (not including dividends).

The merits or cost of holding money in liquid form and investing it in one's own business or in shares, etc., can be measured in terms of the rate of interest on irredeemable gilt-edged Government securities. If rates are low, due to the high price of stocks, then the money will be invested in shares pending a fall in share prices. On the other hand, if the price of stocks is low (which means the interest rates are high), there will be a tendency to buy stocks, particularly as they are likely to rise in price.

Although there is no magic formula for making money on the share market and the art of investment is not a science, there are general points which are useful to know. First, never risk money you cannot afford to lose. The costs of investing in shares are such that a rise of about 5 per cent is necessary before an investor can expect to break even. Hence a reserve should be kept, and money which was intended to be put aside for emergencies or short-term needs should not be invested. The extremes of over-diversification or over-concentration should also be avoided. It is a good idea never to have more than 10–20 per cent of one's capital locked up in one security or class of shares. Investing in a broad spectrum of companies minimises the risk of loss, but unless considerable capital funds are available, it is better to concentrate on about ten to fifteen securities so that each one is given the attention it requires. Next, unless a person is a financial genius or lucky, it is generally unwise to invest all the capital in one security—in other words to put all the eggs in one basket.

There is the basic consideration of what to buy, depending on whether one is interested mainly in regular income, capital appreciation or quick profits. Shares can be grouped according to this broad criterion. If regular income is the aim, one would be advised to invest in firms which have an assured place in the economy, a record of good dividend and increasing yields, great financial strength and secure markets for well established products. These are called "blue-chip" companies. Usually fairly large, they are regarded as relatively safe for investment: for example, I.C.I., Marks & Spencer, Unilever. At the end of a boom period investors tend to switch to stocks or shares in this category, which are likely to be less affected by a slump. This is called "defensive switching."

One may be more interested in capital appreciation, in shares that perhaps offer more modest yields but better prospects of a gain in price. Here some research is necessary to ascertain the firms that have developed new methods and techniques to meet new needs or tastes. If interested in successful speculation to make quick profits, then look for shares expected to gain sharply in price over a short period (price appreciation). Sometimes one can discover in advance forthcoming fashionable investments due to general industrial, political or technical developments. Professional investors may look for a particular sector of the market which is underrated and may perform well in the future. Some of the sectors listed in the *Financial Times* are banks, breweries, building, chemicals, engineering, hotels, industries and mining. They will then look for shares in that field which seem more valuable than their current selling price, and which they can discover before their competitors. Eventually, as the word spreads around, the price rises to a level which reflects the value of the company more accurately, and shares are then sold at a profit.

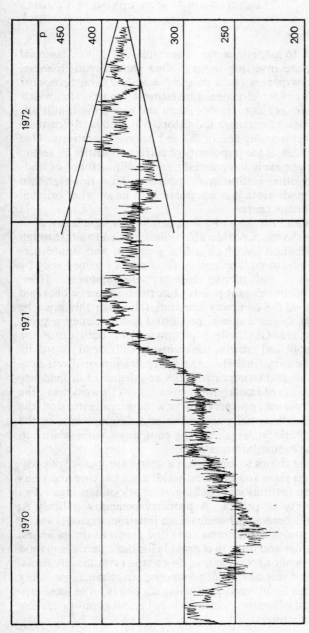

Fig. 19. *Chartist's graph for the price movement of a share*

Professional investment analysts can be broadly grouped as fundamentalists or chartists. The former tend to concentrate on studying the workings of particular sectors and companies. These techniques are described on p. 156. The chartists believe that the best way to locate a trend is to study price movements. They argue that these frequently form repeated clear patterns from which, going on past experience, the next step can be predicted. An example is given above.

Choosing shares

It is important to undertake some research since it is essential to investigate before investing money. One should read financial magazines and newspapers (such as the *Financial Times*, *Economist* and *Investor's Chronicle*) and special investment reports, etc., which may give some guidance as to how political and economic conditions will affect securities. Economic indicators will frequently provide early clues to a forthcoming rise or fall in business conditions. One may obtain some idea of the popularity of certain securities by seeing which companies appear in the greatest number of portfolios of leading unit trusts or other institutional investors. This, however, can only be a rough guide since it is not possible to know what original price they paid for the shares.

The conditions and fortunes of a firm can have a significant effect on the price of its shares. Considerable skill is needed to sift through all relevant information by which a firm's present and future performance can be measured, and crucial facts may be gained only by careful interviewing and piecing together of fragments. Here, briefly, are some of the relevant points. Information can be obtained from an analysis of the company accounts (although this must be treated with care), balance sheets, profit and loss statements, prospectuses, reports, etc. Gradually a picture will be built up of the current rate of profit and growth, the company's dividend record, its position in the industry (including the concentration or diversification of interests), its marketing capabilities and degree of dependence on exports, its quality of management (its strength or weakness), the marketability of shares, prospects of new developments, and the influence of various external phenomena and developments in the economy or the world at large, *e.g.* the company's vulnerability to political action or industrial unrest.

There are certain things to look for in a share: the quality of earnings, price earnings ratio and dividend yield, asset backing and gearing, cash flow and institutional backing. Quality of earnings refers to the dependability of profits. A property company is likely to have solid earnings because it benefits from inflation, its assets are let for long periods and it enjoys reversions and renewals on its leases. Insurance companies and firms that provide for basic needs, *e.g.* food firms, have high profit dependability. In contrast commodity firms, rubber growers and primary metal producers, etc., have a low rating because profits can be affected by fluctuating prices. The same applies to the cyclical industries, which include capital goods producers and textile manufacturers.

The price earnings ratio (P.E. ratio) is equivalent to the current rate of the share—say 34p—divided by the previous full year per share earnings—say 2p. Thus the P.E. ratio 17:1 measures the number of years' earnings which would be needed to pay for the share. A company that has a high P.E. ratio usually has more growth prospects than a company possessing a low one. A P.E. ratio higher than about fifteen might be thought the size of a growth company, but it is salutary to reflect that today's prices on today's profits may not necessarily be good indicators of the future.

There is a financial axiom that stock market conditions follow where money conditions lead. Given the long-term rate of interest, ordinary share prices generally reflect published equity earnings and dividends declared. The current or historic P.E. ratio is based on last year's reports and earnings. However, prices will also be influenced by changes in expectations regarding dividends and earnings in the year ahead. The reason next year's earnings are used to compute the prospective P.E. ratio is because investors who purchase and sell the shares do so on the basis of next year's estimated earnings.

Dividend yield is the annual return on each £100 invested. One multiplies the percentage dividend by the nominal value of the share and divides by the market price. Thus if a company pays a 10 per cent dividend on 25p shares standing at 50p the yield will be:

$$\frac{10 \times 25}{50} = 5\%$$

A low dividend generally depresses share prices, but not necessarily, for retained profit may be used to finance capital investment and hence to increase the volume of capital and profits in the long term.

If the current price of a share is high the dividend yield is low. An investor may accept a low yield if the growth prospects of the company are good and if he expects to reap the benefit from increases in the value of the share itself. Sometimes if the price is high the shares are split in order to attract more buyers, who might be discouraged by high share prices. Imagine that you own 100 shares in a total of 1,000 shares in company A.T.C., each with a market value of £5. If the shares are split on the basis of three to one, there are now 3,000 shares, market value £2 each, and you have 300 shares. In actual practice, the price of a split stock sometimes advances and dividend increases, and one gains as a result.

The next fundamental is asset backing, which acts as a buffer for a share price if a firm runs into hard times. The important point to note is the composition of a firm's assets. The more liquid a firm's assets and the less hampered by loans, the less likely the chance of a relapse in share price. Gearing is the ratio of a company's fixed interest borrowings to its equity (debentures, loan stocks, preference shares).

A company is low geared if it has a small proportion of fixed interest borrowings and high geared if the proportion is large. This can have an important bearing on the fortunes of a company. For example, a high gearing may result in more than average share price fluctuations in boom–slump conditions, and increases the likelihood of a decline in trade proving disastrous to a company. A high percentage of prior charges makes such companies unattractive to ordinary shareholders when times are bad.

In the case of a high-geared company, the preference shareholders are taking almost as much risk as the equity holders since, if profits were to fall, even their fixed dividends payments could not be met. Another effect of high gearing is illustrated by the example below, where total shares in the company are 100, and profits distributed in the form of dividends are 10, 11 and 9 respectively.

	Shares	Distribution of profits	Profits up 10%	Profits down 10%
Equity	10	4·6	5·6	3·6
Preference (fixed at 6%)	90	5·4	5·4	5·4
Total	100	10·0	11·0	9·0

It can readily be seen that high gearing causes instability and a comparatively small change in profit makes a comparatively large percentage change in dividend equities. A company geared in this fashion would therefore be subject to speculation. In fact it would be most unlikely that any company would be set up in this way, as this is an extreme case to illustrate a point. However, the whole question of gearing must be considered when one is analysing the performance of a company to determine why share prices and dividend payments have varied in the way they have. The gearing is worth watching when a company is first formed. In general, most companies are well balanced in relation to the form of financing chosen. It is important to bear in mind other forms of ratio analysis, which are covered in Chapter V.

The greater the confidence the stock market has in a company's future the higher the share value will be. The company, too, wishes to see a high and increasing value of its shares because it can raise capital for expansion by issuing new shares, or it can take over another company by offering its own shares in exchange for those of the other company. This may well depress the share value, but only, it is hoped, for a limited period.

Another important point is cash flow—a firm's annual cash

generating capability. If money is tight, this can result in a fall in asset value, since a company may have to sell off property. A drop in cash flow mainly reflects lower sales, lower profits or a build-up of stocks.

The timing of investment

The problem of what to buy needs to be balanced by the other essential consideration of when to buy. A share that was a good buy at a certain price level may become a sale at a higher price level. If one is interested in taking advantage of share price fluctuations (the changing fortunes of growth of speculative enterprises) rather than in holding on to shares to receive a regular income, then buying and selling securities are basically a question of being familiar with the time element and the trends. This implies understanding the political and economic conditions responsible over a period of weeks, months or years for causing the bulk of shares either to rise in price (giving a "bull" market) or to decline (a "bear" market). The price tendencies over these three periods are called minor, intermediate and major trends respectively.

Sometimes it is an advantage to go liquid, *i.e.* to sell most, if not all, of one's shares, particularly if one is interested in major trends. Such years, at high peaks of the share index, were 1951, 1955, 1961, 1964 and 1968. Appropriate years for reinvesting capital were the slump periods in 1949, 1952, 1958, 1962, 1966 and 1970–1. If one is impatient for quicker results, then specific market conditions responsible for minor movements need to be studied. An example of a possible factor is an industrial strike. Here there is usually an advantage in buying when it occurs and in selling when it is settled.

One safeguard against serious loss due to an error in forecasting is the dealing in share options. It is the right obtained, in return for a fee, to buy ("call") or sell ("put") a share at an agreed price. With a call option the price at which the broker undertakes to sell that share is normally $1\frac{7}{8}$ per cent above the current price. The investor, in addition to paying the cost of a call option, has to pay the option fee plus the broker's commission of $1\frac{1}{4}$ per cent of the total value of the shares under option. With a put option, the agreed price is the current bid price. Using a simplified example, if a buy was placed on 100 £1 shares, total cost 10 pence per share, and the shares appreciated to £120, the broker would pay the client £10, having taken £10 for costs.

Shares will be affected by the level of industrial activity, by the general level of confidence of the investors in the economy, and by various current political conditions in the country or abroad. A close link exists between interest rates and fixed-interest Government stocks. In turn, in addition to the choice as to whether to retain money in liquid form or in stocks, investors have to decide on the respective merits at various times of holding money in stocks rather than shares, and vice versa.

Despite all the financial and technical sides which can be used, the process by which investors decide to buy or sell stocks and shares is far from scientific. The whole process, in fact, hinges heavily on the psychological make-up of the persons doing the guessing.

In summary, here are a few points to bear in mind as criteria for investing:

1. Find the right sector.
2. Look for companies which appear underrated. (Note the quality of the management.)
3. Ensure that the timing is right.
4. Discover what other people are doing.

V. COMPANY ACCOUNTING

INTRODUCTION

The term accounting covers such a wide range of activities that an attempt at definition would not at this stage aid the reader's comprehension. Instead, let us consider the types of activity which are either performed by, or are usually considered to be, the responsibility of the accountant. Amongst these are:

1. The recording of financial transactions in an accurate and systematic manner.
2. The responsibility for collecting and paying monies owed to or by the organisation.
3. The preparation of statements to show financial achievements and financial position.
4. Analysing and interpreting the financial results of an organisation, and providing guidance on financial performance.
5. Establishing and running systems of accounting within the organisation to establish and control costs.
6. Assisting in the preparation of plans, forecasts, and budgets.
7. Monitoring and reporting on progress against plans and budgets.
8. Assisting in the process of decision-making, by performing financial investigations and reporting thereon.
9. Devising and installing systems for the accurate recording and processing of financial transactions.
10. Providing a check, *i.e.* audit, of the accuracy of financial systems and accounting data.
11. The provision of statutory information to government.

These activities are not intended to provide a comprehensive listing, but an indication of the scope of accounting. Within this Chapter, we shall not attempt to cover all of the above activities, but instead shall concentrate primarily on examining the construction and analysis of the following financial statements for private enterprise companies and public corporations.

1. The Balance Sheet.
2. The Profit and Loss Account.
3. The Funds Flow Statement.

Systems of planning and control will also be referred to in this Chapter. Other aspects of accounting are covered in different Chapters, and the reader is referred to Chapter IX, Leadership and Decision-Making, for an examination of the provision of financial data for decision-making within the organisation; and to Chapter IV, Money, Banking and Investment, for aspects of Finance.

PRESENTATION AND MEASUREMENT OF FINANCIAL PERFORMANCE

The Balance Sheet

The Balance Sheet is a statement of the financial position of an organisation, at a given point in time. It is a statement of assets, the resources owned by the enterprise; and liabilities, the amounts owed to individuals and entities outside the enterprise. The Balance Sheet is constructed from the accounting records of the firm where transactions are valued at their historic cost, *i.e.* the cash value on purchase or sale. Therefore the Balance Sheet is based upon historic cost value, and it does not purport to measure economic value, or any other type of value.

In recent years, due to the impact of inflation, there has been considerable debate as to the validity of historic cost as the valuation base, and proposals have been developed for inflation accounting. These will be referred to later at p. 189.

The Balance Sheet, has been described as showing a picture, or snapshot, of the firm at a particular point in time. It may be illustrated in a simplified horizontal format as in Fig. 20. The terms in this Figure represent the basic classifications of assets and liabilities which are explained below.

LIABILITIES (Amounts owed by the enterprise to outsiders)	ASSETS (Resources owned by the enterprise)
Owner's equity Loan capital	Fixed assets
Current Liabilities	Current Assets

FIG. 20. *Simplified Balance Sheet*

Fixed Assets. A fixed asset has a life of longer than one year, and has been acquired for continuous use in the enterprise.

Examples of fixed assets are land and buildings, production machinery, and motor cars.

Current Assets. Current Assets are those which are used for day to day trading purposes, and which are therefore subject to constant change. They are sometimes referred to as Working or Circulating Assets. Examples of such assets are raw material stocks, finished goods stocks, debtors, *i.e.* amounts owed to the enterprise by outsiders, and cash.

Current Liabilities. These are the converse of Current Assets, being short-term in nature and likely to change from day to day. Examples are creditors, *i.e.* amounts owed by the enterprise to outsiders for the supply of goods or services, and bank overdraft.

Loan Capital. Loan Capital represents money lent to the business for long-term financing. In the case of companies, long-term loans are usually referred to as Debentures.

Owner's Equity. This represents the owners financial stake in the firm, and would consist of any input of money by the owner as an investment, plus any profits earned which have been retained within the enterprise. For a limited liability company, Owner's Equity consists of share capital (ordinary and preference shares), plus reserves (*e.g.* retained profits).

It is now possible to examine certain balance sheet relationships.

1. Total assets (*i.e.* fixed assets plus current assets) equals Total Liabilities (*i.e.* owner's equity plus loan capital plus current liabilities). It is from this relationship that the term balance sheet is derived; assets balance with liabilities. Another way of looking at the Balance Sheet is that liabilities show the *sources* of funds to the enterprise, and assets show how these funds have been *invested* or *applied*.

2. Total assets minus current liabilities equals owner's equity and loan capital.

3. Total assets minus current liabilities and loan capital equals owner's equity.

Balance Sheet examples

The X.B.C. Company has the following assets and liabilities at 31st December 19 . . , Land and buildings: £10,000; machinery: £4,000; stocks: £3,000; debtors: £2,000; cash at bank: £2,000; owner's equity: £15,000; long-term loan: £3,000; creditors: £3,000. The Balance Sheet laid out in a horizontal format is as in Fig. 21.

X.B.C. Company
Balance Sheet as on 31st December 19 . .

	£		£	£
Owner's Equity	15,000	Fixed Assets:		
Long-Term Loan	3,000	Land and Buildings	10,000	
		Machinery	4,000	14,000
Current Liabilities:				
Creditors	3,000	Current Assets:		
		Stocks	3,000	
		Debtors	2,000	
		Cash at Bank	2,000	7,000
	£21,000			£21,000

FIG. 21.   *Balance Sheet—horizontal format*

From the Balance Sheet, it can be seen that the relationships noted above hold true. Thus:

1. Total assets of £21,000 equal total liabilities of £21,000.
2. Total assets minus current liabilities (£21,000 − £3,000 = £18,000) equal owner's equity plus long-term loans (£15,000 + £3,000 = £18,000).
3. Total assets minus current liabilities and long-term loans (£21,000 − £3,000 − £3,000) equals owner's equity (£15,000).

X.B.C. Company
Balance Sheet as on 31st December 19 . .

Fixed Assets:	£	£
Land and Buildings	10,000	
Machinery	4,000	
		14,000
Current Assets:		
Stocks	3,000	
Debtors	2,000	
Cash at Bank	2,000	
	7,000	
Less Current Liabilities:		
Creditors	3,000	
Net Current Assets		4,000
Net Assets		£18,000
Represented by:		
Owner's Equity	15,000	
Long-Term Loan	3,000	£18,000

FIG. 22.   *Balance Sheet—vertical format*

COMPANY ACCOUNTING 165

Because of the above relationships, it is possible to present a balance sheet in a number of different ways. Many organisations prefer to prepare their balance sheet using a vertical format as illustrated in Fig. 22.

Both the vertical and horizontal formats use the same items of information; the only difference is in their arrangement. The vertical format also enables additional information to be seen at a glance. Thus, net current assets, also known as working or circulating capital, can readily be ascertained. The net assets of the enterprise and the long-term financing are also clearly disclosed.

Transaction Recording and Profit Measurement

Let us examine the effect on the balance sheet of X.B.C. Company, of some typical trading transactions.

1. Stocks are purchased on credit at a cost of £1,000.
2. Debtors pay the company £500.
3. The company pays £1,200 to creditors.

Commencing with the opening balance sheet, the increase or decrease in values relating to each transaction, followed by the new closing balance sheet, are shown in Fig. 23

X.B.C. Company

	Opening Balance Sheet (1) £	Transactions 1 £	2 £	3 £	Closing Balance Sheet (2) £
ASSETS					
Fixed assets:					
Land and Buildings	10,000				10,000
Machinery (Net)	4,000				4,000
Current assets:					
Stocks	3,000	+1,000			4,000
Debtors	2,000		−500		1,500
Cash at Bank	2,000		+500	−1,200	1,300
	£21,000	£+1,000	—	£−1,200	£20,800
LIABILITIES					
Owner's Equity	15,000				15,000
Long Term Loan	3,000				3,000
Current liabilities:					
Creditors	3,000	+1,000		−1,200	2,800
	£21,000	£+1,000	—	£−1,200	£20,800

FIG. 23. *Effect of transactions on opening Balance Sheet*

It can be seen that, after each transaction, total assets and total liabilities remain equal. Thus, for transaction 1, the purchase of goods on credit results in an increase in stocks and creditors, and therefore total assets and total liabilities, of £1,000. For transaction 2, debtors pay money to the company, so cash increases and debtors decrease by £500, *i.e.* a net change in total assets of zero. Transaction 3 refers to the company paying a debt of £1,200; cash at bank therefore decreases by £1,200, and creditors, having been paid, also decrease by £1,200. Thus total assets and total liabilities have decreased by £1,200.

These transactions show the double entry nature of transaction recording. That is, for each transaction an adjustment is made to more than one item of value, such that in total, assets and liabilities remain equal. It is, however, impractical for most businesses to enter each transaction directly to the balance sheet. The number of transactions engaged in would make this impossible. Because of this, transactions are recorded on a double entry basis in separate accounts.

Suppose that X.B.C. Company engages in a further transaction, selling stocks which cost £1,500 on credit for £2,100. The effect on the balance sheet is shown in Fig. 24.

	Previous Balance Sheet (2) £	Transaction £	Closing Balance Sheet (3) £
ASSETS			
Fixed Assets:			
Land and Buildings	10,000		10,000
Machinery	4,000		4,000
Current Assets:			
Stocks	4,000	−1,500	2,500
Debtors	1,500	+2,100	3,600
Cash at Bank	1,300		1,300
	£20,800	£+600	£21,400
LIABILITIES			
Owner's Equity	15,000	+2,100 −1,500 +600	15,600
Long-Term Loan	3,000		3,000
Current Liabilities:			
Creditors	2,800		2,800
	£20,800	£+600	£21,400

FIG. 24. *Effect on Balance Sheet of selling stocks on credit*

After the transaction it can be seen that closing owner's equity is £15,600, *i.e.* total assets of £21,400 less long-term loan of £3,000, and creditors of £2,800. The increase in owner's equity between the two balance sheets of £600 represents profit. Profit or loss can therefore be defined as the amount of the change in owner's equity. The only modification to this definition relates to the investment or withdrawal of cash from the enterprise by the owners. If the owners invest or withdraw money from the enterprise then the value of owner's equity will increase or decrease correspondingly. Such inputs or withdrawals must be deducted or added back to closing owner's equity before measuring profit. If this is not done, then profit will be overstated by the amount of the owner's new investment. The converse applies if the owner withdraws cash from the enterprise during the accounting period.

In summary, therefore, profit and loss may be defined as follows: profit and loss for a period of time equals closing owner's equity (adjusted for any input or withdrawal of cash by the owners during the period), minus opening owner's equity. In practice, as previously explained, it is impractical to adjust values on the balance sheet for each transaction, and profit is usually measured independently of owners equity via a Profit and Loss Account as illustrated in Fig. 25.

X.B.C. Company
Profit and Loss Account

	£
Sales	2,100
Cost of Goods Sold	1,500
Gross Profit	600
Less Expenses	—
Net Profit	£600

FIG. 25. *Profit and Loss Account*

The above assumes for simplicity, that no expenses relate to the sale. A more detailed analysis of the Profit and Loss Account follows in the next Section.

Although it is normal practice to measure profit via a Profit and Loss Account rather than owner's equity, this must not obscure the basic understanding of profit measurement. The determination of profit depends upon valuing assets and liabilities and thereby measuring changes in owner's equity. Thus, different approaches to the valuation of assets and liabilities would lead to different measures of owner's equity and therefore different measures of profit and loss.

If, for example, rather than using historic cost as the basis of valuation, replacement cost were used, then markedly different measures of assets and liabilities, ownership equity, and profit would be likely to arise. Profit measurement should not therefore be viewed as a mechanical process leading to an exact, unchallengeable measure. The use of alternative value bases will result in the derivation of different profit measures, even though the mechanical basis of recording and processing transactions remains the same. A considerable part of the skill of the accountant therefore lies in his knowledge and understanding of the accounting data, of alternative approaches to measurement, and in his ability to interpret and communicate his findings, to managers, investors, and other interested parties. In the remainder of this Chapter, unless otherwise stated, the basis of valuation will be taken to be historic cost.

The Profit and Loss Account

To derive the profit earned by an organisation all expenses which have been incurred in obtaining the sales and of running the business during the accounting period must be matched against the sales revenue. A definition of profit, using a Profit and Loss Account approach to measurement is: profit equals sales revenues less expenses. After the figure of profit is derived, the amount due to the Inland Revenue in taxes is deducted, and the balance remaining may either be paid out to the owners (as dividends in the case of limited liability companies), or retained as part of owner's equity within the organisation.

In essence a Profit and Loss Account consists of three sections. The first section is a Trading Account in which the expenses incurred in getting the goods into a saleable condition are deducted from the sales revenue to give gross profit. An example of such an expense is the cost of the goods sold, which might consist of material costs and, in a manufacturing firm, direct wages. Once the gross profit is ascertained, we come to the Profit and Loss Account proper, in which the expenses of running the business and making the sales for the particular period are deducted to derive net profit before tax. From this figure is deducted taxation on profits to give net profit after tax. The next section of the account is known as the Profit and Loss Appropriation Account, for it is in this section that appropriations of profit, such as dividend payments, are shown, as well as any other appropriations such as the transfer of profit to specific revenue accounts. In the appropriation section are also shown the undistributed profits, *i.e.* retained earnings, of previous years.

COMPANY ACCOUNTING

Taking the example of the X.B.C. Company, let us suppose that in addition to making a credit sale for £2,100 at a cost of £1,500 (Transaction 1), the following also relate to the current accounting period:

2. Salaries and wages of £150 were paid in cash.
3. Other expenses of £50 were paid in cash (including loan interest).
4. It was estimated that machinery declined in value by £100 during the period due to wear and tear (this is known as depreciation).
5. Dividends of £100 were paid to the owners in cash during the period.
6. Taxes on profits, paid by the company in cash at the end of the period, were £150 (normally tax would be paid in a subsequent accounting period).
7. The company purchased on credit, a new machine at a cost of £1,200.

Using the above information, the Profit and Loss Account and closing Balance Sheet would be as in Figs. 26 and 27.

X.B.C. Company
Profit and Loss Account for the period ended . . .

		£
Sales		2,100
Less Cost of Goods Sold		1,500
Gross Profit	£	600
Less Salaries and Wages	150	
Other Expenses	50	
Depreciation	100	300
Net Profit before tax		300
Less Tax		150
Net Profit after tax		150
Add Retained Earnings of Previous Periods		—
		150
Less Dividends		100
Retained Earnings		£50

FIG. 26. *Profit and Loss Account after sundry transactions*

Note that transaction 7 does not affect the Profit and Loss Account. It is the purchase of a new long-lived fixed asset. As such this is called a *capital* rather than a *revenue* expenditure. Revenue expenditures are charged to the Profit and Loss Account. Capital expenditures are treated as assets and shown in the Balance Sheet as such. Transactions 1 to 6 are all items relating to the profit and loss account, and the balance is therefore attributed to owner's equity. Note that from the above, profit can be measured according to the original definition relating to the change in owner's equity. Opening owner's equity from Balance Sheet 1 was £15,000. Closing owner's equity is: £22,050 − £4,000 − £3,000 = £15,050. Adjusting this for the withdrawal of cash by the owners gives £15,050 + £100 = £15,150. Profit after tax for the period therefore equals £15,150 − £15,000 = £150 *i.e.* the figure shown in the Profit and Loss Account.

Cash flow

The terms profit and cash do not have the same meaning. The Profit and Loss Account, and the accounting records of an organisation are based upon *accrual accounting*. Under accrual accounting, sales revenue is recognised when a sale is legally made, not when the cash is received. Similarly if the organisation receives the benefit of the use of a good or service, this is recognised in the accounts even if the cash payment has not been made. Examples of this in the X.B.C. Company illustration are the sale of £2,100 not for immediate cash but on credit, and the purchase of stocks on credit for £1,000.

This fundamental distinction between profit and cash is of major importance. The cash position of an enterprise will be subject to constant change as monies are received and paid to debtors and creditors, to employees, and invested in fixed assets. The failure to plan for cash can lead to profitable businesses being unable to meet their financial obligations, resulting in their liquidation.

A useful way of examining how an enterprise has generated and used financial resources is to prepare a Statement of Sources and Applications of Funds. Such statements are usually included in the annual report of public companies. The purpose of statements of sources and applications of funds is clear from the title. They aim to show from where the business has obtained funds, and how these funds have been used during the accounting period. They may also be used to reconcile the opening and closing cash positions of the enterprise

There are a number of sources of funds for an enterprise. Amongst these are funds generated from trading; the investment of cash by

X.B.C. Company
Balance Sheet as at . . .

	Opening Balance Sheet (2) £	1 £	2 £	3 £	4 £	5 £	6 £	P & L £	Closing Balance Sheet (4) £
ASSETS									
Fixed Assets:									
Land and Buildings	10,000								10,000
Machinery	4,000							+1,200	5,100
Current Assets:									
Stocks	4,000	−1,500							2,500
Debtors	1,500	+2,100							3,600
Cash at Bank	1,300		−150	−50	−100	−100	−150		850
	£20,800								£22,050
LIABILITIES									
Owner's Equity	15,000							+50	15,050
Long-Term Loan	3,000								3,000
Current Liabilities:									
Creditors	2,800							+1,200	4,000
	£20,800								£22,050

Fig. 27. *Balance Sheet after sundry transactions*

shareholders; money lent to the enterprise; the receipt of additional credit from creditors; and disinvestment by the enterprise in either fixed or current assets. Applications of funds include the payment of dividends and taxes; investment in assets; the repayment of loans; and a decline in the financing of the enterprise by outsiders such as creditors. An example of a Sources and Applications of Fund Statement based upon the accounting period between Balance Sheet 1 and Balance Sheet 4 of the X.B.C. Company is shown in Fig. 28.

X.B.C. Company
Sources and Application of Funds for the period . . .

	£	£	£
Opening Cash Position			2,000
Sources of Funds:			
Net Profit before Taxation	300		
Add Non-Cash Expenses: Depreciation	100		
Funds From Operations		400	
Stocks (£3,000–£2,500)		500	
Creditors (£4,000–£3,000)		1,000	
Total Sources of Funds		1,900	
Applications of Funds:			
Purchase of Machinery	1,200		
Debtors (£3,600 − £2,000)	1,600		
Taxation	150		
Dividends	100		
Total Applications of Funds		3,050	
Excess of Applications over Sources			1,150
(Net Cash Outflow)			
Closing Cash Position			£850

FIG. 28. *Sources and Applications of Funds Statement*

A Sources and Applications of Funds Statement reveals directly information not readily discernible from the Profit and Loss Account or Balance Sheet. In the above example it can easily be seen that more funds were used during the period than were generated, thus accounting for the decline in the company's cash position. If the company continued in future accounting periods to have an excess of applications of funds over sources it would eventually be unable to meet its financial obligations and would be forced into liquidation. This could occur even if profits were earned. In relation to the compilation of the statement, it should be noted that depreciation, because it is a non-cash expense (being the amount deducted from the value of fixed assets to allow for the decline in value through use, etc.), is added back to net profit to derive the funds from operations. This does not mean that depreciation is a source of funds; it is not. Depreciation is added back so as to ascertain the correct amount of the funds generated from the trading activities of the business. Stocks, in the above example, are a source of funds because the company has reduced the value of stocks thereby releasing funds. Creditors, by giving more credit to the company are also a source of funds. The converse for stocks and creditors also applies. The purchase of fixed assets, *i.e.* machinery, is clearly an application of funds. Similarly, an increase in debtors means that the company has to finance more goods not yet paid for by customers. However, if the company sold fixed assets, or reduced their investment in debtors, then the relevant amounts would be sources of funds. The payment of taxation and dividends result in an outflow of funds from the company, and are therefore applications of funds.

Depreciation

Fixed assets, such as machinery, cars, and so forth, which are purchased to enable the business to provide goods or services, decline in value through use (wear and tear), and the passage of time. As previously illustrated, depreciation is the allowance made in each accounting period for this decline in value. The depreciation itself is charged to the Profit and Loss Account thereby reducing profit, and deducted from the cost of the asset on the Balance Sheet to derive the net book value (sometimes referred to as written down value) of the asset. All things being equal, if the depreciation charge has been correctly calculated and charged in each accounting period, then at the end of the life of the asset the net book value will be zero, *i.e.* acquisition cost less total or accumulated depreciation equals zero.

The objective of the depreciation charge is to match the decline in value of the asset with the relevant accounting period. In practice this is difficult to do as the accuracy of the depreciation charge in any one accounting period will depend upon two factors. These factors are:

1. the accuracy of the estimate made of the life of the asset, at the time it was acquired and of any residual or scrap value;

2. the accuracy of the method used to compute the depreciation charge for each accounting period.

It is unlikely that any estimate of depreciation will be completely accurate due to the difficulties inherent in estimating decline in value. The aim should therefore be to make as good an estimate as possible.

There are a number of approaches used to estimate depreciation. The two most common methods are:

1. *Straight line depreciation.* An estimate is made of the expected life of the asset and of its final scrap or resale value. The scrap value is deducted from the acquisition cost to give a net value. This value is then divided by the number of years of estimated life to give the annual depreciation charge. Under this method, the depreciation charge for each year is the same.

2. *Reducing balance depreciation.* A fixed percentage of the net value (*see* 1. above) is taken as the depreciation for the first year. The same percentage is taken on the remaining balance for the second year, and so on through succeeding years. To ensure that total depreciation covers the net value of the asset, it is eventually written down in one or more final stages. The reducing balance method has a particular attribute in that in the early part of its life, when maintenance costs are at a minimum (perhaps nil under guarantee) the depreciation is at its highest value. As time progresses, maintenance charges tend to increase whilst depreciation decreases.

Comparing the straight line and reducing balance methods, the depreciation in succeeding years on a fixed asset originally costing £1,000 with a nil scrap value, could be as in Table XII.

TABLE XII
TWO METHODS OF RECORDING DEPRECIATION

Depreciation in	Straight line five-year life	Reducing balance at 20%
First year	200	200
Second year	200	160
Third year	200	128
Fourth year	200	102
Fifth year	200	82
Sixth to ninth years	nil	82 (change to straight line method)
Tenth year	nil	nil

Whichever approach is adopted towards accounting for depreciation, it should be consistently applied from year to year. A change in method should only be made for very good reasons and with the consent of the company's auditors. Otherwise an unscrupulous management could manipulate profit and asset value from year to year merely by changing the method of accounting for depreciation.

COMPANY ACCOUNTING

In the balance sheet of limited liability companies, the total acquisition cost of each type of fixed asset is shown; from this figure is deducted the total (accumulated) depreciation relating thereto, which has been charged in the current and previous profit and loss accounts. The net figure for each type of fixed asset is then shown.

Intangible assets

Intangible assets are possessions of the enterprise which do not have physical form. An example of such an asset is goodwill. Goodwill may be considered to be the value of the enterprise over and above that recorded in the financial accounts and shown in the balance sheet. The accounting value of the enterprise is based upon historic cost and it may well be that the "real" value of the firm is different from that recorded. For example, the ability of an organisation to earn profits may mean that its value to a potential purchaser is greater than the balance sheet value. In such a case the business may be said to possess goodwill. Another way of explaining goodwill is to say that it represents the difference between balance sheet value and the value now (present value) of future earnings. In the general sense, attempting to measure goodwill means trying to measure something which is subjective, *i.e.* future value.

Because of this, goodwill, if it exists at all, is intangible. Accountants do not usually measure or record intangible assets because of the problem of proving that the value is correct. However, if an enterprise is purchased at a value in excess of that recorded in the accounts then evidence of goodwill and its value exists and the asset can be both recognised and recorded. Goodwill would therefore be valued at the difference between the net book value of the enterprise and its purchase price. If for example, the ownership equity of a company recorded in the accounts at a value of £60,000 was purchased for £95,000, then goodwill of £35,000 exists and can be recorded. There is now evidence of its value, because the company has been purchased by an outsider.

Goodwill is therefore frequently recognised on purchase. However, because of the difficulty in future accounting periods of checking on the accuracy of the value recorded (*i.e.* the value may be accurate on purchase, but how can one check that it is still accurate in, say, three or four years time), it is frequently written off as a charge to the Profit and Loss Account within a few years of purchase.

ACCOUNTING SYSTEMS AND TECHNIQUES

Accounting conventions

The compilation of the Profit and Loss Account and Balance Sheet are based upon a series of accounting conventions or assumptions. Amongst these are:

I. *Entity*

The enterprise is assumed to have a separate existence, as an entity, from the owners. In the case of a limited liability company this is recognised by statute.

II. *Stewardship*

The management of the enterprise act as stewards on behalf of the owners, and the accounts are prepared to show the results of this stewardship.

III. *Objectivity*

The objectivity convention requires that definite verifiable evidence be provided as the basis for recording a transaction in the books of account. In most cases, objective evidence of a transaction is taken to be the cash movement caused by a transaction, with the invoice relating thereto as the documentary evidence.

The main reasons for the existence of this convention are as follows:

1. To provide definite evidence of the existence of a transaction, which is capable of independent verification.
2. To eliminate, so far as is possible, the inclusion of subjective judgement in the determination of the value of a transaction.

The application of the objectivity convention, with the reliance upon cash movements as evidence of a transaction, results in the use of historic cost as the valuation base for financial accounting purposes.

IV. *Conservatism*

Where more than one possible value may be attributed to an asset, the application of the conservatism convention results in the lower of the alternative values being recorded in the accounts, *i.e.* where doubt exists as to the value of an asset, it is conservative to record the asset at the lower value. This convention is justified on the grounds of financial prudence; it being considered preferable to understate the value of assets and profits rather than to overstate.

Conversely, if doubt exists as to the extent of a liability, a conservative valuation will result in the higher value being recorded in the accounts.

Conservatism is presumed to operate in the interests of shareholders by reducing the possibility of overstating profits and therefore of paying dividends out of capital. The convention supposedly helps to preserve the financial strength of the company. Lenders and creditors are similarly presumed to be less likely to suffer loss if their decisions are influenced by financial statements based upon conservative estimates of value.

V. *Realisation*

This convention requires that profits or revenues should not be recognised in the books of account until they are realised. A problem may arise in determining when a gain is realised, but in general, gains are not recognised until the complete series of events has occurred which caused the gain to come into being. For example, if the current sales price of goods held by a company exceeded the purchase price, the gain (*i.e.* the quantity held, multiplied by the difference between the current price and the bought-in price), would not be recognised until realised (*i.e.* by the sale of the goods).

However, while profits and revenues are generally not recognised until realised, losses are recognised. Thus, if the current price of materials held by a company were below the purchase price, (historic cost), then the materials would be revalued at the lower price. Similarly, if a loss is expected to occur in the future, (such as the failure of a debtor to honour his commitment), the expected loss would be recognised in the financial accounts although it was not yet realised.

The realisation convention reinforces that of conservatism. The object is to be conservative, and understate the amount of profits and the value of assets rather than to overstate them. Like conservatism, this convention aims to protect shareholders, lenders and creditors.

VI. *Matching*

This convention is based upon the notion that if a fair assessment of profit or loss is to be obtained, costs should be matched with the revenues they have helped to earn. The origin of the convention lies in the need to prepare and publish financial accounts annually, *i.e.* the division of the life of the company into yearly accounting periods. At the end of any one accounting period there are likely to be a number of transactions which are incomplete. For example, a depreciating asset such as a production machine may have been used during the accounting period to produce output which has been sold. Some part of the original cost of this asset should therefore be matched against the sales revenues of the period. If, however, some of the output is unsold at the end of the accounting period, then some part of the original cost may be matched against the closing stock and carried forward to the next accounting period as an asset.

The present system of financial reporting is based upon accrual accounting, which is derived from the application of the matching convention.

VII. *Consistency*

The computation of profits or losses and the values attached to assets and liabilities could be affected from one accounting period to the next by changes in accounting methods. If companies were able to change their accounting methods at will, it would thus be possible to manipulate the computation of profit or loss and the values shown in the Balance Sheet.

In order to prevent this from occurring, companies are expected to consistently follow the same methods of accounting from accounting period to period.

VIII. *Going-Concern*

The convention of objectivity largely results in asset values based upon historic cost. However, the realisation convention, as explained above, may result in a value lower than historic cost being attributed to an asset if the market price is less than historic cost. The going-concern convention represents a constraint on the application of the objectivity and realisation conventions. It may well happen that a company will acquire, for example, a long-lived asset, the resale value of which falls below the price paid immediately it is acquired. Examples of such assets are specially constructed machines and motor cars. Similarly, if the company were liquidated, it may be the case that the sale values of certain assets would be less than the written-down historic cost. If, therefore, the values of such assets were recorded in the accounts on the basis of the realisation convention then in many cases the valuation attributed to an asset would be less than the value to the company as a continuing entity.

This convention is therefore related to the fact that a company is a legal entity with an indefinite life. So long as the life of the company is indeterminate, then generally liquidation values are ignored.

IX. *Full Disclosure*

This convention requires that the financial accounts disclose all relevant information in order that the user is not misled. In practice,

COMPANY ACCOUNTING

companies tend to conform to the legal disclosure requirements of the *Companies Acts*, Accounting Standards and Stock Exchange disclosure requirements where applicable. Furthermore, the information supplied is based upon the conventions outlined in this section.

X. Materiality

The materiality convention affects published financial reports in two ways. Firstly, it may be viewed as a qualification of the full disclosure convention, *i.e.* that the published financial accounts need only disclose those items that are material for an appreciation of profit or loss or assets and liabilities. Secondly, that the accounting treatment of a particular item will be affected by considerations as to whether it is *material* or not. Thus, an acquisition such as land and buildings, will be treated as a long-lived fixed asset. However, the acquisition cost of certain other long-lived assets may be written-off to the Profit and Loss Account in the year of purchase if not considered material. For example, the accounting cost of treating the purchase of a pencil sharpener as a fixed asset may exceed the benefit obtained. The treatment of such an item as a fixed asset is not material for an appreciation of profit or loss or assets and liabilities, and hence it will be recorded as revenue expenditure.

Ratio analysis

A ratio is a figure expressed as a percentage or proportion of another figure.

Ratios are a very useful aid in diagnosing the financial strengths and weaknesses of an organisation. The approach must, however, be used with care recognising the advantages and limitations for analytical purposes.

The prime advantage of ratio analysis is that figures are related to others thereby enabling relative measures of financial performance or position to be obtained. Thus, for example, insights may be obtained into profitability and the use of capital, by relating profit to sales and capital employed.

The main usefulness of ratios lies in making comparisons between the same ratio for different periods of time. Such comparisons may be on a single organisation basis, or between organisations. For such comparisons, the analytical value of the ratios lies in examining the direction of movement and possible reasons therefore. A single ratio is by itself almost meaningless.

The main areas for which it may be useful to calculate ratios are as follows.

I. *Return on Capital Investment (Capital Employed)*

By expressing profit as a percentage of capital invested, an assessment may be made of the rate of return.

Comparisons of rates of return over time and between organisations may assist in making judgements regarding organisational and managerial efficiency, and the profitable use of funds.

Capital Investment (or capital employed) may be defined in different ways. In each case a figure for profit which is consistent with the basis for calculating capital must be used. The main measures of capital investment are as follows.

1. *Total Capital Investment*, represented by total assets, *i.e.* the total of all assets without deduction of any liability. This definition of capital investment is usually used when overall managerial performance is to be measured. The relevant profit figure is defined as profit before deduction of loan interest and corporation tax. Neither loan interest nor corporation tax are deducted as the relevant measure is total return achieved in relation to total investment. If financing costs and taxation were included the assessment of managerial performance, in terms of how effectively total funds have been used, would be obscured.

2. *Net Capital Investment or Net Assets*, measured by deducting current liabilities from total assets. This is a measure of that part of total investment represented by long-term finance. It consists of shareholders investment, as measured by owner's equity and long-term loans. The measure for profit is the same as that for total capital investment, with the exception that interest on short-term loans or overdrafts (which are current liabilities) is deducted to arrive at the relevant profit figure.

3. *Ordinary Shareholders Investment*, represented by ordinary shareholders capital plus reserves. The appropriate profit figure is the profit attributable to ordinary shareholders, *i.e.* profit after deduction of all costs, including interest expense, after corporation tax, and after payments of dividends to preference shareholders This therefore provides a measure of returns to ordinary shareholders investment.

II. *Profitability Ratios*

These ratios are obtained by expressing the major items in the profit and loss account as a percentage of sales.

COMPANY ACCOUNTING

III. *Utilisation of Assets*

This ratio is obtained by expressing assets (capital invested) as a proportion of sales.

The overall profit to sales ratio combined with the utilisation of assets ratio explain the percentage return on investment and may be illustrated as in Fig. 29.

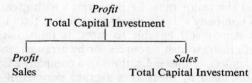

FIG. 29. *The percentage return on investment*

As indicated above, changes in the ratio of profit to sales, or sales to capital investment will in turn be reflected in the overall ratio of return on investment *i.e.* profit to capital investment.

IV. *Gearing/Financing*

As explained in the previous Chapter, the gearing of a company will affect the financial risk. A high level of loans or borrowings means that a high level of interest charges must be met before the company earns a profit for its owners, the shareholders. In extreme circumstances, if the company is unable to pay the interest charges on the loans when due, it may be liquidated, the shareholders losing some or all of their investment. Ways of measuring gearing include relating the amount of the loans to shareholders equity, and loan interest to operating profit prior to charging interest. The higher the proportion of loans to shareholders equity, and the lower the interest cover, *i.e.* the fewer times the interest is covered by the profit, then the greater is the financial risk.

V. *Liquidity*

It is clearly important that an organisation be able to meet its financial commitments. Failure in this respect will finally result in liquidation. Cash management is vitally important, as a business may be profitable and still go into liquidation because of being unable to pay its debts when due. Ways of measuring a company's liquidity position are to calculate:

    1. The Current Ratio—the relationship between current assets and current liabilities.

2. The Quick (Liquid) Ratio—the relationship between cash plus assets, which can be quickly turned into cash, and current liabilities. This ratio is usually based upon the relationship between cash plus debtors to current liabilities.

If both current assets and liquid assets exceed current liabilities, then the business would appear to be in a position to meet its current commitments. However, neither this nor the converse may always apply and the ratios must be interpreted with great care. For example, a company's liquid assets may be less than its current liabilities, but it may still be able to meet its immediate commitments either with its own cash resources, or by arrangement with its bank or other lenders. Other indications of a company's liquidity position may be obtained by measuring average periods of credit given or received (on debtors and creditors), and the stock levels kept by the company. If, for example, a company wished to improve its cash position, it might be able to do so by releasing funds tied up in stocks and debtors, or by obtaining longer periods of credit from suppliers. The current and quick ratios are useful measures of liquidity, but should not be thought of as providing definitive assessments. Without exact knowledge of a company's financial commitments and their timing the ratios can only be used to provide crude liquidity measures. However, in conjunction with Statements of Sources and Applications of Funds they may provide useful indications of trends, and possibly provide warnings in advance of a liquidity crisis.

Calculation of ratios

There follows an example of how ratios may be calculated from financial data, and their interpretation. Some of the ratios are based upon year end information as shown in the balance sheet. In these instances, it is assumed that the balance sheet figures are the best available for calculative purposes. However, it must be remembered that a balance sheet figure is valid only for a given point in time. The year end stock figure, for example, may not accurately reflect the usual level of stocks held throughout the year. Such possibilities must be borne in mind when interpreting ratios.

X.Y.Z. Co. Ltd.
Profit and Loss Statements year ending 31st December

	19X1 £000	19X1 £000	19X2 £000	19X2 £000
Sales		600		750
Cost of Goods Sold:				
Direct Materials	150		200	
Direct Wages	60	210	75	275
Gross Profit		390		475
Less Expenses:				
Indirect Wages and Salaries	60		70	
Depreciation	40		50	
Other Expenses	150	250	215	335
Operating Profit		140		140
Less Debenture Interest		10		10
Net Profit before Taxation		130		130
Less Taxation		65		65
Net Profit after Taxation		65		65
Less Preference Share Dividend		4		4
Net Profit for Ordinary Shareholders		61		61
Less Ordinary Share Dividend		31		31
Retained Earnings (Reserves)		£30		£30

Fig. 30. *Profit and Loss Statements for two consecutive years*

Note: There were no changes in Sales Prices between 19X1 and 19X2. The treatment of taxation has been simplified. It has also been assumed that tax, dividends and debenture interest have been paid during the relevant accounting periods.

The Profit and Loss Statements and Balance Sheets used in this example are shown in Figs. 30 and 31 respectively.

1. (*a*) *Return on Investment*

		19X1 £000	19X2 £000
(*i*)	Total capital invested (total assets)	560	690
	Operating profit before taxation and Debenture Interest	140	140
	Operating Profit: total capital investment	25%	20%
(*ii*)	Ordinary Shareholders equity	310	340
	Net profit for ordinary shareholders	61	61
	Net profit for ordinary shareholders: ordinary shareholders equity	20%	18%

Overall profitability related to total capital investment has declined,

X.Y.Z. Co. Ltd.
Balance Sheet as at 31st December 19X1

	£000		Cost £000	Accumulated Depreciation £000	Net £000
Ordinary Shares:		Fixed Assets:			
Authorised and Issued Shares					
200,000 at £1 fully paid	200				
Reserves	110	Land &			
	—	Buildings	230	—	230
Ordinary Shareholders Equity	310	Machinery	200	80	120
£1 Preference Shares at 8%	50		—	—	—
Shareholders Equity	360		430	80	350
Debentures—10%	100				
	—	Current Assets:			
	460	Raw Material Stocks		35	
Current Liabilities:		Finished Goods Stocks		35	
Creditors	100	Debtors		80	
		Cash		60	210
	—				—
	560				560

X.Y.Z. Co. Ltd.
Balance Sheet as at 31st December 19X2

	£000	£000		Cost £000	Accumulated Depreciation £000	Net £000
Ordinary Shares:			Fixed Assets:			
Authorised and Issued Shares						
200,000 at £1 fully paid		200				
Reserves		140	Land &			
		—	Buildings	230	—	230
Ordinary Shareholders Equity		340	Machinery	300	130	170
£1 Preference Shares at 8%		50		—	—	—
Shareholders Equity		390		530	130	400
Debentures—10%		100				
		—	Current Assets:			
		490	Raw Material Stocks		45	
Current Liabilities:	£000		Finished Goods Stocks		75	
Creditors	100		Debtors		170	290
Bank Overdraft	100	200				
		—				—
		£690				£690

FIG. 31. *Balance Sheets for two consecutive years*

as has the return for ordinary shareholders. This decline in performance may be explained by an examination of asset turnover, and profitability in relation to sales. The relevant profit figure for 19X2 should strictly be calculated before deduction of any interest on the bank overdraft. However, this cannot be done above, as no figure of interest payable is given in the accounts.

COMPANY ACCOUNTING

(b) *Asset Turnover*

	19X1 £000	19X2 £000
Sales	600	750
Total assets	560	690
Sales ÷ total assets	1.07 Times	1.09 Times

The turnover of assets has improved slightly, *i.e.* for every £1 of assets in 19X2 there was £1.09 of sales, compared with £1.07, in 19X1. The decline in return on investment must therefore be accounted for by a fall in profitability to sales.

(c) *Costs and Profit Sales*

% of Sales	19X1 %		19X2 %	
Direct materials	25		27	
Direct wages	10		10	
Gross profit		65		63
Indirect wages and salaries	10		9	
Depreciation	7		7	
Other expenses	25		29	
Operating profit		23		19
Debenture interest	2		1	
	79		83	
Net profit before taxation	22		17	
	100		100	

Note: Addition errors are caused by correcting each percentage figure to the nearest whole number.

Operating profit to sales has declined from 23% to 19%, a decrease of 4%. Net profit before taxation to sales has fallen by 5%. The main causes of the decline in profitability are the increase of 2% in the direct material costs, and of 4% in other expenses. The increase in other expenses appears particularly high.

2. *Gearing/Financing*

	19X1 £000	19X2 £000
(a) In relation to ordinary shareholders:		
Long-term loans (debentures) plus preference shares	150	150
Ordinary shareholders equity	310	340
Long-term loans and preference shares ordinary shareholders equity	48%	44%

	19X1 £000	19X2 £000
(b) *Fixed interest cover:*		
Operating profit	140	140
Debenture interest	10	10
Operating profit ÷ debenture interest	14 Times	14 Times

(c) *Total financing:*

	19X1 £000	%	19X2 £000	%
Ordinary shareholders equity	310	55	340	49
Preference shareholders equity	50	9	50	7
Debentures	100	18	100	15
Bank Overdraft	—	—	100	15
Creditors	100	18	100	15
Total Assets	560	100	690	100

Note: Addition error caused by correcting each percentage figure to the nearest whole number.

There has been a relative decline in the financing of the business by ordinary shareholders, and by long-term capital as a whole. Short-term financing (overdraft and creditors) now provide 30% of total funds, compared with 18% in 19X1. While the fixed interest cover appears satisfactory, the interest payable on the bank overdraft has been included in other expenses and deducted before arriving at the figure for operating profit. It is not therefore possible to assess the interest cover on short- and long-term borrowing combined.

The new reliance of the company on short-term borrowing from the bank is a potential cause for concern. The interest charges on the new borrowings are a probable cause of at least part of the increased cost of other expenses, and therefore a contributory factor to the decline in profitability and return on investment.

3. *Liquidity*

	19X1 £000	19X2 £000
(a) *Current Ratio:*		
Current assets	210	290
Current liabilities	100	200
Current assets : current liabilities	2.1 : 1	1.45 : 1

	19X1 £000	19X2 £000
(b) *Quick (liquid) ratio:*		
Debtors and cash	140	170
Current liabilities	100	200
Debtors and cash : current liabilities	1.4 : 1	0.85 : 1

Although the current ratio shows an apparently acceptable level of current assets to current liabilities there has been a considerable change in the relationship.

The effect of this is revealed by the decline in the quick ratio. In 19X1 liquid assets exceeded current liabilities; but at the end of 19X2 for every £1 of current liabilities the company had only 85p of liquid assets. This is primarily due to the investment of the cash available at the end of 19X1 and the incurrence of the bank overdraft.

COMPANY ACCOUNTING

Other factors affecting liquidity concerning the periods of credit given and received by the company, and stock turnover are examined below.

(c) *Credit given and received*

(i) *Credit given*

	19X1 £000	19X2 £000
Sales	600	750
Debtors	80	170
Turnover rate (sales ÷ Debtors)	7.5 Times	4.4 Times
Credit period (52 ÷ Rate)	7 weeks	12 weeks

The company appears to be giving five weeks more credit to its customers in 19X2. This additional credit period must be funded and therefore contributes to the additional borrowing requirement of the company for 19X2.

(ii) *Credit received*

	19X1 £000	19X2 £000
Direct materials and other expenses	300	415
Creditors	100	100
Turnover rate (direct materials, etc. ÷ creditors)	3 Times	4.15 Times
Credit period (52 ÷ Rate)	17 weeks	13 weeks

The above is a very crude approximation of the credit period received, due to a lack of detailed information on the expenses on which credit is received. However, the credit period, even if not totally accurate, appears to indicate that the company is receiving four weeks less credit from suppliers. Such a fall in the period of credit received must be funded by the company.

(d) *Stock turnover*

(i) *Raw materials*

	19X1 £000	19X2 £000
Direct materials cost of goods sold	150	200
Raw materials stocks	35	45
Turnover rate (direct materials ÷ stocks)	4.3 Times	4.4 Times
Turnover period (52 ÷ rate)	12 weeks	12 weeks

(ii) *Finished goods*

	19X1 £000	19X2 £000
Cost of goods sold	210	275
Finished goods stock	35	75
Turnover rate (cost of goods sold ÷ finished goods stock)	6 Times	3.7 Times
Turnover period (52 ÷ rate)	9 weeks	14 weeks

While there is no major change in the rate of raw material stock turnover, the rate for finished goods has increased by five weeks. The additional five week holding period must be financed by the company, and is a further factor contributing to the incurrence of the bank overdraft.

4. *Summary of Performance*

Although sales volume in 19X2 was 25% greater than that achieved in 19X1, no additional profits were earned. Return on Investment has fallen even though asset turnover marginally improved. The cause of the decline in relative profitability is the fall in Operating Profit and Profit before Taxation to Sales, which is accounted for by:

(*a*) an increase in direct material costs of 2%;
(*b*) an increase in other expenses of 4%.

The considerable increase in sales volume should have led to increased profitability. However, not only were greater profits not achieved, but the previously strong liquidity position of the company has changed to one of potential weakness. This is due to major investments in fixed assets during the year, and the utilisation of additional funds in such current assets as finished goods and debtors. Although trading activities have increased, working capital (current assets minus current liabilities) has declined from £110,000 in 19X1 to £90,000 in 19X2. This decline adds further emphasis to the concern over liquidity. The company has financed a large part of its expansion programme with short-term borrowings.

The company should therefore attempt to improve its liquidity and working capital position, and profitability. Attention should be directed at releasing money tied up in stocks and debtors; ascertaining the causes of the increased costs; and correcting these if possible.

Using ratios

Ratios do not in themselves necessarily give answers to improved or weakened financial performance. They may however highlight areas of strength or weakness which might otherwise go unnoticed. For external users, such as investors, potential lenders, or suppliers, insights may be obtained which will influence the decision to invest or sell shares; to lend money; or to supply goods. Such decisions, however, are unlikely to be made solely on the basis of the ratios. The value of the ratios lies in their use as a diagnostic device raising questions for further investigation. Ratios may also be used as a

COMPANY ACCOUNTING

planning aid; for example by management setting a target rate of return on capital employed.

When interpreting ratios, due regard must be paid to their likely level of accuracy. Many of the figures available to an external user are likely to be aggregated, or relevant only at a particular point in time. The interpretation of ratios based upon such figures must therefore be subject to qualification. In certain cases it must be recognised that it is only possible to obtain a crude approximation of a set of information.

An example of such an approximation, based on the above example, is the period of credit given to customers. In 19X2 this is estimated as 12 weeks, based upon the year end figure for debtors. It may be however, that the average figure for debtors throughout 19X2 varies considerably from the year end figure. If this were the case, then the real credit period may differ considerably from that based upon the year end balance sheet.

Inflation accounting

The system of financial reporting is primarily based upon recording and reporting on transactions at their original exchange value, *i.e.* historic cost. So long as prices remain stable over time the items recorded in financial accounts are comparable one with another in terms of their exchange-value. However, once prices change over time, the financial accounts represent a conglomeration of items, recorded in terms of a common unit of currency, but which relate to transactions at different price levels and therefore at different levels of purchasing power. Thus, for example, depreciation calculated on the basis of an acquisition at one price level will be matched in the profit and loss account against sales revenues relating to other price levels. The unit of currency, the pound sterling, is the same, but the value of the currency at different points in time will differ. This has been referred to by one writer, R. S. Gynther, as being " . . . as illogical as adding chestnuts to coconuts and recording the result as 'nuts'."

It has also been suggested that in periods of high inflation, profit measurement and asset values based upon historic cost may become highly misleading. The provision for depreciation for example, may be considerably below the figure required if the assets are to be replaced at the end of their useful lives. Similarly, the raw material costs charged in the profit and loss account may be less than the replacement cost of the material consumed.

Two possible approaches to accounting for inflation are outlined below.

1. *Adjusting for changes in the general level of prices.* Using this approach the figures in the profit and loss account and balance sheet are adjusted for general price changes by means of an official index such as the Retail Price Index (sometimes referred to as the cost of living index). This approach was recommended by the major accounting bodies in 1973. Following this recommendation the government set up an inquiry into Inflation Accounting, leading to a report generally known as the Sandilands Report.

2. *Current Cost Accounting.* The Sandilands committee recommended a new basis of valuation known as Current Cost Accounting. Under this system, the majority of assets in the balance sheet would be valued at written-down replacement cost, and a figure of operating profit would be established after the value of assets consumed during the period had been charged. In the main, this would mean that the profit and loss account and balance sheet would be based upon a form of replacement cost accounting. The Sandilands recommendations represented a radical departure from the existing basis of financial reporting as they introduced a totally different concept of value to that of historic cost.

Following the Sandilands Report, the major accounting bodies established an inflation accounting study group. This group proposed a detailed system of current cost accounting based largely upon the Sandilands recommendations. The report, entitled Exposure Draft 18, Current Cost Accounting, was published in December 1976 and resulted in considerable controversy amongst the accounting profession, leaving unresolved the question of how, if at all, inflation adjustments might be incorporated into published financial statements.

MANAGEMENT ACCOUNTING

We have so far been concerned with what is frequently referred to as financial accounting, *i.e.* the recording of financial transactions and their assembly into the profit and loss account and balance sheet. The analysis and interpretation of such statements using ratios has also been examined. Management are clearly concerned with such statements which represent to the owners and other interested parties the achievements and financial position of the company. However, for management to operate efficiently, more financial information and other forms of financial analysis are required within the company.

Management accounting may be viewed as the provision of financial data to assist management in their role as decision-makers.

COMPANY ACCOUNTING 191

It embraces the areas of forecasting, planning and control. One area of management accounting deserving specific mention is cost accounting. Cost accounting is concerned with establishing internal costs for locations in the company, departments, products, and so forth. It provides a data base for management accounting. To take an example, the use of cost accounting procedures may enable the accountant to assess what it has cost to provide a service in the past. This cost may then be used as base data to predict future costs, and to decide upon the *level* of services to be provided in the future.

Management accounting is a wide subject which will not be fully surveyed in this chapter. For marginal costing and capital investment decision-making, readers should refer to the relevant sections of Chapter IX, Leadership and Decision-Making. The remainder of this chapter will survey budgeting and standard costing.

Budgeting

Most people are familiar with the concept of budgeting, either in a personal sense in the planning of individual finances, or as in the national budget prepared by the Chancellor of the Exchequer. A company budget is basically the same. It represents the plans of the organisation in money terms, showing planned earnings and expenditures for each segment of the business, concluding with the planned profit and loss statement and balance sheet. Most companies would prepare a detailed budget for the forthcoming financial year, and possibly a less detailed budget or forecast for the longer-term of, say, three to five years.

Budgeting should have a number of advantages for the company. The budgeting process requires the specification and agreement of the objectives of the firm by top management, as well as the evaluation of alternative policies and strategies. Whilst this process may be exceedingly difficult to perform, and never in an ideal sense achieved, it should at the very least focus the attention of management on the major issues facing the company. It is more likely that opportunities will be taken and major problems avoided if budgeting exists than if management merely waits upon events. The process of forward planning should also assist management in making the best use of resources and avoiding waste.

In a commercial organisation, such as a manufacturing company, a series of budgets will be prepared leading to the production of the Budgeted Profit and Loss Statement and Balance Sheet. An illustration of the type of budgets involved and budget interrelationships is given in Fig. 32.

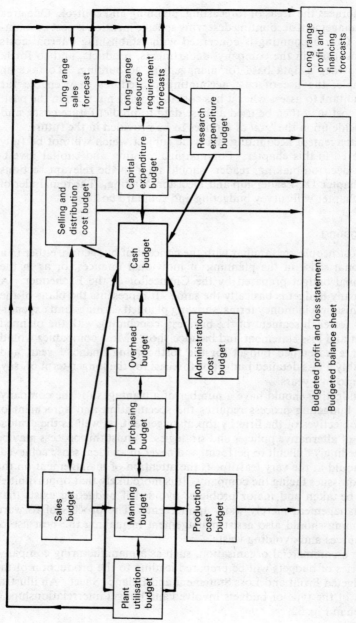

Fig. 32.

Budgetary control and standard costing

The comparison of actual results with a budget provides the basis of budgetary control. The difference between actual results and a budget, called the variance, is established for each item of sales revenue or expense in each budget. Significant variances from a budget are investigated, the causes of variation established, and corrective action taken.

Standard costing, for control purposes, has identical objectives as budgetary control. The operations of segments of the organisation are broken down into their constituent elements and predicted costs are established for them. These predicted, or standard costs, represent the level of cost that should be incurred if operations are performed at a given level of efficiency. Comparisons are made between actual and standard costs, and variances established, which form the basis for investigation and action. For example, assume that a single product is manufactured in a particular department. Standards could be established for each of the following:

1. *Materials.* The type of material, the quantity of material to be consumed per unit of output, and the material price. At the end of any control period, if all things proceeded according to plan, standard cost should equal actual cost. However variances could exist and would be calculated for each deviation from standard, *i.e.* price variance and quantity (usage) variance.

2. *Labour.* The rate of pay for the specified grade of labour and the labour time per unit of output. Deviations from standard could result in a rate of pay variance and labour efficiency variance.

3. *Overheads.* An hourly rate of overhead absorption for overheads that vary with output, *e.g.* variable overheads such as power, and a rate for overheads such as rent and rates which tend to remain fixed over a given output range. For both variable and fixed overheads, variances could be calculated for any deviation from standard performance, such as taking longer to produce the output than laid down by the standard time.

Standard costing, budgeting, and budgetary control are all interrelated. The standards may be used to build up the budgets. For example, a budget forecast to produce so many units of output may be converted into a labour manning requirement and budgeted cost by multiplying the forecast units by the standard labour time and rate of pay in each department. From the budget, however, are derived the variable and fixed overhead absorption rates for each department. For control purposes variances will be established by using both budgets and standards. Standards may also serve other purposes. For example, standard product costs may be used as a basis for sales pricing and stock valuation.

The control process should be based upon the idea of responsibility accounting. This means that an individual is held accountable only for those items the level of which he can completely or largely control. An individual should not be held responsible for items outside his authority as a manager. Whilst this principle may appear to be self-evident it should be remembered that accounting exists to serve a large number of purposes. A system designed to fulfil one set of purposes may not satisfy another objective. The design of a budgetary control system must therefore take this into account.

A final point relating to budget preparation and financial control is the need to be fully aware of the importance of the human factor. In recent years there have been a number of developments in behavioural accounting. Target setting via budgets, and control via budgetary control and standard costing will affect the motivation of managers and other employees. The aim should be to motivate performance at work directed towards achieving the goals of the organisation. A good planning and control system will go some way towards achieving this objective. A bad system may result in the opposite. An example of such dysfunctional behaviour would be if an employee were encouraged to spend money unnecessarily in the current period because of his expectation that lower spending in this period will result in a lower budget allocation in the next. Another example would be the employee who was discouraged from trying harder because of a performance target that was set at an unrealistically high level. The accounting system cannot be viewed as something independent of the people that it serves. The human factor is all important, and must be carefully considered in system design, implementation, and working.

VI. MANAGEMENT INFORMATION AND DATA PROCESSING

DATA AND INFORMATION

Management information may be presented in a number of different ways. They range from a simple listing or tabulation of latest results, such as sales achievement by region or production output by factory, to a comprehensive statement supplying the manager with all conceivable data he may require in the form he needs to enable him to take the best possible decisions. The former is exceedingly common, the latter, in the strictest sense, virtually unattainable.

Data may be numeric or it may be descriptive: a selection of words, not necessarily forming sentences, which aid comprehension. It is from data that information comes, but data by itself can never be information. It becomes so if it is capable of interpretation and translation so that action may be taken and/or a decision made. For example, it is data to know the speed limit in a built-up area; it becomes information only when the person with that knowledge is driving a car through the area and is required to conform to that speed limit.

A most prodigious provider of numerical data is the computer. It is able to absorb numbers at a very high rate, to perform arithmetic upon, sort and store them at fast speeds, and then spill out the results in a wide variety of ways. A manager may regard the computer as a necessary evil, preferring to leave its control in the hands of the computer department staff. Such control over the technical aspects and operation of the computer is absolutely essential, but it can sometimes happen that, perhaps from a mixture of hope, faith and fear of a complex machine which he does not understand, the manager accepts without question whatever the computer provides, with little regard to his real needs of managing. In its turn, the computer department may provide data which it sincerely believes is needed and which is convenient to produce. Most data is useful sometimes and it is very difficult to predict which data will always be required. Unless the computer installation incorporates some form of visual display unit (known as V.D.U.) or other on-line inquiry device, *i.e.* connected directly to the computer, it is not possible to interrogate the computer's store of data without modification to computer programs, which can be expensive. In order to avoid being left in the position of not having access to certain data on occasions, albeit few, when it is critical for him to have it, the manager may ask for more computer output than he can reasonably use. Such reports from the computer are frequently referred to as "Management Information," but in reality they can be little more than collections of data, for which management have no clearly defined purpose.

It is far easier to criticise the presentation of data than it is to construct rules by which information, as we have defined it, should be compiled. We should not minimise in any way the considerable task that faces management if we ask the apparently simple question, "What information do you need to enable you to make the best decisions?" The most likely answer is, "All information," and perhaps justifiably so. However, "All information" can so easily turn out to be "All data," which leaves the manager sifting though a pile of reports to find what he needs at the time when he most wants a quick answer.

Exception reporting

A method by which total volume of data can be reduced is that known as "exception reporting." To illustrate the technique let us assume that a forecast is made periodically of the number of dining-room chairs that a company making furniture expects to sell. It may be that sales conform to a pattern and that a mathematical formula can be applied, taking previous weeks' sales as parameters from which to extrapolate into the future. The forecast helps to determine the production schedule, how production resources should be deployed, whether men should be asked to work overtime, the quantities of raw materials to be purchased perhaps way in advance, the price at which the chairs should sell, the amount of money that can be spent on new designs of chair or even welfare facilities, and the total profit of the company as a whole. The forecast is one of the important factors on which management must base their decisions.

Provided the sales when they actually occur are close to forecast, the plans of management, at least as far as sales are concerned, are satisfied. The question arises as to how frequently should management examine results in detail, and what action should they take whenever there is a deviation from plan. There is little point in examining reports in great depth if sales are on target, although one might argue that if sales are as planned then there is room for more effort and an improved performance. However, leaving such comment aside, all that management need to know is that all is well. Such information can be communicated by the fact that management receive no report at all. In other words it is only informed about the exceptions, and hence the phrase "exception reporting."

We might pursue our furniture company a little further to see what type of exceptions would be reported. It is just as important to know that the company is overselling as to know that it is underselling. But in either case, by how much, and over what period of time? Is there an oscillatory effect, that is underselling for a while, then overselling and then back to underselling? Are there reasons beyond the immediate control of management to explain sales behaviour, such as a "go slow" by the postal workers causing a delay in the receipt of orders, or should the method of forecast itself be modified to take account of current trading conditions? A well-thought-out exception reporting system would be able to highlight most of these possible situations and would present information to management on which they could act.

What might be considered a hidden and unexpected advantage of exception reporting is the necessity for management to say precisely what an exception situation is. Having identified an exception they must then decide in advance of it actually occurring what possible alternative actions they can take, and what additional information they will need at that time. On occasions, such detailed analysis has led to action being taken which has prevented the exception condition ever occurring, and has removed the need for any further reports on the subject at all.

THE COMPUTER

Trials and tribulations

An excellent tool for providing analyses of data is the computer. Its existence within a company greatly facilitates the provision of information in the form that management require it, but management must take full responsibility for ensuring that such information satisfies their needs before they receive it. It can be time-consuming and costly to make modifications to computer programs and the computer can soon gain a reputation for inflexibility.

An advantage of the computer, often cited, is the standardisation of procedures, coupled perhaps with centralisation of the company's accounting systems. Such centralisation can mean that information can only be obtained by communicating with a computer at a distant location. The managers who are not physically placed close to the computer may be tempted therefore to develop locally their own clerical methods which, although duplicating some part of what is already being processed on the computer, provide information which satisfies their own particular needs and which is under their own immediate control.

It is possible that full and thorough systemisation, which is so necessary when introducing a computer and can be the cause of a dramatic improvement in efficiency, will bring with it what will appear to the manager to be unnecessarily complicated procedures. He must be more precise and must specify exactly not only what output he requires from the computer but also the input for which he is responsible. The manager who makes full and proper use of the computer must be willing to discipline himself; as a result he is likely to think more clearly and perform more ably. The computer can provide information which reports upon the activities of all divisions of the company, thus giving a good overall picture instead of the more insular one which the individual manager might have if left to his own devices. In return he must conform to the procedures of the system, such as supplying data in the exact form the computer requires by a specified time of the week. The computer may become an additional link in the communication chain and as a result the manager may feel he is losing direct control, but it is a price worth paying perhaps for better and faster information.

Delays which have been accepted as inevitable by a company for many years may be found to be unnecessary when analysed prior to the installation of a computerised system. In a similar way, the need for reports by a certain deadline might be found to be due solely to the fact that many years ago the chairman of the company liked to know his latest trading results before meeting his counterpart from a rival company for lunch at the club. Traditions die hard and even though the club may no longer exist, the provision of the information, no matter what the cost, continues. Although a computer study will highlight such anomalies, once it is installed and has become a part of the company's way of life, it, too, can become a tradition and can introduce delays and deadlines of its own.

Management must take care not to allow this to happen. It is easy for any department to become bureaucratic, which can result in a reduction in efficiency on the part of the department itself and a loss of confidence by those who use its services. Since information is the life blood of any organisation it is essential that the computer department be fully alive to the needs of management and be an active, reactive and integral part of the company as a whole.

Human similarities

The computer is a machine which has been likened to the human brain on many occasions. In terms of some limited functions which the computer can perform, this is an acceptable comparison. But as far as actually carrying out a recognisable process of thought is concerned, the comparison is less applicable. Computer specialists themselves often complicate the picture by defining some of the functions of the computer in terms of human capabilities. The computer is said to have a memory. It can read data and it can write information. It is able to evaluate possible courses of action and it can take decisions. It is also said to be able to communicate in a conversational mode, either machine to man and vice versa, or machine to machine. It can recognise certain pattern structures, and identify handwritten numbers and shapes and even pictures of human beings. Such claims to human behaviour can be justified only if we are prepared to accept a degree of limitation on the more usual ways in which the words are used.

Binary base

Broadly speaking, any capability which the computer has is provided by its ability to sense whether or not an electric current is present. It is for this reason that arithmetic with binary base is of such importance. It is either there or it is not. The French scientist Pascal in the 17th century and the British mathematician Babbage in the 19th, both acknowledged originators of the principles of the computer (although Babbage is the predominant), did not limit themselves to binary and both produced mechanical calculators of some complexity. Their ingenuity could not, however, be matched by the engineering skills which had developed at that time and so further progress had to wait until the discovery and development of electricity.

Although binary may seem inefficient and clumsy compared with decimal, with which we are more familiar, the advantages of using a binary base are immense when the requirements of designing an automatic calculator are considered. Computers are powered by electricity because it makes commercial sense for them to be so. It may not be beyond the realms of possibility to conceive of an alternative means of providing energy for computation and so develop "computer thinking" on a different base. It may be argued that the human brain breaks down its thought processes into basic "yes" or "no" decisions—or binary ones—at least if we consider only those types of decision which are quantifiable. But it is of interest to speculate to what extent this view of human thinking and decision-making is conditioned by the manner in which computing equipment has been designed, yet the design is governed by the latest technical developments and commercial convenience. Pascal and Babbage suffered limitations in design and, albeit at a higher level, modern scientists do as well.

Computer decisions

We must therefore keep in perspective the decision-making ability of the computer. If it is possible to reduce a problem to number form and to define and measure all of its parameters, then the computer is an ideal tool with which to solve the problem and in the strictest numerical sense it is capable of taking decisions. It is sometimes said that if a computer can guide man to the moon, land him there and bring him back home again, surely that same computer can be fed with a mass of data on company behaviour and so decide upon the optimum strategy for producing and marketing a range of goods. After all, the company problem is an earthbound one, whereas who knows what might happen on the moon.

The answer to this apparent paradox lies in the fact that we do know exactly what is going to happen on the moon, whereas we do not know back on earth. This is well illustrated by the way in which it is possible to pinpoint within yards the location on the moon where the spacecraft will land, but the point of descent of the astronauts on earth can be far less accurately determined. Similarly, there are no take-off delays on the moon due to external causes, whereas they occur relatively frequently on earth. The reason is that on earth we suffer the natural elements, but no such phenomena exist on the moon. It is possible to quantify exactly what will occur on the moon and accordingly take decisions on numerical fact, but not so on earth. The day may come when we shall be able to fit an exact mathematical equation to the behaviour of the elements, and great strides are being made in this direction. But it is no easy task.

Of similar complexity are some of the problems facing the business enterprise. It, too, suffers from the turbulence of external forces: the whims of customers, the behaviour of competitors and the variable availability of raw materials. At least in trying to predict weather patterns there is a wealth of past data on which to base research, but there is little past evidence to guide the businessman when, for example, he decides to introduce a new product. Many fashion stores in New York and elsewhere suffered badly because they jumped on the bandwagon of the midi skirt too soon in 1970. Their decisions were based on their knowledge, understanding and flair for the business, their entrepreneurial skill. In this particular case they fared badly—man (and perhaps woman?) is often an illogical creature—but in others they make considerable profits.

In an attempt to introduce scientific judgment, we could observe how frequently a particular businessman is successful and how often he is unsuccessful. We could grade his success and lack of success in certain categories and levels. We could analyse the data so obtained and predict with some confidence how often he will make the right decisions in the future, and how often he will make the wrong ones. We might even be able to tell him, over a period of years in the future, how much profit he is likely to make if he continues to perform in the same way as he has done up to now; but what we cannot say is how any particular decision will turn out, whether his customers will like his latest product and how many they will buy; yet the businessman must convert a basically unquantifiable problem into a quantifiable one so that he knows how much and how many raw materials to buy, the extent to which he should tool up his factory and the number of people he should employ.

The businessman, in deciding whether or not to produce and/or sell a new line, must make a final yes or no decision—although there may be various grades of yes, each identifiable by the quantities he first produces and stocks. This final decision is a binary one: yes or no, on or off, go or stop.

It may be that to arrive at this binary decision it is necessary to progress through a series of lower level binary decisions. It is beyond the scope and purpose of this book to develop such theory any further, but in practical terms it is not always possible at the time of decision to analyse the problem in such depths or to analyse and identify meaningful sub-levels. In the event, the businessman may simply" play a hunch," or try to lead and direct the market. His decision may even be based on little more than the toss of a coin, which after all is a very effective binary decision-maker.

Data input

Data can be recognised by the computer only if it can be sensed as electrical impulses. Just as messages can be transmitted over telegraph lines in Morse code, so numbers in code, made up in a binary pattern, are handled by the computer. An electrical sensing device can tell, for example, whether a hole exists in a piece of card or not. Other types of mechanism, similar to the tape-reading head in the home tape recorder, can sense the presence or not of a magnetised spot on magnetic tape or on disc. Data is contained on these devices in magnetic and binary form, written serially. The disc, with data located on concentric circles, has an advantage in that its data may be accessed more quickly by a movable reading head or pick-up arm. But just as one might compare the suitability of a tape recorder with that of a record player and choose the one which better suited one's needs, so there are advantages peculiar to tape and to disc to be evaluated before either is used within a computer system.

There are other ways for a computer to accept data. It can, for example, recognise pencil marks made on card. The cards are mechanically fed at high speed through a sensing device which feels for each end of the pencil mark and uses the carbon in the mark itself to conduct electricity. If the mark is there the circuit is made, otherwise it is not. The pencil mark must be placed with some precision since its location on the card determines its numeric value as data.

A further step in sophistication is to read handwritten numerals. A scanning device systematically traces out the shape of the character written on the paper and compares it with known shapes which it holds in its memory. Provided the character is sufficiently well recognised to a degree determined by the design of the reading machinery, it is accepted as that number. If it does not reach the required standard it is rejected for human opinion and correction. As an example, no character is accepted by the sensing device if it is written with a break. A "5" with the horizontal top line separated from the vertical and the bottom loop would fall into that category. In similar fashion, it is not possible for the device to recognise the difference between the letter B and the number 8. At considerable cost of improved design such recognition could be achieved, but at the present time it is not commercially viable.

There are other ways of getting data into the computer, and there will assuredly be more developed in the future. But one of the most common is through punched cards, which are the size of a large postcard with eighty columns by length and twelve rows by width. This means that eighty decimal units can be represented on one card, although the card may be subdivided into groups of columns to accommodate numbers larger than ten and to cover units, tens, hundreds and so on. Such a group is called a field, and is illustrated in Fig. 33. There are twelve positions in each column, which are two more than are needed for the ten decimal units, zero to nine. These additional two enable other characters to be coded in a column, for example, any letter of the alphabet may be represented by two holes

MANAGEMENT INFORMATION

punched in one column. A full set of characters is shown in Fig. 34.

The cards are fed into the computer by means of a card reader, which pushes them through a device that senses the existence of the holes in their respective positions. The equipment is exceedingly well engineered to achieve a high reading speed of three or four hundred cards per minute.

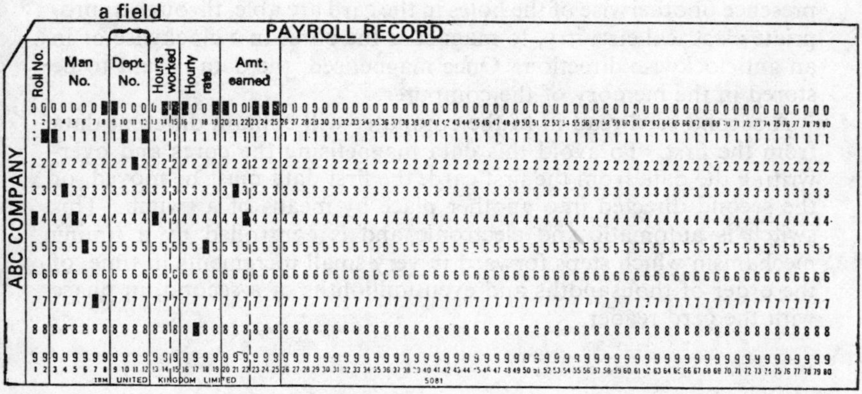

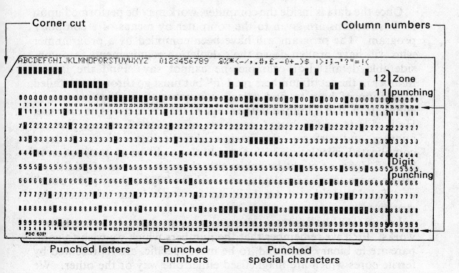

FIG. 33. *A payroll record card*

FIG. 34. *Characters on a punched card*

Memory

The coded numeric data from the card is transmitted as electrical pulses into the memory of the computer. The memory is made up of many tiny pieces of iron, often as many as a million or more, which are known as "ferrite cores." They are circular and they can be magnetised in one direction or in the other. The pulses caused by the presence or otherwise of the holes in the card are able, through appropriate electrical circuitry, to magnetise the cores in a clockwise or in an anticlockwise direction. Once magnetised, the data is said to be stored in the memory of the computer.

A second card read in to the computer will contain different data from the first. To avoid this data magnetising the cores and overwriting the data from the first card, the first data must be moved, or the second directed into another place by means of a switch. This switch is automatic and electronic and is controlled by a timing mechanism which steps forward in very small increments in time, of the order of thousandths and even millionths of a second, in phase with the card reader.

Program instructions

Once the data is inside the computer, work may be performed upon it. Instructions are given to the computer by means of a computer program. The program will have been compiled by a programmer who will have broken down the calculation requirements into considerable detail. For example, he cannot say "Find the largest number in the set of numbers read in" but must go through a detailed exposition of how to find a largest number through a process of elimination. He is limited in the scope of the instructions he may use. He is able to add, subtract, compare, move data from one place to another, and perform other basic arithmetical operations. A more complicated calculation such as multiply might be an instruction in its own right, or might be achievable through a series of additions. Other more involved calculations such as "Take the square root" or "Take logarithms" are built up from the basic arithmetic instructions.

Let us take the compare instruction as an example to see how it works. First we remember that the numbers which we wish to compare are in binary form and, to be more specific, are represented by ferrite cores which are magnetised either one way or the other. We assume that magnetisation in one direction represents the binary number 1 and in the other represents the binary 0. The compare instruction itself consists of three parts:

1. the part which defines it as a compare instruction as distinct from any other instruction;
2. the address or location in memory of the first number to be compared;
3. the address of the second number.

The instruction is reached by a scanning mechanism within the computer which steps sequentially from instruction to instruction. The definitive part of the instruction acts as an automatic switch which sets up the required circuitry to carry out the instruction. At the same time, the locations of the numbers to be compared are sensed by means of the address parts of the instruction, which also activate switches.

A comparison between two numbers can result in either one answer or its opposite: either they are equal or they are not; the first is bigger than the second or it is not. Either possibility can be considered as a binary result. If we have the possibility of three states—less than, equal to or greater than—it becomes a higher level comparison which is composed of a sequence of lower level ones.

To conduct the comparison, corresponding digits of the two numbers are checked. The scan begins from the left or highest order digit. If corresponding digits are contained in ferrite cores which are magnetised in the same direction, the numbers are equal. As soon as a position is reached where they are different, the one containing the 1 is the largest. At this stage the comparison is complete and a pulse is generated by the result of the comparison which sets further switches, transferring control back to the process of scanning the program instructions. The point at which the instruction scan begins again, however, depends upon the result of the comparison. If the numbers are equal, the scan moves on to the next sequential instruction. If they are not equal, it misses the next instruction and goes on to the one after that. In this way different action can be taken in the program as a result of the comparison, but such action must be decided before the result of the comparison is ever known.

This is an extremely important point when considering the computer as a provider of information and as a decision-maker. It is doubtful whether we would say that a train with a fog-sensing mechanism takes a decision when it stops automatically as soon as the fog reaches a predetermined intensity. Not even if, instead of the train stopping, the mechanism automatically changed points which were ahead to re-route the train, would we really accept that the train had taken the decision. It would have gone through a series of mechanical and electronic testing mechanisms with a finite number of possible outcomes and the action to be taken on each outcome would have been known well in advance. Just as the train mechanism senses fog so the computer compares two numbers, and it is this attribute of comparison which makes the computer appear to take decisions. In a limited sense it can take decisions, but we cannot thereafter deduce that it can take more complicated decisions, including those of a qualitative as well as a quantitative nature.

All other instructions which can be used by the computer, such as add and subtract, are set up in a similar way to the compare instruction. The definitive part of the instruction causes appropriate switches to be set for the result of the calculation to be achieved. Although said in few words, the design of computer circuitry requires considerable ingenuity and technical skill, particularly in view of the very high speeds at which computers operate and the degree of miniaturisation which is possible today.

Computer output

There are two types of output that a computer produces: that which it provides for its own or other computers' use at a later time, and that which is required to be seen and read by human beings in recognisable language. The former can remain in computer digestible form and be output on to magnetic tape or disc, just as it may have been read in. The latter needs to be printed in some way, presented visually on a display unit, or even communicated through speech.

Permanent copy

The most common means of providing output is by printer. Binary coded characters from within the computer memory are transmitted to the printer in much the same way as a teleprinter receives messages: the major difference is the speed with which it is done. It is possible for the printer to print upwards of 3,000 characters per second, which is ideal for large-scale invoicing and dispatching, required for example by mail order companies, and it is for this kind of reason that such high-speed equipment was designed. Such speed, however, can be abused; it is not uncommon for companies to produce regularly each week reams of paper from their computers, the purpose of which is open to doubt.

Audio and visual records

Audio output from the computer is glamorous, but except for a few cases lacks practical use. It is not difficult to pre-record syllables of human speech, usually numbers, and, instead of the computer sending electrical pulses for a type bar on the printer to be struck, it directs a pick-up arm to the appropriate recordings and strings the syllables together to make sentences, just as letters strung together make words. Speech communication from the computer in this way has been very successful in notifying credit ratings on customers in department stores. The assistant dials the customer's number on the internal telephone and, confidentially and without the customer knowing, the voice from the telephone says how much credit the customer may have. Audio can also be used to give details of latest stock positions in, say, an engineering company, but there are few applications where a more permanent record of an inquiry would not be better.

Visual display units, V.D.U.s, consist of a cathode ray tube device on which numbers, words and even pictures may be presented. The astute programmer very soon learns how to instruct the computer to draw his favourite cartoon character and even achieves some animation, but the real purpose of a picture display is to see the effect of changes: for example, changes in engineering design. It is possible to program a computer to show on the screen the view of a new design of motor car from various angles, even though initial designs may be from front, rear and side only. Any change introduced for engineering reasons, such as a need to raise the height of the grille to accommodate a larger radiator, may easily be checked to see that it does not spoil the overall appearance, without incurring the expense and time of making a new scale model whenever a change is proposed.

A more recent innovation is the use of the light pen to modify diagrams on the V.D.U. Each point on the screen is identifiable by a system of co-ordinates and can be represented in binary form as either lit or unlit. Touching the screen with the light pen registers that illumination is required at that point, while those points which are not touched remain unchanged. If a control key on the V.D.U. is depressed, the light pen can take on the opposite role: it removes light from the screen at each point on the screen it touches.

Man/machine conversation

A more generally applicable use of the V.D.U. is the presentation of numeric and alphabetic characters. V.D.U.s are normally fitted with a keyboard that enables the operator to communicate with the computer, which must first be programmed to accept input from the V.D.U., interpret questions which may be raised by the operator and present them on the screen in the way that the operator understands. This means that the programmer must know in advance what type of questions will be asked and what data will be needed to answer the questions.

A question will be in the form of a requirement for a simple calculation. It may be a request for an item of data contained within the computer's memory, it may involve a search for the largest number in a set of numbers, or it may require a lengthy calculation to be performed on data already held by the computer. Whatever the question, it is entered into the computer in coded form in such a way that it becomes part of the current program, placed so that the instruction scanner deals with it immediately.

Just as a question may be asked of the computer, so the computer may ask a question of the operator. It writes on the screen its requirement, such as "Enter in via the keyboard the latest buying price of product X." Product X may be a commodity such as wheat, whose buying price varies from day to day due to fluctuating market conditions. It is not strictly necessary for the V.D.U. to have been programmed to display its requirement in English but it helps, particularly the new inexperienced operator; all that is really required is for the computer to stop and wait for data entry at the appropriate point in its program. Instead of keying in the price in numerals, the inexperienced operator may be tempted to reply in English with "The latest buying price is 27p per kilo," when perhaps 540 is the answer required because it is conventional to state the price in twenty-kilo lots. If the computer is programmed to check whether the data it receives is alphabetic or numeric it will reject the operator's sentence and wait until it receives a purely numeric answer. In this particular case the question from the computer could have been phrased more precisely to reduce the possibility of operator error, which illustrates how carefully the original program must be written to ensure that the questions are asked in the right way to receive the right answers. Further questions to the computer on clarification would not be permissible because it would not have been programmed to accept them.

High-level languages

The language of the computer is binary, but it would be unworkable for the V.D.U. operator to communicate in binary, particularly if he was a busy manager. Equally it would be extremely time-consuming and tedious for the programmer to have to write all his programs in binary. Programming methods have therefore been developed, known as "high-level languages," which avoid this necessity.

A high-level language is a half-way house between binary and ordinary English. It contains a number of restrictions on the use of ordinary English words, but they are imposed only to avoid ambiguity. High-level languages such as COBOL, FORTRAN and ALGOL can considerably reduce the total time taken to write and test programs, but they lose a little in computer efficiency. They are far easier than binary to read and comprehend, particularly after a long absence from the program, a change of programmer or a need to modify an existing program. The very fact, however, that a number of different high-level languages exist indicates that as yet no single one is best suited to all the needs of the programmer, nor is one sufficiently powerful or descriptive. (FORTRAN and ALGOL are usually applied to scientific or technical problems, COBOL to commercial use.)

The calculation of the roots of a quadratic equation is shown in typical high-level language program form in Fig. 35. The equation is represented by

$$ax^2 + bx + c = 0$$

whereby
$$x = \frac{-b \pm (b^2 - 4ac)^{\frac{1}{2}}}{2a}$$

unless the discriminant $b^2 - 4ac$ is negative, in which case the two roots are imaginary.

The procedure the computer follows is to begin at 1 by reading a card with the values of A, B and C punched upon it. It cycles through the program and back to 1 to receive another card with fresh data for calculation until no more cards remain, when it stops. The program as written needs little explanation: it is almost self-descriptive, which illustrates the strength of the high-level language. It bears no comparison with the string of binary digits of which the program would otherwise comprise. Nevertheless, inside the computer, the program becomes a string of binary digits, having been translated by an intermediary program known as the "compiler."

Organisation of data

The computer is capable of storing vast quantities of data on magnetic tape or on disc. These two media augment the computer's memory, which, although more limited in size than tape or disc, can still hold relatively large amounts of data. Data which is already within the computer's memory is accessible immediately, but it

```
1. READ A, B, C
   D = B**2 - 4.0*A*C
   IF D LT. 0 GO TO 2
   X1 = (-B + SQRT(D)) / (2.0*A)
   X2 = (-B - SQRT(D)) / (2.0*A)
   PRINT X1, X2
   GO TO 1
2. PRINT # ROOTS IMAGINARY #
   GO TO 1
   END
```

FIG. 35. *Typical high level language computer program*

takes time, albeit measured in milliseconds, to transfer data from tape or disc to memory so that arithmetic may be performed upon it. It is therefore necessary to arrange the data on tape or disc in such a way that it may be retrieved as quickly and as conveniently as possible whenever it is required. This is particularly so of magnetic tape, since data stored, say, in the middle of the tape takes time to reach. Data on disc is easier to locate by means of the access arm.

Just as the choice of music for the home record player and tape recorder is very large, so the quantity of data stored on tape can be almost limitless. It must be set up and arranged in discrete lots and maintained in library form for ease of reference. A library of such data is often referred to as a data bank and this term is frequently

MANAGEMENT INFORMATION

coupled with the expression "management information." Care must be taken not to consider them as synonymous.

The data needs of management

Other chapters describe the functions and responsibilities of the divisions of management and Chapter XII, by presenting a case study with related questions, provides opportunities to make decisions based on the kind of data which is commonly available to management. Table XIII gives some of the data requirements of manage-

TABLE XIII
MANAGEMENT DATA REQUIREMENTS

SALES	Customers: names, location, ownership, attitudes, credit limits, items purchased, payment records, discounts, delivery needs. Products: price, discounts, range. Employees: number of salesmen, territories, quotas, commission, welfare. Plant: Environment: sales by region, competitive activity, advertising.
MARKETING	Customers: names, location, ownership, items purchased. Products: price, range, competitive products, promotions, packaging, raw materials. Employees: wage rates, welfare, sales incentives. Plant: capacity. Environment: sales by region, competitive activity, advertising, market research.
DISTRIBUTION	Customers: names, location, items purchased. Products: packaging, perishability. Employees: number of delivery men, wage rates, welfare. Plant: depots, vehicle utilisation and maintenance. Environment: vehicle routing, sales volumes.
FINANCE	Customers: name, location, payment records, credit limits. Products: total costs by each function. Employees: wage rates, welfare, efficiency. Plant: depreciation, capital expenditure, utilisation. Environment:
PRODUCTION	Customers: Products: sales volume, range, packaging, raw materials. Employees: wage rates, welfare, efficiency. Plant: capacity, utilisation.
PERSONNEL	Customers: Products: Employees: wage rates, welfare. Plant: Environment:

ment, categorised by divisional responsibility. There is an overlap of data required by each division, which suggests that common data files might be generated to serve several purposes. Frequently, however, files which should be identical are maintained by a company in more than one place and by departments who have each accumulated their data from different sources. This lack of co-ordination can lead to divisions taking decisions on what is purported to be the same evidence, yet is either out of phase (*i.e.* one part of the company has more up-to-date information than another) or slanted towards the interests of each particular division.

If data which is common to more than one department is compiled centrally instead, perhaps for inclusion in a computerised data bank, considerable care must be taken in deciding who will be responsible for updating and maintaining it. The least troublesome way is to give that responsibility to the company's computer department, if only because it is in control of the machine which manipulates and stores the data. Any other department which might update the files within the data bank would perhaps have a greater interest in that part of the file which directly concerned itself and would pay less attention to the requirements of others; furthermore, the reasons why other data was required would be less well understood. As an example, consider the accounts department, which needs to know precisely how many goods at which prices were delivered to each customer so that the correct invoices may be dispatched. If quantity is known but for some reason the specially negotiated discount price is not, processing the data and updating the files may be delayed; yet replenishment of the depots with stock may depend upon notification through the computer that previous sales demands have been fulfilled. To maintain customer service, speed of notification of sales is essential and to this end a measure of inaccuracy can be tolerated, but no invoice may leave the accounts department if it is known to be wrong.

The computer department is no better qualified to understand the data needs of every department in the company, but at least it is impartial—or should be; although it is probably true to say that a computer department which reports to the financial arm of the company will be influenced by the needs of finance and accounting. To give responsibility to just one department always raises the danger that possible improvements in providing and handling data will be overlooked and that existing methods will become traditional and hard to break. Probably the answer is that whoever requires the output should be made responsible for the input as well, although with the overlap discussed earlier, this is sometimes hard to achieve.

MANAGEMENT INFORMATION

Of one aspect we can be sure: if bad data is put in, bad results will come out. "Garbage in—garbage out," or GIGO, is a common computer maxim.

Computer justification and data bank

A company needs to be of sufficient size before it can gain full benefits from installing data-processing equipment. There are no hard and fast rules, and frequently that size is determined by the degree of accounting which the company has. Accounting routines and procedure are frequently the first applications to be placed on a computer, with the promise that from the data which is provided for and by accounting, a data bank may be formed as the basis for a management information system. Sometimes the cost of the installation is offset by savings in clerical staff, more efficient procedures and a better system, perhaps simply because effort has been expended in analysing and improving the way the work was done before. Unfortunately direct savings of this kind do not always accrue and they may need to be bolstered by intangible benefits such as data bank, systemisation, co-ordination and more of relevant information.

A further justification for the computer is when a company grows in size. It takes on more customers (not necessarily the case, but we will assume so), increases its range of products and sets up additional distribution points. Without proper control, one of the first areas to suffer is the accounting function: invoices may go out progressively later and there may be insufficient time to check credit-worthiness. The volume of clerical work grows, it is repetitive, and the comparative nature of the arithmetic required, for example, to apply discount policies or to test customer credit limits makes invoicing and credit control ideal first applications for the computer, providing data which forms a firm foundation for the data bank.

Commercial documentation and credit control

Invoicing requires that comprehensive and detailed files be maintained of customers and products, and involves far more than the relatively simple matter of sending out a bill to those customers who have received goods. The company must be sure that all the goods have been delivered and that any products which are unable to be supplied on the first call because of stock shortages have been subsequently dispatched. A typical consumer goods manufacturer might have some 10,000 customers and 300 products, if different sizes of packs are taken into account as well as the product itself, and each of the 10,000 customers might be invoiced in different ways. For example, a large national multiple expects to receive a composite invoice each quarter of all products supplied to all its retail outlets, broken down by outlet type such as supermarket and counter service, or urban and rural. In this way the multiple is using the supplier as a means of providing data of importance to itself and so reducing its own costs. Such detail is not all loss to the supplier, however, since it is useful data to hold on the customer file. At the other extreme there is the small retailer with one shop which he owns himself. He is probably invoiced on delivery and may be asked to pay immediately for his goods. If he is not, he will be expected to pay in a much shorter time than the large multiple.

Discount policies relate to quantity of goods purchased and customer category. With 10,000 customers and 300 products there are potentially a large number of possible prices, aggravated by the fact that salesmen and their immediate managers are keen to negotiate the most attractive terms for their customers in order to win the sale, particularly if there is pressure from competitors, which can result in a further proliferation of prices. Companies normally set limits on discount strategies, but this still allows for many possibilities.

Very often the place of delivery is not the same as the place to which the invoice is sent: for example, companies with several retail outlets and wholesalers with more than one warehouse. This type of dispatch information must be held on the customer's file, together with any special delivery instructions such as times at which goods cannot be accepted by the customer. The supplier might also keep a record of times when delivery is difficult, such as when large consignments arrive from other companies and queues occur.

The customer normally expects to receive with the goods a confirmation of what has been delivered, called a dispatch note. It should relate exactly with the invoice which is sent at a later date and is usually a direct copy, without cost details. This means that co-ordination of the accounting function with distribution and dispatch is necessary, the more so if there are several depots. A terminal inquiry station or V.D.U. at each depot with direct access to the computer could be of value in keeping orders and dispatches matched together, the prime purpose being to inform the computer when the order has been fully satisfied. It would also play an important part in communicating the initial customers' orders between centre and depot. An alternative approach might be to take a physical stock

MANAGEMENT INFORMATION

check at short and regular intervals, which would tighten up the system sufficiently to ensure that the stocks held at each depot were precisely those quantities recorded by the computer. It is then possible to adopt the method of pre-invoicing instead of the more straightforward one of post-invoicing; the computer produces an invoice and an identical dispatch note, the latter acting as an instruction to the depot to deliver, while the invoice is sent directly to the customer for payment without a check that the stock actually exists. If it does not, the company will be inundated with demands for credit notes and customers will eventually refuse to pay their bills. If pre-invoicing is employed, a tight control of stock is absolutely essential.

There may be a satisfactory reason for not delivering to a customer goods which have been ordered. This could occur when, for example, the customer orders in cash terms more than a predetermined amount, known as a credit limit. Goods are not normally paid for on delivery and it frequently takes a month or so for an invoice to be sent and payment to be made. It is not possible to permit customers to owe an unlimited amount over this period and it usually happens that the smaller the customer the smaller the debt he is allowed to incur.

Before a delivery is made to a customer, it is important that his credit status be checked and a decision taken whether or not he should be supplied with the goods. In practice it is difficult to make such a check in the time available between receipt of order and promised delivery date, unless the credit status of each customer is held on a customer file which is accessed at the time the delivery note is prepared. It is important that credit status be kept continually under surveillance, since it is not unknown for customers to have credit ratings which may have been appropriate in the past but due to changing fortunes are no longer so. It is usually the sales division who can most easily recognise a customer's current standing, but it is accounting who make use of the credit rating; neither may feel responsible for updating it. The accounting department may, for example, take action against a customer because he has been slow to pay, yet that customer may be an important one to sales whom they do not wish to upset.

An important function of credit control is to press for payment of debts. The cost of a computer can sometimes be justified on the savings which can be made from its encouragement of prompt payment of debts: the computer is able to send statements of account at regular intervals and keep up to date with defaulters. Customers who do not pay can automatically be sent letters of increasing severity until they eventually pay, or legal action is instituted. This procedure is known as "dunning."

Distribution by value

There is a widely accepted rule of thumb, known as the 90–10 rule and expounded by Peter Drucker in *Managing for Results* (Heinemann, 1964), which says that 90 per cent of a company's turnover is provided by the sales of 10 per cent of the company's products. The 90 and 10 may vary by a few per cent in any given company, but in general the statement is frequently found to be true. In other places it is possible to see the 90–10 rule in operation. Approximately 10 per cent of the books in a library are likely to be out on loan 90 per cent of the time. Over a given period, 90 per cent of all the audiences at a cinema will probably be attracted by 10 per cent of the films shown.

From the data bank, which contains data compiled as a result of invoicing and credit control, it is possible to extract a list of all products, sorted in descending order of sales volume by cash value. This listing is known as "distribution by value" and is a very good means of identifying the sluggish products as well as the high flyers. Figure 36 is an illustration of a distribution by value, with relatively few high sellers and many steady plodders with low-volume sales. The items in the list are a selection from the complete product range: it would be tedious to include them all.

To illustrate the distribution by value concept, it can be seen that item number 2979 has the greatest annual sale in cash terms and represents 0·06 per cent of the items, of which there are 1,537. Item number 2473 has the fifth largest annual sales of £19,254, but it does not rank fifth in terms of annual units (unit volume ranking is not shown).

For this particular example we may assume that, as the result of a previous listing, the very low-volume items have already been removed from the range so that the 90–10 position no longer applies: it has become instead the far more healthy situation where 89·5 per cent of the total sales is achieved by 48·8 per cent of the products, *i.e.* almost a 90–50 result. The listings should be supplemented by an enumeration of the amount of profit contributed by each product.

A decision to prune the product range because it is too large should be reached only after consultation with all functions within the company, and many factors must be taken into account. For example, production might need to redeploy its resources of machines and labour; sales might lose a loss leader, *i.e.* a product which does

MANAGEMENT INFORMATION

not contribute much profit, perhaps even a loss, but without which other products would sell less; distribution might find that with the absence of a particular product it would be carrying uneconomical loads. Products which are not selling well now may gain a new lease of life in the future and this too must be considered.

Item number	Item count	% of items	Annual units	Unit £ cost	Annual £ sales	Cumulative £ sales	% Cumulative £ sales
2979	1	0·06	12,413	2·07	25,695	25,695	1·2
2473	5	0·32	3,626	5·31	19,254	107,032	4·9
0354	8	0·52	1,572	11·19	17,591	162,373	7·4
2493	13	0·84	7,819	11·70	13,292	235,065	10·8
2467	31	2	3,377	2·76	9,321	434,717	19·9
2790	45	2·9	5,095	1·56	7,948	557,721	25·5
1917	76	5	8,223	0·69	5,674	753,942	34·5
1822	154	10	4,848	0·70	3,394	1,093,143	50·5
1388	308	20	4,567	0·41	1,872	1,470,944	67·3
0300	413	27	1,263	1·12	1,415	1,639,350	75
1349	545	35·4	392	2·55	1,000	1,795,964	82
2561	750	48·8	1,334	0·46	614	1,954,716	89·5
2566	1,162	75·6	284	0·93	264	2,123,810	97
2860	1,470	95·6	455	0·22	100	2,179,849	99·8
4582	1,537	100	12	0·49	6	2,183,919	100

Notes
1. The top 13 items (under 1%) account for over 10% of the annual turnover.
2. The top 45 items (approx. 3%) account for over 25% of the annual turnover.
3. The top 76 items (approx 5%) account for over 34·5% of the annual turnover.
4. The top 154 items (approx. 10%) account for over 50% of the annual turnover.
5. The top 413 items (approx. 27%) account for over 75% of the annual turnover.
6. The bottom 5% of the items account for only 0·2% of the annual turnover.
7. The bottom 25% of the items account for only 3% of the annual turnover.
8. The bottom 50% of the items account for only 10·5% of the annual turnover.

FIG. 36. *Distribution by value*

On its own, distribution by value is simply data which has been removed from the data bank and sorted into a convenient order. It is only when other relevant data is introduced that it becomes transformed into information on which action can be taken.

Levels of reporting

Data accumulated in the data bank as a result of customer orders and receipts is of considerable benefit to the marketing and sales divisions. At frequent, regular intervals it is possible for the sales department to know by region, by area, by territory and by customer, if they so wish, how much of each product has been sold. In fact, so many tables of sales achievement with references can be compiled that it could take most of management's time to read them. The volume of paper may be reduced to manageable proportions by setting up a system of management levels to which sales results are sent. The first level might be top management, perhaps the sales director, who receives the sales figures by area, and so on. This type of reporting structure works quite effectively until the sales director wishes to know, say, the outcome of a sales drive in a particular part of the country, details of which he does not possess. His request may be accommodated by sending him reports which are normally sent to lower management levels, but a more sophisticated answer would be to provide a V.D.U. with which he could make direct inquiries into the computer store. Alternatively, additional tables might be printed each week and distributed only if they are required. There is no guarantee that even then what is asked for will be readily available.

The method of providing progressively consolidated reports at management levels is most appropriate when reporting financial results. The higher the level of management, the more it is concerned with overall achievement of financial targets and the less with detail. When financial detail is required, it is relatively easy to identify what form that detail should take. This is not necessarily so when presenting sales achievement. It is more difficult to specify in advance what the areas of interest will be, or what facts will be needed to help diagnose the problems which might arise and which will need management attention.

This situation might be likened to the police detective following clues—each clue leads him on to another until he finally solves the crime. When he starts he has only a limited concept of the path he will take, guided by the events he sees around him. Step by step he improves his knowledge, sometimes turning in the wrong direction but eventually arriving at a solution. In the same way management will want to decide what additional information they require only when they know the effect of the information they already have. Although management should know the purpose of each item of data in the data bank, the possible ways in which the data might be interpreted and the range of decisions that might be taken as a result of being made aware of that data, it is unrealistic to expect too precise a statement from management before the data is actually used.

Factors of control

Before sales results can have any real meaning, they must be compared with both a target figure and the rate of sales which management expect: these two are not necessarily the same, since the former

MANAGEMENT INFORMATION

may be to satisfy an agreed profit objective while the latter recognises more recent market states. The difference between actual and target can be measured, but two questions emerge. By how much can actual differ from target before management intervene, and, if the difference exceeds that amount, what action will management take?

As an example, we will assume it has been decided that if sales drop below 90 per cent of target, a pre-planned sales campaign is set in motion which offers special discounts for quantity orders. The decision is an automatic one, triggered by low sales; all preparations have been made before the event. Production and distribution departments are informed immediately by the system so that they can react quickly enough to the expected surge in demand. The activity of competitive companies and the counter measures they take are carefully watched, and all relevant data is collected. If the sales campaign is particularly effective, competition may redesign their packaging materials, introduce a new product or a new size, or simply reduce prices. To enable management to monitor the effects of the campaign, such data on competitive behaviour is essential, yet particularly hard to obtain sufficiently far in advance for worthwhile action to be taken upon it.

We have described a purely hypothetical case and it is doubtful whether any management would allow a business decision of such magnitude to be taken in such a mechanistic way, which bodes ill for the "total management system," as it is sometimes called. Perhaps a compromise can be reached through man/machine interface with V.D.U.s, provided the computer system on which it is based is suitably flexible and reactive. If such a system exists it is of interest to reflect upon which factors would trigger the completion of the sales campaign, just as sales less than 90 per cent of target began it. To suggest there should be a return to normal operation once sales were back on target would ignore the fact that in all probability market conditions would have changed as a direct result of the sales campaign and subsequent action. There is no way of telling in advance what these effects would be, although estimates could be made of what they would be likely to be.

Far less attention is paid to sales being over target as opposed to being under, yet being over target can sometimes be almost as harmful as being under and can have a particularly bad effect on other products in the company's range. Not only may similar but more profitable lines suffer lower sales, but both production and distribution can be severely disrupted in attempting to satisfy the increase in demand. The overall effect can in extreme cases be a reduction in profit. Seldom are salesmen measured on profitability, most commonly it is by sales turnover and quantity sold. The reason may be that to provide sufficient data to measure profitability is a considerable task, but to count up total quantity sold is a relatively simple matter. Yet high sales, particularly if achieved by high discounts and overtime working, may well mitigate against increased profits.

Sales forecasting is a particularly good example of the delegation by management of control to the computer. It is discussed more fully in Chapter VII.

MANAGEMENT INFORMATION SYSTEM

The purpose of a management information system is to provide management with all the information they need to enable decisions to be taken which produce optimum results. The system should be capable of reacting to actual events and, within predetermined limits, capable of readjusting control parameters to maintain optimum performance. For example, if sales are increasing and the system is able to deduce that they will continue to do so for some time to come, not only will the production department be required to make more but a major recruiting drive may be proposed for new salesmen as well as for extra staff in most other functions. Such a system is not unlike the process of automation described in Chapter VII, but it is applied there to an inanimate mechanism, whereas the management information system is more akin to a living organism. It is expressed diagrammatically in Fig. 37.

Few companies can claim that they have actually installed a full working management information system and those which do either have special circumstances, for example, an airline seat reservation system, or define their system in a limited way. As an example of the latter, the method of forecasting described in Chapter VII is self-sufficient when applied to stock control; it can take corrective action to keep stocks at the right level by adjusting safety stock as a result of its measure of forecast accuracy. It can also identify when sales demand is so different from forecast that management intervention becomes advisable.

A problem which faces the proponent of the management information system concept is that the information needs of each division within the company are different. They may not only be distinct, but even where the same data is applicable to two departments, its form of presentation and the emphasis placed upon it can be different. The point is particularly relevant in relation to management accounting data, as introduced in Chapter V. It can mean that the total system becomes a series of interrelated sub-systems, each with its own data requirements and objectives. If these objectives are consistent with one another and take fully into account the effects each department has on all others, the agglomeration of the sub-systems produces a workable total system. But if, as is usually the case, the objectives of the sub-systems are contradictory, some compromise is required to arrive at an acceptable total system. Companies tend to tackle their problems in sequence, as the need arises. Each department has its turn when its problems are the most pressing ones, a solution is found and its operation is optimised, perhaps to the detriment of others. The case study described in Chapter XII can be used as an example of such behaviour if one considers the attitudes of each division to stock-holding, and then the objectives of the company as a whole. A management system requires that an overall solution be found, or in other words all problems be considered simultaneously in parallel instead of sequentially. It must be sufficiently flexible to sense changes in market conditions and other factors which cause the relative importance of divisional needs to be modified.

A simple real-life example of sub-optimisation and potential conflict is the design of a company's product list, which is printed on an order set used by the salesman to record the quantities of each product ordered by each of his customers. One copy is left with the customer, a second is sent to the supply depot and acts as a dispatch advice note, a third is sent to central accounting to be subsequently processed by the computer and a fourth is retained by the salesman for his files. It is convenient to have these four copies to avoid duplicating the order at a later date for each of the departments who need to take action on it. But the customer and the departments require the products to be printed on the order form in the sequence which best suits their own particular needs, as described below.

1. The customer wants the list to be either in alphabetical order so that he can quickly check back to see the quantities he has ordered, or in product groups because he lays his shelves out in that particular order, or because there appears to be a logical connection, such as pepper with salt or soap with detergent.

2. The depot would like the products to be listed in picking sequence, which enables them to assemble the goods from the racks in one continuous tour of the depot without back-tracking to collect items they have passed. The order in which the goods are laid out in the depot may be dictated by the physical characteristics of the depot, the way in which the goods are supplied

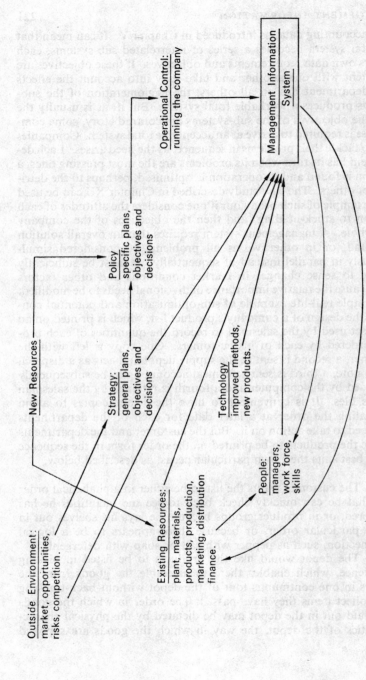

FIG. 37. *Management information system—data flow*

from the factories or the way in which they are packed in bulk.

3. The computer department requires the list to be sequential, with the most active ones at the head, that is in the sequence determined by distribution by value, as discussed in an earlier part of this chapter. By the nature of the products, such a listing is likely to be subject to continuous change.

4. The salesman would like the products which give him the greatest commission to be at the head of the list, particularly those on which there are large discounts to help boost sales. Special offers can then be brought much more quickly to the customer's attention, resulting in larger orders.

A decision has to be made on how the product list on the order set should be laid out. It may be company policy that the customer's wishes should be respected and should take preference over the requirements of any single department in the company. This would almost certainly conflict with a second company objective, namely to maximise profit. Such a listing could make it necessary to employ additional depot staff and use more computer time, thus increasing company operating costs. One might argue that a contented customer is worth more than these additional costs; such a justification would be on qualitative rather than quantitative grounds.

VII. PRODUCTION AND MARKETING

The purpose of this chapter is to discuss the various functions within a company which exist to enable the product to be manufactured, marketed and distributed right through to the eventual consumer in the most efficient way. Different industries, even different individuals within the same industry, would see the functions in different orders of priority. The order chosen in this chapter is not meant to suggest that any one function is more important than another, for if a link is missing or is defective in any chain the chain as a whole will surely suffer. It is for convenience of presentation only that this order has been adopted, starting with the purchase of raw materials and ending with distribution of the product to the customer.

FUNCTIONS ASSOCIATED WITH PRODUCTION

Purchasing

The responsibility for purchasing goods for a company, be they raw materials, office furniture or protective clothing, is normally vested in the buyer. It is his job to be fully in touch with market developments and trends and to know which of the many suppliers is the best one with whom to deal. A departmental head will usually have the authority to purchase items up to, say, £25 in value, but any requirement which costs more than that amount will need to be authorised at a higher level, and progressed through the buying department to ensure that the standard and legal requirements of the company are satisfied and the responsibilities and liabilities of both supplier and buyer are properly defined and understood.

Buying is a specialist activity which is a very important part of the company's total operation. Companies which are dependent upon few raw materials, for example, flour milling, which has wheat as its principal ingredient, place buying at a very senior level, even a directorship. Others make buying responsible to production or to finance, sometimes at a relatively junior level. This is probably a mistake for a number of reasons. Buying is not just a matter of running errands with a shopping list, nor of attempting to buy goods at the lowest price. It requires a great deal of knowledge about how the company itself operates, for what purpose the goods are required, how reliable they should be, what servicing facilities are needed for the goods and are offered by the supplier, whether goods of a lower quality and significantly lower price would be acceptable and whether savings might be made by re-specifying the end product in the light of market availability of raw materials. This list of buying responsibilities is by no means exhaustive: no one person would be able to have such a broad view of the company operation, yet a buyer must take these considerations into account if he is to serve the best interests of the company.

Most buyers are responsible for purchasing goods worth a great deal of money, and although they cannot be held responsible for goods which turn out to be below standard yet supplied according to a firm and agreed specification, nevertheless there will always be some reflection on the buyer: as a professional, he is expected to know those suppliers who can be trusted. Considerable time and energy are spent by companies to perfect their marketing, production and sales effort: to reduce costs or to increase sales and profit is a commendable achievement. Too often, however, insufficient attention is paid to the importance of the buyer obtaining the goods at the best price in the first place, where "best" includes weighing the risk of non-delivery or non-performance by a supplier or servicer against the financial advantages which can be achieved by accepting special offers, for example, discounts for bulk, orders by a specific date, or purchases out of season. The buyer may be applauded for reducing purchasing costs, but the consequent additional expense caused by non-availability, obsolete or stale goods and quantities which are inconvenient to store and to handle may offset the savings he has made. The higher up the management tree the buyer is placed, the better able he is to reconcile conflicting ideals.

The buyer in a department store or retail chain has a considerable influence over the success or failure of the total company operation. If he chooses the wrong merchandise, no matter how expert the sales staff may be, the goods will not sell. Not only must the buyer strive to buy the right goods of the right quality at the right price but he must also take great care to uphold the company's image. That image may be one of fair trading and it will apply with suppliers and customers alike. The buyer must be on the alert not to overplay his strength: for a good healthy business relationship it is just as important that the supplier makes a reasonable profit as it is that the buyer gets his full share.

The grain buyer must be aware of grain prices throughout the world, both in the immediate future and in the longer term, up to one year away. He requires grain of a consistent quality and a guaranteed supply. He must consider the time it takes for the grain he buys to leave its country of origin and arrive at his mills, and must make sure that there is no break in supply. He must take care that competitors do not tie up the market and prevent him from satisfying his requirements, and he must not leave it possible for them to buy at all the best rates. Skilful buying will have a major influence on company profits, but mistakes can be costly and so there is a tendency to buy more from the principal sources of supply such as Australia and Canada, even though Poland, for example, may at a particular time be producing grain of far better quality at a better price. Not only is there the possibility that the grain may be insufficient in quantity but there is also the cost to consider of blending it, perhaps at several mills, with existing stocks and future supplies of grain of different qualities from other countries.

Production planning and control

Various techniques exist for the planning of production, ranging from calculations on the backs of envelopes and the use of graphs, charts and tables, to critical path network analysis, scheduling routines and linear programming methods. Each has its use in particular situations, bearing in mind the size of the company concerned, the complexity of its business and the period over which the planning takes place.

Long-term production planning is basically an analysis of which plant facilities will be required to satisfy future demands. Since actual sales will not be available, and neither will the extrapolation of present sales be sufficiently accurate, planning tends to rely upon the assessments made by senior management and information on any economic trends which may be available. On occasions companies have made such calculations only to find that their manufacturing capacity is greater than they really need, simply because they failed to recognise that competition would enter the field as well, thus reducing their sales potential.

The more flexible a production plan can be, the better it usually is for the company as a whole. It is difficult to allow much flexibility in a long-term plan, since it means committing the firm to the purchase and installation of plant and equipment, but a certain amount may be contained in short-term plans. It is possible to allow for some spare machine capacity, raw material and packaging availability and labour adaptability. This is not an easy task, particularly when the production division is measured on plant and labour efficiencies and idle time is frowned upon. Yet it may be important, even essential at times, that certain customers be supplied at short notice: the need is therefore to plan in such a way that machine runs can be interchanged in the light of the most recent sales information, so that there is no occurrence of congestion, bottlenecks and idle time, particularly when other work might be done but cannot yet be started, and so that costs are contained within acceptable limits.

The requirements of the production plan are:

1. To schedule available labour resources, plant capacities, materials and components so that consumer demand can be satisfied at the right time. This can mean arranging to produce and store goods in advance to cater for periods of peak demand when insufficient plant capacity exists; it would be uneconomical to have capacity to satisfy maximum demand if that demand occurs infrequently. Alternatively, extra shifts may be employed, perhaps an evening shift of women workers, often referred to as a "twilight shift." This would require organising the labour force in sufficient numbers for several weeks to make it worth their while.

2. To arrange the schedules so that the flow of work through the various departments remains in phase and does not become unbalanced.

3. To provide the means by which information on progress can be supplied to management so that they may identify and correct potential difficulties before they become serious.

Once a production plan has been put into operation, it is necessary to monitor actual events to see how closely they resemble plan. Standards of performance which have been built into the plan, of both men and machines, are unlikely to be totally accurate and failures are bound to occur as well as mistakes. To enable management to take corrective action, a procedure must be devised whereby significant differences between plan and actual can be detected and therefore a formal method of production control instituted. The way in which management is kept informed of progress may be through periodic reporting by supervisory staff on performances measured against pre-determined standards, or it may be with the aid of progress chasers, men responsible for checking the progress of work through the factory. Either way, or perhaps a combination of both, management will be interested in considerations of cost, quality, machine and labour utilisation, the amount of waste arising from the use of raw materials and the ratio of finished goods to raw materials employed in the manufacturing process.

The more stable the industry, the more precisely may the standards be set. For example, the manufacturer of motor tyres can say with some accuracy what his total raw material usage should be. The builder can tell with less certainty how long it will take to build an individual house, but the manufacturer of a prototype, be it airliner, computer or undersea tunnel, has no precise idea of cost, time before completion, raw material usage or even which problems he may be faced with next.

It follows therefore that a much tighter rein can be kept on production in the well-established stable industries. Experience gained from manufacturing the product can identify when inspection and testing for quality control should take place. It is known how much of each product can be produced by each machine in a given time and how much idle, breakdown and/or maintenance time can be tolerated. Similarly labour efficiency can be closely monitored. In the steel, chemical and other process industries, it is possible for automatic control to be introduced, particularly for continuous flow production. The exact requirements of the process can be set on appropriate controls, measurements of performance taken and from this feedback the controls automatically reset if there is any deviation from standard. Often this form of automation requires a computer to calculate repetitively the effects of changes in the process detected by the measuring devices. The changes are induced by factors such as deterioration in the performance of parts of the machinery, varying qualities of raw materials and fluctuations in power supplies. Automation of this kind allows huge plants for example, an oil refinery, to exist with very few people to operate them. If difficulties are encountered with which the system cannot cope, the remaining staff must be particularly well qualified and competent. *See* Chapter X.

There is a relatively new science called "Cybernetics," which is the study of information systems. It attempts to identify and relate principles of feedback, self-regulation and control that are common to all systems, be they physiological or man-made.

Value analysis and work study

There can be little doubt that with sufficient endeavour almost every human activity could be performed better and with greater efficiency. It is therefore natural for a company to make periodic efforts to see whether it can find improved ways of producing, administrating and marketing its goods at reduced costs. Such reductions can often be obtained through the application of methods and work study, but sometimes it is better to take a broader look. Instead of reducing costs, it might be better to maintain or even to increase them, provided the consumer gains a corresponding increase in value and the product is, for example, more reliable and achieves better market acceptability. This approach, which encompasses the total company operation, is termed "value analysis."

Value analysis requires the formation of a team, the members of which are drawn from various disciplines and departments within the company. A full-time value engineer may be employed by the company who would act as team-leader. The team is asked to investigate a particular problem, say, the diminishing profits earned by a special product which is made up from several components. The team is free to explore any likely avenue but may choose to analyse in depth the manufacturing cycles and/or purchasing procedures for the component parts, beginning with those components which cost the most. Data would be collected on contributory costs and the function and purpose of each component, as well as the final product. No restrictions would be placed upon ideas and suggestions how the product might be improved or how its value might be increased in the broadest sense. The best solution would be determined, proposed to management and, if accepted, implemented. A total approach of this kind is far better than piecemeal unorganised attempts to improve performance or design and reduce costs, but there is sometimes a reluctance on the part of management to accept the all-embracing recommendations of value analysis. If the necessary changes are not made exactly as proposed, many of the advantages that could have been gained may be lost.

Work study is one of the techniques that value analysis is likely to employ. It consists basically of two techniques, method study and work measurement. If work study is used in the office work context, it is usually referred to as organisation and methods. The purpose of work study is to increase productivity by increasing the effectiveness of existing processes. It must be applied with care to avoid antagonising the workforce and it is of benefit to both worker and company, since it improves efficiency and hence the potential for greater material rewards. In factories in which the workers are not doing a fair day's work, if any such factories exist, it will be strongly resisted because it is a considerable threat to easily earned wages and relaxed conditions.

Method study is really the application of common sense in a systematic way. Jobs to which method study is applicable are those with high labour content, where bottlenecks occur, where there is evidence of excessive overtime, low earnings and complaints about working conditions. A heavy and continuing demand for a particular product is also a good reason for a method study to ensure that its production remains as efficient as can reasonably be expected. Once the job for study has been identified, the existing method of operation is recorded in detail and analysed with the help of Kipling's six honest serving men: why, what, when, how, where and who. All possible alternative ways of doing the job are considered, no matter how inappropriate they may seem. From these alternatives a new and better procedure can be devised, presented to management and, if accepted, implemented at a time that will cause the least inconvenience, for example, during an annual holiday shutdown of the factory or a week-end. The labour force will, of course, need to be trained in the new methods, and their managers before them.

Work measurement is the means by which the time to carry out a specific task at a defined standard of performance by a qualified operator is determined. It should normally be applied only after a method study has been conducted and the recommendations of that study implemented. It provides the basic data for production planning and control as well as for financial incentives for work.

The first step is to choose, with the foreman's approval, an operator who is qualified in the task to be measured, but not so experienced that he consistently achieves a higher level of performance than most other operators. He must be at ease and working in a normal fashion. Where appropriate, the job should be divided into separate elements and a note taken of the time he takes on each. The observations should be repeated several times, about thirty, to remove any bias. The average time taken for each element is calculated and they are added together to arrive at a total time. Allowances can be added to this time, such as a relaxation time, usually a minimum of 10 per cent, but it can be over 100 per cent for particularly tiring work. Arbitrary allowances may be added as a matter of policy to increase operator earnings, in which case the resultant time is called "allowed time;" otherwise it is standard time.

The choice of operator is particularly important and is a source of possible trouble if the resulting wage structure from the work measurement is considered by the workforce to be inadequate. Equally the company does not wish to pay more than it need or it should. Accordingly standard rating scales have been devised, of which the British Standard 0/100 scale is one, and this scale is commonly used; the operator is rated on it and his times for the job are multiplied by the resulting factor. This is still a subjective estimate by the work study engineer, but with experience his judgment on the scale becomes extremely accurate.

The performance of an operator can be affected considerably by job motivation, of which financial incentive is an example. An incentive scheme must be easy to calculate and must also be kept up to date by frequently checking the accuracy of the standard times on which it is based. Examples of incentive schemes are piecework (where the worker is paid a fixed amount of money for each piece produced), premium bonus (whereby the worker receives a proportion of the savings he achieves if he manages to complete the work in a shorter time than that allowed him) and measured day work (whereby over a fixed period the average performance of each worker compared with measured standard determines the wage rate to be paid over the next period). It is essential when applying any incentive scheme to have safeguards against poor-quality workmanship; it can be improved by regular inspection of work and comparisons between the quantities of accepted work and rejects. A measure of these results may be built in some way into the bonus earned by the worker.

Patents and registered designs

A patent may be obtained on an invention which is original: no other company or individual may have patented it before and it must have a practical application. Protection is granted for sixteen years, during which time no other person may make the product, or incorporate it in any other product unless he is licensed to do so by the owner of the patent. An invention may be improved upon or modified and the subsequent changes patented, thereby extending the effective term of protection. Many companies earn large incomes by licensing their inventions to other companies throughout the world. Each country has its own independent patent office and patents must be filed separately in every country in which protection is required. This is usually the responsibility of a patent attorney, who describes the invention in as precise a way as possible and carries out all necessary searches, both when filing a patent and when investigating to see whether a new product may be infringing an existing patent. In a similar way, a design may be registered and given protection: a trade mark is an obvious example—words, signatures, letters, symbols or drawings may all be registered as trade marks and are then protected under common law, provided it is evident that they are actually in use. However, no word can be registered which describes a common characteristic or property of the goods, such as "comfortable" applied to an armchair.

Tenders

A tender or quotation is a written offer to supply goods or provide a service subject to stated conditions and at a given price. It is usual for a company requiring service to seek quotations from a number of suppliers, normally three or four, and to choose the one which satisfies all the conditions the company requires at the lowest cost, or perhaps the next to lowest cost. The real question when deciding which tender to accept is whether or not the supplier can actually produce the goods or service on time and of the right quality, even though he may have said so in his quotation. Such a statement, provided it is accepted in writing, constitutes a contract in law and therefore the supplier becomes liable if he defaults. However, it is far better to avoid the risk of lengthy court proceedings if it is at all possible, since it is little consolation to have won the case but to have lost one's own customers as a result of the delays or poor workmanship, however much one may pass on the blame.

A tender should be written in simple English to avoid ambiguity. Suggested contracts or tenders may be obtained from most trade associations and professional institutions, but the following is a guide to what they should contain.

1. *Specification.* The service or goods should be stated as precisely as possible, with drawings where appropriate, and any limitations, such as quality of materials to be used and/or performance criteria, should be listed.

2. *Price.* Including discounts, part payment procedures if appropriate and terms.

3. *Delivery.* Place and date.

4. *Inspection.* How, when and where.

5. *Guarantee.* Spelt out as clearly as possible, including limitations, particularly with regard to maintenance and services provided by third parties.

6. *Penalties.* For non-fulfilment by either party.

7. *Conditions.* Any conditions specified by the customer should be either confirmed or repudiated.

FUNCTIONS ASSOCIATED WITH MARKETING

Market analysis and research

Marketing, in the sense of planning and extracting most out of existing products and resources, can never be considered an exact science, if it is a science at all. A great deal of subjective analysis must be employed, and although it is frequently not difficult with hindsight to see what should have been done, it is quite a different matter before the event. Management will often have pet products, certain that next year sales will improve; or they will be influenced by their own prejudices, beliefs and previous personal experience. It is the responsibility of market research to put forward a case in a logical, well-reasoned way, using a minimum of technical terms but sufficient to give management confidence in the findings which are presented.

The methodology employed by market research is centred upon statistical techniques. The requirement is normally to analyse in some way the performance of a particular product and then to project the findings into the future, suggesting how certain trends might either be avoided or encouraged and at what cost.

One approach is to compile a questionnaire asking consumers detailed questions concerning the product, choosing the interviewees in a random statistical way to avoid bias. The interviewers need to be particularly well briefed, impartial and experienced and the forms particularly well written and definitive, otherwise misunderstandings may occur and quite the wrong result achieved. It is almost impossible to design a questionnaire which does not ask for a view or an opinion to be graded in some way, for example, by taste or colour; even when the question can be answered with complete accuracy, there remains the problem of weighting the answers and arriving at an acceptable consolidated conclusion. It is impractical to ask every consumer his views and would be very costly; accordingly the number of people included in the survey is determined statistically in such a way that the results can be said with, say, 95 per cent confidence to represent the view of the whole.

A second way of obtaining market research data is to employ a panel of people, usually part time, who regularly give their opinions of the product under research. This maintains a consistent and identifiable base from which to work: changes in attitude can be seen as new products are developed or old ones modified, but the danger remains that the panel may be too introspective or too much of a kind and new blood needs to be introduced from time to time.

Typical market research activities include the analysis of the acceptability of new products and of consumer attitudes to existing products, research on competitive products, determination of market characteristics with particular attention to possible market changes or trends, assessment of market potentials, analysis of market share and sales effectiveness, medium- to long-range forecasting and studies of business and economic trends. Other work, but usually in an advisory capacity to another department, would be the study of sales quota systems, sales incentives and territory boundaries, analysis of the costs of physical distribution, research on sales promotions, location of plant and warehouses, studies of export markets. Specialist companies exist to provide data for market research.

Product planning

The objective of product planning is to find those products or services which customers need and will buy and which will utilise the company's skills and resources at an adequate profit. There is little to be gained from placing on the market an item which may have been exciting and interesting to produce but for which there is no demand. Product planning must be principally from the standpoint of the customer, bearing in mind that the customer does not always buy the product for what it is, but often for what it can do. As an example, most people buy television sets because they wish to be entertained, and although a set has some value as an article of furniture and perhaps as a status symbol, nevertheless its principal worth is in its ability to provide entertainment. It would not be kept in the house if it were unable to function in that way. This places the television appliance manufacturer in the business of home entertainment, not just television. If, as an extreme, we all decided to take up playing musical instruments in the evenings and entertaining ourselves in that way instead of relying upon an outside medium, then musical instruments would be a considerable threat and competition to the television manufacturer: his product plans would need to take this into account. But frequently a company sees itself in, say, the electrical appliance industry, unwilling to contemplate the time when its whole industry defined in that way could go into recession, and fails to recognise what it is that the customer is really purchasing when he buys the product. The transport industry is a good example: consider the advent of the aeroplane and its effect upon shipping; or the train upon the stage-coach.

The first step in product planning is to identify a real customer need or simply to have a good idea. Frequently the customer does not know if he wants a product until he has seen it and so there is considerable scope for innovation. However, before any commitments are made on the proposed product or service a systematic study must be made, with the aid of market research, of the prospects for the product in the market-place, and of considerations such as future trends, competitive activity, timing and company image for this kind of product, particularly if it is a new field. If the market research findings are promising, detailed specifications are drawn up and passed to the manufacturing and/or development divisions, who produce prototypes from which are provided initial cost estimates. If these are accepted and if no major production snags are uncovered, marketing must decide upon strategy, based on their forecast of demand for the product (which they may wish to review in the light of modifications that may have been made to the product at the prototype stage) and eventual profits. A test market may be chosen, say, in a particular region of the country or, for a consumer good, with an individual retail chain, and further data may be collected on consumer attitudes to the product, its price, packaging and general presentation. As a result, modifications will be made to the product and eventually it may be launched nationally as a new product.

This procedure does not apply only to new products, as existing ones can be given a new lease of life by systematic modification and improvement of their image. Alternatively, instead of embarking upon a lengthy period of market testing, it may be prudent to launch the product in one part of the country, wait until it is settled and then proceed to the next; or it may be decided that an immediate national launch should be made to steal the limelight from a competitor.

A company which does not introduce new products will eventually go out of business, for no matter how popular an existing range of products is and no matter how long they have been on the market, sooner or later their sales will begin to decline, due either to a change in consumer preferences or to the intervention of competition. Unfortunately little more than 10 per cent of new products go beyond the test marketing stage or become commercially viable when they do. Furthermore, approximately 50 per cent of those which satisfy the test markets subsequently fail when launched nationally.

The timing of the launch of a new product is important. Several products have been unsuccessful simply because they have been put on the market too soon: a delay of eighteen months or so would have made all the difference. During the early life of a product its sales usually climb quickly because considerable effort and money are expended in advertising, publicity and discounts to place it before the consumer. Next comes a period of consolidation, which is a make-or-break situation. Sales will decline, but only, it is hoped, to a level which the product will sustain. From then on it may increase in sales until it reaches a plateau, receiving a number of injections over this time to improve lagging sales until eventually they decline and fade. The length of each part of the cycle will differ from product to product, but a life of five years without modifications would in most cases be a long one. Figure 38 illustrates the life cycle in graphical form.

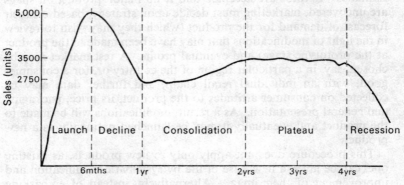

FIG. 38. *Product life cycle*

The sales function

The only way in which a company can recuperate its costs and make a profit is by selling its final product. At one time the salesman was looked upon simply as a channel for dispersing the goods which the company had made, but nowadays, with increasing emphasis upon the marketing activity, there is greater awareness that there are no ready customers and a real sales effort is required to convince the customer to buy. Some aspects of salesmanship are discussed in Chapter X. More and more is the salesman expected to merchandise as well as to sell. He must advise his customer on how to display the goods, which promotional material to use, where they should be placed, how profitable they are compared with others and how frequently stock should be replenished. He must be aware that he is really selling at two distinct levels: to his own direct customer and to his customer's customer. If he is selling components he will succeed only if the final assembly can be sold; if he is selling to retailers he will sell more only if the retailer's customers buy the goods.

There must be close liaison between the distribution and sales departments to ensure that the goods are in the right places at the right times. Special efforts can be made by sales if stocks are high in a particular region; equally sales department can ease up and emphasise other lines if stocks are low. Such co-operation is made easier if distribution areas and sales regions have common boundaries, the choice of which may be influenced by the areas served by commercial television stations, if that is a major form of advertising by the company.

One way in which a sales force may be motivated is by a sales target or quota; they may be paid either directly proportional to the sales they make over and above a fixed minimum, or by being given a bonus for achieving a sales target. Individual quotas should be set by considering the potential sales in each salesman's area over a given time period of, say, one year, not determined by simply dividing the target by the number of salesmen employed. If the sales manager requires a special effort with a particular product or customer he may additionally run some form of competition, with the reward of, say, a colour television set for the salesman who sells the most. Salesmen are notoriously reluctant to keep clerical records of their activities, yet the only way in which immediate feedback of competitive activity and sales effectiveness can be obtained is by relying upon the accuracy of their form filling. This can be supplemented by spot checks, but as a result the ratio of salesmen to area sales managers or supervisors will be relatively low.

A sales force may be organised by geographical regions, by product groups or by customer groups, such as all those within an industry or subsidiaries of a parent company. If the company sells few products then a geographical organisation is likely to be the right one, provided the products do not each require specialist expertise. Customer grouping has advantages if the company supplies major customers, for example, a food manufacturer supplying supermarket chains, or if particular skills or knowledge are required for dealing with a trade or an industry.

The principal difference between marketing and sales is that marketing is concerned with the longer term and planning, while sales have short-term operational objectives. Forecasting, for example, would be far more subjective for the sales division (who might also be influenced by opportunities for personal gain) than it would for marketing. That is not to say that the two functions do not overlap: the closer they co-operate the more successful they will be. Whether sales or marketing should be in the forefront depends upon the particular circumstances of the company and its products. A discussion of the information needs of the sales function, and its place in an overall management information system, is included in Chapter VI.

Channels of distribution

The function of distribution is to move the goods from where they are produced to where they are required to complete a sale. This may mean collecting in bulk from factories, storing in special warehouses either owned by the company or hired from a contractor, keeping appropriate stocks at company depots and delivering to final customers. Distribution may therefore be responsible for all finished goods from the moment they leave the factory floor until they are exchanged for cash. Figure 39 shows the various routes the goods can take. The means of transport includes a company's own fleet

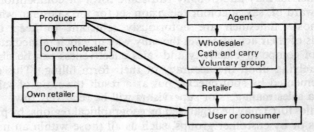

FIG. 39. *Various routes of distribution*

of vehicles, contractors' vehicles, train, air, even canal; the goods may also go by post. Choosing the method by which they are conveyed is a major consideration.

Goods can arrive in a number of ways; in practice there are probably more than are shown in Fig. 39, because on occasion it will be expedient to take paths which are not connected in the diagram, say from wholesaler to own retailer Although the diagram is intended to be self-descriptive, each box can be further expanded. The retailer, for example, may be a national multiple with central warehouses of its own. He may decide that goods be delivered centrally for further distribution to his outlets himself. The producer may, on the other hand, see an advantage in delivering direct to the retail shops because he will have better contact with the local manager and may therefore be able to increase his sales. Negotiations will take place from time to time, terms agreed and delivery arrangements switched. In a similar way a manufacturer may decide to distribute through wholesalers instead of dealing with his customers direct; he may later revert to direct delivery, if it suits him to do so. A company must always be ready to improve its distribution methods, which must therefore be capable of flexibility. In a similar vein it must always be on the lookout to make better and more profitable use of its distribution network. As an example, the milk roundsman is delivering many more products than just milk to the home, sometimes to the detriment of other tradespeople, like the baker.

The choice of the appropriate channel of distribution for a company's goods depends upon a number of factors. In the case of industrial companies selling capital equipment such as machine tools, computers or cranes, the manufacturer will most likely have a direct link with the user, or perhaps will employ an agent to represent and work on behalf of the company. There is less need or desire to employ intermediaries, and marketing aids such as advertising and merchandising are of less value.

The size of the company has a considerable influence on the way it presents its products to the ultimate consumer. Small companies are likely to use wholesalers, while the larger ones will prefer to deliver direct; either may adopt door-to-door selling methods. The general attitude of management may determine the channel, as well may the choice made by competitors. It may be essential for the goods to travel from producer to consumer in the shortest time possible, for example, perishable foodstuffs, in which case a van sales delivery service is appropriate. The more complicated the product the better it is to deal direct with the customer. The size of the profit margin, the price of the goods and the consequent capital tied up in stocks, volume sales and seasonality are all factors to take into account. It may be that a combination of channels should be chosen and that they should be reviewed at regular intervals or whenever fortunes change.

The costs of distribution and selling, including transport, warehousing, handling, insurance, deterioration and obsolescence, can be as high as 35 per cent of the total cost of the product. These costs can be materially affected by the various stages through which the product passes on its journey to the consumer. It may, for instance, be given special packaging for protection and/or display, the cost of which, if the product were not sold in that particular way, could be avoided. It is usually not difficult to make distribution savings of this kind, but in so doing one must be very much aware that other costs will accrue because other compensating forms of distribution and selling will need to be employed, and it is the total cost of distribution which is the prime consideration. Unlike the costs of production, distribution and selling costs are frequently difficult to allocate precisely to the products and the effect of incurring certain expenses is not always known until after the event.

A further channel of distribution is the overseas or **export one.**

The stages through which the goods pass are not necessarily different except that there are additional considerations. Tariffs, quotas, even embargoes may be placed in the way of free trade between countries. Devaluation can occur and the occasional war. Despite these factors, foreign trade can be very profitable, as exemplified by the growth of the many international companies which have set up their own local offices and factories in each country and have become an accepted part of that country's life. Smaller companies may instead employ an import agent in the country to which they are selling and a shipping agent to arrange the passage of the goods. The agent may be dedicated to the one product, for example, a car importer, or he may deal in several companies' products, perhaps specialising in a particular type or a single exporting country. In this way the company gains the benefit of reduced selling and distribution overheads, but regular personal involvement, without interfering in the agent's way of operating, can still reap dividends. The more successful exporting companies usually form separate departments, even separate companies, to handle the differing needs of the foreign markets. These needs range from language and communications, through special legal restriction and an awareness of local customs, to knowledge of the standards which each country may have and to which the products must conform.

Commodity markets

Commodity markets are highly specialised markets where traders sell their goods to merchants for distribution within a country. In Britain they are located in London or in large ports, as is the Cotton Exchange in Liverpool. The three main classifications are food, fibres and metals, examples being grain, wool and copper.

Each commodity has its own special peculiarities. Crop commodity prices are strongly influenced by the size of the season's harvest, and any news of rain or drought can be very significant. Metals are more susceptible to movements in demand springing from changes in the level of industrial activity. Commodity prices fluctuate more widely than share prices because they are sensitive to a wider range of economic factors, political, economic and climatic, on a world-wide scale, which are constantly altering and hence affecting supply and demand conditions.

Because of the uncertainties involved in trading in commodities three types of transactions are possible, each arranged specifically by brokers. A spot price can be agreed for immediate delivery of a product; or a forward price, which assumes that delivery will occur at an agreed future date, can be arranged, making it possible to sell goods in transit or crops not yet harvested; or, with the development of futures markets, goods can be graded sufficiently accurately to make sale by description possible, no samples being necessary. Speculators enter into agreements to buy goods they do not want or sell goods they do not possess, hoping to profit from any price changes which have taken place when the time comes either to reverse or to honour the contract by buying from or selling to another dealer.

Two important techniques used by the speculator are "going long" or "going short." The first is to buy when the prices are low and, hopefully, to sell later when they are higher. The second involves the selling by an investor of a commodity not in possession, at a particular price for delivery at a date in the future. He sells the commodity that he does not yet have because he believes the price will fall before the agreed delivery date arrives. In which case he makes the difference between buying and selling prices, less dealing expenses.

The futures market helps producers to find a ready market in which to sell their commodities at a time which suits them, and manufacturers and other users of commodities to purchase these goods at a time which is convenient to them. In addition to performing the function of bridging the gap between the times when the producer wants to sell and the user wants to buy, the speculators also perform a beneficial role in helping to keep prices more stable than would be the case if the commodities were bought and sold only when actually required. They can protect themselves against heavy losses by placing a stop-loss order to sell the futures contract in the event of the original decision being wrong, with the price moving, say, a few pence the wrong way.

A futures market enables traders to use a protective procedure called "hedging" to minimise losses due to adverse price changes, by entering into an insurance contract in addition to the original contract. For example, an importer contracts to buy raw material to arrive in, say, two months' time. He can protect himself against a fall in the price of the goods by entering into an insurance contract in addition to the original contract. In this he sells the same amount of the raw material. If, in the course of two months, the price falls in his home market, he loses on his main contract, but gains on his speculative contract as he is able to buy up the amount he contracted to sell at a price lower than it was at the time of the contract.

Advertising and promotions

Advertising is one of the tools available to marketing to persuade potential customers to buy their product. An advertisement placed in the "For sale" column of the local newspaper is usually there to sell just one item, and it is an easy matter to see whether the advertisement has succeeded or not. Company advertising, however, has a multitude of purposes. Because the needs, desires and performances of people change during the many phases of their lives and because the population in any given area is continuously being increased or decreased by natural means as well as by personal reasons of choice, advertising keeps the potential users and consumers aware that the products exist. It attempts to persuade them that some products are better than others and if they are already using the product which is being advertised, it reinforces the decision they took in choosing that product so that they will buy it again next time. Advertising does not necessarily sell products, but it increases the likelihood that a sale will be made. The more lasting the effect of an advertisement, the less effort the salesman has to make to sell the product, provided the effect is favourable. It is a way of linking the mass production capabilities of the modern firm to mass consumption, and gaining greater control over demand by smoothing out the peaks and the troughs.

It is sometimes difficult to identify any real differences between one manufacturer's products and those of another. An advertisement will try, therefore, to accentuate any differences there are or to build upon a particular characteristic of the product which may be intangible but which can be associated with it. For example, the product may be presented by a beautiful girl in an expensive car, or it may be implied that without the product the consumer will lose his friends. These situations illustrate the association of sex, status and fear with the product, each of which can be seen regularly on television commercials and other advertising media. Once a theme has been chosen, the technique is to use it repetitively, to concentrate upon one single aspect or advantage of the product and to ensure that in its field that particular advertising dominates.

In common with most forms of consultancy, the advertising agent can provide a specialist service at a cost far lower than that which would be incurred if a company set up its own self-contained department to do the same job; unless the company was particularly large, such a department would also have less opportunity to gather the same experience. Consultants also tend to have greater objectivity as outsiders and often management will accept a recommendation from a consultant which they would not accept if that recommendation had been made from within. The services offered by an advertising agency include the selection of media—newspapers, magazines, television, radio, cinema, direct mail, hoardings or posters—aimed at the appropriate social-economic group, ranging from rich to poor and graded accordingly. For example, the readers of certain newspapers seem to fall naturally into particular types, as do followers of the various television programmes and regular cinema-goers. It is such groups, far more precisely defined, which are termed social-economic. The advertising agency may design the advertisements, choose the theme, produce a film if such is the medium and buy time on television and space in the newspapers. They may also carry out market research activities to test, for example, the acceptability of the product and the effectiveness of the advertising, as well as be marketing consultants.

A benefit which is frequently claimed for advertising is that by creating a larger market it helps to reduce unit costs by taking advantage of economies of scale. There is a cost involved in advertising itself, but this is offset by savings in production, distribution and other overheads. It is sometimes argued that the price of an item could not be reduced even if it were not advertised, because advertising is a very small portion of total costs, far less per item than the smallest unit of currency. Furthermore, advertising acts as a subsidy for commercial television, cinemas, train fares and newspapers, for without advertising each would be far more expensive, perhaps could not even exist. On the other hand, an industry which employs relatively few technical skills and enjoys no protection from would-be entrants by holding, for example, a monopoly on raw material supplies can to some extent defend its position by advertising heavily and thus create a high cost of entry into the market. This can be costly both to the consumer in higher prices and to the shareholder in lower dividends, particularly when there are only two or three companies involved, each trying to increase its market share at the expense of the others. Once a product has reached a level of sales, management are loth to reduce their expenditure on advertising for fear that sales will decrease. As a result, it is possible for advertising to be self-perpetuating. It is an investment from which, like any other form of investment, a return is expected, but that return may only be the maintenance of the status quo.

It is frequently difficult to measure how effective a particular advertising campaign has been. It is usually possible to estimate how many people have read a magazine or watched commercial television, but there is no truly quantifiable way to determine how many of them have actually taken in the message of the advertisement. Advertising is not necessarily the reason for an increase in sales; all the other marketing methods play their part, but it is common practice to measure advertising effectiveness by the amount of money spent on it, related to the increase (or decrease) in sales which has occurred.

Sales promotions can be a substitute for advertising, or a complement. They include simple price reductions for a limited period,

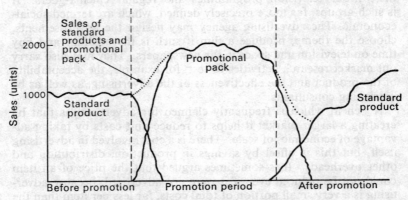

FIG. 40. *Effects of a sales promotion*

offers of free gifts, competitions, additional trading stamps, money off coupons and "two for the price of one." Whatever the form a promotion takes, it is usually notoriously difficult to forecast the effect it will have, particularly at each of the various distribution points. There are basically two kinds of promotion. One is known as a trade promotion, whereby the manufacturer makes a special deal with a particular retailer and he in turn offers the goods at a lower price in a prominent position in his store. The other is known as a consumer promotion, when the manufacturer makes his goods generally available with an added incentive to buy; this takes the form of a modified product which competes directly with the normal or standard product, so much so that for the life of the promotion (assuming that it is sufficiently attractive to the consumer) none of the standard products will be sold.

A principal reason for running a promotion is to increase sales, not only during the promotion but permanently thereafter. Figure 40 illustrates the hoped-for effect on both the standard product and the promotional pack. There will inevitably be a reduction in sales after the promotion has ended because consumers will have stocked up while it was on. Thereafter they are expected to prefer the product

PRODUCTION AND MARKETING

to its competitors, even at the normal prices without offer. An increase in market share is therefore a reason for promoting a product in this way, but competing firms will use similar tactics and the end result may show no change; at worst, promotions will be launched simply to counteract competition in order to maintain a market share. There is also considerable doubt about the continuing loyalty of the consumer to the product once normal terms are restored. Other reasons for promotions are to dispose of excess stocks, to liven up interest in the product, to bring the product to the attention of the consumer, particularly when it is launched for the first time, and to act as a draw to the retail store so that other products may be sold as well, at a higher profit. Products which are promoted in this way are frequently known as "loss leaders."

Public relations

The Institute of Public Relations defines public relations as "the deliberate, planned and sustained effort to establish and maintain mutual understanding between an organisation and its public." More colloquially, it is an organised way of creating and/or retaining a company image, a reputation which may be for reliability or public spirit, or for being a good employer or industry leader, or a solid company in which it is safe to invest.

The methods employed by public relations are not dissimilar to those used for advertising: in fact every advertisement carries with it a responsibility to enhance public relations. But public relations may succeed additionally in persuading newspapers to write about a product (perhaps a motor car or newly announced computer) as news, which may therefore carry more weight as unsolicited testimony and as an endorsement of the product. Public relations work through press releases, arrange for exhibits at trade shows, organise factory visits, receptions, symposia and conferences. For industrial companies for whom advertising is unlikely to be appropriate or effective, of which an example is shipbuilding, public relations can be of considerable importance.

Forecasting

Every company, even the most stable and the most confident of its market, must at least at one time in the year wish to make forecasts, be they forecasts of sales, raw materials usage, labour requirements or profit projections. From marketing's estimate of sales for the year, it is possible to calculate production schedules and distribution needs and from these to determine the likely profits. At this stage, the forecasts which were originally made by marketing become objectives or targets; and although the more recent the data the more accurate a forecast based on that data is likely to be, targets set some months in advance may not be changed except under extreme conditions and so marketing action, perhaps special advertising or promotions, must be taken to influence sales and keep them on target. Industrial companies, as opposed to those which are consumer goods oriented, are less likely to be able to change the course of sales at short notice in this way; any discrepancy in forecasts therefore means a corresponding discrepancy in profits.

A forecast is based on calculations performed on past data. Confusion sometimes exists when, on the record of sales performance, it is evident that targets cannot be met, yet the target is still looked upon as the forecast. If special action is taken to change the natural course of sales, by which is meant the extrapolation of past data into the future, then the forecast must be overruled by means of a prediction. In the case of sales, this is normally provided by marketing. A prediction takes account of factors which are known only by those who are applying them. It must be treated with some trepidation since it is a human failing to show excesses of optimism if the prediction is for some long time in the future and to become increasingly pessimistic as the time draws near.

It is possible in most companies to obtain data on past sales for periods of, say, one week over the previous two or three years. Such data is useful in helping to identify whether there are many seasonal influences on sales which can then be taken into account when making forecasts. There may be some evidence of sales cycles which are not in phase with the seasons and it may be possible to see sales trends, either up or down. What will be clear is that sales will not conform to a smooth pattern; there will be fluctuations from week to week which cannot be explained by seasonality, cycles or trend and which can only be described as noise or random effect. They may not be totally random and very probably if sufficient research were done reasons could be found, such as competitive activity or perhaps an absorbing television programme which stopped most people from shopping at a particular time; but for all practical purposes, effects such as these may be considered to be random.

A further factor which must be borne in mind is that sales data is not necessarily demand since an out-of-stock situation will mean that demand cannot be satisfied. Customers may be willing to wait until stocks are replenished, but usually if demand cannot be immediately satisfied, it may be assumed to be lost.

A simple method of forecasting is to take an average of past data and to use this as the forecast of sales. It may be improved by taking the past sales of a fixed number of weeks and as each new week passes to include that week in the average and to drop the one which is the farthest back. This is known as a moving average. If it is thought that the most recent week is of more importance than the week earlier, and that that week is more important than the week before, and so on back to the earliest week included in the average, and if the weeks' sales are multiplied in that order by decreasing factors, summed and then divided by the sum of those same factors, the forecast so obtained is said to be a weighted moving average. The forecasts obtained by using the three kinds of average, described mathematically in Fig. 41, may be improved further by taking account of seasonality, trend and cycles, if they have been identified.

A most common method of forecasting is known as exponential smoothing. In its simplest form it consists of taking the forecast made for the week just ended and adding to that forecast a proportion, usually one-tenth, of the difference between what actually happened and that week's forecast. In mathematical form:

$$NWF = TWF + 0{\cdot}1\,(AS - TWF)$$

where NWF is next week's forecast, TWF is the forecast for the week just ended and AS is actual sales. This week's forecast will have been derived in a similar way from the forecast for the previous week and the sales in that previous week, as will have been forecasts in all weeks prior to that. This means that exponential smoothing takes account of sales data in earlier weeks and is in effect a form of the weighted moving average with the major advantage that only the last week's forecast need be remembered. Figure 42 illustrates the methodology of exponential smoothing, using the data of Fig. 41.

Another method of forecasting is by linear regression. This means identifying the straight line which passes through a set of points on a graph so that it is the best fit, as illustrated in Fig. 43. In that example, "best fit" means the line which passes at each point in time through the sales quantities, which, when measured from actual sales at those times, provide differences, the sum of squares of which is a minimum.

In more mathematical form, d_i as shown in Fig. 43 is defined as the difference in week i between actual sales in week i and the sales which would have occurred in week i if sales had been on the line of best fit. The line of best fit takes the form

$$\text{sales} = a\,.\,\text{time} + b$$

Sales data	Week no.	1	2	3	4	5	6	7	8	9	10 (now)	Next week
	Sales	204	182	196	210	171	179	220	218	241	217	?

Simple average	Moving average	Weighted moving average
Total sales over all available weeks 2,038	Three-week moving average for week 4 $$\frac{204 + 182 + 196}{3} = 194$$	Factors applied to this week: 3
Average sales 203·8		last week: 2
Forecast sales for next week 204	for week 5 $$\frac{182 + 196 + 210}{3} = 196$$	week before: 1
		Three-week weighted moving average
	for week 9 $$\frac{179 + 220 + 218}{3} = 205\tfrac{2}{3}$$	for week 9 $$\frac{179 \times 1 + 220 \times 2 + 218 \times 3}{6} = 212\tfrac{1}{6}$$
	for week 10 $$\frac{220 + 218 + 217}{3} = 218\tfrac{1}{3}$$	for week 10 $$\frac{220 \times 1 + 218 \times 2 + 41 \times 3}{6} = 229\tfrac{5}{6}$$
	for next week $$\frac{218 + 241 + 217}{3} = 225\tfrac{1}{3}$$	for next week $$\frac{218 \times 1 + 241 \times 2 + 217 \times 3}{6} = 226\tfrac{1}{6}$$
	Forecast sales for next week 226	Forecast sales for next week 226

FIG. 41. *Simple forecasting methods*

where a and b are constants which determine where the line is placed in relation to the sales in each week. The line satisfies the condition that the sum of the d_is, squared, is a minimum, i.e. Σd_i^2 is minimum.

The values of a and b can be found from:

$$a = \frac{w\bar{t} \cdot \bar{s} - \Sigma t_i s_i}{w\bar{t}^2 - \Sigma t_i^2}$$

and

$$b = \bar{s} - a\bar{t}$$

where $\bar{t}$ and $\bar{s}$ are the averages of time and sales respectively, w is the number of weeks, t_i and s_i are week number and sales in week i respectively and Σ means form the sum of the terms immediately following for all weeks.

PRODUCTION AND MARKETING

Sales data	Week no.	1	2	3	4	5	6	7	8	8	10 (now)	Next week
	Sales	204	182	196	210	171	179	220	218	241	217	?

Exponential smoothing formula:
next week's forecast = this week's forecast + 0·1 × (actual sales − this week's forecast)

Assume that the sales estimate for week 1 (before week 1 sales are known) = 200

Then forecast for week 2 = 200 + 0·1 × (204 − 200) = 200·4 (applying the exponential smoothing formula)

Week no.	This week's forecast	Actual sales minus this week's forecast	Next week's forecast
2	201	182 − 201 = −19	199·1
3	200	196 − 200 = −4	199·6
4	200	210 − 200 = −10	201·0
5	201	171 − 201 = −30	198·0
6	198	179 − 198 = −19	196·1
7	197	220 − 197 = −23	199·3
8	200	218 − 200 = −18	201·8
9	202	241 − 202 = 39	205·9
10	206	217 − 206 = 11	207·1
Next week	208		

Note. To simplify the arithmetic, this week's forecast is increased to the next highest whole number.

FIG. 42. *Exponential smoothing*

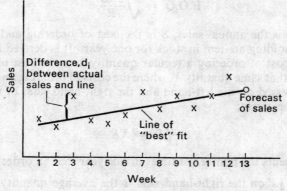

FIG. 43. *Linear regression*

Once the line has been determined, using the formulae above for a and b, the forecast is said to be the sales quantity on the line for the next time period ahead. But linear regression need not only be restricted to measuring variation against time, as Fig. 40 illustrates. Instead of t representing time, it could be, for example, the amount of money in thousands of pounds spent on advertising in previous years.

Advertising expenditure (t)	Sales (s)	$t_i s_i$	t_i^2	
2	60	120	4	Show $a = 8$
3	80	240	9	
4	70	280	16	and $b = 48$
5	100	500	25	
6	90	540	36	

FIG. 44. *Example of regression analysis*

Stock control

If all forecasts were accurate (and we can be sure that they rarely are) stock control would be a simple matter of maintaining levels of stock determined by an exact knowledge of future demand. A balance would be needed between keeping (*a*) too much stock, which is costly in space, tied capital, insurance and other elements, and (*b*) too little, with consequent frequent ordering and handling of goods, which can be expensive. A formula which goes some way to achieving the balance is known as the economic order quantity or E.O.Q. and is expressed:

$$\text{E.O.Q.} = \sqrt{\frac{2AS}{R}}$$

where A is the annual sales, S is the cost of ordering and R is the cost of holding an item in stock for one year. It is derived by equating the cost of ordering a regular quantity X to the cost of holding in stock that same quantity X, where the costs of ordering and holding are expressed on the left-hand and the right-hand sides of the equation respectively:

$$\frac{A}{X}S = \tfrac{1}{2}XR$$

$\frac{A}{X}$ represents the number of times in one year that an order is placed and the $\tfrac{1}{2}X$ on the right-hand side is the average quantity in stock during the year. It is assumed that sales demand is steady and known

PRODUCTION AND MARKETING 251

precisely, which means that orders of the same quantity can be placed at regular intervals. It applies only to stock in discrete lots, either raw materials or finished goods, and has no relevance to work in progress.

A formula such as this is useful only where the stockholder has no interest whatsoever in the costs incurred by the supplier. It is therefore appropriate for a wholesaling operation. If, however, it is necessary to consider the costs of manufacture, or to include the costs of holding the goods in a central location before they are supplied to a local depot, the problem becomes more involved. In the case of the manufacturer, he is concerned to make full and economic use of his plant and machinery and therefore wishes to produce batch quantities which minimise unit costs. These economic manufacturing quantities, E.M.Q.s, are not necessarily compatible with the E.O.Q.s, but may be made to be so.

Sales demand is never as steady as one would like and accordingly it is worth while to record by how much actual sales differ from forecast. If sufficient data is collected, it is possible to say how frequently in the past sales and forecast have differed by given amounts; from these figures, probabilities of the difference exceeding certain amounts in the future can be expressed. It can be seen that this approach is similar to that adopted when taking the average of a set of observations and then calculating their standard deviation. If now it is agreed by management that, say, 95 per cent of the time there should be stock available to satisfy demand (stock to satisfy 100 per cent of demand would mean infinite quantities), it is a relatively simple matter to hold additional stock over and above forecast such that the probability of sales exceeding forecast plus that additional stock is just 5 per cent. The additional stock is known as safety or buffer stock and the management decision on frequency of stockouts is their choice of service level to their customers.

A precise system of forecasting, coupled with a method of stock control and exception reporting (see Chapter VI), provides an example of the beginnings of a management information system. For further discussion on the function of stock and its role in practice, the reader should turn to the case study in Chapter XII.

Automated warehousing, vehicle scheduling and depot siting

Once a system of stock control has been implemented within a company, it is possible to consider more advanced and sophisticated ways of improving distribution efficiencies. Several companies have installed mechanical equipment to automate the warehouse operation, ranging from small electric cars which enable the pickers to collect the goods as quickly as possible, to full automation whereby the goods are selected and customer orders assembled without human intervention. In this latter case, not only is picking automated, but the location of the goods in the warehouse as well; it is under the control of a computer system which is activated by notification of the receipt of goods and of customer orders. Not many companies can really benefit economically from fully automated warehousing: however, considerable savings can be made by an intelligent application of automation principles, such as placing in the most accessible places in the warehouse those goods which are most frequently in demand.

The reasons for siting a depot in a particular part of the country are usually ones of convenience: availability of suitable space, expansion possibilities, access roads and so on. If, however, these considerations are secondary, it is possible to calculate the optimum siting by analysing the costs of delivering the goods to known customers and placing the depot so that the sum of the costs is at a minimum. Assuming that this does not locate the depot in the middle of green-belt land or on the top of a mountain, a weakness in the method is that it is applicable only to existing customers with their present volume of demand for the goods. An allowance can be made for probable variations in that demand in the future, but it could mean that a site which is particularly attractive at one time could become completely inappropriate at a later date.

Computer programs exist to help in depot siting: they exist also to minimise the cost of serving customers from the depot. Each day calculations can be made to route the vehicles in accordance with customer demand so that they operate at least cost. Disadvantages can be that customers are not always served by the same delivery man, each driver has to know a far wider area than if he had a regular journey, and customer orders need to be received sufficiently well in advance to enable the calculations to be made. The greatest advantage to be gained in using a vehicle scheduling technique is in identifying the optimum vehicle fleet size and type in the first place, and then allocating customers to fixed rounds, or routes, by considering expected probable order quantities. It is appropriate to review periodically the composition of the routes, perhaps at six-monthly intervals.

VIII. INDUSTRIAL RELATIONS AND PERSONNEL MANAGEMENT

Industrial relations are concerned with the practices and problems arising from the employment relationship between employer and employee in an organisation and with finding ways of preventing or overcoming internal strife.

Sometimes an emphasis is placed on the economic and legal aspects, industrial collective bargaining, rule-making and legislation, organisation and regulation at the workplace and, in particular, on the workers and their organisations, the employers and their organisations and the relevant Government agencies. The subject also overlaps with personnel management and studies in human relations as applicable to industry. Hence the whole field stands at the crossroads of many disciplines, *e.g.* economics, law, psychology, sociology, political science, systems analysis and organisation theory.

TRADE UNIONS, COLLECTIVE BARGAINING AND THE LAW

History and legal background

The history of unionism in Britain has been one of struggle against industrialists and Parliament to secure legitimate recognition and wage settlement procedures. It was during the time of the Industrial Revolution in the late 18th and early 19th centuries when workers suffered long hours, low wages and poor conditions under the factory system that associations were formed to improve the position. They also campaigned for the abolition of unfair methods of payment under the truck system. Workers were forced to spend a certain amount of their wages in shops owned by their employer, or were paid in goods produced by the firm, which goods they then had to sell to get wages, or suffered long pays (delayed payments), which resulted in the workers getting into debt.

The prevailing attitude of *laissez-faire* handicapped attempts at union organisation. This implied that the maximum social good could be achieved by allowing the citizens to pursue their own interests without state intervention. As part of the unwritten law of the land was freedom of trade, governments did not encourage the formation of unions to counter the power of employers. Unions were considered to be acting in restraint of trade by seeking to regulate wages and conditions of labour, etc., and in the long run their actions, it was thought, would only have damaging effects on the economy. This approach resulted in much hardship for workers, since in a system of complete free bargaining between the individual and his employer the power lay almost wholly on the side of the latter.

Union historians have memories of the *Combination Acts* in force from 1799 to 1824, which forbade all combinations of men with heavy penalties for infringement, and of the experiences of six Dorset farm labourers of Tolpuddle, who were sentenced in 1834 to seven years' transportation to Australia for administering an illegal oath with the aim of forming a trade union.

During the 19th century union organisation became stronger, certain landmarks being the foundation of the Amalgamated Society of Engineers in 1851 and the Trades Union Congress in 1868. However, the legal position of unions was ambiguous and before 1871 they were frequently prosecuted for criminal conspiracy.

In 1871 the *Trade Union Act* for the first time gave unions legal recognition. They were allowed to become registered, with protection for their funds, and were freed from any risk of their actions being deemed illegal for being in restraint of trade. Agreements between individual firms and unions could be made legally binding if the parties wished. Otherwise, under section 4 (4) of the Act, there was no obligation to enforce any collective agreements. Since then unions and employers have tended to prefer this position of having agreements which were binding "in honour only," and which could be broken at any time by either side.

By the *Criminal Law Amendment Act* of 1871 striking was in effect made impossible by the restriction on picketing, but the right of peaceful picketing was restored. Unions grew rapidly after this, and by 1896 some 1½ million people were members of trade unions out of a working population of 12 million.

In 1901 the Taff Vale Railway Company successfully sued a union for £23,000 damages, on the grounds that its members had conspired in a strike to induce workmen employed by the company to break their contracts of employment and to interfere with company traffic. The effect of this decision was to render practically worthless the nominal right to strike. The unions campaigned to improve their position and in 1906 the *Trade Disputes Act* was passed. This gave a broad definition to a dispute to cover a wide variety of circumstances and protected employees and employers from criminal and civil liability for their actions or for any loss or hardship that might be caused to anybody as a result. The right to peaceful picketing was confirmed, though the law did not proclaim a positive right to strike. It gave the trade unions further immunities from the torts that had been established—mostly by judges in common law. Tort is a civil wrong other than a breach of contract. This meant that unions could could not be sued for negligence, deceit, threats of injury, libel, slander, etc., and were not liable for the actions of their own officials.

In 1909 in the Osborne case a railway worker took action against his union to prevent part of his contribution being used for political purposes. The House of Lords ruled against the unions, stating that, according to the definition of a union established by the 1876 Act, any activities other than industrial were illegal.

The unions campaigned to get this position changed. They argued that business interests were well represented in Parliament by Conservative and Liberal members and that the only practical way to secure independent labour representation was through trade union support. In 1913 an Act made it legal for unions to include any lawful purpose in their constitution including political objects (with "contracting out" provisions), provided its principal aims were those of a trade union as defined in the 1876 Act.

After the First World War, 1914–18, there came worldwide depression, which caused high unemployment and low living standards. Unrest culminated in the General Strike of 1926. The Government reacted the following year with the *Trade Disputes and Trade Unions Act*. This Act outlawed strikes, lockouts and sympathetic strikes aimed at coercing the Government directly or by inflicting hardship on the general public. The definition of intimidation was widened, leaving much to the discretion of the courts. It also became illegal to apply union funds to help in a strike or lockout. One had to "contract in" if one wanted to make contributions to a union's political fund, thus weakening the Labour Party. This Act was a severe blow to the trade union movement and remained in force for nineteen years.

It was after the Second World War, 1939–45, that unions started coming into their own with the repeal of the 1927 Act and with the rationalisation of their grouping, increasingly large and comprehensive unions absorbing multifarious smaller ones. From 1945 Britain benefited for about fifteen years from the maintenance of high employment, which strengthened the position of the unions as manpower became a scarce resource. Increases in productivity and increased money wages led to a considerable improvement in the standard of living.

Although there was no major Government intervention in the activities of the unions until the 1960s there were some important developments in the courts. First there was the *Bonsor* v. *Musicians' Union* case, 1955. Bonsor had been expelled from the union for non-payment of dues but theoretically his expulsion had been unconstitutional. This the union conceded. However, the musical industry was a closed shop so Bonsor wanted to claim loss of earnings, but damages for tort could not be given against a trade union after the *Trade Disputes Act*, 1906. The court ruled that a registered union could not be sued for breach of contract as a legal entity, that the expulsion of Bonsor amounted to a breach of contract, and that damages should be taken from union funds, not individual members.

The *Rookes* v. *Barnard* case, 1964, concerned workers at B.O.A.C. who had threatened to strike over a non-union member working in a closed shop. It was ruled that the defendants, the union leaders (although not the union, which was protected by the 1906 Act) were guilty of intimidation through threatening a breach of contract, and could be prosecuted for conspiracy. The *Trade Disputes Act*, 1965, legalised such a threat if it was connected with a trade dispute.

Structure and function of trade unions

The long historical development of the British trade union movement has resulted in a wide variety of union structure. Though there are about half the number of unions that existed in 1919, Britain has a large number compared to other countries, some 12 million members in 491 unions. The large number is partly due to the value placed on independence, and reluctance to keep to one type as a model. There are four main types of unions, craft, general, industrial and occupational. However, owing to its origins in skilled crafts, union organisation developed horizontal rather than vertical patterns (across rather than coterminous with industrial boundaries).

Craft unions have members occupied in one skilled craft, *e.g.* Boilermakers' Union, Printing and Allied Trades. Many have now opened their membership to semi-skilled or unskilled workers, and are thus often multi-craft or general unions. General unions recruit anyone who cares to join, usually among the semi-skilled and unskilled and are important in the newer industries where skilled trades of the older types are less numerous. An example is the Transport and General Workers' Union (T.G.W.U.). Industrial unions attempt to organise everyone in one industry, irrespective of the occupation. Few industries are organised in Britain in this way, though in the United States and West Germany it is a characteristic feature. Industrial unions have often been advocated as the ideal form of organisation. However, there is the problem as to whether, when rationalisation of the confused union structures is attempted, an industry should be defined by product (as in the car industry), by material (as in the cotton industry) or by process (as in engineering). The National Union of Mineworkers (N.U.M.) has extensive coverage in coal-mining. A type of union that has recently developed is the occupational. In this group all members are in one occupation or industry. Examples are the Transport Salaried Staffs' Association (T.S.S.A.), the National Union of Teachers (N.U.T.), and the Amalgamated Union of Engineering Workers (A.U.E.W.).

Another form of classification is between "open" and "closed" unionism. At one extreme, a closed union restricts its area of recruitment to a specific grade of worker or to a particular industry and region, while at the other extreme a union may be open to recruitment of all types of workers.

Unions often try to protect their membership and increase their bargaining power by enforcing closed shops. A closed shop may be "pre-entry" in which case a worker must be a union member before obtaining a job. This type is confined to craft unions who use it to preserve the exclusiveness of their skill. Only those who have completed an apprenticeship are allowed a union card and entry into such training is strictly controlled. The object is to keep their particular skill in demand so that its scarcity value will strengthen their bargaining power.

More common nowadays amongst all kinds of workers, including semi-skilled and unskilled, is the "post-entry" closed shop which requires a worker to join a certain trade union on becoming an employee. One hundred per cent union membership in a factory obviously helps the work force present a united front to the employer. Trade unionists also argue that it is not fair that people who don't join the union and pay its dues should benefit from the improvements in pay and conditions which the union has fought for. Employers often support such closed shops because they help stabilise their relations with their workforce, but some people argue that they encroach on the freedom of the individual and may restrict mobility of labour. Certainly in recent years the closed shop has become a major political issue.

The prime purpose of a trade union is to maximise the economic and social well-being of its members. In 1920 Sidney and Beatrice Webb, leading socialist intellectuals, defined a trade union as "a continuous association of wage-earners organised for the purpose of maintaining and improving the condition of their working lives." Owing to the increase since 1945 in white collar unions (civil servants, bankers, office clerks, teachers, etc.) the definition would have to be widened to include salary earners as well.

Trade unions undertake a number of functions, of which the most important is probably collective wage bargaining which is discussed later. A union helps to counterbalance the weakness of labour when bargaining in the market-place. If there is greater competition among workers for jobs than among employers for workers, the former are in a weaker position for bargaining; and they will be so except possibly under conditions of full employment. If labour is unprotected by a union, employers looking for ways of reducing costs are likely to reduce wages rather than seek greater efficiency through better organisation or greater use of capital, etc. Collective bargaining enables workers together to press for improvements in a wide range of matters, such as conditions of work, overtime, methods of payment and holidays, which an individual would find difficult to obtain on his or her own.

An important traditional role was that of safeguarding the job. The most important was the making of rules about the type and length of training required for a particular skill, an attempt to protect individual skills (demarcation) by insisting on who should perform them, and to control the intake of apprentices. Particularly in times of full employment, when certain skills are becoming obsolete and deployment of labour is needed, this function leads to overmanning and demarcation disputes.

The trade union movement supports the Labour Party and finances its own members in Parliament. The position of the trade union movement in Britain has completely changed in the last fifty years. From being an organisation fighting for recognition it has become a force which has a part to play in the country's affairs. Union leaders accept positions of economic and political authority on boards of nationalised industries and certain Government committees, and are frequently consulted by the Government on matters affecting the economy which have an impact on the social changes and conditions of the people. For example, representatives of the General Council of the T.U.C. sit with representatives of industry and Government on the National Economic Development Council, an influential planning body.

Employers' associations grew up to offset increasing union power and to assist their members (firms or individuals) to fight strikes. They also originated to prevent the undercutting of wages. They developed locally and then combined in industry-wide federations such as the Engineering Employers' Federation. They undertake a number of functions concerned with collective bargaining and industrial relations such as agreement on holidays, standard and overtime wage rates, safety measures and the organisation of apprenticeship and training schemes. About 100 of the 1,400 employers' organisations are national ones and it is chiefly these which negotiate directly with unions. The Confederation of British Industry was formed in 1965 as a centralising institution. It has about 13,000 companies as members as well as over 200 trade associations and employers' federations. It is a national spokesman for manufacturing industry, nationalised industries, banks and service industries and offers advice on industrial affairs to the Government. Other leading associations are the Retail Consortium, the Association of British Chambers of Commerce and the Chamber of Shipping.

Powers of unions

The ability of a union to exert pressure depends on many factors. Much depends on the skill of its officials, the size, financial strength and type of the union, its strength of membership, sense of solidarity and discipline. The skilled union is usually more powerful than the unskilled, especially if its members are key workers, such as electricians or maintenance engineers. They are also in a strong position when they can force a closed shop, as in printing. Much depends on the type of industry. If the union is operating in a contracting industry like cotton or shipbuilding, it will become smaller and weaker. In a growth industry such as electronics the union is in a good position to increase membership and funds, and again it is powerful if the industry is exporting goods (for example, cars and engineering). One of the chief powers of the unions is the ability to limit the supply of labour to industry and to paralyse it by the calling of a strike. As unions support the Labour Party officially and are represented directly in Parliament, this can be an important source of power, though it must be noted that about 30 per cent of the union membership vote for the Conservative Party and a smaller number contract out of the political fund to the Labour Party.

There are clear limitations to the power of unions to raise wages. Much depends on the current state of trade, on public opinion and on the proportion which labour costs bear to other costs. Elasticity of demand for the product must also be taken into account. If demand is elastic an increase in price will lead to a more than proportionate reduction in the amount demanded, a large proportion of the price change being borne by the manufacturer. Thus if a wage increase occurs, to avoid raising the price and hence losing customers, the employer may look for ways of substituting labour by another factor, such as capital if the latter is relatively cheaper. This would significantly reduce the demand for labour and unemployment may result. The power of unions to raise wages is greater when demand is inelastic. Since even a considerable change in price will lead to only a slight change in demand, the greater costs as a result of wage increases can be passed on to the consumer through higher prices and the employees have little need to fear redundancy and unemployment.

A theory once popular with economists which attempted to explain how wages were determined was the marginal productivity theory. It applied the principle of diminishing utility to wages and stated that an employer would employ labour as determined by its marginal utility, $i.e.$ its productivity at the margin. It was based on the idea that the wages paid were determined by the marginal product of labour, so that if an extra man employed added more to production than he did to costs he would be employed, and this would represent the level of wages that must be paid in the firm. Although it is an inadequate explanation of the level of wages, and although there are many problems in measuring marginal productivity, certain general principles relating to this theory can be observed in practice. For example, when an employer tries to estimate the worth of the existing labour force and the costs of employing an extra man in relation to his expected productivity he is applying marginal analysis. Similarly in cases of new purchases care must be taken to estimate the relative worth of different items. The theory also illustrates the point that if productivity can be increased employees can obtain higher wages.

Given the conditions of demand for labour in one industry, a certain number of men can be employed at a wage measured by their marginal productivity. In Fig. 45 DD is the demand curve for labour, showing the marginal productivity. Consequently this is the equilibrium wage rate for a given supply of labour. Thus OM men can be employed at a wage OR. But if the demand for labour, as shown by the demand curve, falls from D to D^1, there are two alternatives. If the same wage is to be preserved, then fewer men, OM^1, can be employed, and M^1M men are unemployed. But all can be employed if the wage is reduced to OR^1. The tendency is for the unions to maintain the previous wage rate at the expense of unemployment. A fall in wages has a harmful psychological effect on workers, who fear that a reduction, once allowed, will strengthen the hands of the employer.

If equilibrium is reached at P, with all the union's members employed, and conditions of demand then change to D^2, owing to an increase in productive activity, the union can force wages to OR^2 if there are no unemployed. But when unemployment exists, the effect of an increase in the demand for labour would not normally be higher wages, but more employed, OM^2, at the same wage OR. However, in Britain during 1971–2 unionised labour was able to secure higher wages partly at the expense of others who have remained unemployed. The model illustrates the position where, if demand increases, represented in a shift of the demand curve to the right from D to D^2, unions will be able to secure higher wages, OR^2, at the expense of MM^2 unemployed. The latter could have been employed if the wage rate had remained at OR.

In practice perfect supply and demand conditions do not exist and hence wages are not determined by principles of marginal productivity but by certain principles largely established by collective

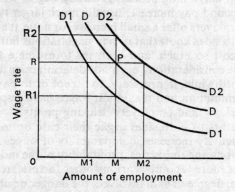

FIG. 45. *Relationship of wage rate to labour demand and employment*

bargaining procedures, and a major factor is the relative power and skill in bargaining of the respective organisation. However, factors determining particular supply and demand conditions for labour and the value of the job done will naturally be important considerations as well.

National collective bargaining (the formal system)

The system of national collective bargaining originated as a result of the principle asserted by the Royal Commission on Labour in 1894, and reaffirmed by the Whitley Committee in 1917, that good relations in industry depend on agreements being made between "powerful trade unions on the one hand and powerful associations of employers on the other." The "Whitley System" is really only influential today in the public sector (the nationalised industries, civil service, teachers, health service workers, etc.). It involves representatives of the employer and the trade unions meeting together on a National Joint Industrial Council (N.J.I.C.) or Whitley Council to re-negotiate their particular national agreement. Agreements used to run for an unfixed period, but nowadays annual reviews have become the pattern. They are not legally binding and cover only broad aspects of working conditions (basic wage rates, hours and holidays). The details are in theory supposed to be worked out in individual plants, offices and workshops by management and through consultative committees. In practice informal bargaining on the shop floor has tended to determine these matters (as we shall see later).

The national bargaining process generally begins when the union claims an all-round pay increase, usually much larger than it expects to get. The employers offer a small increase, or none at all. They then negotiate. Both sides know that if their negotiations fail the resultant struggle will cost so much, and both try to estimate the outcome. Weighing these considerations, each side determines on a certain wage which it is worthwhile, if necessary, to accept or to pay rather than fight. These minimum and maximum wages have respectively been called the workers' and employers' sticking points.

The negotiators of both sides argue their case on many grounds, such as productivity increases, comparability of wages with those of other occupations and industries, profitability of the industry and the need to attract more labour. Various other factors are the value of the work done, degree of skill involved, the danger or unpleasantness of the work and the general conditions of supply and demand. Increased cost of living has always been a point argued by the unions for wage increases. Unfortunately this often results in an all-round escalation in prices and wages. This is because unions wish to maintain the established pattern of wage differentials between workers in different occupations and of precedents set by awards in other industries. Sometimes considerations of social justice are important. In the strike in the nationalised coal industry in 1972 the government was in effect taking the role of an employer. It was forced by the Wilberforce Commission to recognise that the miners' case was a special one, justifying a substantial increase in wages. Where no very clear path is seen, an agreement may be reached to split the difference between the two sticking points or to adopt some other form of conciliatory compromise.

During the nineteenth century developments in trade union organisation and numerous Factory Acts helped to improve wages and conditions in many industries. However, workers in unorganised trades still received unduly low wages while in some industries, *e.g.* agriculture, union organisation was unable to obtain a wage comparable to that of similar grades of workers elsewhere. Public opinion forced the Government to intervene in wage determination.

In 1909 the Government passed the *Trade Boards Act*, creating Trade Boards for certain "sweated" trades (*e.g.* tailoring, paper, box-making, etc.) which suffered from low wages, poor conditions and long hours. They had powers to fix minimum time or piece rates for different classes of worker. In 1918 a further Act applied the Trade Board to other employments in which the workers had no efficient machinery for regulating wages. They were renamed Wages Councils by an Act in 1945 and subsequent legislation, as in 1959, extended their scope.

At present they set a legal minimum wage for over 3 million workers, although lack of efficient inspection means that many employers pay less than the law requires.

Strikes, causes and effects

The "Whitley System" accepted that in the last resort the trade union side could use strike action and the employer's side impose a "lock-out" (now very rare) to force an agreement if negotiations broke down.

It was intended that strikes should only occur when the formal machinery for negotiating wages or settling local disputes had been exhausted. Such strikes would be "official" insofar as they were called by the union leadership who usually set aside part of union funds as strike pay for those involved.

However, since the war the vast majority (well over 90%) of strikes have been unofficial (*i.e.* have occurred without the approval of trade union leadership) and unconstitutional (*i.e.* have occurred in breach of the relevant grievance procedure). Such strikes often develop from small irritations which build up to a flash-point, the last difficulty resulting in a sudden decision by local leaders to strike before adequate discussion of the problems can take place. The majority of these problems are over wages, but may also occur over issues of discipline, dismissals, working conditions, welfare facilities, safety questions or local interpretations of national agreements. They usually last at most only a few days, and are frequently due to the ineffectiveness of industry-wide grievance procedures in resolving local disputes quickly. These procedures tend to take even individual grievances away from the plant to remote districts or even national meetings where decisions are long delayed. A "wildcat strike" is often a quick and effective way to sort out a dispute, to clear the air and reduce worker frustration.

There has been a great deal of argument about the causes of strikes. Some argue that strikes about wages are in fact about other issues like frustration, self-respect and dignity, whilst others have argued that all strikes, whatever reason the strikers admit to, are in fact about money. Some observers see the strike-prone workers as being isolated from society as a whole and having a strong sense of community (miners and dockers). Others contend that technology is a major factor (as in car assembly plant). Certainly strike activity is not spread evenly over industry. A recent study has shown that 98% of all firms are strike-free and that strike activity is commonest in larger firms (over 2,000 employees). Other surveys show that 90% of all stoppages occur in five industries (docks, coal, motor manufacture, transport and shipbuilding) which cover only 10% of the working population.

It seems fairly clear that strike action becomes a habit in some industries, whilst in others it remains an unusual occurrence. However the habit can spread. For instance in the 1970s health workers, civil servants and other previously docile groups have learnt that militancy pays and are much more willing to take some form of industrial action than they have previously been.

Strikes can cause serious damage. Employers suffer disorganisation of work, and loss of output, contracts and customers; and shareholders lose profit. The workers suffer loss of income, because though they may get strike pay from their unions in an official strike, they lose unemployment pay. Workers in other industries may lose their jobs if their work is dependent on the supply of materials from a strike area. The public suffers shortages of the product or service, the union suffers because strike pay reduces its financial reserves. The country's economic development is retarded, with adverse results on the balance of payments.

The informal system and the shop steward

In the past under the formal system the union officers derived their power partly from their skills of leadership and partly from the fact that the relatively weak bargaining position of the workers made them dependent on the union and its officials. However, circumstances have changed considerably in the last twenty years.

Actual earnings have tended to drift away from those established at national level because of a dramatic increase in bargaining activity at workshop level between management and an official known as the shop steward. The shop steward assumed the role of local bargainer, filling a vacuum caused by the lack of official union organisation at the workplace, the multi-union structure there, the shortage of full-time union officials and the inadequacy of national collective agreements. The latter tended to be confined to a narrow range of subjects such as wages, hours and holidays, and in many cases these did not bear any relation either to work done or to the financial needs of the family. The stewards were able to negotiate about all kinds of other matters, often of a local nature, such as disciplinary practices, job rights, recruitment, redundancy and the introduction of machinery.

Full employment conditions in Britain from 1945 to the end of the 1960s have intensified employer competition for labour, and some firms have had to pay more than the centrally agreed rate to attract labour. This has also been a major factor increasing the power of shop stewards, who have been able to employ the threat of strikes to obtain concessions from management, such as informal extra payments and fringe benefits, above the nationally agreed rates. They have acquired largely autonomous power derived not from their trade unions but from the sanctions that the groups themselves are able to impose. Members have also been less dependent on unions and officials than formerly. Strike pay used to be vitally important, and power to grant or withhold it gave the officials a powerful sanction. Today wages are high enough to allow workers to save enough to tide them over during short strikes or else hardship during such periods can be alleviated by social security payments to strikers' families.

The shop steward first came to prominence in the engineering industry during the First World War. He is elected, usually, by a show of hands by the workers, and approved by the district committee. Though he is neither a national nor a local union officer he has been found invaluable as the local representative of union members. His functions are seldom clearly defined, but he is usually responsible for union recruitment, for seeing that dues are paid regularly, for liaising with workers, processing individual grievances, representing union members' interests to management and seeing that agreements between his union and the firm are observed. Sometimes grievances can be quickly discovered by means of the shop steward, who can form an effective communication link upward from workers to management. Firms without shop stewards or with inactive ones tend to find that disputes can flare up suddenly. The shop steward's job of management liaison usually involves shop-level negotiations over pay and working conditions outside the scope of national agreements, plus the role of link man in informing the workers of management proposals such as changes in workshop practices or redundancies.

The shop steward is often an intelligent and competent man, who may have greater capacity than his immediate work demands, and if respected for the job he is doing and treated fairly, he can be a considerable asset to a firm. He fills two roles, one as a worker and the other as elected representative of the workers, and care must be taken to ensure that in any discussions with management it is known which role he is playing. On average a shop steward represents about 40 workers although the size of the work groups they represent varies considerably. Within most largish firms they co-ordinate their efforts by forming shop stewards' committees, often consisting of stewards from several different unions. Usually they elect a convenor or senior steward to act as chairman of the committee and as chief negotiator.

Wage productivity agreements

Conventional bargaining between employees and employers usually brought about an increase in labour costs to the firm as a result of higher wages, without the firm gaining anything in return. In the 1960s many managers started to withdraw from their employers' associations to negotiate special wage productivity agreements with their own employees, preferring to do this than to continue bargaining with full-time trade union officials who were often considered to be out of touch. Management saw these wage productivity agreements as a way of reducing industrial discontent, improving labour production and lowering unit labour costs. The workforce would agree to the removal of restrictive practices in return for, say, increased leisure, higher pay or better fringe benefits, relating perhaps to a firm's pension or sickness schemes. Restrictive practices might include excessive overtime working, rigid demarcation between members of different unions or the overmanning of machines to retain jobs when labour-saving techniques are introduced.

The first important productivity deal was concluded between the management of the Esso Refinery, Fawley, Hampshire and various trade unions in 1960. By 1970 more than 30 per cent of industrial workers were covered by such agreements. Unlike normal collective bargaining, productivity bargaining is concerned with predetermining the division of additional wealth and cost saving which could be created through more efficient working practices and organisations. The Fawley agreement was significant in that management and workers agreed to settle differences by the free exchange of information.

Reform measures

In the past twenty years the voluntary system of national collective bargaining has been increasingly criticised, and has grown acutely complex as one layer after another has been placed on top of the existing machinery. There are now over 1,400 employers' associations, just under 500 trade unions, as well as wage councils, *ad hoc* bodies for special circumstances, etc. The diversity of negotiating machinery caused much confusion, partly due to the growth of the informal system of bargaining at workshop level, leading to conflicts with union officials or with the other sections in the union.

In recent years many have argued that one factor accounting for the instability of the economy has been the unsatisfactory state of industrial relations. The concern of successive governments with stabilising the economy, promoting long-term growth and controlling the two short-term constraints of inflation and balance of payments has involved them more and more in wage problems and collective bargaining matters. During the 1960s Governments tried policies of price control and of limiting the effectiveness of unions to increase wages, an important factor in price determination. For details, see Chapter III.

At the same time there was increased demand from union members for more democracy and freedom to determine their own affairs. They found their actions limited by the spread of Government power and control from the top, and open conflict occurred. Attempts to find appropriate solutions were made by the Government.

The findings, called the Donovan Report of the Royal Commission on Trade Unions and Employers' Associations (established in 1965), were published in 1968. It pointed out that there were two systems now existing in industrial relations, the traditional or formal system, embodied in official institutions, which was now a façade, a pretence, because of the growth of the second, the informal system. The basic problem was summarised as follows:

> *Thirty years ago the gap between nationally negotiated rates and actual earnings was small. Today it is very substantial indeed. And the range of issues effectively covered by national bargaining is almost derisorily small.*

The observations of the Commission related primarily to the engineering and building industries. The Commission itself pointed out that its analysis dealt mainly with the organised male manual workers in private industry and was less relevant to public industry, white collar employees, women and the unorganised.

The Commission proposed a system of collective bargaining whereby company, factory and plant agreements should be the basis of industrial relations in Britain and should be extended to cover various conditions on a more national and coherent basis than at that time existed. It suggested the continuation of the voluntary system since any attempt to make collective agreements legally binding would be "a breach with a long tradition of our industrial relations," which would not improve the position or reduce the number of unofficial strikes.

An *Industrial Relations Act* was proposed whereby all company and factory agreements were required to be registered with the Department of Employment and Productivity. In addition it suggested the creation of an independent Commission of Industrial Relations (C.I.R.), which would help to improve industrial relations by guiding and stimulating the bargainers. This body would deal with problems over the registration of agreements and have the power to investigate both disputes and general difficulties, including recognition problems.

When the Conservative Government was elected in 1970, it felt that stronger measures were needed. Their *Industrial Relations Act, 1971*, was influenced partly by their own policy document "Fair Deal at Work," partly by the Donovan Report and partly from ideas imported from the American system. It sought to reform industrial relations, reduce the number of strikes, create a better balance of power in industry between employers and unions, provide a new framework of courts and tribunals for solving disputes, and promote individual liberty.

Brief details of the Act were as follows:

1. It introduced legal procedures for union recognition, for regulating the closed shop, for disclosure of information necessary for collective bargaining. There was also encouragement for the spread of legally-enforceable collective agreements which were to be legally binding unless they contained a disclaimer clause.

2. It gave employers the right to sue trade unions for "unfair industrial practices." In effect this meant unofficial strikes, sympathy strikes and so on. The intention was to force the trade union leadership to try to control their rank and file.

The State also gained powers to set up a national emergency procedure in the event of industrial action likely to damage the national interest. This included the imposition of a cooling-off period and the holding of a secret ballot before a strike could begin.

3. It gave individuals new rights vis-à-vis their employer (protection against unfair dismissal) and vis-à-vis trade unions (the right to belong or not to belong to a trade union and to natural justice in its internal proceedings).

The success of these measures depended on the willingness of trade unions to co-operate with the Act by remaining in the Trade Union Register, the willingness of the employers to institute proceedings against trade unions and the ability of the Industrial Tribunals, the strengthened C.I.R. and the new National Industrial Relations Court (N.I.R.C.) to enforce the law.

In fact the vast majority of trades unions left the register, even though they lost many of the legal immunities they had traditionally enjoyed. It was a symbolic act of defiance intended to emphasise their hostility to the Act. Employers, for their part, continued to be wary of using the law against trade unions because they felt this might cause long-term damage to their own industrial relations. As for the N.I.R.C., it became involved in a series of spectacular confrontations with trade unions, being forced to arrest five dockers and to fine the A.U.E.W. for contempt. Both cases led to widespread protest strikes and eventually, in the latter case, anonymous donors paid a £47,000 fine, which the engineering union was refusing to pay, in order to avoid a national strike

The *Industrial Relations Act* has been generally regarded as a failure, not only because of the dramatic incidents it provoked but also because it had very little influence in reforming the industrial relations system generally.

In 1974 the newly elected Labour Government repealed the Act, but far from reverting to the traditional abstentionist role of labour law in British industrial relations, introduced, with trade union acceptance, a series of major Acts which, added to the few isolated statutes previously enacted, constitute a complex web of individual and collective employment rights, favourable to trade unions, their members and to workers in general. These rights include:

1. *Recognition*—unions can take employers to the Advisory Conciliation and Arbitration Service (*see* below) if they refuse to recognise them for bargaining purposes.

2. *Closed Shop*—there are now no legal barriers to the closed shop.

3. *Disclosure of Information*—a union has the right to demand that an employer discloses information for the purposes of collective bargaining.

4. *Trade Union Activity*—an employer must not take any action deterring employees from joining a trade union, or from taking part in its activities nor victimise union activists.

5. *Time-off*—shop stewards, etc. must be given time off with pay for union duties and training. Ordinary trade union members must be given reasonable time off without pay for union activities.

The relevant Acts were the *Trade Union and Labour Relations Act*, amended in 1976, and the Acts discussed on pp. 22–3 and 279. In all cases the term trade union refers to a union which has been accepted as an independent body in no way reliant on the employer for its funds or organisation by a new official called the Certification Officer.

At present there is evidence that much of the law operates only on the fringes of industrial relations and that in the important areas of manufacturing industry and in the public sector, unions and collective bargaining are so well established that the provisions of the new Acts are largely irrelevant because unions have already achieved the rights embodied in them. They are already recognised, they have already secured a closed shop, their stewards are already allowed time off for union duties and so they would never allow one of the members to be unfairly dismissed. Admittedly the Acts help the badly organised, the weak, women especially, and immigrants, but these are not the areas where Britain's industrial relations problems occur. The strikes and the unrest, the big wage demands and the bargaining power to achieve them are all concentrated in the large companies and the nationalised industries.

A fundamental problem is how in fact to persuade union officials and their rank and file to strike a reasonable balance between the primary responsibility of their organisation to look after the interests of its members and its public responsibility towards society as a whole, upon which its conduct can have such a profound affect.

The Donovan Commission proposals tried to answer the problem and since the mid-1960s there has been a steady move towards formal plant level bargaining in the private sector. In some ways Donovan no longer seems quite so relevant because in the 1970s the major problem has become industrial relations in the public sector where national bargaining is still the primary means of determining wages and conditions. Until the 1970s the nationalised industries and the public service unions had been fairly restrained considering the massive bargaining power some of them had at their disposal. But inflation and the fact that governments tended to make the public sector bear the brunt of any incomes policy, has led to considerable industrial strike action. All these public sector strikes were official, called by the leadership usually after a ballot of the membership and after agreed negotiating procedure had been exhausted.

So far the only way successive governments have found to try to contain the bargaining power of these groups is to introduce an incomes policy. But experience has proved that it is, at best, only a temporary holding operation. Many observers are looking first to the Advisory Conciliation and Arbitration Services (A.C.A.S.) and secondly to an extension of industrial democracy (*see* pages 288–94).

A.C.A.S. is one of the statutory bodies set up by the new legislation. It is independent of the Department of Employment and gathers together all the advisory, conciliation, and arbitration machinery in one agency. Since the 1896 Conciliation Act the government has recognised that it has a role to play in trying to settle disputes, even if it is only a means by which employers and unions can get off the hook once they have taken up entrenched positions. Usually in peacetime both conciliation (*i.e.* trying to coax the parties into an agreement) and arbitration (*i.e.* making judgment on a dispute and either picking a winner or awarding a compromise settlement) has been voluntary and carried out only by the invitation of the two parties. It has also been relatively unimportant.

Since the setting up of A.C.A.S., which is also mainly voluntarist in its approach, and its severance from the Department of Employment, unions appear more willing to use its facilities to settle disputes with management. In 1976 for example there were 3,500 conciliation cases handled by A.C.A.S., a rise of 35% on the 1975 figure. However, the crucial test of A.C.A.S. comes if it can begin to influence the industrial relations in the big firms. At present most of its cases involve small firms and fairly minor issues. Its long-term aim would be to become involved by invitation in the major disputes.

European trade unions

The increasing scale of multi-national corporations and the development of international economic groupings such as the European Community has led to trade unions exploring ways of co-operating with each other across frontiers. Some of the problems involved in arriving at agreements on wages, productivity, etc., are religious and political differences in organisation and differing monetary and legal systems. So far multi-national bargaining has not extended to wages but has been confined to conditions and redundancies. Philips, Fiat-Citroën and Fokker-VFW are some of the firms which have been affected. Areas where future co-operation may occur include:

1. production transfers;
2. training and retraining schemes;
3. social protection of workers when rationalisation schemes occur;
4. competence of local management.

If a transnational organisation is in conflict with workers in a particular country, it may in the last resort shut down the plant or transfer it to another country. A less extreme measure is transferring production to a plant in another country during the duration of a strike. When unions in different countries support each other through solidarity strikes, they may be able to counter such measures, as the Ford workers in Britain and Germany proved possible during a strike at the Ford factory in Belgium in 1969.

Nearly all European trade unions are affiliated to one or other of the following three organisations:

1. World Federation of Trade Unions (W.F.T.U.), a communist-dominated body;
2. International Confederation of Free Trade Unions (I.C.F.T.U.), formed after 1949 because of the political trends in the W.F.T.U. Most Western European Unions and also the American Federation of Labour are members;
3. World Confederation of Labour (W.C.F.), predominantly Roman Catholic.

In June 1972 the two groups of I.C.F.T.U. member organisations in western Europe, the European Confederation of Free Trade Unions (E.C.F.T.U.) and the Trade Union Committee (E.F.T.A.-T.U.C.) for the European Free Trade Association (E.F.T.A.) agreed to create a single union organisation. In 1973 the European unions agreed to form the European Trade Union Confederation (E.T.U.C.) of national trade union centres. Its aim was to overcome the traditional divisions between communist, catholic and free trade unions.

Belgian unions are divided into two main groups, the Confédération Générale du Travail de Belgique, which is socialist and affiliated to the I.C.F.T.U., and the Confédération des Syndicats Chrétiens Belges (a Christian organisation affiliated to the W.C.F.). There is a third much smaller liberal group. Complications of the Flemish and Walloon division are superimposed on this.

French unions are largely organised on an industrial basis and normally in an industry there are three unions, each belonging to one of the three confederations. The Confédération Générale du Travail, closely linked with the Communist Party, has over one million members. The Christian Confédération Française des Travailleurs Chrétiens has over half a million members and the Confédération Générale du Travail Force-Ouvrière rather fewer, being a socialist "white-collar" union. All workers are free to join or not to join a union, the union shop being forbidden by law. About a quarter of the labour force are members, but French unions are not weak in times of industrial unrest, tending to be supported as much by non-unionists as unionists.

After the Second World War Germany was administered by the Allies and, with help from the British T.U.C., the West German unions were reorganised from scratch. There are sixteen unions representing different industries, and workers in an industry must be members of the union. A strike by law can only be called by a 75 per cent majority in a secret ballot. The Deutsche Gewerkschaftsbund (D.G.B.) is affiliated to the I.C.F.T.U. and has informal links with the Social Democratic Party. The German troops may also join a union. The *Agreements Law* of 1949, amended in 1952, provides the basis for the forming of associations and for collective bargaining.

Italy's unions are relatively badly organised. Collective bargaining tends to be on a national level with no government intervention. The three main groups are the Confederazione Generale Italiana del Lavoro (C.G.I.L.), the largest and affiliated to the W.F.T.U., the Confederazione Italiana Sydicati Lavoratori, affiliated to the W.C.F., and the Union Italiana del Lavoro, formed by right-wing Socialists who broke away from the C.G.I.L.

The Dutch economic and political system, like that of some other continental European countries, has been called corporatism, which defines a situation where power is shared by group leaders who agree on how the resources and benefits of society will be allocated among the groups. The three pillars (zuilen) of Dutch society are the Roman Catholic, Protestant and general or "neutral" group. These three zuilen tend to affect the choice of clubs, organisations, political parties and trade unions for most Dutchmen. Like the political parties, the trade unions are also divided into three groups, socialist, Catholic and Protestant, and the employers' federations are divided into the General Catholic Association, the Protestant Christian and the Central Social Employers.

Since the formation of the Labour Foundation in 1945, representing both sides of Dutch industry, employers and unions have tried to work closely together. The trade unions have benefited from the threefold division of Dutch life, since the officials are well paid and equipped as a result of the way resources are allocated institutionally.

PERSONNEL MANAGEMENT

In industry the role of the personnel manager is not one of managing people directly except within his own department, but of advising and providing specialist knowledge or services to other members of management. Though the personnel function is a specialist staff function it must be stressed that "line" authority has immediate responsibility for personnel administration, for organising and treating individuals so as to obtain the greatest use of their abilities, thus attaining maximum efficiency for themselves and the firm.

Although the personnel manager is concerned with problems in human relations, the scope and significance of his work will differ in one firm from another depending on its size, policy, product and particular problems, and depending also on his competence and influence. In one organisation his chief role may be selection, in another industrial relations, in a third management development. In a few it is still chiefly concerned with social or welfare work, which provided the basis for the early development of personnel management in the First World War and the 1920s. In some it will encompass all of these activities.

Management need to make the maximum use of human resources from the shop floor to the boardroom, as well as to optimise the use of resources such as plant, money and materials. Generally in the nineteenth and early twentieth centuries the human and personal problems of people at work were the most neglected aspect of industrial activity. People were hired and fired as the business demanded, and as there was a constant supply of men from whom to choose, employers gave scant regard to the misery caused by their policies.

Recruitment and selection

Exploring and developing sources of new employees and selecting and training the most appropriate recruits are based upon knowledge and understanding of the firm's needs. A broad plan is developed within which corporate objectives are geared not only to technical and market contingencies but also to human resources. All elements in the firm should work together to establish the broad principles. Manpower forecasts need to be drawn up based on how many people in various jobs should be recruited annually to replace wastage, and on future plans of the firm concerning expansion, contraction, etc. The personnel department helps plan the future manpower needs of the firm and in devising strategic plans to meet them.

The personnel manager plays an important role through liaison with the Department of Employment, and with sources of recruitment such as the employment exchange, schools, other educational institutions and commercial employment agencies. Advertisements are placed in journals and the press. Important details regarding a vacancy are the nature of the job, pay, conditions of employment and qualifications required.

Proper selection and placement of new employees is a prerequisite for the development of an effective working force. The aim is to engage employees in jobs in which they are successful and to which they are suited. In a small firm it may be sufficient to advise the personnel manager that a compositor or junior clerk is needed. However, in a large factory with a multitudinous selection of jobs, each requiring a special skill, something more specific is required.

The practical problem is to discover what human qualities make for success or failure in a given job and to recognise and assess these qualities in candidates for employment. The matching of the two takes great skill. "Job analysis" is a detailed description of how a job is being done and how it might be done in the future. "Job description" (or specification) is a statement of the physical, mental and temperamental qualities required of an individual for the satisfactory performance of the job. It also says to whom he is responsible, who is responsible to him, what his role is and what are the general parameters around his job. Thus individual jobs may require one or more of the following: physical strength, intelligence, creative ability, good colour vision, pliant fingers, an ability to endure monotony, mathematical aptitude, etc. By relating these to the job analysis, a job description can be prepared which will give the personnel manager a clear guide as to what to look for when placing advertisements and interviewing applicants. "Job evaluation" is another important aspect. This has been discussed in Chapter VII.

A standard employment application form is helpful in obtaining essential facts before a candidate is interviewed. This should contain sections relating to personal particulars, education and training, past employment, medical history, spare time activities and job preferences. The interview should be a narrative by the candidate rather than an interrogation by the personnel officer. It should be short and factual and based on a prepared plan. The person interviewed also needs to be given relevant information about the firm as well as details of the job for which he is being considered. The interviewer wants to collect relevant information to enable him to form a picture of the candidate in relation to the job in the future, and he will usually grade candidates into probables, possibles and unsuitables. A short list will be made which is sent with the recommendations of the personnel officer to the manager of the appropriate department, who will make the final selection.

Sometimes tests may be used in addition to interviews, to provide a more rational basis for selection. Intelligence tests usually consist of routine items to demonstrate fluency with words and ability to juggle figures. Aptitude tests which measure physical and mental dexterity are sometimes used. An example is the kind used by data processing departments in many companies to measure a candidate's potential ability as a computer programmer.

A personality or projection test is sometimes used in an attempt to discover personality traits of which the individual is probably unaware himself. Another type is the group test often applied to graduate entries. A task is given to, say, ten applicants. In the discussion as to how these tasks are to be accomplished, those who have superior organising abilities and other useful qualities can be recognised by the group as its informal leader.

Induction records and labour

The personnel manager usually has responsibility for induction, which involves the introduction of new staff to the practices, policies and purposes of the organisation. Although this properly begins when the newcomer starts work it really commences with his first contact with the organisation, his reception, interview and initial treatment. The personnel manager will keep all the information considered relevant by the firm concerned in order to give an up-to-date picture of every employee's career. Basic information will probably include a personal history sheet, the original application form, medical reports, timekeeping records, assessment reports, records of internal movements (transfers and promotion) and any relevant personal information.

Records are kept of absenteeism so that the underlying reasons can be discovered and remedied if possible. A gross absence rate can be calculated as:

$$\frac{\text{Number of man hours (or half days) lost}}{\text{Total number of possible hours (or half days)}} \times 100$$

Labour turnover, if excessive, is a hidden source of inefficiency and can be very costly to a firm. The rate of labour turnover during a period can be calculated as:

$$\frac{\text{Number of employees who have left}}{\text{Average number employed}} \times 100$$

People leave jobs for a variety of reasons, *e.g.* promotion, redundancy, disorderly conduct, retirement, etc., some of which are "controllable" by the firm and others of which are "uncontrollable." The personnel department ascertain reasons why staff leave. Analysis may reveal conditions which can be remedied, such as the inefficiency of selection procedures, poor working conditions or low morale.

Labour turnover can be affected by external community influences, including the employment situation in related industries, population movements, changes in age groups and the prosperity of the community. Labour turnover tends to decline with increasing age, the acquisition of special skills and the length of service with the firm.

Sometimes the personnel manager is involved in meetings to discuss whether or not someone should be sacked, or to advise on the interpretation of rules which have been infringed. This has become more widespread since 1971 when the law began to protect employees from unfair dismissal. If a certain employee is no longer required by a certain department on the grounds of redundancy, and his report is good, personnel are required by the terms of the *Redundancy Payments Act*, 1965, to try to transfer him to another department.

A useful technique for finding out how management and workers respond to their jobs and conditions is an attitude survey by means of a written questionnaire (*see* Fig. 46) or confidential interview. It can serve as a means for uncovering sources of irritation, which if known can be rectified, and as an aid for the formulation of new policies and improvements. Sometimes, if surveys are used too frequently, staff may feel they have to write something, even if they do not have any particular complaints. Their answers are known as "invented grievances." However, careful checks are usually made so that trivial or unjustified comments are eliminated.

Training, welfare and health

Personnel management is concerned with getting the best out of people at work at an economic level and in ensuring that the social system in the company does not militate against this.

After the *Industrial Training Act*, 1964, the education and training of all staff, from apprentices to senior managers, received a tremendous impetus. It has become recognised as an important lifelong process, given the conditions of modern society, which is complex and ever changing. Large firms have specialist training and education officers involved in this work. The challenge set by the increasing complexity of industry is being met by the response of a rapidly

---

JOB COMMENTS SHEET

Code No.: _____ Floor: _____ Date: _____

Please record below any occasions when aspects of your work were particularly satisfying *or*, alternatively, particularly frustrating.

WHAT HAPPENED?   *Satisfying*   *Frustrating*

HOW FREQUENTLY DO SUCH OCCASIONS OCCUR? (Tick appropriate frequency)

                Daily   Few times/month

                Few times/week   Less than once/month

FIG. 46. *Job comments sheet used by a firm in a secretarial survey*

developing educational technology, utilising the aid of television, overhead and slide projectors, tape recorder, etc.

Some companies train their young apprentices, etc., in areas other than those directly related to the job. Many firms accept training in activities likely to lead to earlier maturity, and in the development of leadership qualities through their participation in charitable and service activities. Social activity is regarded as part of "attitude" training. Outward-bound courses help to train graduate apprentices, potential managers and supervisors for positions of responsibility, and to develop self-discipline, confidence and expertise in man-management and human relationships. Social activities, clubs, sport, competitions, dances, outings, company magazines, etc., help to make the organisation less of a mere workplace and more of an environment where employees can develop a wider social life. Adequate canteens should be provided or perhaps luncheon vouchers in lieu of them.

The personnel manager should be available to give or secure advice on a host of employees' problems, without becoming too deeply immersed in the employees' lives outside the factory or office. He will also be responsible for running savings schemes and dealing with superannuation and pension funds. He should never be fully identified with either management or employees but should stand midway between the two groups, trying to weld them into one common unit. However, this is exceedingly difficult; on the one hand his job is by definition a management function and he may be seen by workers as a management lackey; on the other hand if he puts the union view to management, managers may assume he is siding with the workers.

He has the job of seeing that the provisions of the Factories Acts and other industrial regulations are observed. Regulations cover such matters as physical working conditions, safety, first aid provision, hours of work for women and young people, and notification and investigation of accidents and industrial diseases. Under the *Health and Safety at Work etc. Act*, 1974, trade unions have the power to appoint safety representatives and demand disclosure of safety information and the setting up of safety committees within the office or factory.

INDUSTRIAL SOCIOLOGY

This section discusses selected fields of social psychology and sociology which are relevant to problems of industrial organisation, supervision and management.

Needs and motivation

A person's ability, the quality of his tools and materials, the nature of the work environment and the job, and efficient managerial co-ordination of the efforts of the workforce all assist the effective performance of a job. It also depends on the worker's motivation and morale, which are variables partly dependent on the above factors and partly independent of them. A person's basic needs and wants determine to a large extent his actual behaviour, and if they could be identified and measured for relative importance, it might be possible to design an organisation in which the employee satisfied them by contributing to the overall aims of the organisation.

There is some agreement that motives can be divided into physiological needs and psychological wants. The former relate to such physical or basic needs as hunger, thirst, shelter and sex, and are common to all regardless of social environment. The latter seem infinite in number and it is difficult to find any wants that are common to all mankind. A number of sociologists have followed the American, A. H. Maslow, in classifying needs as follows: physical, safety, social and self-actualising; and in maintaining that people tend to satisfy their needs in this order of priority. These needs can be looked upon as motives for work since it is by working that sufficient money can be earned to make their satisfaction possible.

A person living at the bare subsistence level of existence works solely to satisfy his basic needs for survival, the actual quantities required varying according to such conditions as climate, work, etc. Another important aim is to seek protection from danger, threat and deprivation, to look for security for oneself, one's family and possessions. Today safety needs are met fairly adequately in modern industrialised society. However, industrial trouble still occurs when job security is threatened by changing economic conditions which cause unemployment.

The loss of freedom due to industrial work is an important cause of discontent. Motives tend to become "monetised," since workers are likely to feel money is the solution when something is wrong, and to try to satisfy their needs outside the place of work. As a result employers have been apt to think that industrial harmony is only a question of paying sufficiently high wages to satisfy lower-level physiological and economic needs. This was one drawback of the classical approach, which is discussed shortly. Primary emphasis was on obtaining efficient task performance, the feelings, morale, psychological life and intellectual capabilities of the staff being considered secondary.

For most people the lower-level needs are reasonably satisfied, and they have begun to look for the satisfaction of their other needs, not merely indirectly by what money can buy for them in their free time, but directly from their working life. In any case the law of diminishing returns may apply to such material incentives as "money" after a certain income level is reached. Workers may start increasing their absenteeism, since the need for money may become secondary to the need for leisure.

One important need is for socialisation, the opportunity to associate with and be accepted by others and to belong to a group. The social atmosphere is just as real and as important in industrial life as the physical environment. This fact was discovered by Elton Mayo, an American social psychologist who carried out one of the earliest studies of behaviour within work groups, which is discussed in detail shortly.

However, at a later period some researchers and organisation theorists began to argue that motivation is not a question of man's social needs alone and to place more emphasis on the organisation and the job itself. They maintain that worker satisfaction is not achieved merely by improving working conditions (for example, by having better canteen facilities, air conditioning, longer holidays—a classical approach), or by recognising man's social needs, but by providing opportunities for the workforce to achieve its higher-level needs. If these needs are recognised by management through their efforts to make work more meaningful for the men, they will elicit greater involvement and hence improve overall worker effectiveness. These needs are (*a*) egoistic (the need for reputation, status, self-esteem, self-respect, self-expression and achievement), and (*b*) self-actualising (the need for a sense of complete intellectual, spiritual and psychological fulfilment).

Some of the methods which have been tried by firms to increase job enrichment and to meet needs for self-expression are discussed in the rest of this chapter. Here one particular study by the American psychologist, Fred Herzberg and his associates can be noted, carried out with accountants and engineers, who were asked to say what was going on when they were feeling both particularly good and particularly bad about their jobs. It was found that genuine motivators were usually connected with accomplishments and the feeling of growth in job competence. What made them feel bad were background considerations such as inadequate salary, poor working conditions, insufficient job security, poor supervision, etc., which Herzberg called "hygiene" factors.

It is necessary to point out that what a particular man wants from his job cannot be quantitatively determined for all time. The needs of the young married executive between twenty-four and forty are usually at a maximum, as his expenses are highest. However, except in occupations where rewards are linked directly to physical effort, he tends to earn most money between fifty-five and sixty when his children have left school and his wife may have started a part-time job.

There is no single ideal incentive, because incentives vary from one society to another and from one individual to another. Young men tend to look for challenging posts and opportunity for promotion while older men often prefer routine and security rather than change. One man values money most, others leisure, achievements, friendliness of supervision or opportunities for promotion. Some may be just content to hold on to their jobs and to avoid trouble in any form.

Not all behaviour is determined by basic needs. Social and economic forces within or outside the firm or factory community can also be important determinants of behaviour. Examples are the influences of childhood experiences, education, national culture, geographical location, loyalties and friendships.

Three possible approaches to organisation have been called Classical, Human Relations and Systems. Though all three approaches cover aspects of organisation which cannot be ignored, they each emphasise factors that sometimes pull in opposite directions.

The Classical School

The classical approach is to study the activities that need to be undertaken to achieve objectives. Once these activities are identified, they are grouped to form individual jobs, sections, etc., the aim being to obtain efficient specialisation and co-ordination without physically overloading supervisors or managers. People are linked together in a chain of command, each knowing his specific responsibilities, and certain rules or principles of organisation are developed. Some of the writers associated with this approach are Fayol in France, Taylor in America, Urwick and Brech in Britain.

Early investigators in industrial psychology believed that if the tools of production were improved through the use of the incentives of money and the environmental conditions of work (temperature, noise, etc.) or the fear of unemployment, productivity would increase. Frederick W. Taylor founded a school of thought in the United States in the 1900s which believed in what was known as "scientific management." He considered that motivation was largely an individual matter, and viewed employees in machinelike terms. He believed in selecting the best man for the job, instructing him in the most effective methods to use and giving him adequate wage incentives through payment by results. Broadly the idea was that if the load or frictions were decreased (the job made easier or lighter), or if economic incentives were introduced, output per man would increase, just as a machine will go faster if the power is turned up. By applying these principles Taylor reduced the number of workers needed to load wagons at the Bethlehem Steel Company, and increased the wages of the remainder and the profits of the owners.

Further details about the contributions of classical writers to management studies are discussed in Chapter X in the the section on organisation structure.

The Hawthorne Studies and the Human Relations School

A weakness of the classical approach is that when work is unskilled and simplified as in the process line and automated industries, workers may become alienated by the lack of job satisfaction obtainable from the firm. This may cause them to be unduly concerned with monetary incentives, which is likely to result in a greater frequency of strikes and other disturbances than in more interesting occupations.

Many social psychologists and sociologists have criticised the classical school for not taking sufficient account of people's likely behaviour under different organisational arrangements and the influence of informal groups. They argue that unless a manager understands the expectations of his workforce and the conditions necessary before they contribute maximum effort, their skills and capacity for co-operation will be under-utilised. The originator of what became the human relations approach was Elton Mayo, who was called in by the Western Electric Company in the United States in the 1920s to give advice on its labour problems. The conclusions of his study upset the prevailing notions of how workers reacted to authority and how production could be stimulated.

Mayo carried out a series of investigations at the Hawthorne Works in Chicago between 1927 and 1932. In the Relay Assembly Test Room experiment a group of five girls doing light assembly work were isolated in a separate factory location. Mayo started on the assumption that improved output would follow improved physical and financial conditions. His research team made experimental changes in their working conditions, such as improved lighting, a shortened workday and rest-breaks, and they offered better wages. While carrying out this the researchers asked the workers for their views and advice, thus arousing an interest in what was going on, and output gradually increased.

In the famous twelfth experimental period all the changes which presumably improved conditions of work were gradually withdrawn. It was now found that the girls worked even better. It was concluded that improved output had been due to social and psychological factors. A sense of responsibility and mutual co-operation with the researchers combined with growing group cohesiveness had motivated the girls rather than financial incentives or good work conditions.

What conclusions were made from these various tests? First it was discovered that productivity was directly related to opportunities for active participation in small groups by employees, who felt they were making meaningful contributions to the aims of the firm. Mayo also found that there was no simple correlation between increased group cohesiveness and improved productivity. Cohesiveness could lead to output restriction and effective opposition to management goals. In the bank-wiring room of the Western Electric Company he found male workers disregarding financial incentives. He discovered that the informal group had selected a leader who was not the same person as the official one. There was an unofficial code of behaviour which exerted a strong influence over group members and impressed on them certain rules. Examples were the idea that one should not turn out too much work, or tell a supervisor anything to the detriment of a work-mate. Thus it was recognised that an informal structure of social relations existed behind the formal organisational structure.

Professor Douglas McGregor of Massachusetts Institute of Technology (M.I.T.) in his book *The Human Side of Enterprise* formulated the concepts Theory X and Theory Y to refer to two possible outlooks held by people regarding human behaviour. He argued that employers had regarded the average man as basically lazy and averse to work, so that he had to be coerced to ensure his working towards organisational goals. These assumptions, which formed the traditional philosophy of direction and control he called Theory X. This he believed to be basically wrong, since it was founded on a misinterpretation of human behaviour. People were not by nature passive or resistant to a firm's objectives, but became so as a result of experience in an organisation. He thought that most people found work satisfying if it was voluntarily performed and as natural as play or rest. A man would exercise self-direction in the service of objectives to which he was committed, and would respond to "carrots" rather than "sticks," money being by no means the most effective carrot. This was his Theory Y.

People cannot easily be fitted into neat categories. For example, one can look at needs in relation to incentives, time, circumstances, cultural conditions, etc. The field of human behaviour and motivation is a difficult one and many theories put forward are subjective and incapable of scientific proof. The problem with much research is that generalisations tend to be made, the assumption being that the conclusions drawn from experiments in particular situations have general applicability. As long as research findings are treated with care, and note taken of the particular conditions under which they were conducted, some can be useful in adding to our knowledge and understanding of human nature in certain situations, and hence of benefit in problem situations at work.

Informal groups

Following the Western Electric studies, research began on the influence of social groups within organisations. A short summary is made here of some of the findings referring to group behaviour.

Managements may try to develop or retain a situation in their firms in which the only important relationships are between individuals or between formally organised work groups. Formal groups will have leaders placed in authority by management, and such groups may coincide and overlap with informal social groups. However, even when no formal groups exist, unofficial groups will tend to develop spontaneously, with natural leaders who have risen with the active support of the group. Rather than being thought artificial or unrepresentative they should be regarded as natural developments of personal relationships, and an important element in the fabric of the firm. Leaders of such informal groups may not be the same as the officially appointed leaders, and in such cases may well have greater power and influence with the workers than the latter. Thus the informal group should be recognised as an important source of control.

Informal groups in industry may develop on several different levels, for example, according to job, work proximity, seniority, age, union associations, personality likes and dislikes, race and religion. Perhaps the two most important groupings represent those identifying with management and those identifying with the employees. An example of the first would be a group of supervisors who, though spatially separated during working hours, meet in the canteen or socially after work; and of the second, young employees who, though similarly separate during the working day, form associations which do not coincide with the formal groups in which they work.

The sum of the attitudes and behaviour of several individuals is not equal to the group behaviour of those same individuals. A person may adopt a role within a group which he would not hold independently of that group. For example, a member may feel less tolerant towards management, reflecting the ethos of the group rather than his own opinions. Group pressure can be brought to bear on individual members to ensure that they fulfil the roles expected of them. Extreme measures can take the form of ridicule or violence, though such measures are rarely required, since members wish to retain the respect of their comrades. The tendency to conform to group pressures can be strong. In one experiment by the American psychologist S. E. Asch, a number of people were instructed to agree on a judgment concerning the length of certain lines which was clearly wrong. Other people found the task of assessing the length of the lines easy when left alone, but when each had to voice his opinions aloud in company with the majority, who had been told to take another standpoint, there was a strong tendency for the odd man out to fall in line with the majority view.

Since the behaviour of individuals can be affected by their group membership, management are wiser to try a policy of establishing a sense of common purpose in group standards rather than of improving the attitudes of members of a group as individuals. An important factor here is morale, which tends to be a group phenomenon, since an employee may well be prepared to mobilise his energy and interest in the enthusiastic and active pursuit of a collective venture in which he would have little interest at the individual level. Group loyalty may result in a greater loyalty to the whole organisation than would have resulted from the sum of individual loyalties.

Primary groups contain about a dozen members. Their chief characteristic is face-to-face relationships, and the difficulty of extending this form of communication to a large number limits the size of the group. To be effective such groups have a distinct identity, acceptable and capable leaders, a sense of common purpose, standards of behaviour, quality of achievement and a structure based on a system of roles and relationships whereby people know what appropriate behaviour is expected of them according to their status position.

Status implies a position within the group. A worker may be a member of more than one group in the firm, his position being different in each case. His status is based on the degree to which he helps the purposes of the group and is derived from his skills, knowledge and intellectual or personality characteristics. Considerable significance is attached to external signs of status: a man tends to be assessed by his wage, grade, position, size of office or desk, etc.

Many traditional "prestige ratings" exist that give informal status to the worker which is unknown to management. The status situation is one of the commonest causes of strikes. Many industrial disputes indicate that it is the wage differential between various jobs that is significant rather than the absolute wage rate, for it is the differentials that establish prestige.

The business firm, no less than the small work group, constitutes a setting for the actions of its members. The modern large firm is more than a physical structure for organising production and distribution. It is a community within the community, having a genuine social and psychological structure of its own.

The Systems School

In recent years more empirical investigation has been made into the impact of organisation structure, controls and technology on behaviour. It has been found, for example, that mass production and continuous-process production involve different types of human relations problems. At this point a summary of the classical and human relations approaches to work organisation would be useful before discussing the systems approach.

The classical approach tended to study the job which needed to be done, to treat the machine itself as the system and to organise the workforce accordingly, with specialisation and division of labour, etc. The human relations approach placed the primary emphasis on the workers and on studying how work could be shared among them so that it could be made more meaningful and interesting. It was no easy task to match jobs to the abilities of men and to bring contentment and interest to work, since the division of labour had become so fragmented in many jobs that it was difficult to make them exciting. One of the suggested methods of increasing satisfaction and morale and relieving monotony was the training of a worker to do several jobs hitherto done by separate individuals, so that responsibility for several different operations would enable him to finish the making of a complete part. This is known as "job enlargement." Another method, called "job rotation," was to give a group of workers the chance of learning the tasks of others so that they could change round from one job to another from time to time. The objective was to design each job so that it would be a challenge and an incentive to effort, thereby reducing frustration and the possibilities of industrial strife.

The systems approach tends to stress the importance of studying how work should be shared between man and machine. A developing field is ergonomics, the study of the interaction of physical and human systems. It aims to produce the right kind of relationship between man and his environment, whether in a factory, office, shop or other place of work, and to increase efficiency by ensuring satisfactory working conditions and relieving the worker from distracting influences and unnecessary stress. Specifically it refers to the "man–machine" system, to emphasise that a system often consists of both man and machine. Thus machine parts need to be designed with human physiology in mind: controls, for instance, have to be placed where they can be reached comfortably and scales and dials have to be designed for effective reading.

The systems approach emphasises that for any study there is an appropriate system to be investigated, and the aims of the study determine both the boundaries of the system and the sub-systems. A system is regarded as a set of interdependent parts which together form a united whole that carries out some function. A change in any one may cause one or more of the others to alter. As emphasis is placed on the decisions that need to be made to achieve the firm's objectives, and as decisions depend on information and information on communication, the organisation is created from an analysis of information needs and communication networks. Focus is centred on decision-making rather than on activities or departments, since it is through the decision-making process that objectives and policies are established and action taken which results in either success or failure. An attempt is made to simplify decision-making through appropriate organisation so that minimum reference is necessary to higher authority. This approach is discussed in Chapter X.

For some years many have been aware of the need to reverse the trend towards reducing the discretionary content of work by subdivision of task and the assembly line (the classical method). An interesting experiment is a recent decision by Volvo in Sweden to build a complete motor-car plant on the principle of self-contained teams or workshops, each responsible for the assembly of a section of a car. The workers will have full responsibility for organising production and the division and pace of work and its control.

Worker participation and involvement

Various methods have been tried in recent years to make staff feel a greater identification with their firm, and generally to improve morale. One technique has been by altering the method of remuneration. Individual methods of payment are broadly of two types, a time basis (usually an hourly rate) and piecework; it is sometimes possible to pay a piece wage based not on the output of each individual but on the combined output of the group workers. If the group is small, so that each worker is in close contact with the others, the effect of this method will be to encourage co-operation between them. Under group schemes, the earnings of a group are pooled, each member receiving a proportion of the value of any output beyond a standard amount.

These methods have merits, depending on the conditions and nature of work to which they are applied. If one method is found impracticable, others can be tried. For example, many disputes caused by piecework problems at the Longbridge plant of British Leyland resulted in 1972 in a switch to a flat-rate system. Since 1967 Norsk Hydro A.S., a Norwegian shipping company, has adopted a novel scheme of job rotation as part of a policy of achieving better work relationships. Workers are encouraged to master new groups in addition to their own, pay being based on the number of groups a worker can handle.

Another method is a formal profit-sharing scheme by which a

fixed percentage of the net profits as defined by agreement is paid as an annual bonus. One variation is co-partnership, by which the workers are annually given a share of the profit in the form of ordinary shares in the business, capitalised from the company's profits. This arrangement has the advantage of giving the worker the rights of a shareholder and the benefit of receiving financial documents relating to the business. In many cases managers have the opportunity of purchasing shares at low prices.

In France companies have to devise ways of giving workers a greater share in the rewards of industry, and in the nationalised aircraft and car companies workers can become stockholders. The aim of all such arrangements is to boost the morale of the staff by helping them to feel that they belong to the organisation, and to encourage them to stay with the firm in addition to accumulating capital. It is agreed that they are an incentive to company growth, improve staff work and reduce turnover of labour.

One problem with many profit-sharing plans is that the worker rarely sees how his bonus is related to his own efforts. Another, concerning typical suggestion plans, is that many individuals will not submit key suggestions because they do not wish to be singled out from their group, particularly as it is recognised that ideas often evolve through the collaboration of many. Joseph Scanlon devised a scheme to overcome these difficulties by the use of group incentive plans, where workers could see a connection between their own efforts and the rewards they obtained as a group. The Scanlon plan involved the submission of suggestions for the improvement of work procedures to committees consisting of both management and labour. If a suggestion was adopted and resulted in reduced costs of production, the savings should be returned to the workers as soon as possible as a percentage of their basic pay rather than as a flat bonus.

The idea of worker participation in management has often been put by left-wing supporters as a move towards some form of industrial democracy in Britain. At one time the T.U.C. strongly opposed the idea as it threatened the role of the trades union. Instead they wanted an extension of their powers so that more questions would become subject to negotiation with management. Instead of simply covering basic matters like pay and conditions of work, negotiation and joint control should cover such things as safety, redundancy, dismissals and the implications of mergers (*see* page 291 for recent developments).

There are a number of objections to workers' participation in major decision-making. For one thing, they are not experienced or trained in the necessary skills. Secondly, if they sat on the board, a clash of loyalties might occur between the interests of the firm, which might dictate mechanisation and labour-saving, and those of the workers, who would be opposed to the unemployment which might well be the result. Thirdly, it can be argued that the union's role is not to secure representation in management but to see that management power is not abused or used against the interests of labour. Fourthly, there is the danger that if workers' representatives are included in management bodies, the meetings will become perfunctory, with the real decisions taken beforehand by the managers alone.

To a greater extent in future management will have to take decisions with the active agreement of their workpeople. The labour force is more mobile, better educated and has greater job opportunity than before.

West Germany has a form of worker control in some industries. After 1945 a number of works councils were created and built round the principle of co-determination or *Mitbestimmung* (deciding together) as a way of bridging the gap between management and labour, and of reducing trade unions' influence in the factory. A recent law extended the power of works councils, allowing them the right to veto dismissals until the employee's case has been investigated by a body created for this purpose. In Holland and Germany there is also the worker-shareholder supervisory board in addition to a board of management. It is the upper tier of a two-tier board of directors. Representatives decide on general policy, but not on day-to-day decisions of management. At shop-floor level workers' participation is fairly effective. In West Germany it is quite customary for a worker to refer to his company as "we" and to feel a part of it, in contrast to the situation in Britain where few companies attract such personal loyalty. The European Commission has proposed that all member states adopt the system of a supervisory council.

In Britain managers are usually aware of the advantages to be gained from allowing workers to take responsibility. There are many methods. Minor ones are grievance committees, which hear employees' complaints, and discipline committees, where workers help to judge and penalise fellow-workers for misdemeanours. Schemes which go further include the creation of a democratically elected joint consultative body. This may be a works council concerned with the maintenance of good industrial relations or a joint production committee concerned with discussing methods of increasing productivity or organising technical changes in the factory.

The minutes of meetings should be circulated to employees so that they can see to what extent their own views have been aired by their representatives. Representation should be on a "per grade or status" basis rather than on a "per department or factory" basis. At the table all should be equal, though it is as well to appoint the managing director as nominal chairman and, in practice, to let the chair alternate between two vice-chairmen appointed from the management and employees respectively. The personnel manager is probably best suited to act as joint secretary supported by one of the employees. Among the few isolated examples of full workers' participation in Britain is the John Lewis Partnership.

Gleitzeit ("sliding" or "flexible" time) has been introduced in West Germany. In those firms where it has been tried it has boosted productivity and worker morale and has reduced absenteeism. Two different time elements are involved. One is "core" time, normally from 10 a.m. to 4 p.m., when everybody should be at work. The second is "flexible" time, three optional working hours at either end of the day. Time-recording machines help in the staggering of times of arrival and departure.

Philips in Holland and I.C.I. in Britain are examples of firms which have introduced schemes to make work more interesting and rewarding. I.C.I.'s weekly staff agreement programme (W.S.A.), ratified with the unions in 1969, aimed to give workers more responsibility over their jobs by eliminating supervision and also making their jobs more flexible. Workers were put on a salaried basis, eliminating the division between staff and manual workers. A poll take subsequently showed that the workers felt happier with the job after W.S.A. was introduced.

Some years ago Fred Herzberg undertook a controlled experiment at Bell Telephone, the subsidiary of A.T. & T. Though the girls it employed to handle customers' complaints were well educated, the amount of individual discretion they were allowed was extremely small. The replies to complaints were mostly standardised, since the form of words was dictated in advance by the company's rule book. The job was heavily supervised and the girls were in effect no more than high-class copy typists. A special group of girls took part in the experiment whereby they were encouraged to draft replies to complaints and to use their own words. This reduced the load on the supervisors and it was found in the long run that the jobs of both the girls and supervisors became more interesting.

Both the T.U.C. and the C.B.I. have changed their policies on workers' participation in recent years. In 1973 the T.U.C. advocated a two-tier system similar to the German model. Later they wanted a

50–50 share of power in a single board of directors. The majority report of the Bullock Committee, set up by the Labour Government in 1975, recommended in 1977 that a law should be introduced compelling companies employing more than 2,000 staff to accept workers on to their boards. There would be a unitary board based on a $2X + Y$ formula, the $2X$ being equal numbers of directors appointed by shareholders and employees, and a smaller group Y nominated by the $2X$ element. The minority Report, which the C.B.I. preferred, suggested a two-tier board. The main Bullock proposals were opposed by the C.B.I. and sections of the trades union movement. At one time the C.B.I. favoured legislation to make works council obligatory in larger firms. Their current view is for a flexible approach with the law playing a low role, and for the spread of voluntary "participation agreements" in individual companies, each scheme tailored to meet individual needs.

Conflict and bargaining

The practical man tends to argue that resources are scarce, that some people only live better if other people live worse. Life is seen as a conflict of self-interest over divisions of the cake, or a struggle of distributive bargaining, in which the gain by one side implies the loss of another or in which both partially lose when forced to compromise. In terms of industry, a direct conflict may be seen to exist between the worker's wage claims and the objectives of management to make maximum profits, since unless higher prices are charged any increase in wages is regarded as meaning reduced profits.

These assumptions have been taken over into the field of collective bargaining, which is seen to involve a struggle between two sides, employers and workers' organisations, over how the wealth which has already been created by joint effort should be divided. In this situation there is no clear answer available and bargainers proceed according to subjective criteria.

Some commentators tend to see disagreement as an essential element in industrial relations and in life generally, and they argue that any deep attempt to get to the root of conflict in order to suppress it entirely would result in a restriction of someone else's freedom. In a free society conflicts between individuals and groups are inevitable.

However, it has been argued that such a system does not produce stable results. Certain psychologists and sociologists are inclined to this point of view, stressing the danger of destructive conflict, which would disappear if the individuals were integrated into a harmonious working group within the system, identifying with its interests and values.

It can be argued that the division between management and employees does not necessarily have to result in conflict caused by interests thought to be diametrically opposed. In other words, the workman can feel an identification through membership of the organisation for which he works as well as through membership of the employee group. It can also be claimed that conflict between two groups need not necessarily be resolved to the detriment of one side, but that both sides can gain from the outcome.

Basically both approaches contain an element of truth. Though there is ample area for conflict between employees and management, there is also a wide potential area of common interest. People feel a sense of pride in working for an efficient well-known organisation, and its success is in the interests of both groups.

Conflict may be either rational, involving facts such as statistical data, or irrational, with our emotions and attitudes playing a crucial part. It is an inevitable and legitimate element in human relations. If a dispute occurs, for example, between a supervisor and a work-study engineer over different proposals, they may resolve it not only by compromise but also by an increased understanding of each other's aims and intentions. On the other hand, if the supervisor interprets the work-study engineer's proposals as a threat to his authority, the conflict may soon become an irrational one in which fear or anxiety, or even a sense of failure, may lead to hostile attitudes on the supervisor's part. This may prove capable of solution only through the calling in of a third party, who is able to transform the dispute from a "cake-sharing one" in terms of power to a "problem-solving one." The aim is to get the two conflicting parties to have the same subjective image of reality. If a conflict is analysed deeply, the outcome may well suggest itself.

Some authorities argue that conditions of industrial peace would result if both sides, management and labour, recognised their particular disputes with each other not as unique and insolvable except by establishing positions of strength, but as having features that commonly occur in conflict. If a trained mediator was called in, he would consult with each group in turn, pointing out some of the problems in the field of perception and stereotyped thinking which prevent them from seeing the situation from a common standpoint.

He would use the process known as controlled communication, which is based on the idea that analysis of a problem situation by a third party will reveal, after the perceptions of both sides have been altered, that neither side may have to compromise and that a solution can be found which benefits both parties, a form of integrative bargaining. This has been termed in a role-playing situation a "positive-sum-game," in contrast to a "zero-sum-game" where one person gains at the expense of another. Examples can be found in productivity agreements or in methods to increase worker participation in industry.

IX. LEADERSHIP AND DECISION MAKING

LEADERSHIP

Successful leadership depends not only upon the leader but also upon the group he leads, and the environment within which he finds himself. The leadership section of this chapter discusses the types of leadership there are, the characteristics of those who are being led, the span of control a leader may have and the extent to which he should delegate his responsibilities.

Every employee works within the confines of the objectives of his company and managers must operate with these objectives fully in mind. It is for this reason that objectives and responsibilities of the firm are discussed here, although they could equally well have appeared in other parts of the book. Similarly, innovation is necessary for the growth and even the survival of many companies, and it is through innovation that some of the most striking management and leadership achievements have been attained. The NASA missions into outer space and landings on the moon are a good example.

Although specific topics have been chosen to be included in this section on leadership, it will be necessary to call upon other relevant sections of the book to provide a broader picture.

Leadership types

It is commonly assumed that a leader possesses certain characteristics or traits which distinguish him from other members of the group, for example, superior intelligence, organising ability and lively personality. But the qualities and skills required in a leader are determined to a large extent by the situation in which he finds himself: some are better equipped to lead in one situation than in another and Sir Winston Churchill is an example of a good war leader who may have been less capable in times of peace. The best leader is the one who is able to rise to the occasion by making the right decisions swiftly and by organising others to carry them out, thus helping the group to achieve its objectives.

The most effective leader is the one who most nearly satisfies the needs of his followers or subordinates, as well as achieving agreed objectives set for the group. Research has shown that there can be identifiable differences between managers who achieve high-level performances from their employees and those who do not do so well. In his *New Patterns of Management* (McGraw-Hill, New York, 1961), Rensis Likert has found that managers or supervisors with the best records of performance focus their attention on the human aspects of their subordinates' problems, and on building effective work groups who are set high achievement goals. He calls them "employee centred." The good leader sets standards which are attainable, but not easily. High standards help people experience a sense of greater achievement, provided the standards are realistic, sensible and well understood by both manager and subordinate alike.

In contrast, Likert argues that managers who expend their energies on improving productivity by concentrating upon "keeping their subordinates busily engaged in going through a specified work cycle in a prescribed way and at a satisfactory rate as determined by the standards" tend in reality to have lower productivity results. He calls such managers "job centred." They may become personally involved in doing the work themselves instead of encouraging and training others and listening to their ideas. The most consistently productive departments are those in which men feel the least supervisory pressure. Likert distinguishes between close supervision, in which workers are told exactly how to execute a job, and general supervision, in which managers make clear the objectives and then leave their subordinates to carry out the tasks in their own way, with minimal supervision. A connection exists between high productivity and general supervision and between low productivity and close supervision.

There are three basic styles which a manager may adopt. He will not fall precisely into any one of these categories, but will display characteristics of each in dealing with situations during his working day. He will, however, tend more strongly towards one individual style, due to his own particular personality.

    1. *Dictatorial*. The manager will decide what action to take and impose his decision upon his subordinates without discussion.

    2. *Pseudo-democratic*. The manager will describe the situation to his subordinates, allow them to state their views and then form his own conclusion.

    3. *Democratic*. The manager will put the case for and against to his subordinates, take a consensus of opinion and act accordingly.

A manager is influenced by his own sense of values, the extent of his confidence in his subordinates and his own leadership inclinations. Some managers function more comfortably and naturally as highly directive leaders. The resolution of problems and the issuing of orders come easily to them. Others perform more ably in a team role, where they share many of their responsibilities with their colleagues and with their subordinates. Much depends on the level of security which the manager feels in an uncertain situation. Once a manager releases direct control over the decision-making process, there is less predictability of the outcome. Some managers have a greater need for predictability and stability in their environment. The dictatorial approach is sometimes the more effective since it is closer to the style of the entrepreneur, who takes both the decision and the responsibility for its eventual success or failure.

The more power there is vested in one individual the more flexible will the decision making be. He is far better able to take decisions on his own, whereas if he were required to report back to a committee for every decision there would be built-in delay and a variety of opinions which would need to be reconciled.

The manager is also influenced by the attitude of his staff in general, who have their own ideas of how they expect the manager to act in relation to them. This attitude depends upon:

1. the value placed on independence and readiness to take responsibility;
2. the ability to tolerate potentially ambiguous situations: some people prefer to be given clear-cut directives than to be presented with a situation which requires them to evaluate alternatives;
3. the extent of the interest taken in the problems of the business;
4. the extent of the understanding and identity with the goals of the company;
5. the extent of the knowledge and experience to cope with any problems which may arise;
6. the expectation of a share in decision making;
7. the influence of senior management and the type of company;
8. the environment in which the company exists.

If a general feeling of confidence in and respect for a manager prevails, he has greater freedom to adapt his behaviour to the needs of the situation. He does not feel that he is perceived as an authoritarian on those occasions when he has to make the firm and sometimes unpleasant decisions which occasionally arise.

Organisations, like individuals, have values and traditions which inevitably influence the behaviour of people who work in them. The factors may be environmental, such as traditional company policies, the nature of the work group or the activities of competition. Some people believe that the manager should be dynamic, persuasive and autocratic, since the structure of the organisation is basically authoritarian, with command levels rather like the military. On the other hand, many organisations allow considerable scope for a two-way flow of ideas in a "democratic" way, placing emphasis on the importance of the executive's ability to work effectively with people.

Before a group is given responsibility for making decisions, certain factors need to be considered. It is more likely to work effectively as a unit if it has been in existence for some time and the members have been allowed to develop habits of co-operation and confidence in themselves. A group in which people have similar backgrounds and interests generally work better together than one with dissimilar backgrounds.

A subordinate, assuming that he accepts responsibility for his work, will do so in one of two ways. Both have an effect upon how the manager should respond as a leader.

1. The subordinate will agree to do his best, and will work according to his own standards to do what his manager has requested.

2. He will accept full responsibility for achieving results and objectives.

No matter how strong the leadership characteristics of the manager, he needs a commitment to task from his subordinates before the job will be done. The manager must take care not to assume that a commitment is made. The subordinate may, for example, qualify his understanding and acceptance of the job with "as long as" or "if" or "but." In effect, he is saying that he does not feel capable of doing the job asked of him, at least in the terms in which it has been explained, but he does not want to say he will not do it. The manager is being asked to help, and an apparently type 2 situation above is changed to a type 1. It is the manager who is saying that the subordinate is capable, not the subordinate himself, and the manager must therefore keep a very close eye on progress.

A manager frequently operates in an organisational environment which is not necessarily of his own making or choosing. There are two extreme ways in which a company can be structured and they may be called organic and inorganic respectively, the latter similar to the organisation called "mechanistic" by Burns and Stalker in *The Management of Innovation* (Tavistock Publications, 1961). This type of organisation is discussed later. Any one company will be somewhere between these two extremes. In an organic organisation, individual managers have no precisely defined terms of reference and a man may be put in the job "to see what he makes of it." He tends to develop his own terms of reference and is the only person who can really say what he should be doing. He will eventually either merge in with the rest of the organisation, or cause friction until he is eventually removed. An organic structure of this kind initially makes the senior manager's job much easier since he does not have to define precisely what his subordinates should do, although he is hard pressed to adjudicate if different forceful opinions are expressed by his subordinates about a given situation. It becomes an inflexible organisation, because there is no overall strategy or control whereby parts can be extracted, modified and replaced without upsetting other managers' concepts of their own roles. On the other hand, the inorganic structure, like those of the army or the civil service, can be very flexible, simply because the top executives know exactly what are the responsibilities of their subordinates, and can change them relatively easily; it is far easier to pinpoint the blame or give credit where it is due. An inorganic structure will accommodate political manoeuvrings far less readily than an organic one would do and will plainly develop and allow to flourish a different kind of manager and leadership type.

Burns and Stalker, in their study of the attempt to introduce electronics development work into traditional Scottish firms, found that a mechanistic organisation experienced considerable difficulty in adjusting itself to taking on new methods and processes. They defined a mechanistic organisation as one in which individuals carry out assigned, precisely defined tasks, and where there exist a clear hierarchy of control and an insistence upon loyalty to the company. In contrast, an organic type of organisation is more appropriate to unstable conditions and a changing environment where there is a continual adjustment and redefinition of individual tasks; organisation charts showing exact responsibilities and terms of reference are seldom found.

According to Max Weber in *The Theory of Social and Economic Organization* (Free Press, Illinois, 1947), there are basically three types of authority.

    1. *Traditional*—authority conferred by the accident of birth; e.g. that of the Royal Family, the Chairman's son.

    2. *Legal/rational*—a hierarchical structure, as found in the armed forces, a company reporting structure or a social club committee.

    3. *Charismatic*—the following achieved by individuals, such as John F. Kennedy and Adolf Hitler. They can also have an

opposite effect on some people, which is just as irrational as the hero worship.

These three categories are not necessarily totally distinct. There may be considerable overlaps, for example, a member of the Royal Family may be extremely popular, as well as holding a high rank in the armed forces which he has earned for himself. The person who accedes to a position of authority must have had the opportunity to do so, the good fortune to have been around when that opportunity arose, an awareness that the opportunity was worth taking and the ability to carry out his responsibilities and exercise his authority in an appropriate manner—not necessarily in that order.

Delegation

A major function of the manager is to delegate the work for which he is responsible to his subordinates and to monitor and advise them on the progress they make. Coupled with this is the overriding requirement that the department or division for which the manager is responsible should operate effectively. This means that delegation should take place in such a way that as a result the department is relatively better off. A manager may be more competent than his subordinate to undertake a particular task, but if he delegates it and the job is done well enough while he is released to do more effective work elsewhere, then the delegation of that job was the right decision to make.

A good example of delegation is that conferred upon a supervisor by his manager. A manager is responsible for a wide range of activities, discussed in more detail in Chapter X, whereas the supervisor is concerned with planning and control in the immediate future. The sales supervisor is usually the senior salesman in a particular area or district responsible for the selling activities of a group of more junior salesmen, and the warehouse supervisor directs and controls the work of a small number of operatives in the warehouse.

Delegation implies responsibility coupled with authority within reasonable limits, enough to ensure that the job can be completed on time and within any other constraints imposed upon it, such as cost and resource utilisation. The manager puts the person to whom the task has been delegated in his stead, the only difference being that the manager acts as a further checkpoint before the results of that work are passed on up the chain to the next level of management. It is possible to see this happening in the world of politics whenever a delegation is sent to a foreign power to sound out the areas of possible agreement. If the delegation has done its job well enough the responsible Minister meets his opposite number, and finally, when all is set, the Prime Minister is involved. If it had been thought that the Prime Minister could settle the problem without the preliminaries and if the issue had been important enough for the Prime Minister to devote his time to the early negotiations, then doubtless that would have been done. But, assuming a mutually satisfactory outcome, the most effective results are obtained by going through the various phases of negotiation, delegating appropriate responsibility and authority and thus releasing the more senior man for more pressing tasks at that time, as well as allowing further room for manoeuvre if negotiations should break down at an early stage.

Span of control

Jesus Christ had twelve Apostles, there are eleven players in a football team and ten secretaries make up the Secretariat of the Communist Party, of whom the Secretary-General is the most powerful. The size of most control groups, whether they be advisers, team or direct management, usually lies within the range six to twelve, with eight or nine as the most likely. Few men can effectively control a management group of a size greater than this—any larger and the leader almost certainly loses touch and control gets out of hand.

That is not to say that larger groups do not exist—it depends upon the tasks to be performed. For example, a schoolteacher may handle a class of forty children by himself, but the children are, or should be, more subordinate to the teacher than are the adult employees in the business environment. Similarly twenty or so clerks may be supervised by one person.

The lowest level of management may have a large number of people reporting to him, perhaps between twenty and thirty. His job is one of ensuring that the work is done on time and is of the right quality, as well as advising and training new recruits. To help him in these tasks, particularly the latter, he will have assistants, for example, charge hands on the factory floor, petty officers in the navy or supervisors in the department store. An assistant is a senior member of the general workforce; although paid slightly more, in many respects he may consider himself to be one of them. If a strike should be declared, he is likely to walk out with the workers, whereas his manager will stay with the company. The assistant has responsibility for very limited decision-making: he acts as a troubleshooter and helps to spread the workload equally among his colleagues. At a more senior level, the personal assistant to the managing director may act in a similar capacity, but with added status.

The principal factors which influence the span of control are:

1. the nature of the work: this is the most important factor and it is affected by the complexity of the job, the variety of tasks for which the leader is responsible overall and the range and types of decisions which need to be made;
2. the personality and capabilities of the manager;
3. the personalities and attitudes of his subordinates;
4. the relationship between the manager and his subordinates;
5. the personality and expectations of the manager's manager;
6. the industry in which the manager is employed;
7. the organisation structure of the company.

Business objectives and responsibilities

Naturally each firm will have specific objectives and responsibilities, according to its particular structure, size and nature of product or service. Firms also have broad aims and considerations in common. In Chapter V how profits were determined by standard accounting procedures and the implications of those procedures were discussed. This section looks more closely at the concept of profit, how the ideal of profit maximisation works out in practice, and its relation to other factors which a firm has to consider.

The prime motive of a person starting in a business (an entrepreneur) is pecuniary gain through the purchase and sale of some commodity or through the provision of a service which the community demands. Thus the success of an enterprise is doubly based, initially on the ability to make money, coupled with the ability to provide something for which the public is willing to pay. If he does not make a satisfactory profit, he will wish to withdraw his labour and capital and start another activity or go and work for someone else. Sufficient return on the total capital invested in that business needs to be made to compensate for the risks and worries the entrepreneur has incurred in setting up independently, over and above what he could have earned by the use of his capital and labour elsewhere.

Even in a large company, where directors and employees are more secure in the knowledge that their remuneration rests on a guaranteed salary or wage, rather than on the fortunes or disasters that occur when one is working for oneself, financial considerations are foremost. Profit is one very sure guide to management efficiency, and if a business makes continuous losses it will soon cease to be able to carry on trading, causing its staff to seek posts elsewhere. Managers' prospects are partly based on the way they are able to handle the financial aspects of their departments.

The maximisation of profit is not usually considered an aim, except in the short run, since it is usually a self-defeating process. Charging unjustifiably high prices for a product or service, apart from the moral issue, is likely to result in either competitors trying to supply the same item at a cheaper price, with subsequent customer dissatisfaction, or Government intervention and possible legislation aimed at curbing profits.

Once a business has become established it will be concerned not so much with making quick profits but with making a satisfactory profit on the capital employed, taking into account the risks involved and what could be earned elsewhere. The term "satisficing" has been used by economists to denote this type of profit. Sometimes a business may seek what is known as "minimaxing," *i.e.* seeking the maximum profit while bearing in mind the need to guard against possible losses. One description of this is "maximising the minimum expected gain while minimising the maximum expected loss, taking into account competitors' actions."

In choosing the profit policy a business is usually concerned with ensuring its continued survival. With this end in mind it will adapt to internal changes and to changes in its environment, modifying its goals if necessary, in order to continue in existence. A business will have certain non-profit objectives, which are difficult to evaluate financially; but neglect of them could eventually impair the social standing, technical efficiency and profitability of the concern. These can also be called "social responsibilities of management." They include consumer satisfaction, the security of the staff, the interests of the shareholders and the impact of the firm on the public, particularly the local community, where short-sighted policies in terms of polluting the environment or frequent dismissals could earn the firm a bad name. Management also have to consider how their policies fit in with the national objectives of Government.

An important aim is customer satisfaction through the provision of goods and services in the right quantity, of the right quality, at the right time, in the right place and at the right price consistent with the constraints imposed by cost and profit requirements. A company must have regard for the welfare and interests of its staff, with opportunities for achieving satisfaction through such means as job rotation and job enlargement. Particular attention must be paid to selection procedures, coupled with planned and adequate training and retraining, which have been discussed in Chapter VIII. The communication system must be fast, accurate, official and effective, justice must be seen to be done and there must be a recognisable system of promotion in operation with equal opportunities for all. This all costs money and probably does nothing for short-term profits. But just as a factory might be built as an investment in the hope that it will provide a big return in the future, so such personnel policies are an investment. If they are not implemented, it is never possible to know exactly how much is lost. But that is one of the most important responsibilities of the manager—to make the best possible estimate of the value of the intangible and the unquantifiable and to decide accordingly what course of action he should take.

A firm must pay attention to its technical efficiency, rate of production, research and development. This may result in larger scale operations, which benefit from economies of size. However, the result can be an impersonal organisation, de-skilled work, difficulties in communication and loss of authority and responsibility at lower levels—all of which can be in indirect conflict with the objectives of the individual. Furthermore, if the firm attempts to react to customer demand and technological change as quickly as possible there is a danger that the workforce will become unemployed, or at best will need to be retrained. Wages are a variable cost to management, but they are a source of livelihood to the workpeople. Thus though the necessity for efficiency and perhaps for maintaining a certain profit level may urge redundancy and the laying-off of employees, staff may be retained to preserve good morale in the firm and good relations with the local community. A firm which continually hires and fires labour in contrast to another will soon obtain a bad reputation. Thus regard to public responsibility and corporate image may mean that social factors will outweigh economic ones.

A firm may also be concerned with its position in the market, and prestige and psychological regard for power and influence rather than economic considerations may persuade it to embark on expansion. Some of the factors which could be measured in this area are:

1. the standing of existing products in present or new markets;
2. the need for new products in existing or new markets;
3. consideration of existing products that should be abandoned.

Other objectives exist which are not necessarily compatible with profit, depending upon the time-scale under consideration. The production goal is to produce a quantity of goods which do not vary greatly from one time period to another, yet satisfy total requirements. Warehouse stocks should be kept at an acceptably low level, yet should avoid possible run-out. Sales aim to hit a particular target in absolute terms and they also wish to increase or at least maintain market share; in this respect they are dependent upon competitive activity and pressures. It would be difficult to say that all of these objectives of the subdivisions of the company are always compatible with profit or even compatible with one another. Neither would it be an easy task to quantify the effect of seeking optimisation in any one of these objectives. The sum of sub-optimisation is by no means the optimisation of the whole, as would soon be shown, for example, by the continual purchase of quality items of furniture to furnish a room. Each piece of furniture might well be exquisite in its own right, but taken as a whole the room could be decidedly uncomfortable and even unpleasant.

A company is a collection of individuals, all with differing opinions, aspirations and demands. The latest event that can be shown to be the biggest crisis gets the most attention. Management have limited ability to attend to every problem within the organisation simultaneously and so each subdivision takes its turn to be optimised. When stocks are high, production must cut back to reduce them. When there is insufficient work for the labour force, more effort must be made to sell more and so provide work for them. If customers complain they are not receiving what they have ordered, stocks must be increased, and so on round the circle.

When a company faces financial difficulties, or if it sees ahead a period of recession against which it wishes to take precautions, it is usually possible to find ways of reducing costs. It is sometimes surprising how well a company can continue to operate even without whole departments, which beforehand would have been thought impossible. Less drastic action would be to delay repainting the factory or repairing the surface of the car park. Every manager who imposes an arbitrary 10 per cent cut is eating into the spare capacity which exists in every company, despite objectives to maximise profits. It has been called "organisational slack" by Cyert and March in *A Behavioural Theory of the Firm* (Prentice-Hall, New Jersey, 1963).

Innovation—research and development

The need for innovation in most companies arises from possible threats to stability. A company's products (for example, black and white television sets) may be reaching market saturation point, or competitive activity (in, for instance, detergents) may be forcing a loss in market share, or the products may (like bread) be in a declining market. Company management do not wish to spend their hard-earned profits on research unless they feel that they will get a satisfactory return, which they are unlikely to do in the short term. There is a very strong incentive for management to hold on to what they already have without becoming embroiled in the expense and uncertainty of seeking new pastures through research and invention. An understandable desire of management is to obtain profits with minimum risk, yet innovation is quite the antithesis. Management need to balance the risk of change against the risks of remaining where they are.

A company operating in a stable market is usually able to structure itself with an organisation which is mechanistic, as described earlier in this chapter. Market conditions are known with reasonable precision, there are few problems which have not been encountered before and the role and responsibilities of each individual within the firm can be closely specified. Experience counts, so the older man is found at the top of the management tree. On the other hand, a company which is in a growing or changing market needs to develop new ideas through innovation. New methods and new procedures mean that individual jobs are less well defined. The organisation is an organic one, experience is less relevant and the younger man achieves more rapid promotion by making full use of initiative and special skills and by keeping abreast of current developments. The older man, although still high in the management chain, takes on the role of judge or court of appeal. These observations are developed by Burns and Stalker.

In this age of mass production, considerable effort is expended in finding new and better ways of producing more at a lower unit cost. Because all other companies in the same line of business are behaving in this way too, to innovate is to survive. The management of a company, because of the dispersed shareholder ownership, are both masters and servants and thereby place survival high on the list of objectives. Nowadays a large public company is not just a profit-making device, it is a social institution which cannot go in and out of business as the profit situation dictates. Change needs to be controlled. It is for these reasons that research and development projects receive support; they are seen as the future life blood of the company, its insurance for survival.

Pure research is work which is conducted without necessarily any motive for profit. Investigations are made into new processes or designs simply because they are new avenues to explore. Sometimes a new discovery is made which appears to have commercial viability, in which case it will enter the development phase. Efforts will be made to convert the basic new idea or concept into a commercial proposition, one which will bring a profitable return. It may have been possible to design, say, a breakthrough in computer circuitry in the laboratory and construct it with the aid of expensive precision equipment. But on the factory floor in conditions of mass production, such precision could be prohibitively expensive. It is the job of the development division to ensure that the results of the pure research are feasible in and applicable to everyday life. That is not to say that what development provides is immediately appropriate to production needs. For any new process, modifications are frequently made, encompassing the suggestions and proposals put forward by both the production men who will do the job and the development staff who have taken the research ideas and made them practical and potentially profitable.

The 19th century was a fertile period for new ideas and inventions. It was thought that inventiveness was a product of genius, that it was wayward, uncontrollable and could not be planned. It was epitomised by James Watt sitting in front of his kettle full of boiling water and experiencing the revelation of the steam engine. Individual men would think up new ideas, would themselves manufacture a few prototypes and if successful would set up small businesses. As new inventions came along which superseded the old, the small firms would either have to buy up the new idea or close down.

By 1900 the scientist, as he was then called, had a recognised place in the world; he was for the first time salaried, but working in the environs of the universities. Bright ideas were still forthcoming from outside the universities, but it had become more and more expensive for them to break into the world of big business. The universities maintained a monopoly over research activities until the outbreak of the First World War. In 1917, the Government formed the Department of Scientific and Industrial Research to co-ordinate the research activities which had culminated as a result of the war effort. Government laboratories and research centres were created and since then industry too has followed suit. In 1938 £2 million was spent on research. Twenty years later, spurred on by the impetus of the Second World War, this figure had increased a hundredfold.

During the Second World War considerable effort was expended by research scientists to discover new and more effective forms of armaments; and this continues today, albeit in a more peaceful guise, in space research, atomic energy research and so on. Industry receives a spin-off from these activities in the shape of new technologies which are applicable to civilian needs, as well as of the benefits from undertaking contracts for work which the Government authorities require to be done. Contracts such as these, often called defence contracts, bring know-how into the commercial market, which is an advantage, but they can also tend to make companies, particularly the small ones, too heavily dependent upon the Government of the day.

The most effective form of research is when there exists a close working relationship between the researcher and the eventual user of the end product of the research. Although we have said that research can be considered an end in itself, no business organisation suffers an expensive research department if in the long run it provides not one worthwhile and profitable idea. Research cannot afford therefore to work in isolation; it must feel itself to be part of the total operation. In an organic organisation there can be considerable overlap between the commonly recognised functions of the business. In a changing market, the salesman is less able to sell his wares without technical backing; the design engineers are less able to understand market requirements without being involved in the market surveys: production must appreciate the problems of both.

Technological progress is achieved through scientific discovery, independent of its use. A proper liaison between user and scientist, which can only be engendered by an awareness by each of the work being done by the other, leads to a definition of the practical needs of the user and of the information required by the scientist to provide a design which satisfies those needs. Often the needs which are originally specified are unattainable: in which case compromise is reached which enables both user and scientist to achieve each his ends.

DECISION MAKING

Taking decisions is a necessary part of everyday life. Whatever we do, we are deciding which of several alternatives we shall choose. Even crossing the street is a series of decisions, beginning first with the decision to do so and followed by decisions which enable us to reach the other side. Every decision contains an element of uncertainty. We are never quite sure that what we expect to happen as a result of each decision will actually occur. Techniques have been developed which enable the manager to evaluate alternatives in a rational way, but they always depend upon an accurate assessment and evaluation of the facts beforehand, and that is not easy to achieve.

There are occasions when it is right not to take a decision, to let events take care of themselves. The problem which is foreseen sometimes never happens at all and to react too soon can be as bad as acting too late. Timing is an important consideration in decision making, and to hesitate too long is tantamount to deciding to do nothing during the period of indecision. What seems right for today may simply store up problems for tomorrow, and the success of a business depends upon making the right balanced choice.

Deciding between alternatives

The most satisfactory time to take a decision is when all the alternatives are presented; each can be properly evaluated on a common scale and the best one chosen. Unfortunately this does not happen very frequently and incompatible factors generally need to be reconciled. The discussion on the social implications of maximising profit earlier in this chapter is an example.

Various techniques are available to help in the evaluation of alternatives, but they require an accurate assessment of the input data on which they are based. Frequently the methods can be used only as guides in decision making, and other factors need to be taken into account by the manager concerned. Some of the techniques are discussed below, with examples of their possible use.

There are two basic attitudes which may be adopted to decide between alternatives:

1. to minimise the loss;
2. to maximise the gain, or possible outcome.

Another way of expressing them is:

1. to minimise regret (if objective is not achieved);
2. to maximise security (of achieving objective).

Between these extremes there is a continuum of expected or hoped-for outcomes. In a mathematical sense, it is frequently possible to perform a number of calculations to achieve either of these two extremes, but in reality there are usually too many factors to take into account to arrive at a truly mathematical conclusion.

I. *Competitive activity*

Let us suppose that firm A, in deciding its advertising strategy, has only two alternatives: either it advertises on television or in the national press. Firm B, the only other competitor in the field, can equally decide to advertise on television or in the press. Past experience has shown that no other advertising medium has as great an effect on the product as these two.

Firms A and B are both anxious to improve market share. The market is, however, a static one and the effect of one company achieving an increase in market share is to reduce that of the other by an equal amount. It has been learnt in the past that if both companies advertise on the same medium at the same time, firm A always seems to gain in market share, 2 per cent from television and 1 per cent from the press. It is as though firm B makes the customers aware of the product but not of B's name, and as A is the market leader of the two they buy A's products. On the other hand, if the firms advertise on different media, B on television gains a 2 per cent increase in share but B in the newspapers simply counteracts A on television. These advertising strategies can be sufficiently well isolated from other activities in the company to make the conclusions reasonable ones and valid. Both A and B are frequently advertising in these ways and they have canvass periods which tend to coincide,

		B		
		TV	NP	
A	TV	2	0	Results for A
	NP	−2	1	

FIG. 47. *Percentage effect on market share of A*

thus causing their advertising to occur at very nearly the same times and at the same intensities. Besides, if one advertised and the other did not, the advertising firm would increase its market share by at least 10 per cent.

From the information given above we can compile Fig. 47 showing the effect on the market share of A. Reading across the rows of the table, we see that if A advertises on TV and B advertises on TV, the gain to A is 2 per cent. If, however, B advertises in the newspapers, NP, the gain to A is zero. Similarly for the second row, if A advertises in NP and B on TV, A loses 2 per cent, but if they both advertise in NP, A gains 1 per cent.

The question now remains, which is the best strategy for A to adopt to counteract B, not knowing in advance what B will do? We can solve the problem with the aid of the diagram in Fig. 48.

The left-hand vertical line measures the gain to A if it chooses NP. The right-hand line measures the gain from TV. Line P illustrates the effect of B choosing NP and line Q shows B choosing TV. The point of intersection of P and Q divides each of P and Q in the ratio 3 to 2, which tells us how often A should use TV (and hence how often it should use NP), assuming that the probability of B going for one or the other is the same, *i.e.* 50%: on three occasions out of every five A should advertise on TV. The reader may also wish to show that,

LEADERSHIP AND DECISION MAKING

from B's point of view, B should advertise on TV on just one occasion out of every five. This method of solution is a part of Game Theory.

II. *Decision trees*

Often a manufacturer wishes to know which of several alternatives he ought to choose. He has several stages of choice and at each stage the decision is relatively simple, yet put together they become highly complex. Let us assume, for example, that a company which manufactures and sells small toy cars is considering adding another model

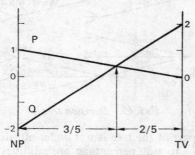

FIG. 48. *Choice of strategy*

to its range. This new model can either be large and not to scale, or small and detailed: in both cases the relative costs of manufacture are the same. The car can be sold at the same price as has always been charged for the range, or it can be more, or even less. There are three possible markets, the U.K., Europe or the world. It can be produced on either of two production lines, each of which has its merits, depending upon the total quantity that will need to be made.

We have: two possible design decisions; three prices; three market considerations; two methods of production. This results in a total combination of thirty-six possibilities. We can draw this out as a tree structure as shown in Fig. 49.

It is now possible to work through the branches, considering each path in turn as though it were the only one. If, for example, we choose the design branch which says "large," proceed along the "same" price and then "Europe," we shall see that the market in Europe with the preceding conditions is likely to be 17,000 (units, dozens, crates, etc.). This will dictate the type of production process to be adopted and hence the total cost and profit figures. If this is done for all possible paths, the one with the highest profit can be chosen as the best.

A further complication would be to introduce what action is

likely to be taken by competition in each of the given circumstances. If, for example, the market figures could be affected by competition, we might add two further branches on to each market branch to identify whether competition is present or not. We could then show the expected market for our product in both these cases, say 17,000 in Europe without competition and 12,000 with.

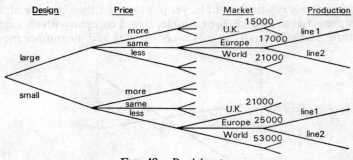

FIG. 49. *Decision tree*

However, this part of the tree is not under our direct control, and so we would have to put percentage probabilities against each of these branches, say, 60 per cent that competition would intervene and 40 per cent that it would not. We might then calculate expected profit, which would be based on a sale of $17,000 \times \frac{4}{10} = 6,800$ without competition and $12,000 \times \frac{6}{10} = 7,200$ with competition. Total expected profit would be based on the sum of these two, 14,000. The section later in this chapter on risks and probabilities discusses these principles further.

III. *Marginal costing*

Although various methods of accounting have already been discussed in Chapter V, marginal costing has been inserted in its present place simply because it is probably the most useful means of identifying for management the effect of the decisions they take. The most important feature of marginal costing is its division of costs into those which are variable and those which are fixed. This is different from other forms of costing in that the fixed element itself is divided into two parts: that which is directly applicable to the product, and that which is not. It is the way these costs are applied which makes marginal costing such a particularly valuable tool.

Fixed costs which are directly applicable to the product are those costs which are incurred no matter how many of the product are

LEADERSHIP AND DECISION MAKING 313

made. It includes such costs as plant maintenance and the wages of the supervisors. In reality, fixed costs are seldom directly applicable: they tend to be so, or they apply within a broad quantity range of total items produced. Costs which are fixed but can be applied to all products, such as factory heating and the cost of the sales force, are

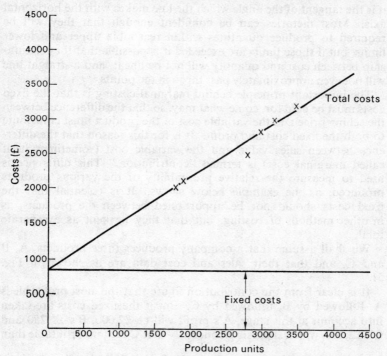

FIG. 50. *Separation of fixed and variable elements*

termed overheads and do not enter into the calculations which follow.

Variable costs are those which tend to vary directly with the volume of goods produced. They include direct labour costs, the costs of raw materials and packaging and other costs such as fuel usage and plant, if they can be directly attributed. It is often difficult to separate with any accuracy the fixed costs from the variable costs and this is particularly the case when it is possible to manufacture a mix of products on the same plant. Only if the same mix stays constant week after week can the relevant costs truly be attributed.

A method of allocating costs is to obtain pairs of figures which record the costs associated with various levels of production. If sufficient of these records are available, they can be plotted as shown in Fig. 50. A straight line can then be drawn which passes as closely as possible through all the points. A more accurate and mathematical approach is described as linear regression under forecasting in Chapter VII. Where the line cuts the vertical axis is the fixed cost, and the variable cost is related to the slope of the line; more precisely it is the tangent of the angle which the line makes with the horizontal axis. Most factories can be confident enough that they will be required to produce quantities within reasonble upper and lower limits, but if those limits are exceeded it is possible that the relationship between cost and quantity will not be linear, and a straight line will not even approximately pass through the points.

The important principle behind marginal costing is that the fixed costs must be paid for, come what may, so that the difference between the selling price and the variable cost of the product must contribute to both the fixed cost and profit. It is for this reason that the difference between sales value and the variable cost (sometimes itself called marginal cost) is termed "contribution." This difference is used to measure the relative profitability of the various products produced, as the example below shows. It is essential that the fixed costs should not be apportioned between the products, as in other methods of costing, but that they be kept as a separate total.

We shall assume that a company produces three products, A, B and C, and that their sales and cost data are as shown in Fig. 51.

It is clear from the contribution figure that the most profitable is A, followed by B, followed by C. But if the fixed costs are taken into account at this stage, A's profit will be £2,000, B's £2,250 and C's £2,500, which suggests erroneously that C is more profitable than

	Product A	Product B	Product C	Total
	£	£	£	£
Total sales revenue	10,000	10,000	10,000	30,000
Variable or marginal costs	5,000	6,000	7,000	18,000
Contribution	5,000	4,000	3,000	12,000
Fixed costs	3,000	1,750	500	5,250
Profit				6,750

FIG. 51. *Sales and cost data*

B, which is more profitable than A. If management now had the opportunity to achieve a further £10,000 worth of revenue and therefore needed to decide with which single product it should be obtained, only marginal costing would have pointed to the right one. This assumes that the company has the capacity to produce additional output for only one of the three products.

The use of marginal costing for the analysis of alternative courses of action can be further illustrated as follows. Assume a retail group has three shops with budgeted profits and losses for the next financial year shown in Fig. 52.

	Glasgow £000		Edinburgh £000		Dundee £000
Sales	100		150		125
Cost of goods sold	50		70		60
Gross profit	50		80		65
Direct fixed costs	20		45		50
Head office costs	20		20		20
	40		65		70
Budget profit (loss)	£10		£15		£(5)

FIG. 52. *Budgeted profit and loss (1)*

The costs directly attributable to each store are the cost of goods sold and the direct fixed costs. The head office costs of £60,000 in total are indirect to each shop and allocated to them at £20,000 each. It might appear in the interest of the group to close the Dundee shop to eliminate the loss of £5,000. However, Dundee recovers its direct costs and makes a positive contribution to the general fixed head office costs. The contributions are:

Glasgow	£50,000 − £20,000 = £30,000
Edinburgh	£80,000 − £45,000 = £35,000
Dundee	£65,000 − £50,000 = £15,000

The contribution figures show directly the effect on group profitability of a closure of Dundee. Far from improving profitability, £15,000 will be lost on closure. Assuming that head office costs are unaffected by the closure of Dundee, the position after closure would be as shown in Fig. 53.

	Glasgow £000	Edinburgh £000	Total £000
Sales	100	150	250
Cost of goods sold	50	70	120
Direct fixed costs	20	45	65
Total direct costs	70	115	185
Contribution to head office	30	35	65
Head office costs			60
Budgeted profit			£5

FIG. 53. *Budgeted profit and loss (2)*

The closure reduces budgeted profit from a total of £20,000 to £5,000, a reduction of £15,000. Assuming no alternative use of the funds invested in Dundee, profit is reduced on closure by the Dundee contribution.

A direct cost approach to the analysis of alternative courses of action will generally be the most useful to management. It is the change in the level of contribution after charging direct costs that will most clearly highlight the effect on profit. This illustrates that it is not sufficient to analyse cost behaviour just in terms of variable and fixed costs. For an activity to be profitable, it must recover all the costs which are directly attributable to it, whether these direct costs are variable or fixed in their nature. It may be desirable to continue an activity that does not appear to recover its full costs, so long as it recovers its own direct expenses. However, it is generally not worthwhile to continue with activities that consistently fail to recover direct costs.

The main uses of the contribution approach lie in providing a framework for the evaluation of such alternatives as setting sales prices; deciding on the acquisition of new capacity; product range rationalisation; determination of sales mix; allocation of scarce resources to competing activities; introduction of new products or activities; and the close-down decision.

IV. *Break-even analysis*

Now that we have introduced the concept of marginal costing, it is a simple matter to extend the discussion into break-even analysis. The break-even point is that volume of output which provides neither a profit nor a loss, so that fixed costs are exactly covered by the contribution. Its value is in setting a lower limit for management below which they should not be prepared to sell the product. Figure 54 illustrates a simple break-even chart, where the intersection of the sales line with total costs is the break-even point. This assumes that the revenue from sales and the costs of providing the product are each linearly dependent upon volume. This is not necessarily the case and a more realistic description of the break-even point might be that shown in Fig. 55. Perhaps surprisingly, two break-even points are shown, the higher one due to the fact that a stage in production is sometimes reached when the more there is produced, the higher become the unit costs, for example, the cost of overtime working. However, the lower of the two points would normally be the one in which management would be interested and for all intents and purposes a linear representation of costs and revenue around this break-even point is acceptable.

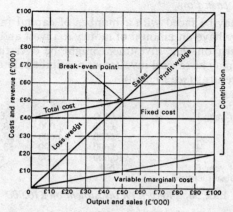

FIG. 54. *Break-even chart (showing contribution)*

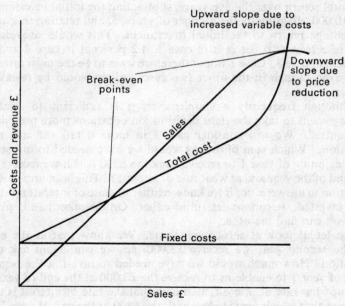

FIG. 55. *Break-even chart, non linear costs*

V. Discounted cash flow

A company may be faced with a number of capital investment decisions. It may have an amount of money to invest and it may know what the return on that investment might be over the succeeding years. There may be several investment possibilities and correspondingly several returns (*see* Fig. 56).

	1	2	3
End of year 1	£600	£100	£500
2	£600	£2,000	£3,600
3	£600	£4,000	£5,000
4	£600	£5,000	£3,000
5	£10,600	£1,000	£500
End of year 6 and subsequently	Nil	Nil	Nil

FIG. 56. *Return on investment on £10,000*

The pertinent question is, "Which of the three investments should the company make?" Which is the best, a steady regular return as in case 1, an early return as in case 3 or a later one as in case 2?

There are simple averages which might be taken, such as summing the total return over the five years, subtracting the initial investment of £10,000, dividing by the number of years, 5, and relating this as a percentage return to the initial investment. This would provide a rate of return of 6 per cent in case 1, 4·2 per cent in case 2 and 4 per cent in case 3. Case 1 would therefore seem to be the most attractive, even though in the other two cases money would be released earlier.

Although frequently a simple average is sufficient to enable management to take the right decision, on occasions more precision is required. We will consider case 3 in more detail and ask the question, "Which sum of money would we have needed to invest at the beginning of year 1 to receive back the £500 which we receive at the end of the year and at what rate of interest?" This is an impossible question to answer since if we know neither the rate of interest nor the sum invested, we cannot determine either. On the other hand, given one, we can find the other.

But let us look at subsequent years. We know that at the end of the second year we receive £3,000, so we can again ask the question "How much would we have needed to invest at the beginning of year 1 to enable us to receive the £3,000 at the end of year 2 and at what rate of interest, assuming that the rate of interest is the same as that which provided us with the £500 at the end of year 1?" We are still unable to answer the question, but we can persevere and ask the same type of question in each of the subsequent years up to year 5. At this stage we have one additional and important piece of information. Since we originally invested £10,000, we know that the sum of all the quantities we have been trying to find for each year is equal to the £10,000. We now have, in theory at least, sufficient information to enable us to determine precisely the rate of interest and the invested quantities we have been seeking. In fact, these invested quantities are known as "present values."

It is possible to describe the previous paragraphs in a more mathematical form. If we put x_i equal to the present value which accrued due to the return shown in the ith year and if r is the percentage rate of return, then

$$x_1 = \frac{500}{1 + \dfrac{r}{100}} \qquad x_2 = \frac{3000}{\left(1 + \dfrac{r}{100}\right)^2} \qquad x_5 = \frac{500}{\left(1 + \dfrac{r}{100}\right)^5}$$

where $x_1 + x_2 + x_3 + x_4 + x_5 = 10,000$

Although there are sufficient equations to find the unknown quantities, the mathematical manipulation which is required to do so is not trivial; it can be a formidable task. However, if similar calculations were performed for each of the three original cases we started with above, the one with the highest rate of return, r, would be the one to choose. This method is known as "discounted cash flow," or D.C.F.

There is another way in which we might have looked at the problem and might have derived a different answer. Let us suppose that we can estimate the rate of return, which for simplicity we specify as the current interest rate on a bank loan. If this rate were applied to the equations above to determine all the xs, the sum of the xs would represent the present value of the return that subsequent years had to offer. The difference between the xs and the original investment of £10,000 would show how much profit was to be made. If this were now calculated for each of the three cases above, the most profitable investment could be determined. From a practical standpoint, if company profits from normal trading had been retained in the business for investment purposes, thus avoiding the necessity to raise a bank loan, rate r should still have been set at a realistic level and not assumed to be zero simply because the money had been readily available.

VI. *Risk, uncertainty and probabilities*

Decisions taken by management always contain an element of risk, otherwise there are no decisions to take, but simply a procedure to follow which can be delegated to a clerk or a computer. Risk implies probability and although, if pressed, management might say, "The chance of success is 60 per cent" or some such figure, in reality there is a probability that the probability stated by management is correct —and so on *ad infinitum*. Furthermore, management usually have only one opportunity of taking a decision: the chance of success may well be 60 per cent, but after the event success either was achieved or it was not. Take, for example, the roulette player who places a large sum of money on the chance of just one number coming up as the winner. Before the wheel is spun his chance of success is one in thirty-six (assuming no zero), but after the event he is either a very rich man or a foolish one. At least in roulette, if he had divided his initial stake into thirty-six and had placed an equal amount on his number on thirty-six occasions, his chance of getting his money back with even a little profit would have been a reasonable one. But roulette is not business (although it undoubtedly is to the croupier); in business, chances cannot be so accurately determined, and continual tries cannot be made or slim chances of success accepted.

Even so, we have a better understanding of the business situation if we are aware of the probabilities involved and we take the time and trouble to assess them. The decision tree discussion above is an example. Of one point we can be sure, the estimated sales of the toy cars calculated on a basis of probability will not actually occur, but it is a guide to our thinking. The salesman who is selling umbrellas and who calculates that the probability of rain on any given day is $\frac{1}{5}$, while his chance of receiving an order from his biggest customer has been $\frac{1}{2}$ when it did not rain and $\frac{3}{4}$ when it did, is deluding himself if he concludes that the probability of making a sale on any given day in the future is $(\frac{1}{5} \times \frac{3}{4}) + (\frac{4}{5} \times \frac{1}{2}) = \frac{11}{20}$. His manager, who may have set a target of making a sale on three visits out of four, will not be impressed by such arithmetical skill. What may seem to be a valid probability on one day will almost certainly turn out to be something different on the next—otherwise why have salesmen at all? They are there to influence the sale and hence change the probability in their favour. This applies equally well to management in general.

Levels of decision

In any business operation a variety of decisions are made. They range from the mechanical to ones of policy and include those taken by the youngest member of the office right up to the managing director.

At the lowest level we may have the most junior office girl who is designated the task of opening the incoming letters each morning. She has minimum responsibilities and simply follows a procedure laid down by her immediate superior. We may call her decisions "vegetative."

Once the letters are opened they may be passed on to a more senior clerk who routes them to the intended recipients. His decisions in this respect are "automatic." If the letters are requests for price quotations which are relatively easy to provide, the decisions are "routine" ones. More complicated requests are passed to a senior level for action; they include inquiries for special products not yet produced by the company and with which there are no rules for dealing. These "unique" requests require "interpretive" action: if it is decided to make the products and subsequently they sell well and become part of the company's range, from then on they are handled automatically as routine because rules have been formulated for them. Whether or not the product range should be enlarged further to embrace an even wider market is a decision of "policy." It may be inspired by the decision-makers at the interpretive level, but it is the prerogative of the most senior management to determine policy.

An illustration of these levels of decision is shown in Fig. 57. The flow of instructions is represented by the downward arrows on the right-hand side and the feedback is received on the left. If a problem can be resolved at a particular level, the solution is recycled without recourse to higher management. Stimuli are received at the bottom of the chart from external influence, such as working relationships and market conditions, and at the top from the most senior management. Experiences gained at other levels from outside the immediate working environment will also affect the decisions taken.

It is of some interest and salutary that the children's poem *The King's Breakfast* by A. A. Milne fits the principles displayed by the chart. It is a lighthearted example of instructions given and the consequent feedback; all goes according to plan as "The King asked the Queen and the Queen asked the dairymaid, 'Could we have some butter for the Royal slice of bread?'"—until the message reaches the cow, which retorts, "You'd better tell His Majesty that many people

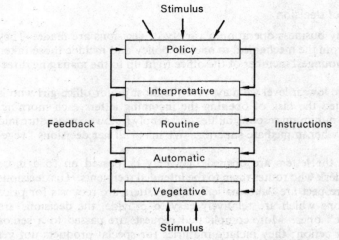

Fig. 57. *Levels of decision*

nowadays like marmalade instead," and the instruction is recycled for a new policy decision.

Decision types

There are three main classes of decision in a company: operating, administrative and strategic. Within each class may be found the levels of decision discussed in the previous section. The definitions which follow are condensed and taken from H. Igor Ansoff's book *Corporate Strategy* (McGraw-Hill, New York, 1965).

Operating decisions are those decisions which must be taken for the normal day-to-day operation of the company. They include matters of allocation of resources, budgets, direct supervision and control. They are concerned with problems of production, marketing, distribution and sales, and they attempt to optimise conflicting ideals under conditions of risk and uncertainty. The problems and some solutions are described in various chapters of this book.

Administrative decisions are ones of organisation, acquisition and future development of employee and physical resources. They deal with company structure, the flow of information, communication and related management responsibilities. They include problems of finance and personnel, and they attempt to resolve conflict between strategy and operations, between individual objectives and those of the firm.

Strategic decision-making is concerned with opportunities and the choice of products and markets to optimise the company's future potential. It sets objectives and goals and determines the diversification, expansion and administrative and financial plans of the company, as well as its future growth and timing. The decisions are non-repetitive and are usually taken in partial ignorance, without full knowledge of all the relevant facts.

Corporate planning

Corporate planning has become increasingly fashionable over the years. It is the means by which management at the highest level formulate their long-term plans for the future. It has brought with it its own terminology, of which "synergy" is a prime example. Loosely defined, synergy is a compatibility between two companies which provides the likelihood of mutual advantage if they join forces: the attributes of one would match in with those of the other so that, once merged, the whole would be an improvement on the sum of the separate parts. Its objective is the achievement of "$2 + 2 = 5$."

Corporate planners are expected to look into the future with none of the inhibitions of operating management. They are able therefore to conceive of the company completely changing course, selling up and investing its capital in more profitable ventures. They are, however, bound by practical restrictions, so that if they make such a proposal it needs to be well and truly justified.

To arrive at any plan it is essential to determine first the objectives of top management: whether management wish to maximise short-term profits or long, whether a centralised or a decentralised organisation is preferred, with consequent cost of profit centres, and so on. Within the constraints imposed by the objectives, a search is made to see whether the company should adopt a strategy of diversification and/or expansion (presumably contraction as well), which may also mean new methods of administration. As part of their objectives, management will have specified the return on investment they expect and so any new investment opportunities exposed by the search will need to conform to that return. Management must ensure that sufficient funds will be available when they are needed and that their objectives are realistic and financially achievable.

In looking for new areas for diversification or expansion, the corporate planners attempt to identify the inherent skills and attributes of the company which they can exploit; to cite an extreme, a baby food manufacturer with a large, competent but under-utilised sales force would be unlikely to wish to get into the earth-moving business, but it might seriously consider making a bid for a toiletry manufacturer because in the main both companies serve the same types of customer. A more obvious and real-life example of synergy is the cement manufacturer who makes a take-over bid for the waste products company. The former digs the holes and the latter fills them up again!

Synergy can exist in a multitude of ways, but for simplicity we can specify four classes: general management, research and development, manufacturing and marketing. It is unlikely that the management of a heavy engineering company producing locomotives would have much in common with a company specialising in underwear, neither would the marketing techniques of the motor-car industry be appropriate to the hotelier. Nevertheless the knowledge and experience of one industry can sometimes be valuable to another: whether or not the intended level of synergy is actually achieved can be recognised by measuring its effect on:

1. profit related to sales turnover;
2. operating costs;
3. capital invested in the business;
4. the rate at which improvements, if any, are obtained.

These factors are important whether or not a company has merged with another, but too often it is assumed by one company taking over or merging with another that considerable advantages will be gained when, in reality, seldom do they accrue. A proper measure of improvements not only identifies the successes, but also stimulates the means of ensuring that the hopes and aspirations of the merger are truly achieved.

X. ORGANISATION AND COMMUNICATIONS

ORGANISATION

The way a company is organised plays an important part in its continuing success. Most progressive companies will adapt themselves to changing circumstances and will take as much advantage as they can of latest technology, market behaviour, available finance and other prevailing conditions. It is not always possible, however, to change an organisation as quickly as a company would like, and human and other factors need to be taken into account. The function and purpose, both long and short term, of departments and of the roles of individuals must be considered, and their inter-relationships must be understood as much as is possible.

Some of these factors are discussed in this chapter, but it is by no means exhaustive. It could be said that organisation is a subject which embraces all activities within a business enterprise, and therefore topics relevant to organisation will also be found elsewhere in this book.

Company ownership

The true owners of a company are the shareholders: in theory they are the ones with ultimate authority to decide how the company should behave. In practice the shares are frequently dispersed among many owners, most of whom have little or no interest in the company as such other than that it pays an acceptable dividend and/or it achieves an appropriate rate of growth in terms of share value. Often the largest shareholder is one of the institutions, such as a major insurance company, and they are traditionally reticent about interfering in the affairs of other companies unless through dire necessity, for example, conclusive evidence of sheer stupidity on the part of the company management. In the large companies there is seldom one major shareholder who can muster enough support to insist that change should take place, although obviously it does and will happen sometimes.

Unless company management are blatantly incompetent and provided they return reasonable results each year, they can expect to continue without any interference from and with only minor interest displayed by the majority of its shareholders. We can reach the situation therefore where the senior executives are responsible not only for running the company but also, if by default, for setting their own objectives to enable them to do so. It might be said that one way of overcoming this apparent anomaly, at least in part, is to allow employees to participate in a share purchase option scheme.

Chairman and Managing Director

Every business organisation requires an ultimate leader, a power at the helm. It need not necessarily be a single individual: some companies have joint leadership in the form of joint managing directors; others, and certain Government organisations are an example, are controlled by committee.

Both the managing director and the chairman are members of the board of directors. The function of the managing director is to interpret the policy laid down by the board and to be responsible for the operation of the company. In that sense he is subordinate to the board, although he is also a full and equal member of it. The chairman is a member of the board who has been elected to take the chair at meetings. Such definition is a clinical statement of his responsibilities; in practice he is frequently the most senior member and a close adviser of the managing director.

Some companies may overlap to some degree the responsibilities of the chairman and managing director. The reasons may be historical and convenient rather than strictly practical. For example, the chairman who is the senior member of an erstwhile family business may take particular interest in long-range planning, while the managing director may concentrate upon the shorter-term operational problems. As well as taking the chair at board meetings, the chairman also represents the company to the shareholders at the A.G.M. and in official notices such as the annual report and accounts.

The positions of chairman and managing director may be filled by the same person; in the case of joint managing directorships it is not uncommon for one of them to be chairman as well. This endows a certain higher level of status upon the individual who is also the chairman as he automatically becomes the company's spokesman to the press and the outside world. Nevertheless, each of the joint managing directors should have clearly defined responsibilities and should be the final arbiter in his own particular spheres. However, those spheres may on occasions overlap and a joint ruling must then be made.

There are advantages to be gained from joint responsibility, one

ORGANISATION AND COMMUNICATIONS

of which is a second view of the company's affairs. From one side it may be clear that a particular course of action should be taken, but if the effect of that action on other parts of the company is considered, it may turn out to be quite the wrong path to take. A compromise which satisfies all parties may be reached, provided each party understands in advance that what it is doing does have an effect on the others and is willing to do something about it. This is not always the case, and one of the greatest difficulties can be that areas of potential conflict will arise without the people involved ever knowing that they have arisen. Even the best-thought-out definitions and delineations of responsibility will suffer under implementation and interpretation. Because loopholes will occur, individuals in employment, and this includes the joint managing directors, need to work well together and complement each other, not only in running the business but as people as well.

The Board of Directors

There are three principal types of director, one who sits on the main board, another who serves on the board of a subsidiary company and a third who is a senior manager without board status. The main board director is in theory appointed by the shareholders but in practice he is recommended to the appointment by the board itself. He may be a well-known, perhaps titled, public figure and industrialist, an influential merchant banker, a senior director from one of the subsidiary companies which may have been merged with the parent company, a member of the family who began the business, a major customer, or one of the staff who has worked his way up through the company hierarchy. The main board director may or may not be a director working in the operating management structure of the company, sometimes known as an executive director. If he is not directly involved in the day-to-day running of the company he will have been appointed principally for his advisory skills and influence in other spheres of interest to the company, such as finance. Whatever the reason for his appointment, he is expected to contribute to the major policy decisions of the company on an equal footing with his fellow directors and to consider each issue with an open mind and strictly on its merits. This can be more difficult for the executive director than for the non-executive director.

The main board is responsible for determining the policy as a direct consequence of the objectives laid down by the owners, however imprecisely we may define "owners" and their objectives. The main board interprets those objectives and applies them in the context of the company. The managing director is answerable to the main board for the success or otherwise of the company—he is the director with the principal task of managing the company and while the main board meeting is in session he has no higher authority than any other main board member. This can cause some difficulty for any one of the main board directors who also happens to be an executive director if, in the normal day-to-day control of the business, he is directly subordinate to the managing director. While acting in the capacity of main board director, the executive director must take a broader view of the company, not just that of his immediate working responsibility.

The director on the board of a subsidiary company is appointed by the main board, which is the representative of the parent company, itself the majority shareholder. He is normally an executive director and is directly responsible for the success or failure of his company, or the part of the company of which he is head.

Directors who are not on the main board, or the board of a subsidiary company, are responsible to the managing director as any senior manager would be responsible to his immediate manager. It is likely that he is called a director to designate his particular seniority, to recognise that he is responsible for a major part of the company's activity, for example, a top staff function, and that he is regarded by the managing director as an essential participant in his working management meetings.

There is no standard reporting structure nor even a common nomenclature for the positions held by directors. This is also true lower down the company scale and to an outsider some titles can be almost meaningless. For example, one large progressive company finds it necessary to employ a manager of unannounced products, together with a sizeable staff. What kind of function each employee needs to fulfil depends very much upon the business in which the company finds itself (and directors are just as much employees as anyone else). A common debating point within a company is what level or rank each manager fills in relation to his fellow employees. Outside the confines of a particular company it is virtually impossible to say how one man in one company ranks with one in another and so the very title of director itself may be misleading.

It is likely that the larger companies will have directors (led by the managing director or chief executive) responsible for at least the following functions: finance, marketing, production and personnel. The marketing function may include sales, or sales may be set up as a major function in its own right. On the other hand sales may exist at director level and marketing may report in to sales. A commercial

ORGANISATION AND COMMUNICATIONS

director may be appointed, responsible in some companies for sales and distribution, in others for general administration. Distribution, though an important function, is seldom thought to warrant an appointment reporting to the managing director, yet a strong case could be made for it to be so. Distribution usually reports to either marketing

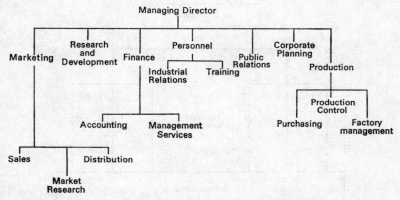

FIG. 58. *A company reporting structure*

or production, with consequent problems either way. It is discussed more fully in Chapter VII. A generalised organisation chart depicting a reporting structure (if it is possible for a general organisation to exist) is shown in Fig. 58.

Organisational structure

I. *Functional*

The concept of functional organisation was first put forward in a formal way by F. W. Taylor in 1903. Taylor is known as the father of scientific management and his collected works were published by Harper of New York in 1947 under the title *Scientific Management*. Functional organisation is expressed diagrammatically in Fig. 59. The principle is a simple one: the lowest level of employee, known as the labour force, is instructed in the various aspects of its work by the managers who are the most expert in their own particular fields. A difficulty which may occur is that the manager with the strongest personality dominates and his interests are those which tend to be given priority. We can see evidence of the functional organisation structure in companies today, but not in the extreme that Taylor advocated. Examples are in quality control and cost estimating.

Perhaps the most important contribution Taylor made to management thinking was not so much in his organisational proposals, but in bringing to the attention of the industrialist the advantages to be gained from specialisation.

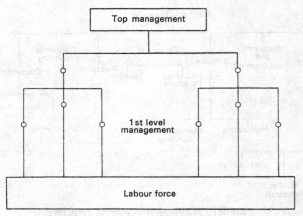

FIG. 59.   *Functional organisation*

II. *Line and staff*

The structure shown diagrammatically in Fig. 60 is known as line and staff organisation and is attributable to Colonel Lyndall F. Urwick (*The Elements of Administration*, Pitman, 1947). It is exemplified in companies today by considering personnel as a staff function. The line management A to D in Fig. 60 might be: A, chief executive of an international corporation; B, chief executive of a national subsidiary; C, general manager of a producing factory; and D, manager of a department within the factory. The factory floor operatives report to D. The corresponding personnel functions, *i.e.* the staff, might range from personnel director for the corporation to departmental personnel specialist.

In theory no link should exist between staff functions at different levels since each has its own immediate superior in line management. The staff man is there to advise his own manager, not to report to his equivalent staff colleague who happens to report to the line manager one level up. In practice there will be a communication link between staff levels, not only because it makes sense for their particular expertise to be disseminated both up and down the management chain but also because a low level staff man aspires to either taking his immediate manager's place or to advising his own manager's manager. If, however, this staff link should become a strong one there is the likelihood that the whole structure could change to a Taylor functional organisation, since staff, with its link directly to the top, might become stronger than the line managers and effectively suppress their ruling. The staff communication chain can often be faster than that of line.

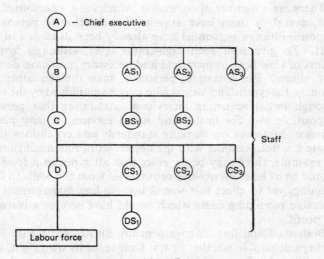

FIG. 60. *Line and staff organisation*

A strong line manager will not encourage too much contact between his own staff and those of his subordinates, as well as those of his own superiors; he will aim to keep his staff as his own direct advisers and to keep them loyal to himself.

Functional relationship

The word "functional" was used by Taylor to describe the one particular way in which he envisaged organisational control, as described previously. This has become the classical meaning of the word in the context of the organisation of the firm, but it has also been used to describe the relationship, the functional relationship, between line and staff within the firm. It is not always easy to see clearly where the line job ends and the staff one begins, and sometimes there is overlap. It could be argued, for example, that the accountant has control over and in a sense directs production because production must conform to the procedures laid down by the accountant. A functional relationship between staff and line is when staff have jurisdiction over line management—although it should occur only in the areas of specialisation of the staff function.

Staff responsibilities

There are a number of companies which have a personnel division and several of them have appointed a director of personnel; the responsibilities of personnel have already been discussed in Chapter VIII. To give staff such high-status level, although from many points of view both appropriate and necessary, can have detrimental side effects. For example, personnel may dictate, albeit unconsciously, the type of individual who may be employed by the company through initial screening interviews. Assuming that personnel is responsible also for health and social services, it may place such stringent measures on working standards and conditions that they create a serious conflict with the objectives of line management. As an example, there may be an edict that all pipes in a food factory should be at least twenty-five centimetres from the walls to facilitate cleaning, yet to effect this would involve line management in considerable rebuilding costs which would have serious adverse effects on profit.

Both staff and line management are illustrated in Fig. 58. It is perhaps debatable whether or not finance, in its own right, is a staff or a line job. It can be argued that a proper control of cash is a requirement similar to the control of the quantities of stock through production and that finance is therefore as much line as is production. On the other hand, finance provides, through accounting, a service to line management and keeps them informed of performance to date and variances.

Corporate planning is a staff job which keeps management abreast of opportunities for expansion and sets the scene for the longer term, say five years and onward. Management services usually covers organisation and methods, work study, operational research and the data-processing divisions. It might be considered a part of finance, but such a link is little more than tenuous and is justifiable only on the slender grounds that data processing in most companies began life as a tool of finance. This illustrates the problem companies have of organising their operations in such a way that they may achieve the greatest benefits from the skills and special abilities of their staff. Research and development and public relations are two further staff functions which for many companies may be luxuries which they cannot yet afford or else may exist within other staff or line responsibilities, perhaps part time. Each of these staff responsibilities is discussed in greater detail in other chapters.

The specialist barrier

If we compare the line management reporting to the chief executive in Fig. 58 with the staff, it is clear that in strictly numerical terms the senior staff functions outweigh the senior line functions by six to four. As a result, the chief executive is in danger of spending too much time receiving advice and too little in running the company. Line management may feel that their call on the chief's time is the more pressing and they can grow to resent the occasions when they are unable to see him because of his prior commitments with his staff men. The situation is known as the "specialist barrier."

A natural desire of an individual in employment is to perform as well as he is able and to be recognised as having done so. To the staff man this means acting in a highly competent and professional way so that whatever the task or service he is asked to perform, he judges his own efforts by standards he has set for himself, not necessarily those of the department in the organisation for which he is performing the service. For example, the training officer may insist that all presentations in the company should be rehearsed several times, irrespective of the level of management to whom the presentation is to be given or the degree of prior commitment or knowledge of the topic by management. He may also require that all visual aids should be drawn by a professional artist. These requirements are undoubtedly desirable in themselves, but they may not always be as necessary as the training manager thinks; in fact, if management were made fully aware of the cost of the presentation it might have an adverse effect on final acceptance. In a similar vein, the operational research specialist may employ a variety of skilled and complex techniques in an attempt to solve a particular problem, when a more simple approach would suffice. If this is taken to too great a length, line management are likely to refuse in future to call upon the services of the staff functions because either they feel that the staff man is "out of touch" or they fear that he is usurping their own position in the organisation. It is sometimes difficult to maintain a proper balance in a staff job, to give a service which is good but not overpowering.

Employee roles

A role in the employment context satisfies a number of human needs. It provides:

1. status and recognition, a sense of belonging;
2. expected patterns of behaviour, a conformity to conventions;
3. an activity with consequent responsibility.

The role which an employee sees for himself does not necessarily coincide with the role that others see for him. Furthermore, the personal attributes of the individual filling each particular job colour the role. It is essential therefore that whenever an effort is made to evaluate a role it is the role itself which is analysed and not the job into which an individual has moulded it by his own flair and initiative, however commendable they may be. Distinguishing between the role and the man becomes even more important when, for example, one company merges with another and a particular position takes on that much more responsibility. The job title may be the same, but the level of management skill required can be considerably more. It is not easy to reject the two natural contenders for one job, *i.e.* the incumbents in the two companies which have merged, in favour of a more capable man from outside, even if one can be found.

Most management positions are filled by men (or women) who have demonstrated managerial ability, but in some circumstances it is professional, technical or academic skills which count. For example, if we consider for a moment a doctor as fulfilling a management role, as soon as he qualifies he is recognised to be the equal of his fellow doctors, capable of taking a position of responsibility in his field. But an older man will have greater experience than the younger and it is possible that the young man may be working to the limit of his capabilities while the more experienced doctor may be finding that his job is under-utilising his real abilities.

Structured conflict

A business organisation is similar to any other kind of human institution: it is made up of people of various types, some of whom get along extremely well together while others find co-operation difficult to achieve. It is possible, however unwittingly, for the organisation itself to have created its own built-in, structured conflict so that whoever were to fill two conflicting roles of this kind, each would soon find reasons for refusing to accept the opinions of the other. An example is the staff man, perhaps with an easier line of access to more senior management, who over the years has been allowed to believe that his advice weighs more heavily than that of other staff men; or the assistant branch manager who, when the branch grew into a district with branches of its own, became a personal assistant to his same manager, now a newly promoted district manager, while other men were appointed as branch managers covering the territories for which he was previously responsible.

The cause of the difficulty is usually the imprecise definition of the responsibilities of the roles which suffer from structured conflict. The result can be:

1. a degree of co-operation, coupled with an aura of "muddling through," and the distinct possibility that neither side will take action when it is needed, each blaming the other for taking or having assumed responsibility; or

2. a built-in quarrel, causing friction at the personal level which can last even after the respective managers have moved on to other jobs within the company, so endangering the smooth running of the company in other spheres as well; or

3. a hidden line of authority whereby the man with the stronger personality gets his own way, irrespective of their relative management levels. In this case the dividing line of responsibility between them shifts towards the weaker of the two men. An equilibrium level is reached, but it can be totally upset if one of the men moves on, when a new balance has to be achieved with a new personality on the scene.

Management responsibilities

Management at all levels, to some degree or another, are concerned with the future as well as with the present. They are responsible for co-ordinating, organising, planning, controlling, reporting and directing, which can be remembered by means of the mnemonic COPCORD.

Co-ordinating is achieved through a proper awareness of the responsibilities and capabilities of subordinates as well as an understanding of the responsibilities of other departments and the objectives of higher management.

Organising means ensuring that objectives set for subordinates are realistically achievable by grouping, defining and delegating tasks and by establishing a proper relationship between an individual's authority and his related responsibility.

Planning is the process by which the manager forecasts and develops objectives or goals. It involves the anticipation of problems and the development of policies and procedures in answer to them, within a related budget. In short, planning is thinking before doing.

Controlling means measuring performance against pre-determined standards, evaluating progress and steering the whole department in the required direction.

Operating is all that work which a manager does in simply being a manager: the execution of the day-to-day requirements involved in carrying out his job.

Reporting embraces the administrative work of the manager, including reporting progress to his superiors.

Directing involves keeping the subordinate properly motivated on an appropriate and meaningful path, best achieved by selecting the right people in the first place, by team building, communication, appraisal, counselling and training.

An equivalent mnemonic found in some management texts is POSDCORB, which stands for planning, organising, staffing, directing, co-ordinating, reporting and budgeting. The responsibilities identified by these words are the same as those which make up COPCORD, but they are defined differently. It will be seen that the elements of POSDCORB are contained within COPCORD and vice versa.

It is a simple truism that without authority, the execution of responsibility is difficult if not impossible to achieve. Authority should be clearly distinguished from power. It is possible to have power without authority; for example, a shop steward may have the power to cause a work stoppage, without necessarily the authority to do so. Responsibility requires related authority, but the possession of power obviates the necessity for authority.

Many managers complain that they have responsibility but not the authority that goes with it. As a minimum therefore management must be given the authority to:

1. allocate tasks to individuals under their control;
2. decide which areas are discretionary and to conduct reviews when they see fit;
3. assess differentially and reward;
4. veto appointments;
5. remove an individual from his role when it is necessary to do so.

The last point is thought by some managers to be their least attractive responsibility and a discussion on role/individual compatibility deserves a chapter to itself. However, it is of interest to note that one way of persuading a person to leave his job of his own accord is to reduce his responsibility in the job, yet leave him at the same salary level. He may become dissatisfied with his own standing or status within the company and eventually quit.

The manager may adopt this approach unwittingly and be pleasantly surprised and relieved when his subordinate does finally go, thus saving him the unsavoury task of reducing salary or asking the subordinate to leave his employ. Equally the subordinate can resent the fact that his responsibilities are reduced and may consequently cause increasing difficulties for his manager. This could lead to a final breach which may force the manager to take positive action and dismiss his subordinate—or again the subordinate may leave of his own accord.

Measurement of management performance

As we proceed through the management chain from director through manager to foreman and supervisor, the responsibilities change from those of long-term planning to those of short-term operations. The lower down the management scale the easier it is to set objectives and measure performance. To take extremes, the foreman on the factory floor may be charged with producing a given number of products within a given time period (this does imply other responsibilities but for the purpose of this illustration we shall not consider them), and the managing director may be contemplating new products, new marketing domains or an increase in production facilities. It would be difficult to say precisely how well the managing director has performed, at least until after the results of his decisions can be assessed, whereas the foreman can be monitored much more quickly.

It is common for performance to be measured in quantifiable terms, yet frequently quantification is difficult to achieve and qualitative methods must be applied. An apparently simple yardstick is performance against budget, but as discussed in Chapter V it depends very much on how the budget has been compiled and whether the manager concerned has full control over the factors which affect his cost effectiveness. Furthermore the budget is often self-fulfilling: either the manager spends up to his budget whether or not he needs to, or he goes over budget, with appropriate justification, by so much that such spending is built into subsequent budgets.

There is frequently a recognisable difference between an official or formal situation and the real life one: in legal terms, we would say on the one hand *de jure* and on the other *de facto*. Further complications are introduced when we consider each individual's behaviour in any particular situation. Two important factors are:

1. the personality and character of the individual concerned;
2. the situation itself.

The situation can be interpreted in different ways by different people and the perception of the situation is of far greater relevance than the situation itself. It might be argued that an unwritten management responsibility is to act as an entrepreneur, at least for management at the higher levels, and that risk taking is part of the job. To what extent should the manager disregard preconceived measures of performance if he sees an opportunity, however risky, to improve his own position and that of his company? Such a question must be borne in mind when determining the discretionary content of a manager's responsibility.

Human activity always involves objectives and the exercise of discretion within limits: the management of a business organisation is no exception. Before management performance can be measured, objectives must be set and agreed between the manager and his immediate superior. This process has become commonly known as Management by Objectives, or M.B.O. The objectives must cover the duties of the manager, the tasks he is committed to complete, the date of completion, the standards he is expected to achieve, the expected results of his labours and the work he must maintain and keep running. They must also specify the limits of his responsibility, how far he can go in taking decisions, the extent of his discretionary powers and the areas in which he is free to use his own judgment and initiative without recourse to higher management. It is helpful, too, if it is known in advance what are the consequences of the manager making marginally poor decisions and how soon it would be known that such decisions have been made. This time period would help to determine the appropriate interval between consecutive review meetings.

It might be said that the formation of so much information on the objectives of each manager in the company would be an almost impossible task and doubtless that is right. However, unless a conscious effort is made to compile such information, any attempt at assessing how well the manager has performed becomes meaningless. It would be wrong to suggest that only if the objectives are written down in the form described above are they sufficiently definitive; many senior managers will say that they know what they expect from their lower levels of management and thereby have defined and specified their objectives. Unfortunately, not always do the lower levels of management clearly understand themselves what are the objectives laid down for them.

It is not the misfit or the continuously bad manager who causes the difficulties, but the marginal performer. It is he who one day may do just sufficiently well and another not well enough. He causes problems by not taking decisions at the time when they should be taken. It is only human to be sympathetic, to be charitable and to sustain hope; it takes time to decide what action is needed concerning the marginal performer.

Time span

As a result of his joint work with the Tavistock Institute of Human Relations and with the Glacier Metal Company in the United Kingdom, Elliott Jaques developed the idea of relating the level of responsibility that an employee undertook with the time between the making of a decision and the discovery that it was a wrong one, if indeed a wrong one it had been in the first place. The time that is of most interest is the one which, when all the decisions made by an individual in his employment have been considered, turns out to be the longest. This is defined as the time span for that individual's job. In his book *Equitable Payment* (Heinemann, 1961) Jaques defined it more formally as "the time span of discretion," which is "the period of time during which marginally sub-standard discretion could be exercised in a role before information about the accumulating sub-standard work would become available to the manager in charge of the role." For example, the girl on the production line soldering the joints on an electrical component will know within fifteen minutes or so whether her work is up to standard. The quality-control inspector will be able to pick it out within that time. On the other hand, the chief executive of an aircraft manufacturer who commits his company to a new design will not know for several years, perhaps twenty, whether or not his decision has been a correct one. Within these two extremes lies the whole gamut of company activity and we can see, according to Jaques, the relative responsibility rating of every individual by using this method.

Table XIV illustrates the relationship between individual capacity, weight of responsibility and conventional pay or reward. The third column includes benefits additional to salary, such as a company car, assistance with housing, a pension scheme and so on. The weight of responsibility is related directly to the time-span concept and is subdivided into blocks or ranks.

Individual capacity is a measure of the capability of the individual to carry responsibility at a given level with competence but without undue psychological stress. It would be hoped that any given individual would fit exactly along a horizontal line drawn on Table XIV at his appropriate conventional pay level, but in reality his position plotted separately in each column would be unlikely to form such a straight line.

TABLE XIV
RESPONSIBILITY RANKING

Individual capacity to carry responsibility at a given level competently and without undue psychological stress	Weight of responsibility (related directly to time-span concept)	Conventional pay or reward (1977 rates)
Rank VI and higher	10 years plus	£20,000 plus
Rank V	up to 5 years	£12,000
Rank IV	up to 3 years	£8,000
Rank III	up to 18 months	£5,000
Rank II	up to 9 months	£3,500
Rank I	up to 3 months	£2,000

The man whose capacity level is below that of his weight of responsibility is likely to show signs of stress. He probably takes work home with him, says "we" instead of "I" and continuously looks for support. Instead of making up his own mind for himself, he seeks confirmation from the boss every time and holds too many meetings with his subordinates. At the other extreme there is the promotion seeker who is capable of more than the position he occupies. Unless he is given the responsibility he deserves, he may encroach upon other people's areas of responsibility and may cause an internal company feud. Otherwise he may use up his extra capacity outside his immediate place of work, say, as a local politician or sportsman; or he may become a highly competent shop steward.

There are some jobs which demand high-capacity personnel who may only need to demonstrate their skills and capacity at infrequent intervals. Most of the time people of lower capacity could do the job just as well, but occasionally the high-capacity man becomes essential. For example, the chief engineer in a fully automated nuclear power station will, it is hoped, spend most of his working life dealing with routine maintenance. But just once or twice it is likely that his decisions could mean life or death to a large number of people. In a similar way the airline pilot will use his major skills only at take-off or landing, or at times of real emergency. These events are relatively so infrequent that there is a real danger that these highly competent and expert men will go stale and not be able to deal with the emergency situations as competently as if they had occurred more frequently. Such situations are avoided by continual retraining and experience in emergency through simulation.

There are some generalisations which can be made about the rankings as shown in Table XIV, but first we should consider the observation that organisations have probably evolved to meet the capacities of the people they employ. This means that ranks will not necessarily have the same dividing lines in different organisations, although there will obviously be some correlation. Rank III management are likely to have around four hundred to six hundred people reporting to them all at one location, while rank IV may have responsibility for dispersed forces with, say, three or four factories under control. Rank II provides the company with its junior to middle management, starting with the foreman and going as high as the departmental manager. Rank I usually contains the manual worker level, which does not have managerial responsibilities, although at the higher end there are the charge-hands and supervisory staff.

The dividing line between rank I and rank II can be identified as the Us and Them line. It is here that one is likely to see the point at which employees consider themselves to be either with the workers or with management. Trade union activity tends to be most forceful in rank I, although that is not to say that it cannot be found in strength at higher ranks. There is the general feeling in rank I that the individual is working only if he is "at work," *i.e.* if he is driving his bus, operating his drill or loading his van.

These observations apply only when the size of rank I is measured by time span and individual capacity. The market forces of supply and demand can inflate or deflate the salary or wages paid to any individual, as can vocational attitudes. It would, for example, be wrong to place the nurse or the teacher in rank I for capacity or time-span reasons, but at least in the early years of their respective professions their salary level would impute so. Similarly there are a number of jobs occupied by women that are relatively low paid because it is common practice for them to be so. The private secretary, may be "worth her weight in gold" but it is unlikely that she is paid accordingly.

Rank II contains the bulk of management; they are responsible for ensuring that the policies of higher management are properly applied, particularly the managers right at the bottom of rank II whose job it is to see that the rank I employees actually implement policy as it affects them. At more senior levels within the company there is a measure of give and take, an acceptance that the subordinate manager may question the instructions he is given, even though he may finally have to accept them without change. At the bottom of rank II, however—or the bottom of the executive chain, as it has been expressed by Lord Wilfred Brown who was managing director of the Glacier Metal Company when Jaques was working there—the manager, perhaps foreman, is told that it is his job to settle the men without recourse back up the chain. The chain likes to hear that everything is running smoothly in the way that it has decreed and so the unpleasant situations at the lower levels are not always properly discussed or mutually resolved; the procedures and methods of operation are imposed from above.

According to Lord Wilfred Brown in *Exploration in Management* (Heinemann, 1961) it is common for a gap in communication to exist between rank I and rank II, not because the lower levels of management are incompetent but because they are powerless to resolve the differences between their subordinates and their management. It is in this kind of situation that the shop steward comes to the fore. He is able to communicate with the men more effectively because he has their direct interests at heart—he is one of them—and he can also speak on behalf of the men with management. The lower levels of management may have considerable sympathy with the case put forward, but they must remember with whom their loyalties must lie. In this kind of situation there could develop unconscious collusion between lower management and the factory floor which, in the long run, might help to find a solution.

Figure 61 illustrates a possible reporting structure laid out to show how the branches of the management tree lie in the different ranks. Manager B has been placed in rank III along with his subordinate manager C. Manager D, who also reports to B, is in rank II. On most occasions the reporting levels bridge over from one rank to another, but the C reporting to B situation is quite possible. When it does occur it is most likely to happen in rank III. The D to B to A reporting structure works well enough, but it is possible for C to recognise his proximity to A and therefore to tend to go over B's head. B has the authority to prevent this from happening but, knowing C's relative seniority, is likely to treat the matter with some leniency. Rank III is particularly susceptible to this kind of situation because it is here that the longer-serving members of the company cluster. They may not have the ability or the capacity to progress into rank IV management so they tend to settle at the high rank III level. Frequently, management consultants descend upon companies which have such rank III management and by pruning produce a more effective management structure. Some few years later, however, as the lower levels of management get older and more experienced, the cluster almost inevitably reappears.

Rank II and rank III managers are likely to be thinking about

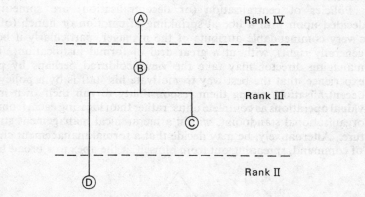

FIG. 61. *Reporting in rank*

their work both on and off the job and, so it is said, will sometimes solve their most pressing problems while relaxing in the armchair at home. In general their thinking is conceptual—they do not need to be immersed in the factory atmosphere to arrive at a solution but they do think in concrete and tangible terms, for example, a new factory layout or a new sales incentive scheme. On the other hand, ranks IV and above need to concentrate upon more abstract considerations such as in which market the company should be, the overall size of the manufacturing plants and how they should be tooled up to meet future demand. They are concerned with the company as a whole, or at the very least a major division of it. In contrast, however, they are likely to be defenders of the status quo, if for no better reason than that they have enough on their plate already.

Centralisation or decentralisation

There are no hard-and-fast rules to guide management in the choice between a decentralised organisation and a centralised one. Which of the two is preferred depends very much upon the moment in time, the particular industry and the attitude of management. It is difficult even to define precisely what is meant by centralisation since many organisations which consider themselves to be centralised (or decentralised) may from the outside appear to be quite the reverse. Furthermore there may be some parts of the business which are considerably more centralised than others, thus making an overall assessment of the extent of centralisation that much more difficult.

Policies of centralisation (or decentralisation) are sometimes decided upon with a liberal sprinkling of emotion or hunch (often a very commendable attribute of the manager, particularly if he is generally right), without a great deal of formal justification. The managing director may take the view, coloured perhaps by past experience, that the best way to motivate his staff is by a policy of decentralisation, giving them responsibility to run their own individual operations as complete units, rather than locating each, from an organisational standpoint, within a hierarchical management structure. Alternatively, he may decide that a formal management chain of command, spreading out from himself at the apex to a broad base

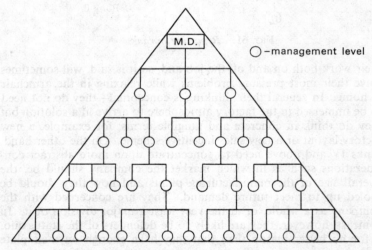

FIG. 62. *Centralised organisation*

at the bottom of a pyramid, is better than a number of self-contained sub-units. Figure 62 illustrates the latter, centralised, approach.

If the company chooses decentralisation it must acknowledge a diminution of operating control from the centre. The group headquarters takes on the task of providing a service to the subsidiary companies, as shown for the hypothetical bakery company in Fig. 63. It could be argued that each of the subsidiary companies is autonomous and has charge of its own destiny. Yet all must accept the service functions offered from the centre because each has specific bakery experience and can operate more cheaply than a similar function called in from outside or one working within each of the subsidiaries. There is therefore a combination of decentralisation and

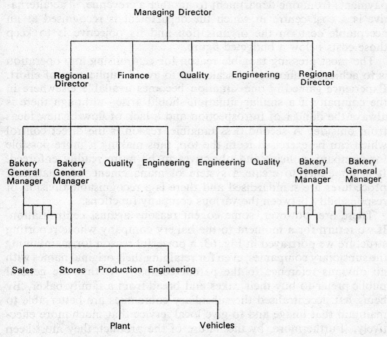

FIG. 63. *Decentralised organisation—bakery*

centralisation, choosing the most appropriate organisation to fit the circumstances.

Central control is usually maintained on matters of finance. Each subsidiary has a target profit on which it is measured and it is not able to make any capital expenditure without approval from the centre. This means that the profits made by each of the subsidiaries can be pooled and a total reserve put aside for capital expenditure. This reserve can be reallocated to the subsidiaries in the way which best suits the long-term interests of the company as a whole. A subsidiary which is making high profits now may not be the best one in which to reinvest those high profits for the future.

A decentralised operation is far more likely to have a profit awareness among the lower levels of management than is a centralised one: each decentralised part of the company may behave as a profit centre in its own right. It is accountable for maintaining an acceptable level of revenue, holding down costs and achieving a target profit. It is possible for any department to be set up as a profit centre in this way, although perhaps unrealistic to consider transfer payments from one department to another as revenue. The alternative is a cost centre in which the department is recognised as an acceptable cost on the organisation and its objective is to keep those costs below a budgeted figure.

The most pressing tangible reason for centralising any operation is to achieve economies of scale and to avoid duplication of effort. Experience gained in one situation becomes available elsewhere in the company if a similar situation should arise—although there is always the danger of introspection and a lack of flow of new ideas from outside. A second, less tangible, reason is the direct control which can be exercised from the top, thus making it more possible for company policies and objectives to be more readily enforced. It is far easier to create a system of management information if procedures are standardised and there is a recognisable division of responsibility between the various company functions.

There are, however, some cogent reasons against centralisation. If we return for a moment to the bakery company whose reporting structure we portrayed in Fig. 63, a powerful reason for maintaining the subsidiary companies, even for retaining their original names with no obvious reference to the parent company, is that the general public prefer to buy their cakes and bread from a family baker. By being left decentralised the subsidiary companies are better able to maintain that image and to give local service that much more effectively. Furthermore, by the nature of the product, they must keep their customers supplied with fresh produce and so a local manufacturing plant and distribution network are essential. However, even the bakery operation is not as decentralised as might at first be thought. The bakery manager has no jurisdiction over price, quality standards or raw materials and little say in the range of goods he provides. All of these factors are controlled from the centre, as also, for example, is centralised buying, which is common in most large companies. The same applies to the large international companies, where local management may not have the freedom to manufacture their products under their own full control. The employees of the company may be nationals of the countries in which they operate and the company may have a national image; but in reality the management are restricted in the major decisions of policy, just like the bakery general manager, and the company may be little more than an import agency, however large.

Some factors which should be taken into account before adopting a policy of centralisation are listed below.

1. *Inflexibility*. Centralisation demands standardisation and uniformity, with laid-down procedures. There is less room for the entrepreneur and hence less opportunity to take advantage of an unexpected situation. It maintains rigidity and induces a delineation of responsibility which can be difficult to disturb.

2. *Complexity*. Standardised procedures are developed to cover every eventuality. The more centralised an organisation becomes, the more standardisation is required and the more difficult it is to accommodate every possible situation.

3. *Bureaucracy*. There are few short cuts and procedures are followed to the letter. Whole departments may emerge to ensure that the proper channels are followed, irrespective of the urgency or the reason for the job in the first place. In time, the procedures themselves may dominate and the reasons for them be forgotten.

4. *Autocracy*. Central control is a valuable asset provided it is not unreasonably excessive. There are times when in the best interest of the company rules should be broken, yet that is sometimes difficult to do in an overtly centralised company. The sparkle of individuality may become lost.

5. *Morale*. Everybody needs to feel that what he is doing is part of a worthwhile whole. He must know why he is doing it and what purpose he serves. The worker on the mass production line may be frustrated and bored, a major source of interest the likelihood of a strike in support of a cause about which he may care very little. Centralisation may reduce responsibility and erode away job incentives.

6. *Redundancy*. In a decentralised organisation individuals become used to doing more than the one job and tend to help their colleagues in times of adversity. Centralisation can mean that each department is self-contained and must employ sufficient people to cater for the peak loads as well as for the occasions, such as holidays and sickness, when additional complementary staff are required.

7. *Delays*. With any system, procedures must be followed and obeyed otherwise the result will be confusion. If there are any priority situations they must be known to the system in advance and be capable of easy identification. It is not always possible to get the priorities ordered in the correct sequence for all eventual-

ities, both present and future. As a result, certain parts of the company may suffer delays from time to time which they may consider unacceptable.

COMMUNICATIONS

Communication is the life blood of a company, heavily dependent upon the way the company is organised to accommodate it. Just as a company may lose business by running short of stock, so a break in the communication chain can have equally adverse effects. It is the duty of every employee to ensure that he is communicating the right information at the right time to the colleagues who need it.

Horizontal and vertical communications

The job of maintaining good communications in a firm can be difficult. Managers are inclined to believe that their own particular system is far better than it really is. Experiments have been conducted which show that information which has travelled down through several levels loses considerable factual content. An average of 20 per cent can be lost through five levels of management, and poor communications can be a serious handicap to the smooth functioning of a firm.

It is through communication that we learn. A knowledge of what other people have done helps to ensure that wasteful duplication does not occur and allows new discoveries to be made, each building upon the one before. Animals are unable to communicate in the way we humans do, except in the simplest form. They are of a lower order of intelligence, but if they were able to communicate more effectively they would probably be able to pass down their experiences from generation to generation. Instead of animals of this age being very similar to those of an earlier time, we might find that they had learned and, presumably, changed in some way. Education is only possible through efficient communication.

Horizontal communication is that which takes place between equivalent levels of management. It avoids duplication of effort, broadens the experience of each manager and helps to co-ordinate departmental activities in implementing company policy. An example of poor horizontal communication is the following situation, which could have occurred in many companies. Raw materials were purchased in bulk by the buying department of a major company because high discounts were offered for large quantities. The factory warehouse manager, keen to reduce his inventory, persuaded the production manager that he should step up production and convert the raw materials into finished goods, which were then to be dispatched to the company's depots. The sales manager, concerned that depot stocks were getting high and were using up valuable space to the detriment of other products, decided that his sales force should make greater efforts, and the stocks were sold off at heavy discounts. As the stocks were being depleted at a fast rate and the production workers were accustomed to full and overtime working, another bulk load of raw materials was purchased and the whole cycle began again.

It is not difficult to see the reasons for this episode. With strong overall management at the top such a situation would be stopped long before any harm could be caused. However, in a complex business organisation which has a well-defined organisation structure and responsibilities, the manager of each department expects to operate in his own interests as efficiently as he possibly can; doubtless each manager did in this particular case. But the real problem was one of communication. They communicated what they wanted to happen, but not the reasons for it. One might cite this example as evidence of the saying, "Good communications are the essence of good management."

The organisation chart is a formal way of depicting how communications should be maintained within a company, but if it were strictly adhered to, the company would surely not survive. A stable organisation with an inorganic structure can tolerate for some while the convention that only managers at equivalent level may communicate: if the subordinate of one manager needs to speak with a manager at the same level as his own, he must do so through his immediate manager. In time this will lead to inefficiencies, although it can be argued that it is an efficient method provided necessary exceptions are allowed.

Downward communication in a firm is broadly of two types, one which instructs staff in the responsibilities of their job, the other which provides more background information about the firm. If too much attention is devoted to the former, employees do not feel involved in or become a part of the firm. Ignorance can be an important factor giving rise to discontent. Frequently the average worker has only a vague idea of the nature of the work of senior executives, and little knowledge of matters relating to his daily occupation, such as the output of his department and its relation to the output of other departments and to that of the firm as a whole. If he does not understand the reasons for orders received, he cannot appreciate the motives behind them; thus instructions are liable to misinterpretation.

Downward communication can be achieved in a variety of ways. Although the written word is more explicit, as it is a statement of what is required and can be referred to at a later time in case of doubt, it can in certain circumstances be less effective than the spoken word since it is impersonal and does not allow for a two-way communication. One drawback of verbal communication is that if A gives B a verbal message which is passed on, C tends to get 90 per cent of it, D gets 80 per cent and so on. No two men respond to a message in exactly the same way. Words are slippery tools, as T. S. Eliot once said, for "they slip, slide, crack and break under strain." Few men use them as precision tools. Items of concern or interest to all employees can be communicated by circular letter, perhaps in the wage packet, by notice board or by public address. If the communication is simply a description of procedures which need to be followed, it can be incorporated in a procedures manual. Each individual who receives the message will be interested only in that which applies directly to him, so there is little to be gained in writing a large number of general points followed by a specific one at the end. It is likely to be missed. Whatever method is used, the words must be appropriate to the audience, otherwise misunderstandings may occur.

Successful communication depends upon more than a common language, the use of a common set of words. Because people vary in their intelligence, experiences and social positions in life, they have widely differing mental attitudes and modes of thought. For example, the language of the trained expert is not that of the layman, the language of the director may not be the same as the worker's. For clear communication between the top and bottom of an organisation, these differences in modes of thought must be recognised.

In both verbal and written communication it is important that ideas are not wrapped up in long words and involved sentences, but are clearly and simply expressed. There can be semantic problems, for words may have several meanings. Vocabulary needs to be carefully chosen so that the person receiving the message understands in the way it is intended. It is far easier for management to communicate downwards than for communication to be in the other direction. However, the upward flow is particularly important because it is with information, the result of communication, that management can take realistic decisions. Even so, it is unlikely that top management really hear what they should; they are often told only that which the lower levels think they ought to know or which hides their own weaknesses, not necessarily what top management themselves would want to hear.

An effective means of getting feedback from one's staff is to go to them, to take every opportunity to hear their point of view on a man-to-man basis. Care must be exercised to prevent any "between levels" of management from feeling that they are left out in the cold, but in moderation this approach can lead to a lowering of any communication barrier which may exist. We have discussed earlier in this chapter the gap in the bottom of the executive chain and how it is filled in part by the shop steward.

In addition to official vertical communication there is informal communication (the grapevine), which can be exceedingly fast and surprisingly accurate. If a particularly important item of information needs to be released only at a specific time, great care must be taken to ensure that it does not leak out in advance and that if several locations are to give the information at the same time, then they are properly synchronised. Communication is not a benevolent act on the part of the employer; it is a recognition of the employee's right to know and if the employee is not informed through official channels he will very quickly learn through the grapevine, perhaps with quite the wrong interpretation placed upon it, however factual the information may be. In contrast, if no information is made available, unfounded rumours may come into existence to "fill the gap." It is important that management should recognise the existence of informal communication so that its contribution is made positive rather than negative.

There is the story which passed quickly to the workers via the grapevine concerning a new table which had been bought for management use for £500. There were muttered complaints among the workers about the special privileges of the management until the real story was told: the previous firm had paid £500 for it, but their own firm had obtained it as a bargain for £3. Only the adverse and mistaken information had leaked through to the staff, not the accurate story.

Communication nets

Many problems of communication are linked to the type of organisation used for the collection and dissemination of information. It is important to use the type of network most appropriate to the circumstances. Here are some examples of possible communication networks.

Where much information has to be correlated from a large number of sources, it is advantageous to have one highly centralised position with others arranged peripherally (as in Fig. 64(*a*)). However, where initiative, creativity and high morale are important, a different arrangement is necessary; otherwise, if all behaviour becomes routine, initiative and adaptation to a changing environment can be weakened.

One can imagine a circle formation of six individuals who, in order to solve a problem, must share as quickly as possible the information each person possesses. Each of the six may send information, in

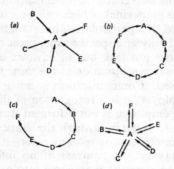

FIG. 64. *Communication nets*

writing, only to his immediate neighbours, the one on his right and the one on his left. Experiments have shown that the number of mistakes made by individuals working in a "circle" pattern can be reduced by about 60 per cent by removing one link and making the pattern a "chain," as in Fig. 64(*c*). Members of a circle pattern are likely to enjoy their task because they can interact, both giving and taking messages; morale is high, but organisation is poor and accuracy is low. In the chain formation, organisation is more stable but morale is low. In the star form (Fig. 64(*d*)) speed of communication is likely to be much better than in the circle or chain. The leadership pattern is clear, immediate and stable, but morale is poor.

Committees

The maximum size for a committee should be in the region of six to eight members; any larger number and there is likely to be a loss of communication between the members and a lack of understanding. It will also be that much more difficult to reach agreement. Committees can be divided broadly into four types from the point of view of information and communication flow.

1. *Informative*. This can be an informal group of, for example, all supervisors in a department, or of departmental heads. It may be a regular meeting or *ad hoc*. The purpose is to explain some new policy or measure of interest and benefit to the staff, for example, a new pension scheme. It may take the form of a "briefing group" system, where each level of management explains what is happening, and why, to the next level down. The purpose is to give pertinent information geared deliberately to have profitable effect on all employees. In this way vagueness and lack of factual information about the organisation can be eliminated. This approach tends to effect a general improvement in morale and the status of foremen and junior managers. By the use of group discussions, staff are able to identify the objectives of management with their own, and their energies are canalised for that purpose. Attempts to change the attitudes of individuals apart from the group are likely to fail, but by the use of group discussions the individual is more willing to comply, by recognising that he belongs to the group.

2. *Joint consultative committee*. The normal form is the coming together of a group of managers with an elected team of workpeople. Where a business or part of the business is trade union organised, the workers' representatives are usually shop stewards. It provides a useful means by which management can acknowledge the views of others before a decision is taken, particularly where advance assessment is needed of the possible reaction to a new idea which it is thought may prove unpopular.

3. *Problem-solving committee*. A committee is frequently constituted so that the responsibility for taking decisions becomes a shared one. There is a chairman whose job it is to see that all points of view get a fair hearing and that all the deliberations of the committee are relevant and to the point. He will, in advance, have prepared an agenda or have had it prepared, and it will have been circulated to all members of the committee in sufficient time before the meeting for them to give proper consideration to the implications of its points. During the meeting ample time is allowed for discussion without it being too much. At an appropriate time the chairman takes a vote, and the decision is made either on a simple majority or on, say, a two-thirds majority, *i.e.* at least two-thirds of the committee must approve for the decision to be accepted. In the case of a tie when a simple majority is required, the chairman has the casting vote. It is important that the members of the committee should be of equivalent rank. Any suggestion of a hierarchical structure limits the freedom of expression of the lower levels; this is particularly so if the manager and a direct subordinate are both members of the same committee.

4. *Advisory committee.* A manager of a department and his subordinates may compose an advisory committee. The staff may play an active part in decision making, or only air their views and opinions so that the manager will be better equipped to come to a decision unilaterally. Since the manager is in a position of ultimate responsibility and authority (unlike a committee chairman, who is really only the committee's spokesman), he may decide to modify the views of his "advisers," just as the President of the United States might do when faced with a major problem.

Perception, semantics and communication

Successful communication, in the sense of total understanding, does not necessarily take place when persons talk to each other, for example, when a supervisor conveys a message to a work group. Communication depends for its success partly on the ability of the communicator to choose the right words and partly on the ability of the recipient to perceive or understand what is being conveyed. Some appreciation of the barriers which can distort communication is important.

There is first the semantic language problem. Words are the symbols or labels, however inadequate, by which we convey facts, ideas and feelings to each other. (Non-verbal behaviour is omitted from this discussion, though the importance of signs, facial expressions and bodily postures as another form of communication is acknowledged.) A breakdown in communication can occur in interpretation as a result of misunderstanding, since words can have various meanings and those used by one person can be interpreted by another in a way contrary to what was intended. An illustration can be taken from the use of the word "profit." Management are likely to see profit as the reward for running a successful business, and perhaps as an opportunity to buy new equipment, to expand and to create new jobs. Employees may see it as unfair, as a surplus amount of money unearned and unmerited. Any attempt to communicate about profits must overcome this barrier of incompatible ideas about the word.

The confusion over words is part of the greater problem of differing social and cultural experiences. Each of us tends to see and understand things in a different way from other people. We form our attitudes (the combinations of beliefs and feelings which influence our behaviour) by a process of assimilating information. In some matters we tend to act in a rational, logical and predictable manner, in others we tend to act in an irrational and unpredictable way;

this is largely due to the emotional elements in our attitudes, and is perhaps the result of such factors as insecurity, fear, anger and prejudice. Our perceptions, the way we see things, are shaped partly by our past experiences and by the inherited characteristics, emotions and instincts which make up our personalities.

In looking at a fact, event or object we rarely see the whole thing, but we tend to abstract, to pick out certain characteristics, and then to assume that this constitutes the whole and to ignore the rest. There is an inclination to discount information which conflicts with our own attitudes, and to accept only those factors which we know about and believe. Sometimes it is in any case difficult to see the whole. Thus witnesses of a car accident are likely to give differing accounts, having seen it from various viewpoints; and this is yet another example of partial perception, where only one aspect of the whole is seen.

There is also the problem of distinguishing between facts and abstractions. A fact is something which is true or concrete in the sense that something exists, or has taken place, about which we can make a definite statement, *e.g.* the price of a car, the production quota of a factory. An abstraction is an idea or quality which is considered quite apart from its concrete expressions, and which therefore cannot be so easily seen to be true or so readily defined, *e.g.* efficiency, morale.

Conversation can take place at a factual level, or at the level of generalities and abstractions. For example, the following is a factual statement. "There was a 30 per cent turnover in the staff in our firm this year compared to a 15 per cent turnover last year." An abstract generalisation or inference from this would be, "Management–staff relations are getting worse in our firm." This is a conclusion, which may or may not be true, based on one individual interpretation of the above fact. A value statement would be, "This is a terrible company in which to work." A comment such as "Something should be done about it" could be called a purposeful communiqué. Most communication tends to take place at the level of such abstractions, and only infrequently at the factual concrete level. The problem is that we rarely make the effort to distinguish between these two levels of reasoning and may give them equal weight as facts intead of seeing some of them as generalisations or subjective evaluations.

It is so easy to form false ideas and prejudices based on wrong conclusions. For example, a foreign worker might conclude, on the basis of working only in the one firm mentioned above, that businesses in this country had poor human relations and that management never cared about their staff, in the same way as a tourist abroad might decide on insufficient evidence that the food was poor or too expensive. When talk is confined to specifics such as the role of the mechanics in a firm, it is easier to verify or deny the statements. However, if talk is confined to various abstract levels, such as mechanics in general, labour or the working class, manpower, etc., it is difficult to refute sweeping generalities, which may well be false although they sound plausible.

It is important to be aware of the pitfalls of language and of false reasoning. Terms such as "workers," "trade unionists" and "managers" are abstractions. Though it is useful and convenient to categorise people as members of such groups, it is difficult to make generalisations about their characteristics, for whatever they have in common, these individuals have characteristics which would identify them also with other groups, *e.g.* national, religious and cultural. One should avoid generalisations based on "black/white thinking," which assumes that things can be classed categorically as right or wrong, "them and us," in rigid polarities, making no allowance for the infinite variations which are possible. An appreciation of the effect of time and space is also important, and an ability to think in "contextual terms." For example, there is no point in believing that worker A or firm B or process C is always efficient, without allowing for changes brought about by time and altered circumstances.

Perfect verbal communication is not possible as this would require the bringing of identical experiences to the same words. However, there are a number of aids to assist clear thinking and improved communication. Harold Leavitt has defined the efficient communicator as "one who shoots information to hit a target and who gets feedback to know the target has been hit." The success of communication can be judged by whether or not the receiver has both understood the message and taken the required action. Simple concise language, containing the essentials and no irrelevant information, is vital. The presence of extraneous information will most likely produce "noise" (defined here as any distortion or error which can prevent the receiver from gaining the message), which will lessen the chances of success.

The communicator is most likely to succeed if he is able to speak or write logically and clearly in the kind of language familiar to his audience. Naturally the diction appropriate to a diplomatic gathering is not the same as that for a garden party or a union meeting. Certainly the qualities of empathy, sensitivity to the problems of others and the ability to imagine oneself in their place and to see things as they do will help a supervisor or manager when talking to a group of employees. One must bear in mind the tendency of people to act irrationally as a result of emotive influences on their behaviour.

When the communicator knows in advance that he is likely to encounter an unfavourable reaction, he needs to frame his message in a way to overcome this barrier. When a communicator is respected his message will be more readily accepted than if he were disliked or distrusted; this phenomenon is known as the "halo effect."

Report writing

There are many types of writing, but they can be broadly placed in the two categories of art and science. The former is personal and imaginative; it is generally divided into chapters for convenience and ease of reading, not organised that way to make a number of points but to relate a story, to develop a topic, to build up biographical material and so on. The latter makes no appeal: the case is stated as succinctly as possible; but unless it stimulates the reader's interest it is unlikely to be absorbed, nor action taken upon it.

The report falls into the science category; it is either investigatory or explanatory. It should be laid out to help the reader understand the main points as quickly and easily as possible. The first and sometimes the second sentence of each paragraph should indicate the idea to be discussed in that paragraph and act as linking sentences between the topics. Sub-headings are useful, provided they are related to the meaning of the text. This is not so in newspaper or magazine reports, which require a more pleasing page layout. Furthermore, journalists sometimes put the more important parts of their account at the beginning so that, if the editor needs to reduce the text at the end, he does not cut out salient parts. The investigatory report should take the following form:

1. *Problem*: the general circumstances leading up to the problem, followed by the particular facts of the case and a statement of the problem.

2. *Summary of conclusions*: the three or four main conclusions and recommendations, briefly stated.

3. *Discussion*: an analysis of the problem, a description of the areas chosen for investigation, with reasons for their choice, and the results of any experiments conducted.

4. *Conclusion*: deduced from the analysis performed, with recommendations made as a result of the conclusions.

The explanatory report can be looked upon as equivalent to the discussion section of the investigatory report. The first paragraph should be a guide or route map, a synopsis of what is to follow. Subsequent paragraphs are descriptive, with intermediary summaries where appropriate. They are not equally important and there may be examples and illustrations to drive the point home. The final summary is not a conclusion in the investigatory sense above; it may be simply the last point made, a highlight or a general observation.

Persuasion

Most forms of communication are an attempt by one person to persuade the other of his particular point of view. This is precisely the role of the salesman; he may be selling a tangible item instead of an idea, but it is the ideas associated with his wares which are likely to settle the deal, not just the presentation of the item itself.

It is unlikely that a sale will be made if the prospective customer does not have some inclination towards the product in the first place. Selling refrigerators to Eskimos will in the long run have the same effect as sending coals to Newcastle: although it may seem to be an admirable sales achievement, in reality it will have harmful repercussions and take up considerable resources which could be more productively employed elsewhere. The customer who is likely to have a desire, however small, for the article which is being sold is therefore the one to approach. The baby food salesman would have a thin time trying to sell to aeroplane manufacturers, but might have some success in a newsagent's shop and would be disappointed if he did not make a sale at a chemist's. There has to be some inclination towards the product in the first place and the salesman tries to convert it into a need.

There are a considerable variety of sales techniques and methods and each salesman has his own way of selling. Personality plays an important part and the best salesman uses the approach which best fits his own personality. "The gift of the gab" is a popular expression for the persuasive talk of the eloquent salesman but he might find that he could be even more effective if he talked less. Until he knows what are his prospective customer's doubts he is unable to assuage them, and so a very important part of a salesman's job is to listen and to be aware of the customer's general attitude. He must be positive and refrain from using words with a negative meaning. An apologetic "Not very large" can more effectively be rendered "Adequate in size," and although no salesman should mislead his customer it is perfectly legitimate for him to stress the advantages which his product has over others. Before he comes face to face with his customer he must anticipate the objections the customer may raise against his product, and must be ready to counter them. He must do so in a polite and efficient way without hectoring, and an occasional compliment is not amiss. Of the many advantages that his particular product will doubtless have, he should choose to discuss with his customer only those three or four which are particularly relevant.

These principles are important not only in selling but in all forms of communication. They make it far easier to put over a point of view, orally or by the written word, whether it be in committee, as manager, as subordinate, as salesman or simply as colleague.

XI. BUSINESS MATHEMATICS AND OPERATIONAL RESEARCH

The beginnings

There are a number of quantitative techniques upon which a manager may call to help him solve particular problems. These techniques may be loosely termed the "tools" of operational research or O.R. The subject of O.R. is a vast one and warrants full-time study in its own right. Here we shall briefly indicate how it can be used. As well as the techniques described in this section, others are discussed in Chapters VII and IX where they particularly apply.

Operational research began during the Second World War as "operations research," *i.e.* research into ways in which the operations of the war effort could be improved. Studies were made, for example, on how to reduce the considerable loss in merchant shipping which was being suffered due to the activity of the German U-boats. The answer was to send the shipping in convoys so that not only could they be defended by the Royal Navy, but as one group in a large sea space they were more difficult to find. Scientists from a variety of disciplines were brought together—psychologists, mathematicians, zoologists, physicists, engineers and chemists among others—who broke away from their narrow disciplines by each concentrating his own particular individual expertise on general problems of planning and organisation.

There is a story, oft related, of the general who told his O.R. team to help work out a plan of attack on a particularly well-defended enemy stronghold. As part of the necessary input data, the O.R. scientists required to know the value of human life, to which the answer was that life has too high a value to be able to place a price upon it. The solution was therefore simple—the general should capitulate. This was clearly unacceptable, but nevertheless he steadfastly refused to set a price. The O.R. men eventually found a way round the problem by calculating the total cost of the protective devices used by the common soldier, airman or sailor, and taking this as the value of his life. Surprisingly enough, the protection afforded to each of the armed forces was very similar. It might be argued that this particular value was an unfair representation of the value of human life, but in the circumstances it was a fair assessment of the worth that society had placed upon the fighting forces. It might be of interest to place a value on our own lives today in a similar way by estimating the amount of money we spend on protective devices in cars, on public transport and in other spheres.

After the war, it was realised that the techniques of O.R. could be equally as applicable to peacetime business and social activities as they had been in fighting the foe. In 1947 the Operational Research Society was formed, and in 1977 it boasted a total membership of 3,000, with probably another 4,000 practitioners who are not formal members of the society. The subject has grown considerably in status, with most universities awarding degrees in O.R. as a fully recognised academic and practical subject.

Operational research techniques

Operational research relies upon scientific methodology to solve business problems. When using a mathematical analysis, it defines the problem in as precise a way as possible, representing the various aspects of the problem as mathematical relationships, or equations, which are known as "constraints." There must always be an end product to an operational research analysis and what is hoped to be achieved must also be capable of being written down in mathematical form, as a mathematical equation. The objective is always to optimise that "end product", *i.e.* either to maximise or minimise, depending upon the requirements of the problem. The particular O.R. technique which is employed is the one which achieves the optimisation in the most effective way.

We see therefore that if a problem is to be tackled in a mathematically based operational research way, it must firstly be reduced to mathematical equations which represent the way in which the company is run. These company rules or "procedures" are the constraints of the problem. It must also be possible to write the solution objectives in mathematical form, and this is known as the "objective function." The procedure is then to optimise the objective function within the stated constraints.

STATISTICS

Statistics is an important topic because it provides, in the mathematical sense, concise data upon which studies may be based. As an example, if we were examining the traffic intensity on a particular road we should be more confused with the knowledge of all vehicular movement on that road than we would with hourly or daily figures. We would suffer mental indigestion with all the data and would probably "not see the wood for the trees" as a result. We are content with the manageable data, but recognise that we may be ignoring other data of importance.

The average

The simplest statistic in a mathematical sense is the average. Instead of placing on view all possible numbers in the set, we can describe them all by adding them together and then dividing by the number of separate entries we have in the set. The average so formed is suitably representative of all the numbers. Or is it?

Let us suppose that there are ten people standing outside the room and we are told that their average height is 1·75 metres. As a result, we might reasonably conclude that there are some slightly smaller than 1·75 metres and some slightly larger. Further, perhaps it would not be unreasonable to assume five smaller and five larger. In making such assumptions we would be using more information than we had strictly been given; we know from common experience that people are about 1·75 metres in height, that it is unusual for them to vary greatly about that height, and that the ten people under consideration have most likely been chosen at random from people around us.

If we were to invite the ten people into the room, we would probably be surprised if we found that the group consisted of five giants and five midgets. We would be equally surprised if nine of them were each 1·50 metres tall and the tenth 4·0 metres tall (the average is still 1·75). We might feel a little cheated if one turned out to be a babe in arms and the remainder all approaching 2·00 metres, and foolish for not realising that the group might consist of five women and five men, with the group of women significantly shorter than the group of men.

The sample

It is clear that the simple average is not sufficient to tell us all we need to know about the original set of numbers. Furthermore, the average of the set we have is not necessarily the average of all the possible numbers from which the set was taken. In the example of heights, we have deduced various "facts," probably erroneously, because the average is roughly what we had expected the average height of all people (past, present and future) to be. If the average height of the people outside the room had been say 1·25 metres or 2·25 metres, we would have been far less surprised to have seen a group of unusual heights enter.

Any set of numbers, be they heights or otherwise, is representative of a much larger set of numbers, which the mathematician assumes to be infinite, which it is clearly not. There has not been, and will not be, an infinite number of people born, but in a practical sense the number is large enough for us to consider it as infinite. To illustrate the concept of infinity further, imagine that you were to count all the grains of sand on a beach, then on every beach in the British Isles, then Europe, then the world. When you had finished you would know precisely how many grains of sand there were in the world and it would be a finite number.

One reason why the mathematician assumes the full set of numbers (the population, as it is called) to be infinite is so that he can say that there exists just one number which is *the* average of the population. Whenever a sample is taken from the population, just as we took the ten people who stood outside the door, the average of that sample is an estimate of what the true average of the whole population really is. It is a sampling of the average taken from the sample of the population. The greater the number of items, or observations, in the sample, the closer we would expect it to be to the real average of the population; but we cannot rely upon it. We may have been unlucky enough to pick for our large sample all the big ones or all the small ones, giving a distorted picture.

How are we to tell how close is the average we have calculated to the true average? All through we have used words such as "most likely," "expected," "estimate" and "perhaps." These words suggest a level of confidence (or even lack of it) of how far we believe the average of the sample is representative of the whole. It is necessary to quantify that level of confidence and to apply a percentage confidence, obviously less than one hundred but greater than zero.

So far we have calculated an average of a sample and found it has given us information, limited information, about that sample, and even more limited information about the population as a whole. We might therefore ask whether taking an average is the most sensible action to take, since what we would truly like to do is to represent the whole by just one number, if we possibly could. There is nothing particularly sacred about an average: in fact various kinds of average have been invented, *e.g.*, harmonic, geometric, and the one we have been using, the arithmetic. There are also the median, the mode, the quartiles and other such measures, but none are as convenient to use mathematically as the arithmetic mean (we called it average) we have just described. Perhaps there is still scope for further invention!

Variation

Given the average value then, we have seen that the elements from which that average is made up may be close to the average, may be equally balanced on either side, but at the extremes, and may be distributed anywhere in between. It would be helpful therefore if we could devise some means by which the dispersion could be measured. Fortunately such a measure does exist.

Each element, or observation, deviates from the average either positively or negatively (there may be observations which are the same as the average and therefore deviate by zero, but we shall assume these to be positive). Since we should like to record the extent of the deviations, we might consider summing all the deviations, positive and negative, and let this represent the deviation about the average of the observations in the sample. A simple check will illustrate that if this were done, the result would always be zero, whatever the dispersion within the sample about the average. However, if the deviations were firstly squared, thus producing all positive numbers since the square of a negative number is always positive, and then summed, the resulting number would be small if the observations were all close to the average and large if widely dispersed. As a refinement, we might divide by the number of observations in the sample, and then take the square root of the result. By adopting this process we have calculated what is known as the standard deviation.

If $x_1, x_2, x_3 \ldots x_{n-1}, x_n$ are numerical observations, then the mean of these numbers is

$$\bar{x} = \frac{1}{n} \sum_{i=1}^{n} x_i$$

The variance is the sum of the squares of each observation subtracted from the mean, divided by n.

Its formula is:

$$\sigma^2 = \frac{1}{n} \sum_{i=1}^{n} (\bar{x} - x_i)^2$$

and the standard deviation is the square root of the variance,

$$\sigma = \sqrt{\left(\frac{\sum_{i=1}^{n} (\bar{x} - x_i)^2}{n}\right)}$$

BUSINESS MATHEMATICS

The average and the standard deviation shown in mathematical form above are just two numbers which have been so calculated to provide considerable insight into all the observations in a sample without actually listing them all. If we return for a moment to our ten people outside the door and we now learn that their average height is still 1·75 metres and they also have a standard deviation of 0·01 metres, we can be confident enough that they are all roughly the same height. Note however that really we have been told three items of information about the people outside: we also know how many of them there are. If there had been one hundred people outside with a standard deviation of 0·01, we should expect perhaps that although most of the heights would be near the average, one or two could be further afield, the effect of the deviation diminished by the large number of observations *i.e.* divided by 100. The number of observations which lie within any given range about the average may be stated with a degree of confidence dependent upon the size of the range. This will become clearer later as we explain why it is necessary to look upon the standard deviation we have calculated as merely an estimate of the standard deviation of the whole population.

In calculating the standard deviation, we found each individual deviation, squared each one, summed and then divided. The calculation so far is known as the variance, a term commonly used in the mathematical treatment of statistics. The standard deviation is derived from the variance simply by taking its square root.

Normal distribution

In 1733 Abraham De Moivre completed the development of the normal distribution curve, long before the study of statistics as we know it today had really begun. Yet the normal distribution function is one of the most important equations in statistics; it allows us to

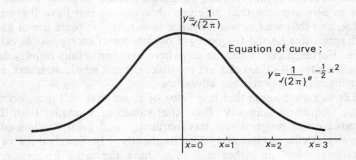

FIG. 65.   *Normal distribution*

draw all kinds of sensible and rational conclusions from raw data, average and standard deviation, provided we do not abuse it. The normal distribution is frequently known as the Gaussian distribution, named after the German mathematician Gauss. In fact, Gauss was born some thirty years after De Moivre's death and later took the credit for rediscovering and for applying it.

The shape of the Normal Distribution Curve, a "bell" shape, is shown in Fig. 65. There is an equation which describes the curve in mathematical terms, which at first glance appears complicated. It is

$$y = \frac{1}{\sqrt{(2\pi b)}} e^{-\frac{1}{2}\left(\frac{x-a}{b}\right)^2}$$

The a and b are numbers fixed for any given curve, so that on the graphical representation we have in Fig. 65, the line of the "bell" shows how y is related to x for specific values of a and b, in fact 0 and 1 respectively.

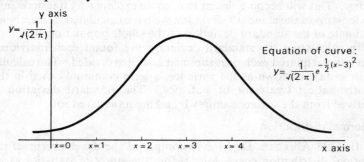

FIG. 66. *Normal distribution, mean = 3, standard deviation = 1*

Let us suppose that we have an infinite number of observations, x. Let us also suppose that different observations can have the same value, and that we know in advance how many xs there are of each different value *i.e.* the frequency of occurrence of each possible value of x. Furthermore, x can lie anywhere between minus infinity and plus infinity: all values of x are possible, not just whole numbers, not just discrete fractions, but all values.

Let us now assume that one value of x, we shall call it x', occurs more frequently than any other: that values of x smaller than this number occur progressively less frequently, and greater values of x likewise occur progressively less frequently. In fact, values of x equidistant and on either side of x' have the same frequency of occurrence. If we now translate these suppositions into diagrammatic

BUSINESS MATHEMATICS

form, we produce a picture which is similar in nature to the normal distribution curve, where x is the value of the observation, and y is the frequency of its occurrence.

It follows that the observation with the greatest frequency of occurrence, *i.e.* the one in the middle, is the average of all the observations. In Fig. 65 the value of x at this point is 0. If we were to slide the "bell" along to the right as shown in Fig. 66, the value of x would increase, in that case to 3. The actual equations of the curves are shown on each respective figure. Note that in the first, the a of the general formula above is equal to zero and that in the second it is equal to 3. These, of course, are the average values of the xs in each respective case. We may conclude therefore that, in the general formula, the value of a is always the average of all the observations, or xs, which that formula represents.

Area under the curve

It happens to be a fact that, for the general normal distribution curve, if we take a slice of area under the curve from $x=a$ to $x=a+b$, 34·1% of the total area under the curve is contained (rounded to the nearest tenth) as illustrated in Fig. 67. From $x=a+b$ to $x=a+2b$

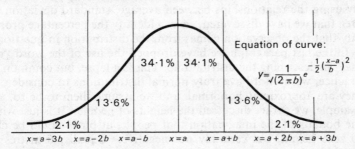

FIG. 67. *Normal distribution, mean = a, standard deviation = b*

the area is 13·6%. Because the curve is symmetrical, the equivalent percentage areas are also contained on the other side of the $x=a$ line, as Fig. 67 shows. Note that this is an absolutely general statement: whatever the values of a and b, it is true. It is true in Figs. 65 and 66, as well as in Fig. 67.

There are many such relationships in mathematics, most of which are merely of academic interest: not so this one. The b of the equation turns out to have a significance of major importance. If it were possible to carry out the standard deviation calculations described previously on all the observations, or xs (remember that there are an infinity of them), about the average a, b would be the result. b is the standard deviation of the observations represented by the normal distribution curve.

What in reality does this mean? It means that, given a normal distribution, 34·1% of all the observations lie between their average and their average plus standard deviation; or 47·7% lie between the average and the average plus twice the standard deviation; and so on. Put another way, if we know the average and the standard deviation of a normal distribution, we can be 68·2% sure that the next observation we encounter at random lies within one standard deviation of the average (34·1% either side).

Identifying the source

Let us now turn the facts around and use them in a different way. Suppose we know the average and the standard deviation, and we have one observation to consider. We wish to know whether that observation has come from the distribution whose average and standard deviation we know. Clearly, any possible value of x could have come from the distribution, but some more likely than others. By using the relationships between average, standard deviation and area that we have discovered, we can identify the percentage probability that the observation comes from the distribution in question.

In the last paragraph we have dropped the use of the word "normal" in describing the distribution. This is a lapse, but common. In practice, we do not have truly normal distributions to consider, but they are approximately normal, and we assume them to be so. For example, we earlier discussed the heights of people. It is just within the bounds of the imagination that people, at birth, could be close to zero height, but certainly not negative. Equally, 6 metres tall would be out of the question. Yet we use the principles of the normal distribution to draw conclusions.

We are also unaware of the true average and standard deviation of all people. Nevertheless, we can make estimates, a most reasonable one being the average of the sample, and the standard deviation. To be strictly accurate, to find the estimate of the standard deviation of the population we should divide by one less than the number of observations in the sample, not by the actual number in the sample, because the "one less" answer gives a better estimate of the true standard deviation of the normal distribution from which the sample is assumed to have come. The proof is complicated mathematically and we shall therefore not pursue it.

BUSINESS MATHEMATICS

Statistics used properly

So far we have merely scratched the surface of the methodology of statistics. There are many formulae and tests which have been devised to improve and measure various estimates derived from data. The objective is always to compress the data into a few, manageable numbers which themselves are assumed to represent a particular curve form, or distribution. Once this is achieved, within probability confidence limits, further deductions may be made about the data without actual reference to it.

Statistics are relevant to operational research and an integral part of it because the collection of numerical data and subsequent analysis is essential. For the right conclusions to be drawn the O.R. worker must fully understand the methodology, implications and limitations of statistical analysis. It has been said that there are "lies, damn lies and statistics," but not in the hands of the conscientious and skilled analyst who measures and declares at all times the confidence he places on the results of his findings.

A distribution problem

Consider a consumer goods distributor who is becoming increasingly anxious about the time his vehicles spend in long delivery delays at certain stores. Perhaps because of special stock checking procedures, insufficient space or simply slow workers, the goods are not being taken off the vehicles fast enough, queues form and vehicles wait. This affects the whole day's delivery schedule and other customers suffer. The distributor may take a number of courses of action to correct the situation. They range from discontinuing supply to the offending customers (difficult to do if they account for a large part of the company's business), calling at times when it is known the queues are shortest, to making special appointments with the customers to ensure that the goods are taken at specified times.

Each of these proposals has its difficulties as well as its advantages. An alternative solution is to accept the situation as it is and build in to the total journey time of the delivery vehicle a contingency factor for queueing. In other words, when planning the delivery route and deciding on how many customers each individual vehicle should call, additional time should be included for delay. But how much?

I. *Collecting and analysing the data*

The first step is to ask each delivery man to record how long he spent at each customer waiting for his turn to unload. For simplicity we shall assume that the data so obtained is of sufficient accuracy, but in practice careful checks would need to be made to ensure that it gave a true picture of what was actually happening at the customer delivery points. After several observations have been recorded we can analyse the data in a formal way and calculate the mean of the delay times at all the customers. We could decide that this value, multiplied by the number of calls made on each journey, is the contingency factor for delay which should be included in the total journey time for each vehicle; but there are two main difficulties. The first is that the mean of delay time over all customers may not give a representative picture for each individual customer; this may be overcome by forming the mean of delay time for each customer and using these figures in our calculations instead of the one. The second difficulty is of more significance in that we can with considerable confidence say that on very few occasions will the mean delay time actually occur; at most times the total journey time will still be different from that which it was planned to be.

To illustrate the point further, there are two possible extreme cases. The delivery man finds at one customer that there are always at least three vehicles waiting when he arrives, but seldom more than five. At another customer it is as likely that there will be no delay at all as that there will be eight vehicles already waiting their turn to unload. Both customers have the same average delay time, but each has different characteristics. It would probably be wrong to serve one's most important customer after the second of the two examples above because it would not be possible to state with reasonable certainty at what time of the day that delivery would occur: only the variation in waiting time in the first of the two examples could be tolerated. We must therefore consider the variation in the data as well as the mean.

II. *Degrees of confidence*

As we have seen on p. 364 we can calculate a statistical measure known as variance, from which we can determine the standard deviation. Knowledge of the standard deviation tells us what degree of confidence we can have in the delay time we have so far determined by taking a simple mean. By assuming expected delay time is equal to the mean, some delay times will be more reliably represented in practice than others; the larger the variance, the greater the variation in delay time. It is therefore useful to know how much confidence we can place in a delay time and how much safety margin we should employ to ensure that for a prearranged percentage of occasions the vehicle is able to move on to its next customer within a given time.

BUSINESS MATHEMATICS 371

By using mathematical formulae derived from the equations of the normal distribution we can state precisely the probability that the delay time at a particular customer will not exceed a given amount. This means that management can decide in advance that it is willing to overrun scheduled journey times for, say, up to 5 per cent of all vehicles each day; the 5 per cent indicates that the delay time to be set for each customer must be such that the probability of achieving it is 95 per cent.

It would be wise to monitor the actual journey times to see that only five per cent of them do exceed plan. If more than 5 per cent consistently do so, it is likely that the customers are taking their deliveries in a significantly different way from that on which the orginal calculations were based. One might draw the same conclusion if a performance better than 5 per cent were achieved, even though the delivery men were receiving justifiable congratulations. If it is management policy to tolerate a 5 per cent overrun then it could be just as wrong to do better as it is to do worse.

III. *Consideration of other factors*

The total time spent with a customer is due to a number of factors such as waiting time, unloading, whether it is morning or afternoon, and so on. Unloading time will depend upon the type and quantity of goods being delivered. In some cases it is therefore appropriate to consider all of these factors instead of their total as discussed above. This can be achieved with the aid of linear regression which is a statistical technique for determining the effect of many factors on final outcome and is described more fully under forecasting in chapter VII. If we were able to collect the data categorised in this way, if it were accurate and if we were confident that the final result we achieved would be better than simply considering total time— and it is reasonable to express doubts on each of these counts—we could calculate the journey time of each vehicle as a function of its load, the characteristics of its customers and perhaps even of its driver. We shall not pursue this line any further here, but we should bear in mind that this kind of data and the statistical techniques we have discussed are of considerable importance in conducting simulation studies, described below (*see* p. 377).

THE THEORY OF QUEUES

Queues are a common occurrence in everyday life. Perhaps the first queue situation which springs to mind is that which takes place at the check-out desk of a supermarket. One of the main reasons for the growth in popularity of the supermarket and the decline of the so-called corner shop has been an awareness on the part of the shopper that considerable savings in time can be made if one's shopping may be gathered personally from the supermarket shelves instead of asking the shop assistant for every single item—assuming of course that the goods one wants can readily be found on the shelves. Because of this emphasis upon time saving, when the shopper arrives at the check-out desk, he or she is much more aware of the time it takes to stand in line waiting for the goods to be checked so that the money may be paid and the goods purchased. The supermarket manager is anxious therefore to provide a quick check-out service, but is equally concerned that the cost of doing so should not be exorbitant.

Ships waiting to enter a harbour are not unlike shoppers waiting in a queue to pay their bills before leaving the supermarket with their purchases. Ships suffer the same kinds of problems because they arrive at the port in an irregular fashion, *i.e.* not according to a rigid predetermined schedule. The requirement of the ship is to be unloaded and/or loaded as quickly as possible so that the ship owners may enjoy the greatest return from their investment in the ship itself and from the crew whom they employ. It is important therefore that the dockers at the berths should carry out their tasks quickly and efficiently. A ship idling outside a port and waiting for entry can be very costly and this must be balanced against the cost of providing better facilities in the form of a larger number of berths which operate more efficiently.

It is frustrating when using the telephone to find that the person whom one is trying to call is continuously engaged. If the person one wishes to contact is already speaking on his own line, there is little that can be done other than to wait until the line clears. Sometimes, however, the reason for the engaged tone is that the telephone switching equipment in the telephone exchange is busy, not the subscriber himself whom one is calling. When a number is dialled on the telephone, a great deal of activity takes place in the telephone exchanges. Every subscriber does not have his own personal line to every other subscriber, and so facilities have to be shared. This being so, a particular piece of equipment may already be servicing an existing conversation, so that when one's dialling activity reaches that stage of the connection the line is found to be busy and the call cannot be made. For obvious reasons of cost, the Post Office does not allow calls which have reached the busy stage to queue although technically it is possible for them to do so. The subscriber must wait a while and attempt to make the call again later. This situation is of interest to us however, because again we have identified a facility which is required to service a customer. To run an efficient organisation, the Post Office must decide just how many of each facility it will provide to ensure an appropriate level of customer satisfaction.

Queue characteristics

We have given three examples above of how queues might form. We might cite many more examples, but we might likely find that they will not be much different in character from the examples we have already given. The queue which forms at the factory store is not dissimilar to that which occurs at the supermarket check-out desk, neither is the body of cars waiting to take up the next available car park space much different from the ships waiting to enter harbour. From the operational research standpoint all these problems are precisely the same.

The objective of the exercise is always to provide a service at an acceptable cost; to satisfy the needs of the members of the queue without spending too much on the facilities which serve them. In the case of the supermarket, the more check-out points there are, the more it costs in manning, provision of tills, and utilisation of space which might otherwise be used to display more goods, yet with too few check-out points customers might well decide to buy their goods elsewhere.

In attempting to reconcile these opposing constraints, we must first collect data which represents the queueing situation which we are about to analyse. There are two principle items of information which we must have, the first is the manner in which people (in the case of ports it would of course be ships) join the queue, and the second is the way in which the customers are processed through the check-out desk (again, in the case of ships it would be loaded/unloaded at the berths). By "manner" and "way" we mean information such as average arrival rate and average service time as well as expected times between the arrival of newcomers to the queue and the expected duration at any time before the customer currently being served is finally dealt with. We should also need to know whether the length of the queue has any influence upon customer willingness to join it, whether one particular check-out point has a greater customer attraction than any other, or whether there is an upper limit, *i.e.* cut off point, on queue length. It will be seen that, in these mathematical terms, the only differences between supermarket, port and telephone exchange are the numerical values of the parameters which define them. The basic characteristics of them all are the same.

Queue control

If we are able to take queue characteristics and treat them in a mathematical fashion, we need firstly to know on what criteria a solution to the queueing problem will be judged: indeed, we must know more clearly what it is that the person in control of the queue is really trying to achieve. No matter how many check-out points are installed, there will always remain the possibility that so many customers will arrive at a given time that the supermarket will be swamped and hence keep customers waiting to pay their bills for longer than might be though desirable. We must therefore look for a solution to the problem which provides for customers waiting on average for no longer than a given time, and for a queue to be of a given average length. Additionally, we must bear in mind that the behaviour of a queue is very much dependent, at least in the early stages, upon its starting conditions. If, for example, many people have already formed a queue before the check-out desk comes into operation, the check-out girl will be hard pressed to reduce the length of that queue. Nevertheless, she will succeed eventually in doing so and therefore, no matter what the starting conditions might be, the length of the queue and the waiting time that an individual will expect to remain in it, will settle down to particular values.

Mathematical analysis

The mathematics of the theory of queues is somewhat complex, yet it is recognised that the mathematical equations which are developed rarely represent a real life queueing situation. The reason for this is the necessity to make stringent assumptions about the behaviour of the queues under study so that the mathematical techniques which we are able to apply can actually be used. This may sound a defeatist statement, but a great deal can be learnt about the behaviour of queues from mathematical analysis, even though the results of such a study may not be directly applicable. The operational research scientist does not of course allow the matter to rest there; truly to solve a queueing problem he adopts the process of solution known as simulation, which we discuss below (*see* p. 377).

The mathematical analysis begins by assuming that, over a very small interval of time, the probability that no one will join the queue is very high, the probability that one person will join the queue is small, and that the probability that more than one person will join the queue is negligible. Those readers who have a deeper understanding of statistics than this chapter can provide will realise that

BUSINESS MATHEMATICS

these assumptions are equivalent to those which generate what is known as a Poisson distribution. Although such an awareness is useful in further analysis, it is not important to our basic understanding of the problem.

The next assumption that we make is that, whenever a customer is being served, the probability that the service will not be completed over a very short time interval is high, and that the probability of completion of service in that same small interval of time is very small. Given these assumptions, it is possible to write down the relationships between them.

Before we do so, however, we must firstly decide what values to give to the "high probability" of no one joining the queue and the "high probability" of the service not being completed. These values are taken to be the average arrival rate and the reciprocal of the time it takes to serve a customer, respectively.

We now determine a number of equations which relate the current queue length to its previous states. Taking the state of the queue in a most general form, we consider the probability that there are n customers in the queue. The way in which this situation could have arisen would be by:

1. $n - 1$ people in the queue and one arrival; or
2. $n + 1$ people in the queue and 1 service completed; or
3. n people in the queue, 1 arrival and 1 service completed; or
4. $n - 2$ people in the queue and 2 arrivals;

and so on.

It will be seen that all we are doing is writing down all possible ways in which a queue of n people could be formed from all possible previous states. Fortunately, most previous states need not be considered because we have initially made the assumption that the probability that two or more people should join the queue within a small time interval or that two or more people should complete service within the same small time interval is negligible. We can therefore exclude from consideration all previous states which have queue lengths other than $n - 1, n$ or $n + 1$. We are then in a position to write the probability equation as follows: the probability that there will be n people in the queue at a given point in time is related to:

1. the probability that there will be $n - 1$ people in the queue in the previous time interval;

2. the probability that there will be n people in the queue in the previous time interval; and

3. the probability that there will likewise have been $n + 1$ people.

From such an equation can be developed a variety of facts about the behaviour of the queue. It is not the intention of this book to explore the mathematics in depth; we shall instead provide the derived formulae which describe the characteristics of the queue.

Some queue equations

The simplest queueing situation consists of one service channel, the units in the queue served strictly in the order of arrival, each unit treated in identical fashion and no limit to the queue length. The probability of the arrival of a unit to join the queue and the probability of the unit which is being served completing that service are each independent of time or the state of the system. In other words, it is just as likely that the next unit will arrive whether the queue length be short or long and whatever the time of day. Similarly, a unit which has been undergoing service for some time has the same likelihood of completing that service within a given time as another unit which has only just started its service.

With these restrictions in mind, it is possible to derive mathematical formulae for the behaviour of queues. The results are exemplified by considering a supermarket operation with one cashier—we assume that the rate of customer arrival remains the same throughout the day although this is unlikely to be so in practice.

On average, say, nine customers arrive every five minutes and the cashier can serve ten in five minutes. Then the average rate of arrival is 1·8 customers every minute, and the average rate of service completions is 2·0 every minute. Let λ be the arrival rate and μ the service completion rate. If we define $\rho = \lambda/\mu$ ($= 1·8/2·0 = 0·9$) as the traffic intensity, we can calculate that:

1. the average number of customers waiting for service is:

$$Q = \rho^2/(1 - \rho) = 0·81/0·1 = 8·1$$

2. the probability that the queue will be greater than ten people is:

$$P(>10) = \rho^{n+1} = (0·9)^{11} = 0·31$$

i.e. 31 per cent of the time the queue will be greater than ten.

3. the probability that a customer may have to wait longer than two minutes for service is:

$$\omega(>2) = \rho e^{-t(\mu-\lambda)} = 0·9 e^{-2 \times 0·2} = 0·60$$

It may be possible to speed up service to twelve in five minutes by relocating the cashier in the store. In which case, $\lambda = 1\cdot 8$, $\mu = 2\cdot 4$ and $\rho = 0\cdot 75$. The effects on Q, P and ω are:

1. $Q = 0\cdot 5625/0\cdot 25 = 2\cdot 25$
2. $P(>10) = (0\cdot 75)^{11} = 0\cdot 042$
3. $\omega(>2) = 0\cdot 75 e^{-1\cdot 2} = 0\cdot 23$

which is a significant improvement in service to the customer.

SIMULATION

Modelling

People make models for a large variety of reasons. We usually think of models as small replicas of life size objects, for example, the model car, the doll, or various kinds of ornaments. The majority of models tend to be made for decorative purposes, or as toys, or to provide us with a degree of pleasure and enjoyment. Nevertheless, there are other types of model which have functional purposes as well, and some which are built solely to investigate how a particular design or operation might work, without any regard to the general appearance of the model.

In the category of models which are both functional and attractive, we might include stage "props." Another example might be the model of a complete town, or of a company's prestigious new office block. It is far easier to appreciate the advantages, and even the shortcomings, of a planned building if one is able to see a three dimensional model of it before it is constructed. It might be argued that with sufficient imagination it would be possible to fully realise what the building will eventually look like from the basic architectural drawings and the plans. But the purpose of the model is to have a better understanding of the total view of the design, especially the relationships of one part of the building to another.

The construction company with a contract to build a new harbour would be foolish if it did not take into account tidal conditions, the importance of building harbour walls in the most effective places, and the purpose for which the harbour was to be built. Unfortunately, however, until the harbour is finally constructed, it is not possible to know whether the harbour will perform as well as was intended. One way out of this dilemma is to build a much smaller version of the harbour, to create artificially the conditions under which the harbour will operate (for example, wave patterns, tidal conditions, arrival and departure of shipping) and to observe the effect of these external influences on the structure. In a similar vein, models are usually made of aircraft before the prototype is built, and the model is subjected to stringent tests. Severe operating conditions are imposed upon the model in wind tunnels and by wing and fuselage stress experiments. The objective of these tests is to identify any inherent weaknesses in the model, and hence in design, so that they may be corrected before the actual project is built. Clearly, such weakness would eventually be discovered even if a model had not in the first place been built and presumably modifications could have been incorporated; but if faults in design do exist, it is usually cheaper and often safer to iron them out in the model stage rather than when the final product is in service.

Mathematical models

We tend to expect models to have an appearance similar to that which they are designed to represent. We expect to recognise the model as a smaller version of the end product. In fact, it is not necessary in some cases to build a physical model at all; we can learn a great deal about the performance of an aircraft from mathematical equations which describe the structure of the aircraft and its relationship to external conditions, such as air flow. These equations in themselves could be considered to be a model of the aircraft, and a great deal of time, effort and cost can be avoided by judicious use of mathematics. Nevertheless, in the case of aircraft design, it would be unusual to rely solely upon the mathematics, and at a particular stage of design a model will be built.

But there are other kinds of mathematical models. Let us assume that a very large factory acts as a central distribution point for several smaller satellite factories. Heavy vehicles continuously arrive with goods from the satellites and other vehicles leave to supply depots throughout the country. Congestion frequently occurs, resulting in delays in supplying goods to the depots and hence to customers. There are a number of possible ways in which the factory and distribution centre could be organised and management wishes to choose the one which allows the smoothest operation.

A way of tackling the problem is to observe how frequently the vehicles arrive and depart, build a scale model of each possible layout, and try to copy or simulate the movements in miniature. Although models of vehicles and factory premises are pleasing to see, it quickly becomes apparent that to describe them in too great a detail is time consuming and wasteful—as much can be learnt by manipulating matchboxes representing lorries around outline drawings of buildings as can be learnt by using exact models. Provided there is sufficient space, it is not the physical characteristics of the vehicles and of the buildings which matter, but the time it takes for each vehicle to carry out a series of well defined movements and procedures. We may focus our attention upon considerations of time, delays, waiting and congestion so that the model need no longer be a tangible three dimensional one, but instead a listing of times that it takes for the vehicles to perform specific tasks, the frequency with which they arrive and depart, the variations in these times and the relationships between the tasks.

The factory distribution point has therefore been reduced to a set of mathematical relationships. We are concerned solely with the problems of congestion, not with the aesthetic beauty of the eventual factory layout that we shall choose. However, if we had built a conventional model of the system, it would be obvious how we might change the layout to reduce congestion and improve efficiency. We allow the mathematical model to change in a similar way, so that other layouts might be considered. For example, in one layout the vehicles may be routed in one direction and unloaded in the order in which they arrive, whilst in another they may be routed in an entirely different direction and unloaded in order of size of load.

Data collection

The kind of data we require to analyse the model, or perform the simulation as we might now call it, consists of information about how frequently service is required and how long that service takes when it is given. This is precisely the problem which was discussed in the section on Queueing, but we assumed there that we knew the mathematical relationship between successive arrivals to join a queue, and the duration of service time. We also had a relatively simple queueing system, *i.e.* servers and queues requiring one particular function to be performed. We are now discussing a succession of queues, each of which does not necessarily behave according to the convenient mathematical way we assume in queueing theory. The methods of simulation are used in practice far more frequently than those of queueing theory.

To illustrate the kind of data collection which is required, we shall return again to the example of the factory with a central distribution point. We need to know facts such as the inter-arrival times of vehicles, and how long it takes to load and to unload them. If a distribution point were already in operation most of these facts might be culled from experience. Usually, however, the project under consideration is a new one and no actual running data is known.

Even when there is some experience to fall back on, it must be remembered that, for example, the vehicle loading times might be related to the layout currently in operation.

Given a particular layout design, we decide in advance how frequently vehicles will arrive and how long it will take to service the requirements of the vehicles; we know load and unload times and how long it takes to manoeuvre vehicles into the correct position for loading/unloading. Rather than compile a list of such times it is often more convenient to assume that the duration between one activity and another can be sampled from a normal distribution. Computer programs would be written to allow the whole analysis to take place, and sub-routines to provide sampling from the normal distribution are readily available.

Simulation objectives

Several layouts of the distribution point can be tested, and eventually one chosen which is most appropriate to the needs of management. It is very important therefore, for management to know what improvements in layout they are seeking and to have defined in advance which result from the simulation run is "best." As an example, it might be possible to reduce the average waiting time, *i.e.* the average time a vehicle spends waiting in the distribution centre, by rearranging the centre facilities in some way. But there is little value if, as a result, the departing vehicles do not have to wait at all and the arriving vehicles wait longer than before. The centre might soon run out of stock and, although there would be no delay for the vehicles feeding the depots, there might in time be no goods for them either.

We implied when we first began to discuss the factory distribution point, that there was a problem of congestion. It is essential for us to define precisely what we mean by congestion, where it occurs, what is tolerable and what is not. For example, it might be acceptable for a given predetermined number of vehicles to queue to enter the factory, and we might wish them to experience no delay on departure. Yet it seems unlikely that we should be willing to tolerate queues entering the system, unless they were contractors' vehicles for which we paid only for the distance travelled to deliver the goods. In which case our concern would be only to ensure that the goods reached their destination at the earliest possible time, not necessarily to achieve maximum vehicle utilisation.

Just as with designing aircraft through the medium of a model, so we cannot be sure that the whole system will work before it is fully

BUSINESS MATHEMATICS 381

built and in operation. Nevertheless, we can learn a great deal about how the system will operate before we invest in costly buildings and procedures. We shall have been able to try out various possible schemes, and decided upon the one which is most appropriate to our needs.

An example of simulation

We assume that vehicles laden with coal arrive at a china clay works. They unload, and the vehicles are washed and then loaded with clay for the return journey. Both on entry to and on exit from the yard, the vehicles and their contents are weighed. The average times taken at weighing, unloading, washing, loading and weighing again for departure are known, as well as the variation about that average. Only one vehicle at a time can be serviced by each facility and so queues form. The one weighbridge is shared by arriving and departing vehicles. Arriving vehicles are given priority if the unloading bay is vacant, otherwise the departing vehicle is weighed first. Times of arrival of vehicles have been noted and the times between successive arrivals are shown in Fig. 68.

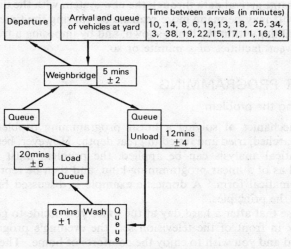

FIG. 68. *Vehicle movement schematic*

The first vehicle arrives 10 minutes after the yard opens. It proceeds immediately to the weighbridge, thence to unload. Assuming average times spent at each facility, after 9 minutes of unloading, the second vehicle arrives. The weighbridge is free and after 5 minutes the first vehicle has moved on to be washed, allowing the second vehicle to move directly to unload. When the third vehicle arrives, the first has been in wash for 5 minutes and the second has been in unload for 3 minutes. When the fourth arrives, the weighbridge is free, but the third has been queueing for one minute to unload, the second requires 3 minutes more to unload and the first has spent 5 minutes in loading. By the time the fifth vehicle arrives, the first vehicle has one more minute to remain on the weighbridge before it departs, so the fifth must wait this time.

In the meantime, the second is halfway through loading and the third has been in wash for 4 minutes. The fourth has been unloading also for 4 minutes, having waited 10 minutes for the third to move on to wash.

A log of times spent in queues may be kept, the maximum and average lengths of those queues, and the total times spent by the vehicles in the system. From this information it may be decided whether the facilities should be improved, for example, whether two loading bays, or two weighbridges, should be provided instead of one. The effect on vehicle times in the system can be determined by running the same arrival data through the new system with the duplicate facilities. It may be made more realistic by varying the times taken in the facilities within the limits shown, and by imposing a travelling time between facilities of a minute or so.

LINEAR PROGRAMMING

Identifying the problem

The mechanics of solving a linear programming problem have been researched, tried and tested in great depth. However, before the mathematical analysis can be applied, the problem must first be identified as of a linear programming kind, and then be represented in mathematical form. A domestic example is discussed below to illustrate the principles.

Suppose that after a hard day at the office you decide to go home and relax in front of the television set: the evening's programmes look good and you wish to enjoy the comforts of home. The TV set is on a bracket fixed to the wall and you intend to place your armchair in a suitable position in front of it. You suffer from eye strain if you sit too closely and, within the confines of the room, you would like to push your chair as far away as possible.

The central heating system in your house is particularly effective.

BUSINESS MATHEMATICS 383

So much so that to be too close to the radiator on the wall which is opposite to the TV set is positively uncomfortable. Unfortunately, there is a draught from underneath the door to the room which on many occasions you have decided to fix, but have not yet managed to do. You wish to keep far enough away from the radiator, out of the line of draught, and suitably placed to view the evening's entertainment.

To add to these hazards, a wall light hangs a little to one side of the TV set. The shade does not function as well as it should and there is a wedge of light which causes a glare, in front of which it is uncomfortable to sit. By suitably manoeuvring the armchair, you eventually find a place in the room to relax without suffering discomfort.

Let us now examine the various aspects of the situation in more detail and consider what was to have been achieved and what were the constraints imposed upon the solution. To assist in the analysis, we have a plan of the TV room in Fig. 69 which identifies the area

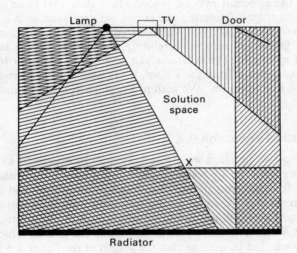

FIG. 69. *Constraints of watching TV*

of the room in which the armchair might rest, and the position marked by a cross where the armchair finally is settled. The shaded parts show where there is too much warmth, a draught, a glare, or simply where the TV set cannot be seen. The only floor space on which the armchair may reside is that which is not shaded, and we call it the "solution space."

Objectives

Firstly we must decide what it is that we are trying to achieve, what is our objective, our objective function. In basic terms we might say that the objective is to watch television, but that might more readily have been achieved by calling in to the first public house on the way home from work. Clearly, if we had done that, other needs would not have been fulfilled, such as eating dinner at home before watching TV, or relaxing in one's own special armchair. When we express, therefore, a desire to watch TV, we take for granted that prior requirements should firstly be satisfied, without specifically saying so. In our minds, "to watch TV" embraces all that we really mean, but to convey the idea to another, we have to be far more explicit.

But once we have reached home, dined, and are about to settle down and relax, we encounter the additional problems, admittedly more localised, concerning the comfort rating of the various positions in which the armchair may be placed. It is clear that once we have reached the stage of entering the room, we are faced with a choice of *how* to watch TV, not just whether to do so or not. In which case, we must find some means of relating various factors so that the optimum setting for the armchair can be found. We want to be as far away as possible from the TV set, yet remain within the room and stay in the line of vision. We wish to avoid glare, draught and excessive heat.

Mathematical expression

The objective function we are seeking may be expressed as "to be as far away from the TV set as possible." If we were to translate that objective function into mathematical terms, we would find it convenient to set the TV room as though one corner, the bottom left hand corner, were at the origin of a graph with the bottom wall along the X axis and the left hand wall along the Y axis, which Fig. 70 illustrates. Let us assume that the length of the room is 5 metres so that the top wall sits on the line $y=5$. The bottom wall is on $y=0$ and the left hand wall on $x=0$.

"To be as far away from the TV set as possible" requires more explanation. Since the TV screen is parallel to the top wall ($y=5$), we shall assume that, given any particular line drawn within the room parallel to the top and bottom walls, any point on that line is equally desirable from which to watch the TV show. In reality that may not be so, and we shall return to discuss that matter later. Nevertheless,

BUSINESS MATHEMATICS 385

if we accept that any point on the line is equally desirable, we may say that our objective is to find the line, parallel to the top and bottom walls, which is the maximum distance from $y=5$. In other words, or in mathematical form, our solution is found when we have determined the line $y=Z$, such that Z is a minimum.

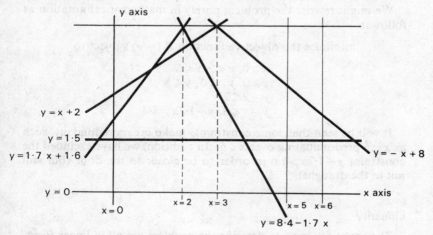

FIG. 70. *Equation of TV constraints*

There are, however, other conditions or constraints to take into consideration.

1. The possible lines from which the optimum solution may be found must all lie within the bounds of the room: *i.e.* $y \leqslant 5$, $y \geqslant 0$, $x \geqslant 0$, $x \leqslant 6$ (the width of the room is 6 metres).

2. The draught from the door runs at right angles to the closed door and follows the line $x=5$. The viewer does not wish to sit in the draught and therefore is constrained to place his chair to the left of the line of draught; *i.e.* in mathematical form, $x<5$.

3. The radiator, which extends along the full length of the bottom wall, emits heat which is unbearable closer than 1·5 metres to it. This means keeping above the line $y=1·5$; *i.e.* $y \geqslant 1·5$.

4. The wall light is located on the top wall, 2 metres from the left hand wall. Its glare covers a span of approximately 60 degrees. The lines which describe the extremities of the glare may be expressed as $y=1·7x+1·6$ and $y=8·4-1·7x$. So to avoid the glare we must site the armchair outside these two lines, *i.e.* either we choose $y-1·7x > 1·6$ or $y+1·7x > 8·4$.

5. The television set is placed right in the middle of the top wall. Its angle of vision is 90 degrees. The equations of its extremities are therefore $y=x+2$ and $y=-x+8$. So to be in a position to watch TV, we need to be within these two lines; i.e. $y-x \leqslant 2$ and $y+x \leqslant 8$.

We might rewrite the problem purely in mathematical notation as follows:

minimise the objective function $Z\ (=y)$ subject to

$$x \geqslant 0, x < 5, x \leqslant 6$$
$$y \geqslant 0, y \geqslant 1 \cdot 5, y \leqslant 5$$
$$y - x \leqslant 2$$
$$y + x \leqslant 8, y + 1 \cdot 7x > 8 \cdot 4$$

It will be seen that some constraints make others redundant, such as $x < 5$ predominating over $x \leqslant 6$. In addition, we have excluded the constraint $y - 1 \cdot 7x > 1 \cdot 6$ in order to be closer to the door (but still not in the draught).

Linearity

The equations used to describe the problem are all in linear form, that is neither x nor y are multiplied in any of the equations by anything other than a known arithmetic value: there are no xys or x^2s. Further, when we described the problem diagrammatically, we found that every line we drew was straight. We have a problem which can be reduced to mathematical formulation in terms of linear inequalities with a linear objective function. It is this kind of problem which can be solved explicitly by means of the technique known as "Linear Programming." The process of solution is discussed below, but before we proceed, there are still some useful observations we can draw from our TV watching exercise.

Reality

Draught from a door does not necessarily flow in a straight line. Much more likely, the air currents will tend to curve, to push inwards into the main body of the room. It would not be difficult to write down a mathematical equation which would describe the extremities of such motion, but it would most certainly be non linear. As we can see from Fig. 71 which illustrates such a hypothetical flow, the line is curved and therefore not linear.

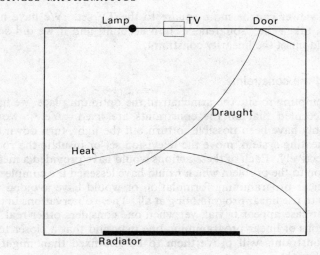

Fig. 71. *Non-linear constraints*

In a similar fashion, the radiator will not cover the full extent of the bottom wall. It would be an unusual radiator if it did so: it is much more likely that it will cover a part of the wall and so emit heat which radiates as a curve from an elongated central point (*see* Fig. 71).

The point of raising these issues is not to criticise the value of the method of solution we have adopted, but to be fully aware that we have made certain approximations. In reality, these approximations may not matter: the solution may turn out to be the same whether we make the equations linear or not. Unfortunately, as soon as we encounter non linear equations, the solution becomes much more difficult to reach. There are suitable non linear solution techniques for specific non linear problems, but not a general method as there is for linear equations through the medium of linear programming.

The intensity of heat from the radiator diminishes the further we are away from it. It does not diminish in a linear way, but as we have described the problem, there is a threshold line on one side of which the heat is bearable, on the other side it is not. In this way we have legitimately created linearity out of non-linearity.

We might consider too the formulation of the objective function. As it stands, to position the armchair anywhere on the line $y = 1 \cdot 5$, out of the glare and the draught, is a satisfactory answer. Yet it would not be unreasonable to assume that the best solution might be found closer to the glare than to the draught. The reason is so that the viewer can be more square to the TV set. We have not, however, taken the "squareness" into account, and if we did so it too would upset the linearity constraint.

Relaxing the constraints

In attempting to site the armchair in the optimum place, we have tacitly accepted that all the constraints are fixed. Yet it would presumably have been possible to turn out the light, turn down the central heating system, move the television set or insulate the room more effectively. Each of these actions would have provided a means of solution to the problem which would have lessened the complexity of the linear programming formulation or would have avoided the necessity to use linear programming at all. These observations in this particular case appear trivial, yet when one considers other real life applications of linear programming one may find that a closer look at the constraints will prove them to be less fixed than might at first be thought.

An application of linear programming

Let us consider a company which produces and markets soup products, among others. It is not possible to make soup to order because

1. the raw materials used as ingredients are available seasonally, *e.g.* vegetables are not easily grown in winter, although they may be frozen and stored at a cost, and

2. once the factory plant has been set to produce a particular variety of soup, the rate of canning is high and for reasons of economy large quantities are produced.

There is only one manufacturing plant and it is capable of producing each variety. Stocks of some lines have to be built up therefore in advance of requirement, and there must be available at any given time at least as much stock as marketing have forecast will be sold before the next occasion when that particular line is produced.

Raw materials are frequently bought in bulk at discount rates. If they are bought in season they cost less than if bought out of season, but they are perishable and if bought only in season they will need to be kept in cold storage at a cost. On the other hand, if they are made up into finished goods, *i.e.* into cans of soup, there is the cost of holding large quantities of finished goods stock which may not be sold for some time. Such stock will need to be handled into storage, maintained in storage and handled out again when required.

Handling charges can be high. We may therefore justifiably ask whether it is more profitable to keep stock in the form of raw materials or finished goods.

A question posed in this way rather assumes that the transition from raw materials to finished goods is a minor consideration. This is not the case since there are production constraints, such as a finite number of working hours, the time it takes to change plant over from working one variety of soup to another, and a minimum quantity that can be made in any one batch. If it is possible to work the plant three shifts, it is normally more costly on labour to run the third shift. The production constraints therefore introduce additional cost parameters and make the balance between stocking raw materials and finished goods that much more difficult.

We have discussed above some of the facts that need to be taken into account by the production planner at a soup-producing factory. With care and some simplification it is possible to write down the production planner's problem in the form of a linear program or L.P., employing detailed costs of production, distribution and storage. The results of the L.P. would be information on which management could act. Over short periods of time we would not expect marketing forecasts to be accurate, although we might expect them to lie within recognisable upper and lower limits. It is therefore very important that the company should have a contingency plan in case of an unexpected market surge, either upwards or downwards. The L.P. method is an excellent medium to long-term planning tool, but difficulties may arise in the very short term when greater flexibility may be needed, combined with skilful management.

The "mix" problem

Problems which are suitable for analysis by the linear programming technique are frequently referred to as "mix" problems. For example, if it is required to produce a particular cattle food with predetermined characteristics of vitamins and proteins, it may be composed of a wide selection of ingredients, each contributing to the total of vitamins and proteins which are necessary. Each ingredient has a cost attached to it, and we simply wish to know which ingredients we should choose to satisfy the vitamin and protein needs, at minimum cost. By analysing and subsequently solving the problem in this way, we take little notice of what the cattle enjoy eating, only what it costs to provide them with sufficient food to grow to the size we want them to be.

It is for this reason, the question of taste, that the linear programming technique has less applicability in the field of human food. It is extremely difficult, if not impossible, to devise a mathematical formula to describe taste, and to compile a formula which is linear is even more unlikely. In an affluent society, we humans can afford the luxury of choosing what we eat for reasons of taste, and any food producer who changes a winning recipe is likely to suffer in lost sales.

Oil refineries have similar problems to the cattle food manufacturer. They have raw materials from which they produce finished goods with precise characteristics and qualities. Crude oil is available from many places in the world, in varying quantities, at different prices, of a variety of qualities. They wish to produce petrol and other oil products at the lowest possible cost.

In the same vein, and to provide a worked example, suppose a smelting company wishes to produce a blend of metal which has 40 per cent lead and no more than 40 per cent zinc. The blend may be obtained from four other possible blends, each with different constitutions and prices, as shown in Table XV.

TABLE XV

BLENDING DATA

Available blends	1	2	3	4	Required blend
% lead	30	50	50	60	40
% zinc	60	30	10	—	≤ 40
% other metals	10	20	40	40	unrestricted
Cost/tonne	43	58	75	73	minimum

The required blend is to be provided at minimum cost.

I. *Numerical solution*

Let y_1, y_2, y_3 and y_4 be the quantities of each of the available blends that will be used in the required blend. Then $x_1 = y_1/(y_1 + y_2 + y_3 + y_4)$ is the fraction of available blend 1 which will be used in the required blend. Similarly for x_2, x_3 and x_4.

$\therefore$ $\qquad x_1 + x_2 + x_3 + x_4 = 1$

Considering the lead requirement,

$$0.3_x y_1 + 0.5_x y_2 + 0.5_x y_3 + 0.6_x y_4 = 0.4_x(y_1 + y_2 + y_3 + y_4)$$

that is $\qquad 0.3_x x_1 + 0.5_x x_2 + 0.5_x x_3 + 0.6_x x_4 = 0.4$

or $\qquad\qquad 3x_1 + 5x_2 + 5x_3 + 6x_4 = 4 \quad . \quad . \quad . \quad . \quad . \quad (2)$

BUSINESS MATHEMATICS

Considering the zinc requirement,

$$0.6_x y_1 + 0.3_x y_2 + 0.1_x y_3 \leq 0.4_x(y_1 + y_2 + y_3 + y_4)$$

that is
$$0.6_x x_1 + 0.3_x x_2 + 0.1_x x_3 \leq 0.4$$

or
$$6x_1 + 3x_2 + x_3 \leq 4 \quad \ldots \ldots \quad (3)$$

Now x_1, x_2, x_3 and x_4 must all be greater than or equal to zero. If we introduce a fifth unknown, x_5, which is also greater than or equal to zero, we may rewrite equation (3) as

$$6x_1 + 3x_2 + x_3 + x_5 = 4 \quad \ldots \ldots \quad (4)$$

The cost of the required blend is $43y_1 + 58y_2 + 75y_3 + 73y_4$, which must be minimised by choosing values of y_1, y_2, y_3 and y_4 which also satisfy equations (1), (2) and (4).

By dividing this cost by $y_1 + y_2 + y_3 + y_4$, we can write the cost/tonne of the required blend as

$$Z = 43x_1 + 58x_2 + 75x_3 + 73x_4 \quad \ldots \ldots \quad (5)$$

We have so far developed the following equations:

$$x_1 + x_2 + x_3 + x_4 = 1 \quad \ldots \ldots \quad (1)$$
$$3x_1 + 5x_2 + 5x_3 + 6x_4 = 4 \quad \ldots \ldots \quad (2)$$
$$6x_1 + 3x_2 + x_3 + x_5 = 4 \quad \ldots \ldots \quad (4)$$

and $Z = 43x_1 + 58x_2 + 75x_3 + 73x_4$ is to be minimised subject to the restrictions of equations (1), (2) and (4) and x_1, x_2, x_3, x_4 and x_5 all greater than or equal to zero.

We have three equations in five unknowns, so that if we were to put x_4 and x_5 equal to zero, we could find x_1, x_2 and x_3 explicitly. It so happens that the solutions for x_1, x_2 and x_3 are all greater than zero and therefore such a solution is a feasible one. In fact, we can rewrite equations (1), (2) and (4) as

$$x_1 = \tfrac{1}{2} + \frac{x_4}{2} \quad \ldots \ldots \quad (6)$$

$$x_2 = \tfrac{1}{4} - \frac{3x_4}{4} - \frac{x_5}{2} \quad \ldots \ldots \quad (7)$$

$$x_3 = \tfrac{1}{4} - \frac{3x_4}{4} + \frac{x_5}{2} \quad \ldots \ldots \quad (8)$$

This is known as expressing the equations in canonical form, where the unknowns on the left-hand side, x_1, x_2 and x_3 do not appear on the right.

A solution is therefore:
$$x_1 = \tfrac{1}{2};\ x_2 = \tfrac{1}{4};\ x_3 = \tfrac{1}{4};\ x_4 = 0;\ x_5 = 0$$

x_1, x_2 and x_3 substituted into Z provides

$$Z = 43\left(\tfrac{1}{2} + \tfrac{x_4}{2}\right) + 58\left(\tfrac{1}{4} - \tfrac{3x_4}{4} - \tfrac{x_5}{2}\right) + 75\left(\tfrac{1}{4} - \tfrac{3x_4}{4} + \tfrac{x_5}{2}\right) + 73x_4$$

which reduces to:

$$Z = 54\tfrac{3}{4} - 5\tfrac{1}{4}x_4 + 8\tfrac{1}{2}x_5$$

A cost/tonne of the required blend which can be achieved is therefore $54\tfrac{3}{4}$, but on inspecting the equation above for Z, it is clear that by increasing x_4, *i.e.* by making x_4 greater than zero, it is possible to reduce Z further.

But an increase in x_4 increases x_1 in equation (6) and reduces x_2 and x_3 in equations (7) and (8) respectively. The most we can increase x_4 is by $\tfrac{1}{3}$, which reduces both x_2 and x_3 to zero if we still maintain x_5 at zero. Either equation (7) or equation (8) will do, but we shall take equation (7) and put

$$x_4 = \tfrac{1}{3} - \tfrac{4x_2}{3} - \tfrac{2x_5}{3} \quad \ldots \ldots (9)$$

Substituting this value for x_4 into equations (6) and (8), we have:

$$x_1 = \tfrac{2}{3} - \tfrac{2x_2}{3} - \tfrac{1}{3}x_5 \quad \ldots \ldots (10)$$

$$x_3 = 0 + x_2 + x_5 \quad \ldots \ldots (11)$$

and in Z:

$$Z = 54\tfrac{3}{4} - 5\tfrac{1}{4}x\left(\tfrac{1}{3} - \tfrac{4x_2}{3} - \tfrac{2x_5}{3}\right) + 8\tfrac{1}{2}x_5$$
$$= 53 + 7x_2 + 12x_5$$

An increase from zero of x_2 or x_5 will only increase Z, so the minimum value of Z subject to the original constraints of equations (1), (2) and (4) is 53.

The solution is to make up two-thirds of the required blend from available blend 1 and the remaining one-third from available blend 4. Blends 2 and 3 are not used.

II. Graphical solution

We know that in equations (6), (7) and (8), x_1, x_2 and x_3 are each greater than or equal to zero; in which case,

$$\frac{x_4}{2} + \frac{1}{2} \geq 0$$

$$-\frac{3x_4}{4} - \frac{x_5}{2} + \frac{1}{4} \geq 0$$

$$-\frac{3x_4}{4} + \frac{x_5}{2} + \frac{1}{4} \geq 0,$$

which can be represented graphically with x_4 and x_5 as axes as shown in Fig. 72.

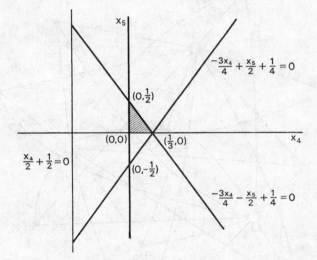

FIG. 72. *Linear program graphical solution*

The area contained within the triangle formed by these three lines is the solution space, but there are additional restrictions. These are that x_4 and x_5 cannot be less than zero and so only the shaded area is applicable.

The value of Z is $54\frac{3}{4} - 5\frac{1}{4}x_4 + 8\frac{1}{2}x_5$ and the family of lines of which this is a member is $-21x_4 + 34x_5 + C = 0$, where C can take any value. The line from this family which cuts the shaded space at its lowest point is the one which passes through $x_4 = \frac{1}{3}$ and $x_5 = 0$.

This is the required solution, which, on substitution into the original equations, yields $x_1 = \frac{2}{3}$; $x_2 = 0$; $x_3 = 0$; $x_4 = \frac{1}{3}$; and $x_5 = 0$, as before.

Transportation

Another common example of the application of linear programming is that known as transportation. It takes this name because it is generally associated with transport type problems, although there are other problem areas to which it is applicable.

Imagine that a one-product manufacturer has three factories, each of which can supply any one of ten warehouses (*see* Fig. 73). The

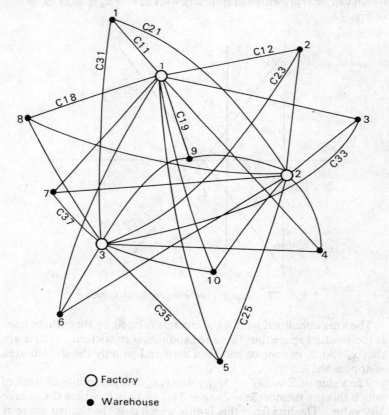

FIG. 73. *Transportation network*

cost of carrying each unit of produce from each factory to each warehouse is known. Assume the cost from factory i to warehouse j is C_{ij}. Let X_{ij} be the number of goods delivered from factory i to warehouse j. Then $X_{ij} C_{ij}$ is the cost of taking the goods from factory i to warehouse j. The sum of all these $X_{ij} C_{ij}$ terms is the total cost of supplying all the warehouses, and the objective is to minimise this quantity by choosing appropriate values of the X_{ij}, and hence how much is sent from each factory to each warehouse.

This objective function is constrained by the quantities which are required at each warehouse, and which are available from each factory. We have that the sum of the X_{ij} for each fixed i is a constant (factory constraint) and the sum of the X_{ij} for each fixed j is similarly constant (warehouse constraint).

The solution to this linear programming problem can be achieved by conventional means. However, because of the simpler format the problem takes (for example, none of the X_{ij} in the constraints equations is multiplied by a factor other than 1), a faster method of solution is possible.

Summary

It will have been noted that each linear programming problem described above consists of constraints and an objective function. Each of the constraints and the objective function can be represented in linear form. If this were not so, a solution could not be found. Unfortunately, relatively few problems can be described in such a way that they may be treated by the linear programming technique, but nevertheless, that still leaves a large number than can. It is often possible, with sufficient insight, to be able to approximate well enough to a linear formulation. Care must be taken, however, not to force the problem into a linear programming one just because it is possible to solve it by the techniques we have discussed. There is no advantage to be gained by mathematical excellence if it is applied the wrong way. Equally, one should take care not to take into account all global influences but use only those which truly matter.

THE THEORY OF GAMES

Definition of a game

We each have, no doubt, a clear understanding of what we mean by a "game." It is basically a competitive activity between two or more players, or teams of players, who conform to predetermined rules which state precisely how an eventual winner is to be decided.

It would be most satisfying if there could be developed a total theory of all possible games. Regretably, this has not yet been achieved. Certainly computer programs have been written to enable machines to play games such as draughts, and with particularly devastating effects. It is now possible for a computer, by means of a pseudo-learning process, to compete effectively with any human opponent, and to win. Clearly, a thorough understanding of the principles of the game of draughts has been developed. Analyses of the game of chess have been less successful, although computer programs exist which can compete effectively with chess players of moderate ability. Knowledge of other games is available to a greater or lesser degree.

In operational research terms, the "Theory of Games" applies to a very special kind of game, and to that kind only. It considers competition between two players, each of whom is able to choose just one of a pre-determined number of possible strategies. Each player makes his choice without any knowledge whatsoever of the choice that his opponent will make. Once the choices have been made, the gain or loss to each player is immediately identifiable.

Zero sum games

Figure 74 shows the possible outcomes of strategies which might be adopted by two players A and B. The strategies of A are represented as the rows of the matrix of Fig. 74 and the strategies of B

A \ B	1	2	3	4
1	12	3	8	2
2	6	3	6	10
3	5	4	7	5
4	9	2	10	16
5	8	1	1	13

FIG. 74. *Zero sum game*

are the columns. If A were to choose strategy 3 and B were to choose strategy 2, the result of that round of the game would be the score shown in the third row and second column position of the matrix, *i.e.* the value of 4.

The array of Fig. 74 showing the results of related strategies is called the "gain matrix." The gain is always for player A. If, therefore, the result of the 3,2 strategy is a gain to A of 4, as we have seen, then there is a corresponding loss to B of 4. A minus figure shown in the gain matrix implies a loss to A and a gain to B.

These scoring rules mean that we are describing a "Zero Sum Game." A gain to A is a loss to B and vice versa. The gain and loss when added together make zero, so we see that no greater rewards can be won from playing the game, only those which are already in the possession of A and B collectively. We might liken the situation to a game of cards between two players; each is trying to win money from the other and whatever strategies they each adopt, under no circumstances can they collectively gain from a third party.

If we were to take the part of A in playing the game of Fig. 74, we should need to choose a particular strategy, without knowing before we adopt that strategy what action B might take. We are in the fortunate position of knowing before the event the outcomes of all possible strategy pairs. B is likewise in a similar position.

We make a fundamental assumption that the decisions B takes in choosing his strategies will be rational. He similarly makes the same assumption about us. That being so, we now proceed to select strategies which, over many playings of the game, should provide A with the highest average outcome.

It is important to note that the game is expected to be played many times, in fact to be pedantic, an infinite number of times. If A and B were to choose their strategies just once, the outcome would depend entirely upon the degree of risk that each were prepared to countenance, and would no longer depend upon rational thinking and decision making.

Non-zero sum games

A good example of a non-zero sum game is that known as the Prisoner's Dilemma.

Imagine two prisoners, A and B, each of whom is accused of jointly committing a crime, and each is in separate police cells. They are told that if they both confess to the crime, each will receive an eight year jail sentence. If neither confesses, evidence is so strong against them and the judge is likely to be so antagonised, that they will receive ten years in jail apiece. If, however, one confesses and the other does not, the one who confesses will receive a fifteen year jail sentence, and the one who does not confess will escape with a mere one year sentence. Clearly, the decision to confess or not confess depends entirely on what decision the other party takes. Yet the police ensure that there is no means of communication.

There is no straightforward solution to this dilemma (other than perhaps remaining honest citizens in the first place), but it does illustrate an example of a non-zero sum game.

Dominant strategies

It is sometimes appropriate for a player in a zero sum game to choose just one strategy from a selection of strategies, and to keep solely to that strategy, in which case it is termed "dominant."

Consider the gain matrix in Fig. 75. From player B's standpoint,

Players A \ B	1	2	3
1	-4	-2	5
2	3	-1	2
3	6	-4	-2

FIG. 75. *Dominance*

column 2 is always a better choice than column 3: it ensures that the gain to A is lower, whatever choice A makes. Since both A and B are assumed to take rational decisions, A realises that B will always prefer column 2. He therefore excludes column 3 from consideration.

It follows that row 2 is more sensible than row 3 because the return to A is always greater (we have excluded column 3). The matrix is now reduced to rows 2 and 3 and columns 1 and 2. At this stage it is clear that B will still choose column 2. In column 2, A chooses row 2. This means that A will always choose row 2 and B will choose column 2. The result of the game is that A will receive -1 (or B receives $+1$).

As rational players, both A and B, no matter how many trials they conduct, will always keep to the same choice of strategy. If A makes any other choice, the gain could be less (or the loss more). If B chooses another strategy, A may gain more (or lose less). B minimises his potential regret, whilst A maximises his potential security.

Saddle points

To the gain matrix shown in Fig. 76 has been added a column which lists the minima of the rows. The additional row shows the maxima of the columns.

A would wish to choose his strategy so that his return is a maximum, if A knew in advance (which A does not, according to the rules) what strategy B would adopt. A's objective therefore is to achieve a solution from the "column maximum" row. Likewise, B wishes to choose his strategy so that A's return is a minimum (without knowing in advance what A will do) and therefore hopes for a solution from the "row minimum" column.

Players A \ B	1	2	3	4	Row minima
1	12	3	0	2	0
2	0	3	6	10	0
3	5	4	7	5	4
4	9	2	0	16	0
5	8	1	1	13	1
Column maxima	12	4	7	16	

FIG. 76. *Saddle points*

If A were to choose just one strategy, he would prefer row 4 in the hope of gaining 16, but knows that B would not allow him to do so (B would be expected to choose column 3). If however A chooses row 3, it is apparent that B would choose column 2 because B could ensure that A would gain the least as a result of the row 3 strategy. Yet given a choice of column 2 by B, A would choose row 3 because it maximises A's return.

It follows that because the maximum of the row minima coincides with the minimum of the column maxima, that is the result of the game, and the necessary strategies of both A and B (assuming rational behaviour).

Mixed strategies

We have already discussed an example of a mixed strategy in game theory (*see* p. 309). Dominance and saddle points, if they exist, identify strategies where both A and B choose, continuously, just one strategy, known as a "pure strategy." Mixed strategies mean that for some of the time one strategy is used and at other times other strategies are used.

The objective of game theory is to determine the frequency with which each strategy should be applied. The strategies are adopted at random (*i.e.* without allowing the opponent to identify a pattern), so that over very many plays of the game, the expected or average result is that which the game theory has calculated, given the particular choice of mixed strategy.

Critical path planning

Critical path planning, or C.P.P. as it is known, is really an extension of the ideas of Gantt, or bar charts. Any construction work or other similar operation consists of a large number of sub-tasks. If those tasks are arranged in a logical fashion, some in sequence and others in parallel, the total job will be completed faster, probably more cheaply and certainly more efficiently.

Firstly, all sub-tasks must be identified. Although apparently a statement of the obvious, it is often the need to identify the sub-tasks in a formal way which uncovers potential trouble spots, allows corrective action to be taken and provides the greatest benefit. Associated with each sub-task which we shall now call by the more usual name of "activity," is a duration of time over which the activity is due to last. The start of an activity and the end of an activity are known as events. Since some activities precede others, the event which is the end of one activity is also the start of any activity which immediately succeeds it and which is dependent upon the completion of the preceding activity before it may begin.

In critical path planning we are concerned with the order in which activities take place as well as their time duration. Diagrammatically, the line which represents the activity is not drawn of a length equivalent to the time duration of the activity, as it is with the Gantt chart.

Figure 77 illustrates a conceptual network, showing activities in

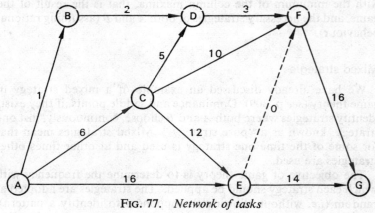

FIG. 77. *Network of tasks*

sequence and those which may run in parallel. Where more than one activity emerges from one event, not one of those activities may commence until the end of all preceding activities entering that event has been reached.

Events are identified as circles, designated by the capital letters A to G. Activities are those lines which join events. The time duration of each activity is shown by the figure. The dotted line activity E to F has a time duration of zero, and this is the conventional way of showing an activity with zero time duration. It is known as a dummy activity and is there simply to ensure that activity F to G does not begin until those which end at E are fully completed. Activities which end at event F must likewise be completed before activity F to G may commence.

Event A is at the start of the activities and event G is at the finish. It is evident that event B cannot occur until at least one time period has elapsed; likewise C cannot occur until at least 6 time periods have elapsed and E must wait for at least 16. Event D cannot take place until both A to B to D has occurred and A to C to D. The former takes $1 + 2 = 3$ time periods, the latter $6 + 5 = 11$ time periods. Event D must wait at least 11 time periods, therefore, before it can take effect.

By a similar argument we can show that event E will not be fully satisfied until at least 18 time periods have elapsed. Carrying these calculations through to the final event G, we find that the earliest time that the whole project can be completed is at time period 34. We now tabulate the earliest occurrence of each of the events as shown in Table XVI.

TABLE XVI
EARLIEST OCCURRENCE

Event	Earliest occurrence
A	0
B	1
C	6
D	11
E	18
F	18
G	34

The earliest occurrence of the project, which we have also called previously the earliest completion, is at 34 time periods. This also represents the total time that the project will take if it is to be conducted in the most efficient way.

Working backwards from G, we can see that F must have occurred by time period 18, otherwise G will not be reached by time period 34, *i.e.* $34 - 16 = 18$. Taking the direct path from E to G, we see that E must have taken place by time period 20. But considering that E precedes F which in turn precedes G, E is also constrained by the E to F to G route which takes $0 + 16 = 16$ time periods. From that direction, C must have been completed by time period 18. Given that the latest occurrence of F is at time period 18, it means that the latest occurrence of D must be 15 ($18 - 3 = 15$). Event C is the starting point for three activities, of which the most critical is activity C to E. It will be seen that C must have occurred by time period 6 to enable E to be reached by time period 18. If C is satisfied by time period 6 then F can be reached by time period 18 with 2 to spare, and likewise D will have a reserve of 4 time periods. Table XVII below incorporates the new latest occurrence times we have calculated.

TABLE XVII

LATEST OCCURRENCE

Event	Earliest occurrence	Latest occurrence
A	0	0
B	1	13
C	6	6
D	11	15
E	18	18
F	18	18
G	34	34

The above table identifies those events which cannot afford to suffer delay; any delay in those events will mean that the full project will not be completed in the minimum time of 34 time periods. The events to which we refer are those for which the earliest occurrence is the same as the latest occurrence: they are events A, C, E, F and G.

Figure 78 highlights these events by showing the activities which join them as heavier lines. It will be seen that these activities are the most critical ones because any delay in these activities will delay the whole project. They are said to lie on the "critical path" of the network. The numbers which have been inserted in the circles which represent the events of the network are: on the left, the earliest occurrence and on the right, the latest occurrence of each respective event. The difference between these two numbers represents the amount of delay or "slack" as it is called, which the preceding activities may enjoy without delaying the project as a whole.

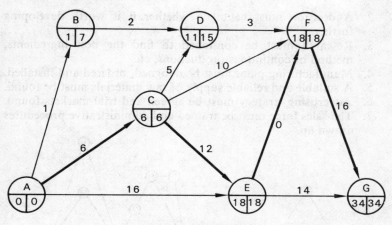

Fig. 78. *Critical paths*

New product launch

Critical path planning has proved itself to be invaluable to the construction industry and was, for example, used extensively in planning the Victoria Underground Line in London. It can be just as useful however for the smaller job, and preparing the lunch or making a pot of tea or coffee might be completed a little more efficiently if the sequence of tasks were firstly drawn out as a critical path diagram. Let us however consider just one practical example of critical path planning.

Suppose that a company is considering the introduction of a new line into its product range. There are several stages of development which have to be considered, many of which may overlap. The sooner the new product is launched, the quicker will be the return on the capital spent in developing the product, and the less time there will be for competition to prepare for its own similar launch. Management therefore have two principal objectives, first, to get the product on the market as soon as possible, and secondly, to do so within a predetermined budget. Some of the work which needs to be carried out before the new product can be put on the market is listed below.

1. There must be sufficient research to determine whether or not the product is feasible.

2. A decision must be taken whether it is worth developing further.
3. Research must be continued to find the best ingredients, method of continuous productions, etc.
4. Manufacturing plant must be designed, ordered and installed.
5. A suitable and reliable supply of raw materials must be found.
6. Advertising strategy must be agreed and trial markets found.
7. The sales force must be trained and administrative procedures drawn up.

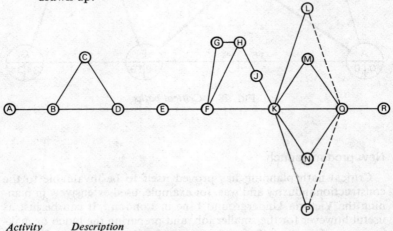

Activity	Description
AB	Basic research on product feasibility
BD	Market research
BC	Product research
CD	Plant design for trial quantities
DE	Product costings
EF	Decide upon trial
FH	Order raw materials
FG	Order plant
FK	Design advertising schemes
GH	Install plant
HJ	Run local trials
JK	Decide whether to go national
KM	Order more plant
KP	Order raw materials
KL	Train sales force
KQ	Prepare documentation
KN	Choose advertising medium
NQ	Design packing
MQ	Install plant
QR	Launch product
LQ/PQ	Dummy tasks, *i.e.* tasks with no duration, used only to define the order in which jobs should take place

FIG. 79. *New product introduction*

Clearly there is considerable work to be done before the product reaches the consumer.

The sequence of work leading up to the new product launch can dramatically affect the date of completion. Several tasks can be overlapped and it is important that this be done, provided the resources for each job are available. For example, it may be that clerical staff are required for two separate jobs, but that there is an insufficient number of clerks. Two such jobs cannot therefore be run together.

The diagram shown in Fig. 79 illustrates a possible sequence for the work. It can be seen that certain jobs, from the standpoint of logic, can take place at the same time. There may, however, be resource constraints which prevent this from being so in practice, as, for example, the clerks mentioned above. The time a job takes to complete depends to some extent on the resources that are applied to it. If expected job durations and available resources are allocated to each job, it is possible to identify that sequence of events which takes the longest time, and hence those jobs which are the critical ones. Resources which are applied to jobs that are not critical would be better used on the critical ones to reduce the overall time, although such redeployment of resources would only be made up to the point at which the non-critical job is made to be critical.

Resources are most likely to be labour and plant, but cash too can be considered as a resource. As a generalisation, the more labour and plant we use, the shorter the time an individual job takes and the more it costs. The objective is to balance time, costs and other resources so that the new product can be put on the market with a significant lead on competition but at a cost which provides an acceptable profit.

Resource allocation

We have seen in the example of the new product launch that the time that an activity takes is dependent upon the resources allocated to it. The times are, of course, estimates of the duration of each activity and are usually based upon resources known to be available. Once the critical path is identified, it becomes evident (unless the scheduler is particularly fortunate) that certain resources could be better deployed elsewhere to either speed up the project, or smooth out the demand for total resources.

If little attention is paid to resource allocation at the planning stages, it is likely that resources will be required in peaks and troughs. Unless the employer is prepared to adopt a policy of hire and fire, he will want his labour resources, for example, to be set at a constant level. It is the function of resource allocation methods to achieve this smoothing and to highlight when resources should be transferred from one activity to another to achieve a less costly and more efficient total operation. The approach is usually to employ the services of a computer, for which several programs have been written for resource allocation. The computer is used to carry out the tedious arithmetic whilst the scheduler with the aid of the critical path planning techniques already discussed analyses and produces approved resource allocation solutions.

P.E.R.T.

P.E.R.T. stands for project evaluation and review technique. It is basically the same as the critical path planning method that we have so far discussed but it attempts to pay greater attention to estimating the duration of each activity. These time estimates are doubtless the most critical and sensitive part of the whole critical path planning methodology. If the time estimates are wrong, conclusions drawn about the total length of the project and the identification of the critical path are of limited value.

P.E.R.T. was first developed by the U.S. Navy in the early '60s. The idea is that whoever is responsible for making the time estimates for each activity should provide not just one figure (*i.e.* that person's best estimate), but three sub-estimates. These three figures are his most optimistic, his most pessimistic, and his most likely estimate. Some kind of weighting is then applied to these three figures *e.g.* $[(3 \times \text{pessimistic}) + (4 \times \text{the most likely}) + (3 \times \text{the optimistic})] \div 10$, and the resultant figure is treated as the estimate which is then used for the purposes of the critical path planning, as before. Because weights have been applied in this way, it is possible to assume that we have a distribution of estimates for each activity, a distribution in the sense that we have discussed in the chapters on Statistics. From these distributions we can deduce a crude measure of standard deviation. As a result, not only can we identify the critical path of the total project based on the durations calculated from the original three estimates, but we can also determine the range in which the true project time will lie, within statistical confidence limits, by taking due account of the standard deviations.

The principle advantage claimed for P.E.R.T. is that the time estimates for the durations of the activities will be more accurate within a range. This may be so, but from a practical standpoint, it is probably even more difficult to obtain three estimates from the individuals responsible for each activity, than it is to obtain just one estimate. Furthermore, if estimates must be obtained from several individuals responsible for groups of activities of the project, there remains the danger that each will base his estimates on different premises. Taking three estimates per activity might simply mean several additional and different assumptions on which the estimates are based.

XII. A CASE STUDY

The XYZ company manufactures, markets and distributes a range of toiletry products and patent medicines, including health drinks. These two divisions of the company were formed one year ago from a merger of two separate companies, each of which was known nationally and had significant market shares for its products, which, although still high, are showing signs of declining. Each company had one factory in which its products were made and so the XYZ company inherited two factories, one at which twelve toiletry products are made and another producing eighteen types of patent medicines. Nearly all products are made in three sizes and so the total number of lines is towards ninety.

The toiletry factory is located in Manchester, the patent medicine factory in North London. Of the seventeen distribution depots with which XYZ began, three have already been closed and it is intended that a further five should be taken out of operation by the end of the year. The remaining nine depots are distributed throughout the country, each covering an area for which it provides a van delivery service. A difficulty has arisen whereby there is just sufficient space in some of the fourteen depots which still remain and it is thought that a further reduction to nine would aggravate the situation so much that it would be unworkable. On the other hand the savings to be made by reducing to nine are considerable and the distribution manager maintains that it is feasible, provided the stocks can be kept in balance throughout the depots and provided sales and production keep in phase. At the moment some depot managers are hoarding supplies in case a shortage should arise and on some products sales are down although production continues to produce more.

When the two original companies merged, a firm of consultants were employed to propose a reporting structure, which was implemented as shown in Fig. 80. The structure for production and distribution was dictated principally by the existing set-up in the patent medicines company. Long experience had shown that the company could sell all that it produced and so distribution was considered to be an adjunct of production. Toiletries on the other hand were more marketing oriented; competition was that much fiercer.

Marketing have always been considered a most important division and it was concluded that they should be organised in two separate

A CASE STUDY

parts. A reason for the merger had been the opportunity for each to penetrate the market of the other and it had been recognised that there were two quite distinct markets, retail grocers and retail pharmacists. Accordingly all customers of both companies had been pooled and then subdivided into grocers and chemists. A clear distinction emerged between the products sold principally to pharmacists and those sold to grocers. As a result, two marketing forces were created, each with a range of products spanning both factories. Obviously grocers and pharmacists are customers for some common products and so no salesman is debarred from calling on any potential customer, be it grocer or pharmacist. There is no product overlap for the two sales forces and therefore a customer may receive a call from two salesmen from the XYZ Company. If both promise early delivery yet make their sales call on different days, the distribution function, which make no similar distinction between sales products, find that they either fail to deliver one salesman's products on time or make two visits to the one outlet, which is costly.

Creating two marketing forces in this way considerably helped the problem of how to deploy the resources of the two original companies. Some consideration has been given to forming just one sales force but no definite plan has been drawn up. It is said

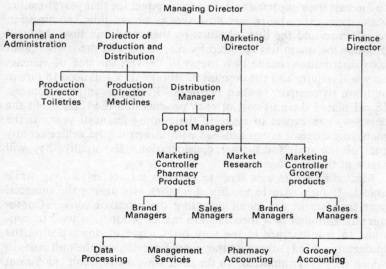

FIG. 80. *Reporting structure of merged companies*

that one sales force would lose the flexibility which the organisation has at present; less promotional activity would be possible and marketing would become less personalised.

Finance are responsible for data-processing and management services, both of which they inherited from the toiletries company. After one year within the XYZ company they have managed to provide compatible procedures which are acceptable to both sides, but there is a distinct slackening in their involvement in the company's activities now that the merger has become effective. Previously in a smaller company, they reported directly to the managing director and he was an influence on the work they did. Now they expect to be called in only when a problem or a requirement for data processing is recognised by the various parts of the company.

Also reporting to Finance are the accounting functions for pharmacy and grocery. The operating costs for the two factories have been split proportionally between pharmacy and grocery, as have the costs of distribution, administration and services. The accountants report on the performance of the two parts as though they were separate companies. This means that they align themselves with their respective marketing controllers, who in turn consider themselves to be running their own companies, responsible for profit achievement.

Six months before each financial year begins marketing are asked to forecast their expected sales of each product for that year, together with their expenditure on advertising, promotions, commission to salesmen and the like. Production then work out how they will produce the quantities required by marketing and the costs. Similarly distribution decide how they will deliver, the size of vehicles they will require and the amount of storage they will need to hire in addition to company-owned premises. From this information can be calculated the unit cost of each product and the total profit the company can expect to make in the coming financial year. If the managing director is not satisfied with this profit, he will reject any part of the plan for further consideration. Eventually they will arrive at the right figure.

Marketing's forecasts tend to become targets set a long while ahead. If they wish to modify their forecasts during the financial year they are in danger of upsetting the profit objective. Consequently although new forecasts are made, production tend to continue to manufacture in the way originally laid down during the budgeting period; otherwise they would not achieve the unit costs to which they are committed. In the same way, distribution charge out

A CASE STUDY

their costs according to the budget, even if sales volumes have changed; they argue that they cannot react quickly enough to dispose of labour and equipment, or hire more, in time to bring their charges more into line with actual product sales performance.

Included in marketing's forecasts is an allowance for the promotions they expect to run during the year. At this stage it is not necessary to say precisely what the promotions will be—perhaps a money-off offer, a simple trade discount, special advertising or gift vouchers; the main requirement is that production should have available at the right time sufficient extra capacity. It is difficult to predict with any accuracy how well a promotion will go and, if anything, there is a tendency for marketing to be optimistic, particularly between six and eighteen months ahead of the event. Furthermore, the branch managers are young and inexperienced. Production and marketing liaise sufficiently far in advance on the exact details the promotion needs, but it is not until marketing produce a circular stating the reasons for the promotion and how the salesman can gain the best advantage from it that distribution are really aware that it is to take place. It is left to distribution to decide how the stocks should be allocated to the depots, first the quantities recommended from the centre, and subsequently those ordered by the depot managers themselves, as they usually do for all other products. The allocation of the initial stocks is particularly hazardous because neither of the territories of the two sales forces has common boundaries with the other territory or with the areas covered by the depots; nor are the boundaries planned to be common when the number of depots is finally reduced.

Production produce according to a schedule fixed by marketing's original forecasts of demand. Marketing try to be more reactive to consumer preferences and therefore they seldom require their goods in exactly the same quantities as they originally specified. The result is that distribution rest in the middle, at times taking in far more stock that was planned or is needed, at others not having enough stock to satisfy demand. Operationally the latter situation is the easier to deal with as it is clear what action must be taken, whereas it is far more difficult to decide that there is too much stock; marketing are always optimistic that sales will pick up and production are loath to change plan, particularly if it may lead them into difficulties in the future if there is a delayed action on sales. Distribution is content to absorb stocks provided there is not so much that it forces them to exceed budget. There is money available with which to hire space in contractor depots and this is particularly necessary when production are stockpiling for a seasonal peak. However, the plan is to use as little outside storage as possible to compensate for imbalances between production and marketing: it is better to iron out the imbalances instead.

Four of the eighteen patent medicine lines are health drinks, which began life some fifty years ago as medicines but which in time have become generally accepted by the consumer as health-giving drinks and now compete on an equal footing with fruit squashes, mineral water and other popular drinks. A summer seasonal demand pattern is emerging and senior management are convinced that the future of these products lies in these mass markets, in time losing their health image but transmuting this asset to gain general acceptance as high-quality beverages. When the drinks were first manufactured, a large amount of capital was spent on plant, ultra-modern machinery with considerable spare capacity for expansion. Unfortunately the products did not take off as well as had been hoped and this is one of the reasons why the company acceded to the merger with toiletries.

In an effort to make better use of the spare plant capacity, the XYZ marketing director decided as soon as the company was formed to manufacture own label products for the supermarkets at reduced prices. "Own label" in this particular case means that the product is exactly the same as the standard line and is packaged in the same way, but has the supermarket's own name and label instead of the normal one. He reasoned that it was far better to receive a contribution to plant overheads by making own label products, thus increasing the profitability of his standard lines, than to leave plant and labour idle, costing money yet earning nothing in return. The supermarkets had forced a hard bargain but one which he was willing to accept. Furthermore, it enabled him to get a bigger foothold in the supermarket, which he wanted for his other products. As a result the standard line of drinks, the branded products, sell in the supermarket at a higher price than the own label ones, yet are of the same quality. The branded lines are not selling anywhere near as well as had been hoped whereas the own label products are on target, if erratic. The supermarkets order huge quantities at a time with short notice and then do not order more for long periods. They are presumably stocking up, perhaps at a central distribution point.

Own label products are made on fixed contract prices and it is difficult to increase them. Yet it will not be long before own label has a bigger market share than the original product. If and when this happens, either the branded product will have to be so highly

A CASE STUDY

priced that it is forced off the market, or the line will be a loss-maker. This point has not been reached yet, but all the signs suggest that it is a real possibility.

The company's marketing research department are particularly anxious that the drinks side of the business should be well established since it is the main area of the company's potential growth. Few competitors have comparable knowledge in this field, and marketing are convinced that if they could find the right new product it would be a considerable boost to the company. Unfortunately the products which the research department have tried up to now have not been successful but they are not disheartened.

An additional worry at the patent medicines factory is that no particularly profitable product is made there. It has been argued that the factory itself is an expensive one to operate, but there is a good and reliable work force with few industrial problems and it is also well positioned as far as distributing the goods is concerned. The toiletries factory on the other hand is a highly profitable one and it has been suggested that two of the products, for which replacement plant will need to be purchased soon, should be moved to the patent medicines factory. The board is expected to make a decision on this matter at its next meeting.

One way of reducing the costs at the patent medicines factory would be to schedule the production so that (a) the ingredients which make up the products are kept in stock in as small quantities and for as short a time as possible, (b) production is continuous yet compatible with demand, without entering into overtime which is expensive, and (c) distribution costs are kept to a minimum by not producing quantities which must be kept in storage for long periods. To arrive at an optimum schedule, various costs need to be calculated and allocated to the stages through which the product passes. The management services department have recently been asked to advise, and they have carried out an initial investigation and are due to report back. The drinks plant is self-contained, with a dedicated workforce, and because of the own label products the production runs are in batches. Since there are now ten own label products as well as the four standard ones, in practice fourteen separate batch runs are required for each size, of which there are three. (The four remaining patent medicines make eighteen in all, but they are not manufactured on this production line.) The forecasts are somewhat unreliable, but marketing are making efforts to improve them and are willing to give weekly forecasts updated as frequently as they possibly can. To compensate for the erratic demands on the products, marketing ask that six weeks' stock be available nationally at all times.

Questions

The case study described above could continue indefinitely. It has been broken off at this particular point because it has already provided sufficient food for thought and material on which to base a number of worthwhile questions. Very few numerical facts have been given and those provided are there only to make the description easier. The case is not an actual one, but every part of it can be shown to exist in some company or another.

The lecturer who chooses to use this case study as a basis for discussion may wish to fit his own data to it: that would not be too onerous a task. The questions given below have been phrased to persuade both lecturer and student to follow a particular discussion path but there is no reason why both should not stray. There are no exact or best answers, particularly since in any description at least half the story must be left out. Even if a complete treatise had been included on, say, the behaviour of competitive companies, that would be no guarantee that the student and lecturer would have interpreted the situation in identical ways, nor would it have ensured that competition would behave in the same way in the future. No answers to the questions are offered because it would be too easy to look upon them as final solutions and it is hoped that both student and lecturer will not feel restricted; and because the purpose of the case study and the questions is not to discuss the XYZ company only as it has been presented. The opportunity should be taken to develop other aspects of the company within the framework which has been set.

1. What advantages are to be gained from merging two companies? What are the disadvantages? Is the XYZ company likely to be better off as one company, compared with its previous state of two separate companies? Does "better off" necessarily mean more profitable and if so over what time period? Discuss the types of customer XYZ serves and the future growth potential of the company.

2. What kind of savings would be expected by reducing the number of depots in the company? What information is required to make such a decision? Is it possible to determine an optimum number of depots and if so, how? What are the disadvantages of reducing the number of depots?

3. Will fewer depots require a tighter control of stocks and how

can that be achieved? Can depot rationalisation be considered as an isolated distribution problem or is it necessary to study the other functions as well? If so, to what extent? Is distribution seeking to reduce stocks or to maintain a stock balance throughout the depots?

4. What are, or what should be, the objectives of marketing, distribution, production and finance? Are they compatible?

5. What do you think were the reasons why the consultants proposed the XYZ reporting structure? Is it an appropriate one? Are the vertical links sufficiently strong and is the horizontal communication effective enough? Discuss the ways in which production, distribution and marketing are organised.

6. Should the XYZ company combine its two sales forces into one? Consider how a salesman spends his time. Would the company be able to reduce its total sales force significantly? Would each salesman be able to cope with an increased product range and would he be able to absorb new products into that range as and when they were announced?

7. Should Sales be a part of marketing, should it be the other way round, or should each report separately to the managing director? What relationships should there be between brand managers and the sales force? What are their respective responsibilities?

8. What are the advantages and disadvantages of data-processing and management services reporting to the financial director? To whom else could they report and why?

9. In what other ways could the XYZ company organise itself? What would it gain and what would it lose?

10. Whose needs are satisfied by the method of accounting used by the XYZ company? Are profits correctly portrayed and can management take decisions based on the accounting facts, divided into two parts, which are presented to them?

11. How does each function within the company arrive at its budget figures for the year? What are the disadvantages of such methods? Can they be improved? How should the managing director decide when the budget is acceptable?

12. Annual operating costs are determined by the budget, which in turn depends upon forecast of sales. What are the arguments for and against recalculating costs during the year as better forecasts become available?

13. Does the XYZ company get the greatest benefit it can from running promotions? Could it improve the way they are set up? If so, how?

14. Why do companies embark upon promotions? Who should

be responsible for their success or failure? How is it possible to tell whether a promotion has been successful or not?

15. What are the arguments for and against areas covered by depots being compatible with sales regions?

16. Consider the costs incurred by distribution in trunking finished goods from the factories to the depots and to and from outside storage contractors, delivering to customers and maintaining appropriate stock levels. How should these costs be allocated to the products?

17. "There are advantages for each of production, distribution, marketing and finance in having high stocks." Discuss.

18. Was it a correct policy decision to become involved in manufacturing for the own label market? What are the advantages and the disadvantages to (a) the manufacturer and (b) the retailer? What should the XYZ company do in the present circumstances?

19. What information should the board of directors be considering to help them decide whether or not they should move the manufacturing of a product from one factory to another? What advantages would they gain? What else might they do to improve the profitability of the patent medicines factory? Is factory profitability a worthwhile objective?

20. Management services are likely to propose using linear programming to improve production scheduling at the patent medicines factory. What data will they need? What are the shortcomings of this solution by management services? Discuss other solutions which embrace better customer relations and modified production methods.

APPENDIX I

QUESTIONS FROM EXAMINATION PAPERS

The following selection indicates the scope of questions set by some examination boards and professional institutes. Grateful acknowledgment is made to:

The Institute of Chartered Secretaries and Administrators (C.I.S.)
The Institute of Bankers (I.B.)
School of Management Studies, Portsmouth Polytechnic, Diploma in Management Studies (D.M.S.)
University of Cambridge Local Examinations Syndicate (U.C.)
Joint Matriculation Board (J.M.B.)
Bournemouth College of Technology, Higher National Certificate (H.N.C.)
Oxford and Cambridge Schools Examination Board (O. & C.)

Economics, business law and international trade

1. Outline the principal features of a public limited liability company. Compare it with a partnership.
2. Outline the ways in which a contract may be ended.
3. Why should the law allow business enterprises to operate under different forms of legal identity?
4. The following data are the market supply and demand schedule for a certain commodity:

Price in shillings per lb.	Demand in lb.	Supply in lb.
12	20	60
11	25	55
10	30	50
9	35	45
8	40	40
7	45	35
6	50	30
5	55	25

(a) Measure the elasticity of supply at the equilibrium price and show clearly how you have arrived at your answer.
(b) State precisely over what range of prices the demand schedule is (i) elastic and (ii) inelastic.
(c) Explain what you would expect to be the main factors governing the elasticities of supply and demand for various goods and services.

5. Write notes on *two* of the following:

   (*a*) marginal cost;
   (*b*) comparative costs;
   (*c*) the supply of money;
   (*d*) the multiplier.

6. The supply curve shown in textbooks suggests that firms will increase output as prices rise. If rising prices can therefore be expected to create economic growth, why is inflation usually regarded as undesirable?

7. Explain briefly horizontal integration and vertical integration, and discuss the comparative merits and demerits of increasing the size of business units by these methods, and by mergers.

8. Discuss the case for decentralisation in large scale business organisations.

9. "The Common Market encouragement of multinational corporations promotes rationalization and higher productivity, but the consumer may suffer because of the increased scope for monopolistic and oligopolistic practices." Discuss this statement.

10. "The rising trend of unemployment in the British economy indicates that development area policies have failed." Discuss this statement.

11. "There is too much preoccupation with the monthly trade statistics." How useful are these as indicators of Britain's economic position?

12. (*a*) In 1960, the total domestic expenditure at market prices in the United Kingdom was £25,491 million. Exports and income received from abroad totalled £6,475 million, imports and income paid abroad was £6,734 million, taxes on spending amounted to £3,405 million and subsidies totalled £489 million.

   (*i*) What was the Gross National Expenditure at market prices? Show how you arrived at your figure.
   (*ii*) What was the Gross National Product at factor cost? Show how you arrived at your figure.
   (*iii*) State what other information is required to enable the Net National Product at factor cost to be calculated.

   (*b*) Discuss the principal reasons why the Government tries to evaluate the various aggregates of income in an economy.

13. To what extent do you consider the amount of Government intervention in economic matters at both macro- and micro-level is justified?

14. Describe and criticise the international system of exchange rates and parities which has operated since the end of the Second World War. Outline briefly the main alternative arrangements which have been suggested.

15. "So long as inflation in Britain does not get out of line with that of our principal trading competitors, our balance of payments position will not be weakened." Discuss.

QUESTIONS FROM EXAMINATION PAPERS 419

Banking, money and finance

16. What functions are usually carried out by a central bank?

17. Distinguish between fiscal and monetary policy. Is it possible to combine a restrictionist monetary policy and an expansionist fiscal policy?

18. Why is the rate of interest very much higher today than it was twenty years ago? Do you expect the rate of interest to rise or fall during the next five years?

19. If a medium-sized manufacturing firm required £250,000 to finance an expansion of its capacity, what alternative sources of finance would be available to it?

20. Explain the main sources of information available for evaluating the ordinary shares of a quoted company.

21. What is "capital gearing" and what is its likely effect on the equity earnings of a company?

22. Discuss the factors which should be taken into account in the selection of a portfolio of investments for a childless widow aged 50, who has capital of £100,000 and no other source of income.

Accounting and management mathematics

23. Discuss the main effects of a period of general price rises on the information provided by conventional financial accounting statements. How might accounting practice, in relation to changing price levels, be changed in order to provide "better" information?

24. It has been recently argued that firms should pay much greater attention to "cash flow" and that "accrual" accounting, by which debtors, creditors and other items are allowed for at a balance sheet date, can be misleading. Explain what you understand by these two terms and discuss the uses of each, taking particular account of the question:

   Is a firm operating at a profit or loss, and will it continue to do so?
   Can a firm meet its liabilities and commitments as they fall due now and in the future?

25. (*a*) Discuss the use of Standard Costing as a means of controlling operation costs.

(*b*) A product requires 4 units of material at a standard price of £1 per unit. Standard labour costs amount to 2 labour hours at 50p per hour.

In a period a batch of 1,000 units were produced the actual costs of which were 4,200 units of material for £3,990 and labour hours 1800, costing £1,125.

Calculate the variances and comment on their significance to management.

26. From the following information relating to a manufacturing company, construct a break-even chart:

Production Capacity	50,000 units
Fixed Costs	£15,000
Variable Cost per Unit	50p
Sales Value per Unit	100p

Comment on the facts shown by the chart. What are the uses and limitations of break-even analysis?

27. A construction company frequently wishes to submit tenders for projects. The amount of work involved in drawing up the tender is believed to be related to its value. The following data refers to tenders drawn up within the last 12 months. (Time in weeks)

Value of tender £1,000s	Time to draw up tender	Value of tender £1,000s	Time to draw up tender
70	7	40	3
50	6	40	4
50	5	60	7
40	5	70	6½
25	4½	20	3
20	4	60	5
80	8	50	4½
60	6	30	4
80	7	70	8

Is the firm justified in believing that a linear relationship exists between value and time?

A tender of approximate value £75,000 is contemplated, how long would you expect the construction company to prepare it?

28. Discuss the function of statistics as a method of quantifying uncertainty. In what ways do you conceive this could assist management in making decisions?

Production, marketing and distribution

29. A canned food company distributes its products nationally by way of regional depot stocks, through which individual retailers are supplied. Discuss the factors to be considered in deciding upon the stock levels to be maintained at the depots, and the type of transport to be used for the movement of goods from the factory to the depots.

30. Consider the problem of layout of facilities and suggest how you would proceed when asked to lay out a supermarket.

31. With reference to a production system with which you are familiar (or an imaginary one) describe the controls which you feel are necessary, and indicate how these controls might be achieved.

32. Explain how co-ordination between production and selling is achieved in an organisation of your selection.

33. What are the factors which determine the expenditure which a manufacturing company is prepared to incur on research?

Leadership, organisation, communication and industrial relations

34. What in your opinion are the essential qualities (apart from academic and professional qualifications) required by a person in order that he or she may become a successful business executive? In your answer discuss the extent to which training can develop these qualities.

35. "Managerial efficiency is what business computing is about. Managerial activity is characterized largely by the making of significant decisions." Discuss with particular reference to the use of computers in the public sector.

36. Describe the types of organisation known as "line," "staff and line" and "functional." Indicate in which circumstances you consider each type to be appropriate; give the reasons for your choice.

37. What is meant by "informal organisation"? "Informal organisation bedevils the formal organisation!" Explain carefully why you agree or disagree with this statement.

38. Why is it useful for the Manager to understand the phenomena of "perception"?

39. At a meeting of departmental heads it has been suggested that communication between management and employees is not as effective as it should be. Prepare a memorandum for submission at the next meeting outlining the steps that should be taken to improve the dissemination of information and generally to ensure the maintenance of good communication within the organisation.

40. What attributes should a supervisor have? Give reasons.

41. "What is a shop steward?" Discuss the role of the shop steward in British industrial relations today.

42. Explain and comment on the distinction made by the Royal Commission on Trade Unions and Employers' Associations 1968 (the Donovan Report) between the formal and informal systems of collective bargaining in Britain.

43. "Productivity bargaining is not only the negotiation of an improvement in wages and benefits in return for a change in working practices, but is also an attempt by management to regain control of the working practices of its employees." Discuss this statement critically.

44. "Interviewing and selecting candidates for posts and promotions is basically a subjective process." Discuss.

45. What motivates men to work well?

APPENDIX II

BIBLIOGRAPHY

Ackoff, R. L. *A Concept of Corporate Planning* (Wiley, New York 1970)
Ansoff, H. Igor *Corporate Strategy* (McGraw-Hill, New York 1965)
Agyle, Michael *The Psychology of Interpersonal Relationship* (Penguin Books, Harmondsworth 1967)
Argyris, Christopher *Integrating the Individual and the Organisation* (John Wiley, New York 1959)
Armstrong, E. G. C. *Industrial Relations: An Introduction* (G. C. Harrap, London 1969)
Bates, James and Parkinson, J. R. *Business Economics* (Basil Blackwell, Oxford 1969)
Batty, J. *Management Accountancy* (Macdonald & Evans, 4th Edition, Plymouth 1974)
Buckner, H. *Business Planning for the Board* (Gower Press, London 1971)
Burns, Tom and Stalker, G. M. *The Management of Innovation* (Tavistock Publications, London 1961)
Coyle, R. G. *Decision Analysis* (Nelson, London 1972)
Cyert, Richard M. and March, James G. *A Behavioural Theory of the Firm* (Prentice-Hall, Englewood Cliffs, N.J. 1963)
Davies, Alan and Coy, John *Economics from Square One* (George Allen & Unwin, London 1967)
Donald, A. G. *Management, Information and Systems* (Pergamon Press, Oxford 1967)
Drucker, Peter F. *Management* (Heinemann, London 1974)
Eddison, R. T., Pennycuick, K. and Rivett, B. H. P. *Operational Research in Management* (English Universities Press, London 1962)
Edey, Harold C. *Introduction to Accounting* (Hutchinson, London 1963)
Falk, Roger *The Business Management* (Penguin Books, 4th Edition, Harmondsworth 1970)
Frean, David *The Board and Management Development* (Business Books, London 1977)
Freear, John *Financing Decisions in Business* (Prentice-Hall, London 1973)
George, F. H. *Cybernetics in Management* (Pan Books, London 1970)
Glantier, M. W. E. and Underdown, B. *Accounting Theory and Practice* (Pitman, London 1976)
Hague, D. C. *Managerial Economics* (Longman, London 1969)
Herzberg, Frederick, Mausner, B. and Synderman, B. *The Motivation to Work* (John Wiley, New York 1964)
Hinel, O. S. *Business Administration* (Longman, London 1969)

BIBLIOGRAPHY

Hopwood, Anthony *Accounting and Human Behaviour* (Prentice-Hall, London 1974)

King, J. R. *Production Planning and Control* (Pergamon, Oxford 1975)

Levitt, Theodore *Innovations in Marketing* (Pan Books, London 1968)

Likert, R. *New Patterns of Management* (McGraw-Hill, New York 1961)

Loveday, R. *Statistics: A First Course* (Cambridge University Press, 2nd Edition, Cambridge 1971)

Maslow, A. H. *Motivation and Personality* (Harper & Row, New York, 2nd Edition, 1970)

McClelland, David C. *The Achieving Society* (Van Nostrand, Princeton 1961)

McGregor, D. M. *The Human Side of Enterprise* (McGraw-Hill, New York 1960)

Moroney, M. J. *Facts from Figures* (Penguin Books, London 1951)

Nicholson, T. A. J. and Pullen, R. D. *Computers in Production Management Decisions* (Pitman, London 1974)

Pigors, P. and Myers, C. A. *Personnel Administration* (McGraw-Hill, 5th Edition, New York 1947)

Pugh, D. S., Hickson, D. J. and Hinings, C. R. *Writers on Organisations* (Hutchinson, London 1964)

Richardson, K. *Do it the Hard Way* (Weidenfeld and Nicolson, London 1972)

Rivett, B. H. P. *Principles of Model Building* (Wiley, London 1972)

Rodger, Leslie *Marketing in a Competitive Economy* (Hutchinson, London 1965)

Savage, C. I. and Small, J. R. *Introduction to Managerial Economics* (Hutchinson, London 1967)

Sisk, Henry L. *Principles of Management* (South-Western Publishing, Cincinnati 1969)

Tredgold, R. F. *Human Relations in Modern Industry* (Duckworth, 2nd Edition, London 1963. Methuen, University Paperbacks, London 1965)

INDEX

Absenteeism, 276, 280, 291
Abstraction, 355
Accelerator, 78–80
Accepting houses, 131, 136
Account,
  current, 119, 121–2, 138
  deposit, 121, 138
  loan, 122
  savings, 121
Accounting,
  conventions, 176–8
  cost, 191
  financial, 161
  management, 190
Accrual accounting, 170, 178
Acquisition, 176, 322
Acts of Parliament,
  Bank of England Act, 1946, 127
  Bills of Exchange Act, 1882, 132
  Charter Act, 1844, 125
  Combination Acts, 1799–1851, 254
  Companies Act,
    1844, 11
    1855, 11
    1862, 11
    1907, 12
    1948, 12, 15, 19, 179
    1967, 12, 179
    1976, 13
  Conciliation Act, 1896, 263
  Contracts of Employment Act, 1963, 22
  Criminal Law Amendment Act, 1871, 254
  Distribution of Industries Acts, 86
  European Communities Act, 1972, 24
  Factories Acts, 23, 266, 279
  Fair Trading Act, 1973, 63
  Health and Safety at Work etc. Act, 1974, 279
  Hire Purchase Act, 1965, 21
  Industrial Courts Act, 1919, 263
  Industrial Development Acts, 1966, 86
  Industrial Relations Act, 1971, 22, 269, 271, 278
  Industrial Training Act, 1964, 2, 86, 92, 278
  Law Reform (Enforcement of Contract) Act, 1954, 20
  Limited Partnership Act, 1907, 10
  Local Employment Acts, 1960, 1963, 86
  Misrepresentation Act, 1967, 21
  Monopolies and Mergers Act, 1965, 62
  Occupiers' Liability Act, 1957, 17
  Partnership Act, 1890, 10
  Race Relations Act, 1968, 23
  Redundancy Payments Act, 1965, 22, 92, 277
  Registration of Business Names Act, 1918, 9
  Resale Prices Act, 1964, 62
  Restrictive Trade Practices Act,
    1956, 61
    1968, 62
  Safeguarding of Industries Act, 1921, 113
  Sale of Goods Act, 1893, 20
  Terms and Conditions of Employment Act, 1959, 267
  Town and Country Planning Act, 1947, 86
  Trade Boards Act, 1909, 1918, 1945, 1959, 263
  Trade Descriptions Act, 1968, 21
  Trade Disputes Act,
    1906, 254, 256
    1965, 256
  Trade Disputes and Trades Unions Act, 1927, 255
  Trade Union Act,
    1871, 254
    1876, 255
    1913, 255
  Trade Union and Labour Relations Amendments Act, 1976, 270
Administrative Staff College (Henley), 1
Advertising, 46, 171, 242–6
Advisory Conciliation and Arbitration Service 271
Agreements Law, 273
Aid, 116
ALGOL, 209
Analysis,
  break-even, 48, 316
  marginal, 260, 315
  market, 232–3
  ratio, 179–89
  security, 145
  subjective, 232
  value, 229
Ansoff, H. Igor, 322
American Federation of Labour, 273
Amstel Club, 133–4
Anti-monopoly Laws, 57
Aptitude tests, 276
Arbitration, 263–5
Articles of association, 13
Asch, S. E., 285
Asset backing, 157
Assets, 162
  capital, 140
  circulating, 163
  current, 162–3
  fixed, 162
  intangible, 175
  liquid, 123, 126–7, 181, 182
  net, 164
  net current, 164, 165
  tangible, 16
  total, 163
  undervalued, 55
  working, 163
Associations,
  banking, 135–6
  British Chambers of Commerce, 259
  employers', 262, 268
  International Bond Dealers, 111
Audio records, 207
Auditors, 161
Austria, 134
Authority, 274, 299–300, 335, 336
Average,
  cost, 43
  moving weighted, 247
  product, 30
  revenue, 47
  statistical, 361

Babbage, 198
Bahamas, 57
Balance of Payments, 70, 102, 138, 264, 267
Balance sheet, 162–6
Bank,
  cards, 120
  credit, 119, 127, 139
  Giro, 120
  notes, 118–19, 121, 124–5, 138–9
  rate, 125–6, 130, 141
Bank of England, 14, 95, 109, 120–1, 123–31, 138, 149

425

Bank, types of,
  commercial, 119–20, 122, 125–9, 141
  deposit, 119, 130, 135, 138
  foreign, 133
  joint-stock, 119, 122
  merchant, 129, 131, 134, 136
Banking,
  international, 134
  school, 124
  Trade Associations:
    British Bankers' Assn., 135
    Fédération Bancaire, 136
    Société Financière Européenné, 135
Bankruptcy, 20, 125
Banks,
  Bank of America, 135
  Bank of London and South America, 134
  Barclays Bank Ltd., 120–1, 147
    International Ltd., 134
  Baring Brothers, 134
  Chartered Bank, 134
  Chase Manhattan Bank, 135
  Child & Co., 121
  European Banks International Co., 135
  Hoare & Co., 121
  Hong Kong and Shanghai Bank, 134
  First National City Bank, 135
  Lloyds Bank Limited, 121
  Lloyds Bank International, 135
  Midland Bank Limited, 121
  National & Commercial Banking Group, 121
  National & Grindlays Bank, 134
  National Westminster Bank, 121
  Ottoman Bank, 134
  Rothschilds, 134
  Royal Bank of Scotland, 121
  Schroders, 134
  Standard Bank, 134
  The Orion Group, 135
  Warburgs, 134
  Williams & Glyn's Bank, 121
Bargaining,
  collective, 270
  distributive, 291
  informal system of, 266
  integrative, 294
  national collective, 261
Barlow Report, 83
Barter, 26
Base rates, 130
Bear market, 159
Behavioural implications of accounting, 193
Belgium, 24, 65, 134
Beveridge, Lord, 83
Bills of exchange, 16, 19, 120, 123, 131–4, 139, 146
  documentary, 132
  negotiation of, 132
Bills of lading, 133
Binary, 199
Board of Directors, 327
Board of Trade, 13, 61, 62
  Companies House, 12
Bond, 142
  British savings, 152
  premium, 231
  property, 169
Bonsor v. *Musicians' Union*, 256
Bonus, 231
Brech, E. F. L., 282
Bretton Woods Conference, 107, 111
British Institute of Management, 1
Brokers,
  bullion, 131
  stock exchange, 150–1
Brown, Lord Wilfred, 342
Budget,
  average family, 144
  balanced, 82
  interim, 96
  purpose of, 96
Budgetary control, 192, 337
Budgeting, 191
Building societies, 119, 129, 139, 141, 146
Bull market, 41, 159
Bureaucracy, 347
Burns, Tom, 298, 306
Business,
  definition of, 6

Cambridge economists, 137
Capital, 13, 28, 29, 51
  appreciation, 155
  circulating, 165
  depreciation, 73, 142, 146–9, 154
  expenditure, 170
  goods, 6, 75, 78
  investment, 57, 145–6
  marginal efficiency of, 78
  market, 150
  working, 165, 188
Capital investment, 180
  total, 180
  net, 180
  ordinary shareholders', 180
Cartel, 60
Case study, 220
Cash–credit ratio, 123
Cash Deposits Scheme, 129
Cash flow, 146, 156, 158–9, 170
  discounted, 318
Central Clearing House, 120–1
Centralisation, 343–8
Certificate:
  of incorporation, 13
  of registration, 9
Chain,
  communication, 348, 352
  management, 337
Chamber of Commerce, 12
Chamber of Shipping, 259
Charge hands, 301, 341
Cheques, 16, 119, 120–1, 125
  travellers', 120
Chicago School, 138
Churchill, Sir Winston, 295
City of London, 20, 104, 131, 134, 151
Classical economists, 80–2
Clayton Act, 1914, 61
Clearing house, 120
Closed shop, 256, 257, 259, 270
COBOL, 208
Coins,
  standard, 118
  token, 118
Collateral security, 122
Collective bargaining, 253, 257, 258, 261, 264, 269, 293
Command levels, 298
Commission for Industry & Manpower, 94
Commission on Industrial Relations, 271
Committees,
  discipline, 290
  grievance, 290
  joint production, 290
  types of, 353–4
Commodity buying, 225
  markets, 240–1
Common market, 24
Commons, J. R., 50
Communications, 303, 322, 330, 359
  breakdown in, 354–6
  controlled, 293
  downward, 349–50
  gap in, 342
  horizontal, 348
  informal, 351

INDEX

nets, 331
speed of, 352
verbal, 350
vertical, 348
written, 350
Companies and Corporations,
Agfa-Gevaert, 58
Associated Electrical Industries (A.E.I.), 62
Bell Telephone Company, 291
Bowmaker Leasing, 147
British Broadcasting Corporation, 14
British Insulated Callenders' Cables, 62
British Leyland, 63, 288
British Railways, 56
British South Africa Company, 11
Cadbury Schweppes Ltd., 54
Dunlop-Pirelli, 58
Elliott-Automation Systems, 63
English Electric, 63
Esso, 267
Fiat-Citroën, 276
Finance Corporation for Industry Ltd., 149
Fokker-VFW, 58, 272
Ford Motor Company, 46, 272
G.E.C., 62
General Motors, 56
Glacier Metal Company, 339, 342
Hudsons Bay Company, 11
Imperial Chemical Industries (I.C.I.), 54, 56, 155, 291
Industrial & Commercial Finance Corp. Ltd., 149
International Finance & Services Ltd., 134
International Telephone & Telegraph Co. Ltd., 56
John Lewis Partnership, 291
Joint Credit Card Co., 120
Litton Industries, 56
Marks & Spencer Ltd., 155
Mitsubishi, 56
National Coal Board, 14
Norsk Hydro, 288
Philips, 56, 58, 272, 291
Pilkingtons, 46
Royal Dutch Shell, 56, 58
Siemens, 58
Standard Oil Co., 60
Trust House Forte, 54
Unilever, 55–6, 58, 155
United Dominions Trust Ltd., 134
Volkswagen, 56
Volvo, 288
Western Electric Co., 283, 284
Company,
chairman, 326
finance, 146
holding, 54
insurance, 129, 156
joint stock, 11
limited, 24
multinational, 128, 135, 272
private, 13
property, 156
public, 150, 306
Comparative costs, law of, 100–1
Competition,
imperfect, 46, 49
perfect, 44, 46, 49, 59
technological, 46
Computer, 194–208, 217–19
compiler, 208
handwritten numerals, 201
high-level language, 208
input, 200
lightpen, 206
magnetic disc, 201, 205, 209
magnetic tape, 201, 205, 209
mark sensing, 201
memory, 202, 207
on-line enquiry, 194
output, 205
printer, 205
programming, 203, 207
punch cards, 200–4
visual display unit, 194, 206, 207–8, 213, 217, 218
Conciliation, 267
Confederation of British Industry (C.B.I.), 92, 94, 258, 290
Conflict, 50
direct, 291
potential, 220
rational, 293
resolution of, 322
structured, 334
Conglomerate merger, 56
Conservative Party, 259, 269
Consideration, 18
Consultancy, 242, 343
Consumer, 136, 233
Consumers' Council, 14
Contract, 18, 19, 20, 22, 23
Contribution, 314–16
Control, 336, 346
quality, 329, 339
span of, 301
statutory, 91
Controlled communication, 294
Conveyance, 16
Co-determination, 290
Co-operative movement, 13
Co-operative Wholesale Society, 13
Co-partnership, 288
Copyright, 16, 19, 59
Corn Laws, 113
Corporations (see Companies),
multinational, 56, 57, 272
public, 14
Cost accounting, 191
Costs, 52
average, 30, 43
fixed, 42, 315–16
law of comparative, 100
marginal, 30, 43, 44, 46
opportunity, 29, 100
overhead, 192, 243
real, 29
replacement, 190
social, 90, 303
total, 30, 43
variable, 42, 313–14
Costing,
marginal, 314
standard, 192–3
Council for National Academic Awards, 2
Court of Enquiry, 264
Cranfield College of Management, 1
Credit,
balance, 119
cards, 120
company, 120
consumer, 140
control, 213
documentary, 133
extended, 120
irrevocable, 133
letter of, 122
personal, 133
rating, 206, 214
red clause, 133
restrictions, 129
revocable, 133
short-term, 131, 146
stand-by, 109
trade, 139, 146
transfer, 120
Creditor, 163

Critical path planning, 400
  resource allocation, 405
  PERT, 406
Currency,
  convertible, 119
  inconvertible, 124
  international, 134
  school, 124
Cybernetics, 228
Cyert, Richard M., 305

Data, 194–6, 200–3, 249–50
  bank, 209–10, 215–17
Debentures, 149, 151, 163
Debt equity decision, 149
Debts, 133
  bad, 131
Decentralisation, 343–8
Decision,
  levels, 321
  making, 199, 204, 301, 308, 354
  trees, 311
  types, 322
Deflation, 76, 81, 142
Degrees of confidence, 370
Delegation, 300
Demand, 32, 74–5, 141, 219
  aggregate, 74
  creation, 33, 74
  competitive, 35
  composite, 35
  definition of, 32
  effective, 26
  elasticity of, 37–41, 259
  exceptional, 41
  joint, 35
De Moivre, 365
Denmark, 24
Department of Economic Affairs, 93, 94
Department of Employment & Productivity, 144, 263
Department of Scientific & Industrial Research, 307
Deposit, 122
  safe, 121
  special, 127–9
Depot siting, 252
Depreciation, 169, 173–5
Depression, 66, 81
Devaluation, 103, 108, 240
Development Decade, 116
Diminishing returns, law of, 28, 43, 280
Directors, 328
Discount, 176, 213, 225, 315
  houses, 123, 125, 129, 141
  market rate, 132
Discounted cash flow, 318–19
Dismissal, 337
Dispatch note, 213
Disputes, 263–5
Distribution, 218
  channels, of, 238–9
  by value, 215
Dividend, 169
  annual, 68
  yield, 156–7
Division of labour, 28
Domestic Credit Expansion, 138
Dominant strategies, 398
Donovan Report, 268–9
Double counting, 72
Double entry book-keeping, 166
Drucker, Peter F., 215
Dumping, 114

Economic Development Councils, 92
Economic,
  fluctuations, 137
  growth, 73, 90–1, 268
  indicators, 70–2, 156
  manufacturing quantity, 251
  order quantity, 250
Economic laws, 34
  diminishing marginal utility, 33–4, 97, 260
  diminishing returns, 280
Economies:
  of scale, 51–4, 346
  external, 53
  internal, 51–2
Economy,
  command, 88
  declining, 70
  growing, 70
  market, 26, 89
  mixed, 89–90
  primitive, 26, 88
  static, 70
Eire, 24
Elasticity,
  demand, 38, 40
  income, 38
  price, 37
Eliot, T. S., 350
Embargoes, 240
Employee,
  centred, 296
  role of, 334
Employers' associations, 268
Employment, 80, 83
Entrepreneur, 28
Equity, 15, 97, 135, 147, 148, 158
Ergonomics, 287
Estimation, 368
Euro-companies, 50, 58
Eurocheque, 120
Eurodollar, 110–12
Euromarkets, 128
European,
  Commission, 290
  Economic Community, 120, 272
  Community law, 15, 24, 64, 87
  companies, 56
  Free Trade Association, 273
  Investment Bank, 87
  Parliament, 58
Examinations and Boards,
  Council for National Academic Awards, 2
  Diploma in Management Studies, 2
  Higher National Certificate, 2
  Higher National Diploma, 2
  National Examinations Board in Supervisory Studies (N.E.B.S.S.), 2
  Ordinary National Certificate, 2
  Ordinary National Diploma, 2
Exception reporting, 195, 255
Exchange,
  control, 125
  Equalisation Account, 105, 125
  foreign, 105
Exchange rates, 107, 111
  fixed, 113
  floating, 105–6
  two-tier system of, 112
Executive chain, 342, 351
Executive director, 327
Exponential smoothing, 247, 249
Export, 96, 101–3, 105, 116, 133, 146–7, 239, 259
Exports Credit Guarantee Department, 133
Exporter, 132–3, 134, 147
Extrapolation, 226

Factors, 147
  of production, 28–9
Fair trading, 63, 225
Fawley agreement, 268
Fayol, Henri, 282
Feedback, 228, 350

INDEX

Fiduciary issue, 125
Finance,
  corporate, 145
  houses, 136
  House Association, 129
Financial Times Ordinary Share Index, 143
Financing,
  deficit, 96
  surplus, 96
Fiscal policy, 96, 138
Fisher, Irving, 136
France, 24, 64, 92, 112, 134
Free trade, 113
Friedman, Milton, 138
Fringe benefits, 266
Forecasting, 72, 92, 234, 237, 245–8
FORTRAN, 208
Full employment, 80, 137, 266
  of resources, 82
Function, 287
Functional organisation, 329
Functional relationship, 331–2
Funding, 127
Futures market, 241

Galbraith, J. K., 50
Game theory, 293, 311, 394
  dominant strategies, 398
  non-zero sum games, 397
  saddle points, 398
  zero sum games, 396
GATT, 103, 115
Gauss, 366
Gearing, 156, 158
General Strike, 1926, 255
Gleitzeit, 291
Gold, 117, 119, 124, 125
Goldsmiths, 118, 124
Gold standard, 82, 104–8, 119, 125
Goods,
  capital, 6, 76
  consumer, 6, 7, 67, 75, 78
  durable, 6, 127
  free, 5
  non-durable, 6
  primary, 116
Goodwill, 16, 175
Grapevine, 351
Gresham's Law, 118
Group discussions, 353
Groups,
  chains, 55
  formal, 284
  informal, 285
  primary, 286

Halo effect, 357
Hawthorne studies, 282–6
Hedging, 241
Herrington v. *British Railways Board*, 17
Herzburg, Frederick, 281, 291
Hire purchase, 19, 75, 127, 139, 140, 146
Hitler, Adolf, 299
Human,
  behaviour, 198, 281, 284
  capabilities, 198
  relations, 281–3

Image, 234
Imports, 101–3, 105, 146, 240
Importer, 133
Incentives, 231, 282
Income effect, 33
Incomes policy, 91, 94
Independent Television Authority, 14
Index,
  cost of living, 72
  numbers, 143
  retail price, 163
  share, 159
  weighting system, 144
Individual rights, 269
Induction, 276
Industrial democracy, 289
Industrial Development Certificates, 86
Industrial Ordinary Share Index, 143
Industrial relations, 253–93
Industrial Reorganisation Corporation, 63
Industrial Revolution, 253
Industries,
  building, 45
  chemicals, 52, 114
  coal, 82, 85, 265
  declining, 85
  engineering, 60, 77, 257
  iron and steel, 60, 82, 84, 114, 228
  motor cars, 46, 52, 228, 265
  oil, 45, 52
  printing, 45
  shipbuilding, 60; 77, 82, 265
  soap, 46, 55, 60
  staple, 60, 81
  textiles, 45, 60, 82, 84
  tobacco, 45, 60
Industry, definition of, 7
Inflation, 66, 91, 93, 94, 103, 126, 137, 139, 140, 142, 143, 145, 147, 156, 189, 268
Information, 194–7
Innovation, 295, 305–7
Institute of Public Relations, 245
Institutional investors, 150
Institutionalism, 50
Insurance, 129, 131, 133, 139, 147
  certificate, 133
  contract, 241
Integration,
  horizontal, 55
  lateral, 56
  vertical, 56
Intelligence tests, 276
Interest, 121, 126, 132, 153–4
  rates, 78, 81, 122, 126, 128, 130, 139–41, 149
International Chamber of Commerce, 133
International Monetary Fund, 102, 103, 107, 109, 111–13, 125
International settlements, 102
Interview, 275–7
Inventions, 231, 306
Investment, 70, 75–8, 96, 102, 106, 122, 154–5
  gross, 70
  issuing houses, 134, 150
  management, 145
  timing of, 159
  trusts, 11, 134, 150–1
Invoicing, 206, 214
Italy, 24, 64, 112, 134, 273

Japan, 56, 92, 111, 112
Jaques, Elliot, 339, 342
Job,
  analysis, 275
  centred, 296
  description, 275
  enlargement, 287, 303
  enrichment, 281
  evaluation, 275
  motivation, 230
  rotation, 287–8, 303
  satisfaction, 280
Jobber, 151
Joint Industrial Council, 262–5
Joint leadership, 326
Joint selling agency, 60

Kangaroo court, 270
Kennedy, John F., 299
Keynes, John Maynard, 82, 137–9

INDEX

Labour,
  demand for, 260
  movement of, 86
  supply of, 28, 261
  turnover, 276, 289
Labour Party, 14, 90, 255, 258, 259
Laissez-faire, 89
Law,
  case, 16
  civil, 15
  criminal, 15
  community, 24
  equity, 15
  statute, 16
  tort, 17
  trespass, 17, 18
Leadership, 295
Leavitt, Harold, 356
Legal tender, 119
Lender of last resort, 126
Liability,
  limited, 11
  unlimited, 12
  vicarious, 17
Liabilities, 162
  current, 162, 163
Libel, 18, 255
Liechtenstein, 57
Likert, Rensis, 299
Linear,
  programming, 226, 381
  regression, 251, 317
Liquidity, 181–2, 186
Loans, 78, 122, 126–8, 134–5, 139–40, 146, 162–3
Location of industry, 84
Lockout, 255, 264
Lombard Steet, 124
London gold pool, 108
London & Manchester Business Schools, 1
Loss leader, 216, 244
Luxemburg, 24, 57, 65

Macro-economics, 24, 66
Management, 4, 29, 261–3, 265–7, 289–90, 293, 295, 302
  accounting, 190
  by objectives, 338
  chain of command, 344
  consultants, 343
  definition of, 1
  information, 195, 210, 218, 219, 237
  responsibilities of, 335–7
  scientific, 282
  services, 332
Managing Director, 326, 328
March, James G., 305
Mark-up, 47
Market,
  changing, 308
  overt, 20
  perfect, 44
  research, 232, 234, 243
  share, 243, 245, 305
  stable, 306
Markets, types of,
  capital, 130, 150
  commodity, 240
  Eurodollar, 110–12, 128
  futures, 241
  money, 131–2
  new issue, 150
  Stock Exchange, 148, 150–1, 241
Margin, 31, 260
Marginal,
  analysis techniques, 47
  product, 30–1
  productivity, 260–1
  productivity theory, 260
  returns, 31
  revenue, 45–8
  utility, 34
Marginal cost,
  economist's definition, 43–4
  usage in business, 314, 316
Marginal costing,
  break-even charts, 316
  contribution, 314–17
  importance of, 312
Marshall, Alfred, 44, 80
Maslow, A. H., 279
Mayo, G. Elton, 280, 283
McGregor, Douglas, 284
McKenna duties, 113
Mediator, 294
Memorandum of Association, 13
Mergers, 54, 56, 62, 134
Method study, 229
Micro-economics, 24, 49
Mill, John Stuart, 80
Milne, A. A., 321
Minimum lending rate, 130
Model building, 363
Monetary policy, 91, 112, 125–7, 138–9
Money,
  at call, 123
  bank deposit, 119, 122–3
  characteristics of, 117
  functions of, 117
  hot, 126
  income, 35
  market, 131–2
  paper, 118
  quasi, 119
  supply of, 119, 125, 138
  token, 119
  types of, 118
Monopolies Commission, 61–3, 94
Monopoly, 44, 45, 59–61
Morale, 280, 285, 347, 351
Mortgage, 147
Motivation, 279, 284
Multiplier, 77–8

NASA, 295
National Board for Prices and Incomes, 92–4
National,
  debt, 95, 124, 128
  Economic Development Council ("Neddy"), 92, 258
  income, 68, 73
  Income Commission, 93
  Industrial Relations Court, 270, 271
  Institute for Economic & Social Research, 73
  Insurance, 22
  Plan, 93
  Product, 69, 70, 95, 116
Nationalisation, 11, 14, 60, 126, 135
Negligence, 16, 21
Needs,
  basic, 279
  egoistic, 281
  physiological, 279
  social, 279
  self-actualising, 279, 281
Negotiation, 262, 264, 266, 268
Netherlands, 24, 65, 134, 273, 290
Noise, 246
Non-zero sum game, 359
Normal distribution, 364
Norway, 134

Objectives, 302, 304, 322, 323, 327
Oligopoly, 46
Open-market operations, 126
Operational research, 359
  critical path planning, 399
  linear programming, 381

INDEX

queuing theory, 371
simulation, 376
society, 360
Opportunity costs, 29, 100
Optimisation, 84, 220, 303
Optimum size, 53
Organisation,
  centralisation, of, 343–53
  chart, 329, 349
  classical school, 282
  decentralisation of, 343–5
  functional, 329
  geographical 237
  Hawthorne studies, 282–6
  Human Relations School, 282–6
  line and staff, 330
  mechanistic, 299, 306
  organic, 299, 306
  systems school, 284
Organising, 334
Ottawa Agreements, 114
Overdraft, 122, 126, 130, 146
Overtime, 84, 258
Owner's equity, 162, 163
Ownership, 16, 325

Packaging, 239
Panels, 233
Parities, 107–8
  sliding, 113
Partnership, 9–11, 146
Pascal, 198
Patents, 16, 59, 231
Paterson, William, 124
Payments,
  deferred, 117
  methods of, 118
Pension, 267
  funds, 150
  schemes, 150
Perception, 294, 338, 354–5
Performance measurement, 337
Personality, 302, 358
  test, 276
Personnel, 332
  management, 253, 274–9, 290
  recruiting, 274
  selection, 274
  welfare, 277–8
Persuasion, 358
PERT, 406
Picketing, 254
Piecework, 231, 288
Pigou, A. C., 44
Planning, 334
  corporate, 323, 332
  indicative, 92
  normative, 92
  target, 25
Pool, 60
Population, 28
  distribution of, 70, 91
  total working, 265
Port of London Authority, 14
Portugal, 134
Possession, 16
Post Office, 14, 120
  Giro, 121, 129
Postal orders, 119
Power, 336
Prediction, 246
Premium Bonds, 231
Price,
  control, 268
  cutting, 61
  determination, 268
  forward, 240
  leader, 60
  spot, 240

Prisoner's dilemma, 395
Probability, 312, 320
Product, 31
  average, 31
  marginal, 31
  planning, 234
Production,
  direct, 7
  factors, of, 28
  mass, 306
  means of, 88
  planning, 226, 230
  primary, 7
  returns, 30
  secondary, 7
  specific, 29
  non-specific, 29
Productivity, 262, 272
  agreements, 267–8
  marginal, 260–1
Professionalism, 332
Profit, 102, 167–70, 218–19, 222, 229, 234, 241, 305
  concept of, 302
  different interpretations of, 354
  margin of, 48
  minimaxing, 303
  normal, 28, 48
  satisficing, 303
  sharing, 288–9
Profit and Loss Account, 167–9
  trading account, 168
  appropriation account, 168
Programming,
  computer, 207
  comparison, 204
Promissory notes, 19
Promotions, 244
Prospectus, 150
Psychological stress, 340
Public,
  debt, 129
  nuisance, 17
  relations, 245, 332
Purchasing, 224
Purchasing power parity theory, 106

Quality control, 329, 339
Quantity theory of money, 136–9
Questionnaire, 233, 277
Quotas, 103, 240

Race Relations Board, 23
Random effect, 246
Ratio analysis, 179–89
  asset utilisation, 180, 185
  creditor turnover, 182, 187
  current ratio, 181, 186
  debtor turnover, 182, 187
  gearing, 181, 185, 186
  interest cover, 181, 185
  liquidity, 181, 186
  price-earnings ratio, 156, 157
  profitability, 180, 185
  quick (liquid) ratio, 182, 186
  return on investment, 180, 184
  stock turnover, 182, 187
Rationalisation, 60
Recession, 66
Redundancy 260, 267, 272, 277, 347
Re-entanglement, 140
Reflation, 66
Regional employment premium, 86
Regional imbalance, 85
Register of Companies, 12, 13
Registrar of Business Names, 9
Registry of Restrictive Practices, 63
Report,
  annual, 14, 69

Report—*continued*
  writing, 357
Reporting, 217, 227, 336
  exception, 195–2
  sales, 217
Resale price maintenance, 61, 62
Research and development, 304, 332
Reserves, 163
Resource allocation, 227, 405
Responsibility, 298, 300, 335, 336, 339
Responsibility accounting, 193
Restrictive practices, 60, 61, 63, 267
Retail, 225, 245
  consortium, 259
  price index, 143
Retailer, 238
Retailing, 9, 10, 56, 61
Retirement, 277
Returns to scale, 30
Revaluation, 112
Revenue expenditure, 170
Risk, 320
Rochdale Pioneers, 13
Role, 267, 334
Rome Agreement, 87
Rookes v. *Barnard*, 256
Royal Commission on Labour 261
Royal Commission on Trade Unions and Employers' Associations (Donovan Report), 268–9
Royal Mint, 119

Saddle points, 398
Salaries, 261
Sales,
  cycles, 246
  forecast of, 247
  incentive scheme, 343
  reporting, 218
  turnover, 218, 324
Salesman, 215, 222, 236–7, 242, 358
Sample, 362
Sandiland's Report, 190
Satisficing, 303
Savings, 25, 75–7, 143, 145
  certificates, 95, 119
Says Law, 80
Scanlon plan, 289
Scheduling, vehicle, 252
Schumpeter, J. A., 50
Scientific management, 282
Seasonability, 246
Secretary of State for Employment, 271
Securities, 122, 150–60
  gilt-edged, 128–9
  government, 123–5, 139
  long-term, 127
  non-marketable, 95
  short-term, 127
Select Committee on Nationalised Industries, 14
Seller's lien, 21
Semantics, 354
Shareholder, 11, 135, 158, 163, 289, 306
Share options, 159, 326
Shares, 11, 16, 19, 54, 68, 91, 122, 134, 150–60, 163
  Industrial Ordinary Share Index, 143
  nominal value of, 148
  ordinary, 147–8, 163
  preference, 147–8, 158, 163
Sherman Act, 1890, 61
Shop steward, 265–7, 271, 336, 340, 351, 353
Singapore, 57
Site, 6
  choice of, 84, 252
Slander, 18, 255
Slump, 82, 159
Smith, Adam, 89, 117

Socialisation, 280
Societas Europea, 58
Sole trader, 9, 10, 11, 146
Sources and Applications of Funds, 170, 172, 173
Span of control, 300–1
Special deposits, 127
Special drawing rights, 109–10
Specialist barrier, 333
Speculators, 108, 241
Staff,
  attitudes, 297
  structure, 330
Stalker, 298, 306
Standard,
  costing, 192–3
  deviations, 255, 361, 364
  of living, 50, 70, 73
Standardisation, 196, 227
Stand-by credits, 109
Standing orders, 120, 122
Statistics, 222, 238, 360, 412
  degrees of confidence, 370
  economic, 68
  estimation, 368
  linear regression, 247
  mean, 361
  normal distribution, 364
  sample, 362
  standard deviation, 364
  variance, 363
Status, 286, 334
Sterling, 108–9, 112, 125, 128–9, 131, 133–5
Stock,
  control, 251–2
  Government, 141, 153, 160
  irredeemable, 153
  redeemable, 153–4
  safety, 251
Stock Exchange, 148, 151, 241
Stress, psychological, 340
Strike, 255, 264–5, 266, 273
  General, 255
  official, 264
  pay, 265–6
  procedure, 270–1
  sympathetic, 270
  unconstitutional, 265
  unofficial, 264, 270
Structure,
  informal, 284
  inorganic, 299, 349
  organic, 299
Structured conflict, 334
Sub-optimisation, 222
Subsidiaries, 57, 345
Substitution effect, 33
Supervisor, 300, 341, 354
Supply,
  aggregate, 74
  definition of, 26–7
  elasticity of, 39–40
  joint, 28
  short-term, 39
Switzerland, 134
Synergy, 323–4
System, 287
  closed, 4
  communication, 304
  management information, 219
  sub-systems of, 220
  total management, 214, 220
Systemisation, 197, 212, 220

Taff Valley Railway Co., 254
Takeover, 54, 68, 134
Targets, 219, 237, 246
Tariffs, 53, 58, 103, 114, 116, 240
  McKenna duties, 113

INDEX

Tax, 40–1, 60, 146
  Capital Gains, 96
  Corporation, 96
  havens, 57
  Income, 82, 96, 122
  P.A.Y.E., 98
  returns, 69
  types of, 96–9
  Value Added, 97–8
Taxation, 56, 77–8, 90, 92
Taylor, Frederick W., 282, 329, 331
Tavistock Institute of Human Relations, 339
Tenders, 232
Terms of trade, 101
Time span, 339
  of trade cycles, 66
Theory X and Theory Y, 284
Tolpuddle Martyrs, 252
Tort, 17, 21, 23, 255
Trade,
  associations, 12, 59, 60
  bilateral, 114
  boards, 263
  cycle, 66, 78, 80
  home, 7
  international, 99, 131
  invisible, 102
  marks, 231
  multilateral, 114
  overseas, 7
  restrictions, 113–15
  retail, 7
  visible, 102
  wholesale, 7
Trade Union, 23, 50, 95, 143, 150, 253–74, 289, 341, 353
  American Federation of Labour, 272
  collective bargaining, 253, 257–8, 261, 264–5, 293
  Congress (T.U.C.), 258, 273
  European, 272–3
  International Federation of Christian Trade Unions, 273
  International Federation of Free Trade Unions, 272
  reform, 268, 271–2
  white collar, 257, 273
  World Federation, 272
Trading certificate, 13
Trading stamps, 244
Transfer,
  credit, 120
  telegraphic, 120, 133
Transfer, payments, 69
Transportation, 394
Treasury, 138
  Bills, 95, 123, 125, 127, 129–30, 132, 141
Treaty of Rome, 24
Trend,
  current, 68
  major, 159
  sales, 246
Turnover,
  labour, 276, 289
  sales, 220, 323
  staff, 355

Underwriter, 150
Unfair industrial practices, 269, 271
Unemployment, 61, 67–8, 70, 76, 80–1, 83, 85, 94, 136, 260, 280, 289
Unit trusts, 150
United Nations Conference of Trade and Development, 116
Urwick, Lyndall, F., 282, 330
United States of America, 50, 59, 60, 66, 103, 107–8, 134, 256
Utility, 26
  diminishing, 260
  law of diminishing marginal, 33–4, 97, 260
  total, 34

Value, 26
  analysis, 229
  net present, 319
  statement, 355
Variance, 363
Variance analysis, 192, 193
Variations,
  flexible, 136–7
  rigid, 136–7
Veblen, 50
Vehicle scheduling, 252
Velocity of circulation, 136
Volcker, Paul, 113

Wages, 42, 68, 69, 72, 91, 261–70, 272
  councils, 263
Warehousing, automated, 251
Watt, James, 307
Warranties, 20, 21
Webb, Sidney and Beatrice, 257
Weber, Max, 299
Weights and Measures Inspectorate, 63
West Germany, 24, 65, 92, 112, 134, 256, 272–3, 290–1
White Paper on Employment Policy, 1944, 90
Whitley Committee, 262
Wholesaler, 238–9
Wilberforce Commission, 262
Wolfson Foundation, 3
Work measurement, 230
Work study, 229
Works council, 290
World Federation of Trade Unions, 272

Yield, 141
  dividend, 155–7
  expected, 78

Zero-sum game, 293, 395